Contents

Preface

This book aims to serve the needs of young economists in the 1990s. Throughout, there is an underlying emphasis on data collection, data interpretation, trends and sequences, application of basic economic concepts, decision-making and policy-making. The overall aim of the book is to help students develop economic understanding – to get them to think and act like economists. To help achieve this aim an active approach to learning has been adopted. Each of the 87 units begins with a piece of stimulus material, with accompanying 'study points'. This may be used in a variety of ways: as the basis for full class discussion, small group work or individual work. The purpose of the stimulus is to focus attention immediately on the particular topic and to get the pupils to develop and use the skills needed at GCSE. It is envisaged that each unit will form the basis of one to two hours' study in the classroom.

The basic text is designed to act as a resource for pupils in using their economics. The workings of the British economy are described, and terms, concepts and theories explained. Data are used to emphasise the link between economic theory and the real world.

Questions, called 'checkpoints', accompany each unit. These questions are designed as a basic check of understanding. Each unit also includes a 'coursework suggestion'. For GCSE, candidates have to research and write one or more projects. The suggestions in the book are not intended as project synopses – indeed it would be totally against the spirit of GCSE if such synopses were commercially available. They are, however, there as a starting-point from which pupils can develop their own unique projects. It is hoped that no final project will resemble exactly any of the suggestions given. 'Key terms' are provided as a further resource for pupils. They should prove particularly useful in examination preparation. 'Key terms' for each unit are identified in small capitals and defined in the boxed area on each right-hand page. Italics are used for emphasis throughout and other economic terms may therefore appear in italic.

Interspersed throughout the units are pages of data-response and essay questions. All GCSE examinations require candidates to answer data-response questions. This again reflects the move towards testing a candidate's ability to *understand* and *use* economics as opposed to being able simply to recall knowledge.

The book is ordered in logical sequence. However, there are many paths which teachers and pupils can take through GCSE, and the splitting up of the material into 87 units has been done in part so that teachers can use the book in as flexible a manner as possible.

I would particularly like to thank Ronald Bramham, Julian Stanley and Linda Thomas who made invaluable comments on the manuscript of the first edition and all the editorial staff at Collins who have worked so hard getting this second edition into print in such a short period.

A. G. Anderton

Scarce Resources and Infinite Wants

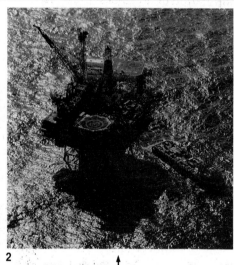

SCARCE RESOURCES

INFINITE WANTS

1

2

3

4

5

6

STUDY POINTS

1 Look at photograph 1. Make a list of the most important items that you think the woman would want to have.

2 What do you think are the ten most important wants of a 20-year-old woman in Britain?

3 What do you think are the ten most important wants of a 10-year-old child in Britain?

4 What wants are illustrated in photographs 3, 4 and 5?

5 Oil is a 'resource' and can be used to produce goods and services which satisfy people's wants. Look at photograph 2. Why is there only a fixed or 'finite' amount of oil available in the world today?

6 Look at photograph 6. Roads are an economic resource, and there are only a finite number of these resources in any area. Why might the situation shown in the photograph be caused?

7 Describe how the photographs show your wants now and in the future. It is an economic fact that nearly all resources in the world are scarce. Explain why many of your wants will never be satisfied.

8 Explain whether you think the wants of a poor person, such as the woman shown in photograph 1, differ from those of somebody better off like yourself.

Scarce Resources

- 'More than half the 20 million rural population of the north east of Brazil suffers from some form of malnutrition.' (*Source*: Adapted from *Financial Times*, 13 March 1992)

- 'Steep increases in world population could lead to catastrophic environmental damage and a loss of species and natural habits.' (*Source*: *Financial Times*, 24 April 1992)

- 'Earnings of 14–16 year olds fell last year. Pocket money from parents went up by 15 per cent but this was more than offset by a 20 per cent fall in income from part-time jobs.' (*Source*: Walls' Monitor)

- 'Up to 20 jobs could go after the plug was pulled on a £3500-a-week subsidy to the fleet of minibuses at Dudley's giant Merry Hill shopping centre.' (*Source*: *Express and Star*, 5 June 1992)

All of these situations have one thing in common. They all illustrate the problem of *scarce resources* or ECONOMIC SCARCITY. There is only a finite (or limited) number of resources such as workers, machines, factories, acres of land and reserves of oil on the planet earth. Because these resources are finite, it is not possible to produce an infinite number of goods and services. So in north-east Brazil, half the rural population doesn't have enough food to eat. By producing more and more goods for an ever increasing population, we are destroying the natural resources of the planet. Closer to home, people are limited in what they can buy because they do not have an unlimited supply of money. Firms have to make cutbacks if they can't afford to run services at a loss.

Infinite Wants

Scarce resources wouldn't be a problem if individuals didn't want more than they have at present. It wouldn't matter that half the population of north-east Brazil was malnourished if people didn't care about the situation.

But human beings do care. They want more resources to be available to them. They want better food, better housing, better transport, better health care, better education . . . the list is infinite. Economists say that WANTS are INFINITE. Whether it is a person struggling to feed herself in the developing world, or a multi-billionaire seeking to increase her fortune in the USA, there is always something more an individual wants.

The Economic Problem

The world's resources are scarce. But human wants are infinite. So there is a problem and it is this problem that is called the BASIC ECONOMIC PROBLEM. The economic problem would not exist:

- if resources were infinite, *or*
- if human wants were limited, *or*
- if all resources were totally *free*, like the air we breathe, *or*
- if we were all Buddhist monks seeking poverty.

If the economic problem were to cease to exist, so too would the study or science called Economics.

World resources are limited. Human wants aren't.

C H E C K P O I N T S

1 What is meant by 'scarce resources' in Economics?

2 Write down ten resources that are scarce in the world.

3 What free resources are there in the world?

4 In three minutes, write down as many items as you can think of that you would like to own or consume. Are there still any items that you would like to have, but didn't have time to write down? Why is it unlikely that you could ever write down everything you want?

5 (a) Give five examples of human wants.
　(b) What is meant by the word 'infinite'?
　(c) Why are human wants infinite?

C O U R S E W O R K S U G G E S T I O N

Take any scarce resource in the world – for example, oil, coal, land, labour. Try to measure how much of this resource is available and show that it is scarce. Then look at the wants of individuals for this resource. What is it used for? How is it used? Would people use more of the resource, if it were totally free? Explain why all this illustrates the basic economic problem. Do you think the scarce resources available in the world today could be better used?

K E Y T E R M S

ECONOMIC SCARCITY – a situation where there is only a limited or finite number of resources available.

INFINITE WANTS – human beings' unlimited desire to own or consume resources.

THE BASIC ECONOMIC PROBLEM – the problem arising because resources are scarce, but human wants are infinite.

FREE RESOURCE – a resource that is not limited in supply for human beings.

Choice, Opportunity Cost and Allocation

STUDY POINTS

1 Imagine you had a place on Youth Training (YT). You live at home with your parents and it costs you £5.00 a week in bus fares to travel to and from your place of work. Draw up a budget as follows, showing how you would spend your money.

2 If the YT grant were increased by £5 a week, how would you choose to spend your extra income and why?

3 The **OPPORTUNITY COST** of something is the benefit lost from the next most desirable course of action. For instance, if Mars bars and Wispas were your two favourite chocolate bars, each costing 25p, and you only had enough money to buy one bar, then the opportunity cost of a Mars bar would be the benefit you give up by not being able to eat a Wispa.

What would be the opportunity cost for you on YT of £10 spent on clothes?

4 What would be the opportunity cost for you of joining YT?

5 YT is paid for by the government mainly from taxpayers' money. Doubling the YT grant to young people to £59 a week would cost taxpayers up to £500 million a year.
(a) Who would be better off as a result of a rise in the grant?
(b) Who would be worse off as a result of a rise in the grant? What might they have to give up in order to pay for the rise?
(c) Should the government double the grant to £59 a week per trainee? Explain your answer carefully.

Allocation of Resources

Here are three sets of statistics relating to the basic economic problem.

- 'People needing hospital treatment in the West Midlands have to wait longer for a bed than the average for the rest of England.' (*Source: Express and Star*, 23 January 1992)

- 'Thousands of teachers will return from the half term break on Monday – to get the sack. Up to 12 500 jobs are set to go because the government failed to give schools enough cash.' (*Source: Daily Mirror*, 25 May 1992)

- 'Coca Cola spend $932 million on advertising in 1990 worldwide.' (*Source: Financial Times*, 16 January 1992)

In Unit 1, it was argued that human wants are infinite. Governments would like to spend more money on hospitals and education. Companies would like to spend more money on advertising whilst consumers would like to buy or be given more goods and services.

But resources are scarce. There aren't enough raw materials, or workers, or time to produce everything that people want. So *choices* have to be made. Individuals, firms, nations, the whole world all have to choose between the various alternative uses of scarce resources. The government has to choose whether to spend more money on health or education. Firms have to decide whether to spend more money on advertising or on product development. Consumers have to decide whether to buy Coca Cola or another product. Economists say that resources have to be *allocated* between all the different uses that those resources could have been put to.

Opportunity Cost

Whenever resources are allocated and choices made, something has to be given up as a result. If the government chooses to give an extra £250 million to education to save 12 500 jobs, then those resources can't be used to cut hospital waiting lists. If you choose to spend £20 on CDs it means that you cannot buy £20 worth of clothes. Economists call what has to be given up the OPPORTUNITY COST of a particular choice. The opportunity cost of a choice is the benefit which is given by the next most desirable alternative that is foregone (given up) as a result of making that choice.

The opportunity cost of a choice is what economists call a REAL COST – 'real' as opposed to 'money'. The money cost of a CD might be £9.99. The real cost is what could have been bought instead – for example, 10 magazines or a T-shirt. The opportunity cost of a choice should always be expressed as a real cost, not a money cost.

Any individual, organisation or nation has to make three fundamental types of choices about how to allocate the scarce resources available to it. It has to decide:

- *what* to produce – food or industrial machinery, books or newspapers, and so on;
- *how* to produce – how many workers will be used, with what machinery, etc.;
- *for whom* it will produce – will some people get a bigger share of resources than others? Will some people get so few resources that they cannot survive, while others live in luxury? Will resources be evenly distributed?

ECONOMICS, then, is the study or science of human behaviour in relation to how scarce resources are allocated and how choices are made between alternative uses.

C H E C K P O I N T S

1 **Indicate how you allocated your scarce resources last week by drawing up a budget. Divide a sheet of paper in two. On the left-hand side, put a title 'Income' and on the right-hand side 'Expenditure'. Then write down all the money you received last week (your 'income') and all the money you spent (your 'expenditure'). Provide as much detail about different types of income and expenditure as possible. If you borrowed money or spent part of your savings, record this under the income column. If you saved money or repaid any loans, record it under the expenditure column. Add up income and borrowing and record the total as 'total incomings'. Add up expenditure and savings and record the total as 'outgoings'. 'Incomings' should equal 'outgoings'.**
   - (a) **What is meant by 'opportunity cost'?**
   - (b) **What was the opportunity cost to you of 50p of your expenditure?**
   - (c) **Why did you face the problem of the allocation of scarce resources last week?**

'If you let **ME** spend our last £5 on this book, I'll hum the tape for you.'

2 **Give three examples of the real cost of a Mars Bar.**
3 **If you were given £10 000 to give to one charity of your choice, which charity would you choose to give it to? Why?**
4 **Why do resources have to be allocated in an economy?**
5 **'Famine in the world today is a problem caused not by finite (i.e. limited) world resources, but by the poor allocation of those resources.' What do you think this means?**

C O U R S E W O R K   S U G G E S T I O N

Consider how a person's time is allocated. Conduct a survey of ten people of your own age. Ask them to keep a calendar record of how they spend their time over two days, preferably a Sunday and a Monday (a day of rest and a day of work). The record should be a detailed one, giving meal times, sleep times, work times (with a breakdown of what work was done when) and recreation times. Compare how different people used their scarce time. What does it reveal about the choices they faced and the opportunity cost of their decisions? Consider whether or not their time was spent in the best way.

K E Y   T E R M S

ALLOCATION OF RESOURCES – how scarce resources are distributed between competing uses.

ECONOMIC CHOICE – deciding between different uses of scarce resources.

OPPORTUNITY COST – the benefit obtained from the next most desirable alternative foregone because of a particular choice.

REAL COST – the cost of an item in terms, not of money, but of the resource, good or service that has had to be given up to obtain that item.

ECONOMICS – the science of human behaviour in relation to the allocation of scarce resources between alternative uses.

Economic Decision-Making

> 'Workers who lost their jobs when a West Midlands factory closed down are taking a bold step to get back into harness. They are planning to buy the factory and run it themselves.' (*Source: Express and Star*, 23 March 1992)

To buy a business that has been closed down requires considerable courage. How do individuals, and indeed organisations and society come to make economic decisions?

Rationality

Economists start by assuming that economic decision-makers act in a RATIONAL manner. What this means is that decision-makers act according to reason, rather than in any odd way. For instance, if a person wanted to increase his or her income, it is assumed that he or she would try to work longer hours, rather than shorter hours. Equally, if there were two identical packets of soap powder on the supermarket shelf, one priced at £2.00, the other on 'special offer' at £1.80, it is assumed that shoppers would buy the cheaper packet.

Maximisation

A second economic assumption is that economic decision-makers attempt to MAXIMISE. This means that they try to get the best out of any economic situation. If a person can choose to work for 38 hours a week instead of 40 hours, everything else being the same including the wage, then he or she will choose to maximise leisure time by working 38 hours. Equally, a business will prefer to earn as much profit as possible, rather than a lower profit, if all other considerations are equal. A government would prefer to spend £15 billion on the National Health Service rather than £14 billion, if there were no opportunity cost involved in this.

Costs and Benefits

In order to decide what is 'best' in any economic situation, a decision-maker

STUDY POINTS

1 What are the benefits of smoking: (a) to the smoker and (b) to non-smokers?

2 What are the costs of smoking: (a) to the smoker and (b) to non-smokers?

3 When a smoker smokes a cigarette, do you think that he or she considers the short-term costs and benefits and/or the long-term, lifelong costs and benefits of smoking?

4 Why do you think people start smoking?

5 Why is it more difficult to give up smoking than, say, going to the cinema or eating chocolate?

6 Would it be better for individuals and society if the government were to make cigarette smoking illegal in the UK?

has to assess the costs and benefits of any particular course of action. For instance, what would be the costs and benefits to the workers who wanted to buy their closed-down factory?

- The cost would be the money they would have to put up to buy the factory from its owners, their former employers. However, costs could be even greater. If the factory started to make a loss, they could not only lose all the money they had put into the firm but also be liable to pay the losses of the firm.

- The benefits would be that they would still be in a job. They would get a salary. What's more, if the company were successful, they could take a share of the profits and see the value of their initial capital investment increase.

These costs and benefits relate to the individual workers who are making the decision about whether to buy the factory. They are examples of PRIVATE COSTS and PRIVATE BENEFITS. Individuals and companies make decisions on the basis of these private costs and benefits.

But there may well be other costs and benefits of a decision. SOCIAL COSTS and SOCIAL BENEFITS are the costs and benefits to society as a whole of an individual decision. For instance, local residents may have been extremely glad that the factory closed down because of the pollution it caused. On the other hand, if the factory were successful, it might take on more workers creating extra jobs and incomes for others. It is these social costs and benefits which should form the basis for decision-making in society as a whole. Social costs and benefits are discussed in more detail in Unit 46.

Six of the workers who decided to buy the factory where they worked when it was faced with closure.
(*Source: Express and Star*, 23 March 1992)

examples of such behaviour.

2 If you were given £5, how would you spend this money? Explain why this would be the 'best' way of spending the money for you.

3 Describe how you spend a typical Monday from getting up in the morning to going to bed at night. Why does this represent the 'best' use of your time so far as you are concerned? What could you do with your time which would be less worth while?

4 Explain the difference between a private cost and a social cost.

5 What are the private costs and benefits to you of spending an evening travelling around your area on a motorbike which you own? What would be the social costs of this?

6 What are the private costs and benefits to you of taking this class this year? What are the social costs and benefits of taking this class? (Consider here the costs and benefits to others of your studying.)

COURSEWORK SUGGESTION

Examine the private costs and benefits of running a motorbike. Describe both monetary and non-monetary benefits. What are the social costs and benefits of motorbikes in the UK? Would it be better for (a) motorcyclists and (b) society as a whole if the minimum age for driving a motorcycle were raised to 18?

CHECKPOINTS

1 What is meant by 'rational economic behaviour'? Give two

KEY TERMS

RATIONALITY – making decisions in a reasoned way.

MAXIMISATION – securing the optimal or best situation.

PRIVATE COSTS AND BENEFITS – costs and benefits paid and received by individual economic decision-makers.

SOCIAL COSTS AND BENEFITS – the costs and benefits which accrue to society from a given course of action.

Spending Wisely

Figure 4.1 Time Diary for a typical week

	Mon	Tues	Wed	Thurs	Fri	Sat	Sun
Sleeping							
Eating							
Paid work							
Household duties							
College or School							
Homework							
Leisure activities:							
Television							
Reading							
Other main activity							
All other activities							

S T U D Y P O I N T S

1 Copy out Figure 4.1 and fill in the time spent on each activity for a typical week.

2 Assume that you are given one hour's extra homework a night and two hours' extra at the weekend.
  (a) What would you give up doing to make room for this?
  (b) What would be the benefits of this change?

  (c) What would be the costs of the change?
  (d) Would the benefits outweigh the costs of the change?
  Explain your answers.

3 The television breaks down and it can't be replaced for another two months.
  (a) How would you use the extra time available?

  (b) Why do you prefer to watch television rather than allocate your time in this other way?

4 (a) What is the opportunity cost for you of time spent doing household duties?
  (b) Do the benefits gained from your doing household duties outweigh the costs (i) for you; (ii) for anyone living with you?

2

'In 1968, Proctor and Gamble launched Ariel, the popular washing powder, onto the UK market. In the same year, Schweppes put out a drink called Cresta and Cadbury launched a product called Appletree. The year also saw Rank Hovis McDougall introduce Scotts' hot cereals in strawberry and raspberry flavours. Today, only Ariel remains a market leader.' (*Source: Financial Times*, 7 March 1985)

Firms launch many new products each year. Most of them are failures, because customers don't want to buy them. Like Cresta and Appletree, they soon disappear from the supermarket shelves. Only a few products, like Ariel, survive to sell year after year. Why is this? Why is it that consumers buy some products and not others? Why is it that consumers allocate their scarce resources in one way rather than in another way?

Costs and Benefits

In the previous unit, we saw that consumers for the most part are rational. So they would consider the *costs* and *benefits* of a particular purchase. Take the purchase of a Mars Bar.

- The cost of a Mars Bar to the consumer is the *opportunity cost* – the benefit gained from the most desirable item the consumer has to give up because of the purchase of the Mars Bar. This may be another type of chocolate bar or an ice cream or a magazine. There may be other real costs. The sugar and fat content of a Mars Bar may damage the health of the consumer. There may be purchase costs as well. Buying a Mars Bar might involve a five-minute walk to a shop, whereas the next best alternative, like a newspaper, might be available there and then.

- The benefits of a Mars Bar would include relief of hunger and the giving of energy (because of the sugar content). A consumer might also like the taste and sensation of eating a Mars Bar. A Mars Bar might also be available there and then, whereas the next most desirable alternative might involve a walk or time cost. In economics, the benefits resulting from the consumption of an item are often called the SATISFACTION or UTILITY to be gained from consumption.

If the benefits of a Mars Bar outweigh the costs, then the consumer will buy a Mars Bar. If, however, the consumer could get better value for money by buying an apple or a newspaper, then he or she will buy the other product.

The Margin

When a consumer makes a decision about how to spend money, he or she will make that decision at the MARGIN. To understand what this means, imagine a housewife going round a supermarket deciding what to buy. She has £100 to spend. She doesn't fill up 10 baskets and then decide which basketful of goods to buy. In other words, she doesn't compare how she is going to spend *all* her £100. What she does is to think about each individual purchase separately. Would it be better to buy this brand of baked beans rather than another? Would it be better to buy pork this week or beef? Is it worth not buying any biscuits so that she can afford to buy some batteries for the radio? The housewife is here deciding how to spend each *extra* pound of her money. She is making a decision at the margin of what she has to spend.

You do the same when deciding how to spend your time. When you decide whether or not to go out to the cinema, for instance, you don't decide how to spend *all* your time for the next week, or month or year in order to make that decision. What you do is to weigh up the advantages and disadvantages of spending this *extra* part of your time. You are making a decision about how to spend your marginal time.

CHECKPOINTS

1 Try to name one product that was put onto the market by a company and that is now no longer sold. Why do you think this happened?

2 Assume that you decide to buy a packet of crisps. What would be the costs and benefits of this action to you personally?

3 Giving examples, explain what is meant by 'utility' in economics.

4 What is meant by 'the margin'?

5 Why might a shopper decide to buy:
   (a) size 1 eggs rather than size 3 eggs?
   (b) a chicken rather than a leg of lamb?
   (c) a Sony television rather than a Philips television?

COURSEWORK SUGGESTION

Ask each member of your household to keep an account of what they spend over a period of time (say, a week). Analyse how spending has been allocated between different categories of consumption goods (see Unit 6 for details of how consumption is broken down nationally). Consider why different members of the household allocated resources in the way that they did. Did each member make the best use of scarce resources? What do you mean by 'best' use?

KEY TERMS

SATISFACTION or UTILITY – the benefit to be gained from the consumption of a good or service.

THE MARGIN – the last (or next) part of a whole. Taking a decision at the margin, therefore, involves decision-making about the last (or next) part of a larger whole.

Measuring Resources

STUDY POINTS

1 Conduct a survey amongst five of your friends. Ask them how much money they received on average per week one year ago, and how much they receive today (e.g. from working, as an allowance, as pocket money). Make a list as in Figure 5.1 and record your results there.

2 Display your results on a bar graph, rank ordering your respondents in terms of income received today. Figure 5.2 is an example.

3 Now convert your figures into **INDEX NUMBER** form. This means that you will call one of your figures '100'. This is the 'base' figure. Then you will compare all the other figures with this base figure and convert them into index numbers in proportion to the base. For instance, converting the figures on the graph (Figure 5.2) into index number form and using David's income today (i.e. £20.00) as a base would give the results shown in Figure 5.3.
Choose as your base figure (i.e. the figure you are going to call 100), the middle figure of today's figures you have collected from your friends. Convert both income today and one year ago to an index with this base.

4 Display your results on a bar chart. What do you notice about this bar chart compared with the first bar chart you drew?

5 Did £1 buy more, less or the same quantity of goods one year ago as it does today? If your income had been £10 a year ago, how much would you need today to buy the same amount of goods and services? (To answer this, ask your teacher for the inflation rate over the past twelve months.)

6 Work out how much each of the people in your survey would have needed to increase their income by to be able to buy at least as many goods and services as they did one year ago. Which people are better off and which worse off compared to a year ago?

7 Calculate the percentage increase in income over the past twelve months:
   (a) in money terms;
   (b) in real terms.

Figure 5.1

Name	Income per week (£)	
	A year ago	Today

Figure 5.2

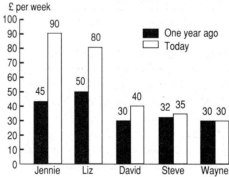

£ per week

| | One year ago | Today |

Jennie 45 90, Liz 50 80, David 30 40, Steve 32 35, Wayne 30 30

Figure 5.3

	One year ago			Today		
	£		Index number £40.00 = 100	£		Index number £40.00 = 100
Jennie	45.00	→	112.5	90.00	→	225.0
Liz	50.00	→	125.0	80.00	→	200.0
David	30.00	→	75.0	40.00	→	100.0
Steve	32.00	→	80.0	35.00	→	87.5
Wayne	30.00	→	75.0	30.00	→	75.0

Money as a Measure

Figure 5.4

	1980	1990
Production of wheat (UK) (million tonnes)	8.5	14.0
Bus passenger journeys (millions)	6783	5682

(Source: CSO, *Annual Abstract of Statistics 1992*)

Consider the data in Figure 5.4. The statistics show that wheat production went up, but the number of bus passenger journeys went down over the period 1980 to 1990. What they don't show is whether the rise or the decline were important relative to each other. To do this, you would need a common measure of both wheat production and bus journeys. Economists often use money as this common measure. It can act as a powerful measuring rod. Figure 5.5 shows the same statistics expressed in monetary values.

Figure 5.5 £ million

	1980	1990
Production of wheat (UK)	891	1451
Bus passenger journeys	1404	2729

(Source: CSO, *Annual Abstract of Statistics 1992*)

The figures look completely different. Both the value of total wheat production and the value of bus passenger journeys have increased. Does Figure 5.5 then show that output has definitely increased in the economy?

Inflation and Real Values

The answer is probably no. Much of the increase in values will have been caused by inflation – a general increase in prices without any corresponding increase in output. If we are to compare like with like, the inflation element of a change in monetary values has to be taken out. Economists call this changing from MONEY VALUES or CURRENT PRICES to REAL VALUES or CONSTANT PRICES.

On average, prices in the UK approximately doubled between 1980 and 1990. So £1 of goods bought in 1980 would have cost about £2 in 1990. That means that £891 million of wheat produced in 1980 and valued at 1980 prices would have cost about £1782 million at 1990 prices (i.e. £891 million multiplied by approximately 2). The 1990 value of £1404 million spent on bus journeys in 1980 was £2808 million (i.e. £1404 million multiplied by approximately 2).

Now we can compare the value of output *after* inflation has been removed from the figures. They are shown in Figure 5.6.

Figure 5.6 — £ million at 1990 prices

	1980	1990
Production of wheat (UK)	1680	1451
Bus passenger journeys	2647	2729

(Source: CSO, Annual Abstract of Statistics 1992)

This now gives the REAL change in the value of money output; or as economists sometimes put it, this shows the change at CONSTANT (1990) PRICES.

The story that Figure 5.6 tells is different from that of Figure 5.4. In Figure 5.4, we saw that wheat production measured in tonnes went up but the number of bus passenger journeys went down between 1980 and 1990. In Figure 5.6, we measure this change in real money terms. It shows that the real (money) value of wheat production fell slightly whilst the real value of bus journeys increased.

Index Numbers

Another way in which these statistics could be presented is in the form of INDEX NUMBERS. An index number is a way of showing proportional changes in a set of statistics. One particular figure is chosen as the BASE figure and given the value of 100. Changes in the figures are shown as changes on this base of 100. For instance, assume there were 30 students in the class at the start of the year and 27 at the end of the year. Taking the 30 students as the base figure of 100, the index of students would change from 100 to 90. The proportions (30 to 27 and 100 to 90) have remained identical.

Going back to the original figures for the production of wheat and bus passenger journeys, and calling 1980 the base year, the statistics would look like those in Figure 5.7.

Figure 5.7 — 1980 = 100

	1980	1990
Production of wheat (UK)	100	166
Bus passenger journeys	100	84

(Source: CSO, Annual Abstract of Statistics 1992)

It is important to realise that wheat production and bus journeys were not the same in 1980 even though we give both statistics a value of 100. The 100 figure only means that that is the starting point for comparing other figures in the same series in other years.

Index numbers are particularly useful when it comes to comparing averages of several figures.

CHECKPOINTS

1 A farmer produces 20 tonnes of apples, which he sells at £400 a tonne. What is the monetary value of the 20 tonnes of apples?

2 A shop sells 1000 pairs of jeans at £30 each. What is the monetary value of 1000 pairs?

3 What is the percentage increase in price in the following examples?

	Old price	New price
(a)	£100	£110
(b)	£100	£150
(c)	£200	£250
(d)	£500	£1000

4 A family spends £400 a month. How much would it need to spend to maintain the real value of its spending (i.e. buy the same amount of goods and services as before), if prices increased by: (a) 10%; (b) 20%; (c) 50%; (d) 100%?

5 A pint of milk cost 50p in 2005. How much would it have cost in 1995, if the price of a pint of milk had increased by: (a) 100%; (b) 50%; (c) 20% over the period 1995–2005?

6 A worker receives yearly increases in wages. Convert these figures into an index, using 1995 as a base year:

	1994	1995	1996	1997	1998
daily wages (£)	20	50	60	100	150

COURSEWORK SUGGESTION

Take a particular set of economic statistics – for example, the gross national product (GNP), the retail price index (RPI) or the current account on the balance of payments. Explain how the statistics are calculated and what they calculate. Explain how money values are used to measure physical quantities. Show how the statistics can be converted to real values and to an index. Discuss the economic significance of the statistics: in particular, how they might illustrate the basic economic problem.

Data Response Questions
Units 1–5

Unit 1 Scarce Resources and Infinite Wants

Fight for school site is lost

Lichfield mayor Councillor Mrs Ann Johnson has lost her fight to save a site earmarked for a new primary school.

Education committee members yesterday decided to release the 2.17 hectares of land at Cappers Lane, Lichfield, for housing.

Councillor Johnson had pleaded for the site to be kept for educational use claiming it was needed to service the 2300 houses in the area.

She said that at present the children had to cross a main railway and two busy roads to get to school.

She accused the council of selling off the land for short term financial gain.

'If this land is lost it will be a blight on the future of our children. If we want to expand primary education in Lichfield there will be nowhere to do it,' she added.

Committee chairman Councillor Roger Wright said there was no need for another school. He said there were vacancies at three nearby schools and no indication that another school would be needed in the future.

A report to the committee says half the land could be used to build 30 to 40 houses and the rest could be left as public open space.

Source: Express and Star, 13 June 1992

1 What 'wants' did Mrs Johnson have according to the article? *(3 marks)*

2 (a) What is meant by 'scarce resources' in Economics?
   (b) Why is land in Lichfield a scarce resource? *(6 marks)*

3 Explain how the article illustrates the basic economic problem. *(6 marks)*

Unit 2 Choice, Opportunity Cost and Allocation

Old folk to pay more for their meals on wheels

Pensioners in Wolverhampton will have to pay more than 40 per cent extra for their meals on wheels. The charge goes up 10p from 60p to 70p at the start of next month.

And at the end of the year the cost will go up another 15p to 85p.

The move is to raise an additional £83 500 a year for Wolverhampton Council's hard-pressed social services department.

A report by social services director Martin Shreeve said that prices rose by 10p at the beginning of February.

He pointed out that the extra revenue was needed as a contribution to the department's cost-cutting measures, and to pay for the growing number of meals likely to be demanded by the town's increasingly aged population.

Source: Express and Star, 12 June 1992

1 What is to be the increase in price for meals on wheels in Wolverhampton according to the article? *(1 mark)*

2 Why are prices going up? *(2 marks)*

3 (a) What is meant by 'opportunity cost'?
   (b) What is the opportunity cost to Wolverhampton pensioners of the rise in prices? *(6 marks)*

4 Explain who might benefit from the £83 500 a year reallocation of resources. *(6 marks)*

Essay Questions
Units 1–5

1 Mr Spencer has £200 saved in his building society account. He wants to buy a washing machine (cost £199.99) and a colour television set (cost £189.99).
   (a) What can Mr Spencer afford to buy with his savings? *(4 marks)*
   (b) Give *two* reasons why he might want to buy the washing machine. *(4 marks)*
   (c) What is meant by 'opportunity cost' and what is the opportunity cost to Mr Spencer of buying a washing machine? *(6 marks)*
   (d) Why does Mr Spencer face the basic economic problem? *(6 marks)*

Unit 3 Economic Decision Making

Protest grows on plan for stores

Opponents of plans to build two out-of-town superstores in Darleston packed into a protest meeting yesterday.

Traders from the local town centres of Darleston and Wednesbury joined councillors and community leaders to draw up their battle plans.

Developers want to build the two superstores on land being reclaimed by the Black Country Development Corporation. The two sites would be within easy reach of a large part of the Black Country especially now that the new Black Country spine road, a motorway linking the M6 with the centre of the Black Country, is under construction.

Source: adapted from the *Express and Star*, 31 March 1992

1 What is an 'out-of-town superstore'? *(2 marks)*

2 What would be the likely costs and benefits to the following if the two superstores were built?
   (a) the owners of the superstores;
   (b) traders from Darleston and Wednesbury;
   (c) workers in the local area. *(9 marks)*

3 Discuss who you think should be allowed to decide whether the superstores should be built. *(4 marks)*

2 Jane Harris, an apprentice engineer, has decided to buy a motorbike at a cost of £750.
   (a) What is the private cost to Jane of buying and operating the motorbike? *(6 marks)*
   (b) What might be the private benefits to Jane of owning the motorbike? *(6 marks)*
   (c) What might be the social costs of Jane using a motorbike? *(8 marks)*

Unit 4 Spending Wisely

Record survey

A survey published this week shows that most people have already decided which album they want to buy before they go into a shop. Only 32% of people questioned in the survey said that they chose records mainly by browsing through stock in shops and even fewer (21%) chose singles in this way. Price seemed to have little influence upon choice of records: 77% of people said that they were rarely put off buying a record because of its price. If a record was expensive, people said that they would still buy even though it meant that they had to buy less of something else. 35% of people said that they bought records because "they were in the charts", 32% because friends had bought the record, 44% because they had heard the record on radio or television and only 5% because the record had been cheap. But price was important in deciding where records were bought. 55% of people said that they bought records from shops where they thought price would be lowest.

1 According to the survey, what made people decide to buy a particular record? *(3 marks)*

2 According to the survey, in what way was the price of a record important in deciding to buy a record? *(1 mark)*

3 What is the opportunity cost of buying an expensive record? *(2 marks)*

4 What benefits or utility might a consumer gain from buying a record? *(4 marks)*

Unit 5 Measuring Resources

Index of consumers' expenditure on food and services (1985 = 100)

	At current prices		At constant (1985) prices	
	Food	Services[1]	Food	Services[1]
1971	28	20	97	80
1981	100	100	100	100
1991	178	282	111	149

[1] excluding rent and rates.
(*Source:* CSO, *Economic Trends Annual Supplement 1992* and CSO, *Monthly Digest of Statistics, April 1992*)

1 What is meant by an 'index'? *(4 marks)*

2 By what percentage did expenditure on food incease between 1981 and 1991 (a) in money terms and (b) in real terms? *(2 marks)*

3 (a) How has expenditure on food changed between 1971 and 1991 compared to expenditure on services?
   (b) Suggest why the change has been different in each case. *(9 marks)*

Patterns of Spending

Figure 6.1 Average weekly household expenditure, 1990
Source: Department of Employment, *Family Expenditure 1990*

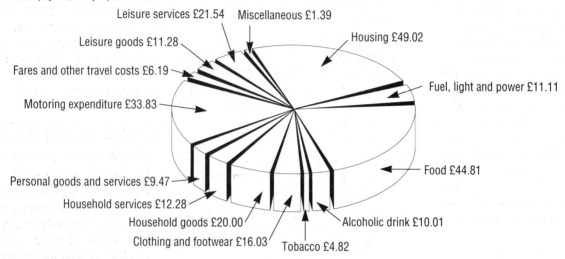

Leisure services £21.54 Miscellaneous £1.39 Housing £49.02
Leisure goods £11.28
Fares and other travel costs £6.19
Motoring expenditure £33.83
Fuel, light and power £11.11
Personal goods and services £9.47
Household services £12.28
Household goods £20.00
Clothing and footwear £16.03
Tobacco £4.82
Alcoholic drink £10.01
Food £44.81

Figure 6.2 Pattern of household expenditure, 1957–90

Figure 6.3 Average weekly household expenditure, 1990
Source: Department of Employment, *Family Expenditure 1990*

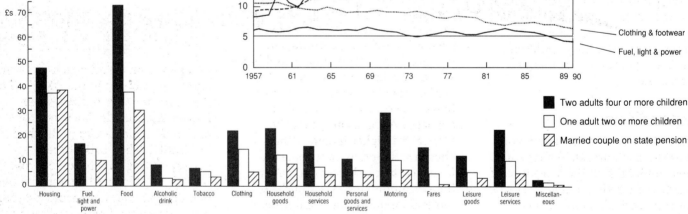

- Food
- Housing
- Motoring & fares
- Clothing & footwear
- Fuel, light & power

■ Two adults four or more children
□ One adult two or more children
▨ Married couple on state pension

Housing, Fuel light and power, Food, Alcoholic drink, Tobacco, Clothing, Household goods, Household services, Personal goods and services, Motoring, Fares, Leisure goods, Leisure services, Miscellaneous

STUDY POINTS

1 Put in rank order, starting with the largest expenditure first, the components of average weekly household expenditure (1990) shown in Figure 6.1.

2 Write down how much your household spends on average in a typical week on each of the categories in Figure 6.1. Draw a pie chart showing your household expenditure.

3 Using Figures 6.1 and 6.3, and the pie chart

you have drawn of your own expenditure, explain why different households spend different proportions of their income on housing, food, alcoholic drink, etc. For instance, why do pensioner households spend so little on housing? Why do single-parent families spend so little on alcoholic drink?

4 Using Figure 6.2, describe how household expenditure has changed over time.

5 What reasons can you think of to explain why patterns of expenditure have changed over time. In your answer, remember that real household income doubled (i.e. households could buy twice as many goods and services) over the period 1957–90. Has there been any difference in spending on necessities and goods and services that could be called 'luxuries'?

The Typical Household

Households face the same basic economic problems common to all economic decision-makers. They have a limited income and therefore can buy only a limited number of goods and services. This unit considers what consumers do buy in the UK and how this has changed over time. Figure 6.1 shows how the average household in the UK spends its money. The figures are taken from the *Family Expenditure* survey. Each year, the government picks about 11 000 households and asks those households to record their expenditure in detail for a two-week period. An average is then worked out for all the households and also for special households, like pensioner or one-parent households. The SURVEY is not totally accurate because:

- the information given by households to the government is not always completely accurate;
- as in any survey, only a *sample* of the population is taken. In 1990, 7000 households from the 11 000 agreed to help with the survey; 17 500 people lived in the households surveyed, out of a total UK population of nearly 58 million. Every effort is made to try to make sure that the households surveyed provide a representative cross-section of the population, but it is not possible to be totally accurate.

Expenditure

Figure 6.1 gives the breakdown of CONSUMER EXPENDITURE in a typical household. Most of the categories of spending are self-explanatory: namely, housing, food, alcoholic drink, tobacco, and clothing and footwear. Of the others:

- 'fuel, light and power' refers to gas, electricity, coal and oil paid for by the consumer;
- household goods include furniture, kitchen appliances like cookers, and small items such as toilet paper;
- household services are services such as insuring the contents of the house, postage, telephone and dry cleaning;
- personal goods and services include handbags, watches, jewellery, medicines, cosmetics and hairdressing;
- leisure goods include television sets, books, newspapers and gardening items like seeds and plants;
- leisure services are services such as cinema and theatre, video rental and holidays;
- 'miscellaneous' is a category which covers any items of expenditure not covered in the other specific categories, and includes pocket money to children.

Trends Over Time

Figure 6.2 shows how the composition of consumer expenditure has changed over time. Households have been spending a larger proportion of their income on housing and a lower proportion on food, clothing and footwear. The fact that households are spending relatively less on food and clothes may be due to the fact that these are NECESSITIES rather than LUXURIES. As households receive higher and higher incomes, they choose to spend extra income on luxuries such as bigger and better housing or on videos or holidays, rather than on food and clothing.

Different Households

Figure 6.3 shows the differences in spending between three different types of household. The first is a large family household with two adults and at least four children. The second is a one-parent family household with two or more children. The third type is the retired couple whose main income is the state old age pension. The stimulus will help you to draw out the difference in spending between these three types of household.

C H E C K P O I N T S

1 Explain the purpose and methods of the *Family Expenditure* survey.

2 Using the categories found in Figure 6.1, say which category each of the following expenditures would fall into: a pair of jeans, a motorcycle, a gas bill, an electric cooker, a weekend break to Paris, a packet of cigarettes, a bottle of lemonade, a magazine, a bed, a can of beer.

3 Give ten examples of services.

4 Explain the difference between a 'necessity' and a 'luxury'. Would you classify (a) housing and (b) food as necessities or luxuries?

C O U R S E W O R K S U G G E S T I O N

Compare your own household with the typical household in the UK. Find out the characteristics of the typical household from the latest edition of *Family Expenditure* (published by HMSO). Then collect the corresponding data from your own household. This will necessitate the members of your household keeping a diary of their expenditure over a short period of time. Collate the data you collect from your household so that it is in the same form as that to be found in the *Family Expenditure* survey. Then compare the allocation of resources between the 'typical' UK household and your own household. Explain why the two differ or are similar. Evaluate whether or not each household is making the 'best' use of its *scarce resources*.

K E Y T E R M S

SURVEY – the collection of data from a representative sample.

CONSUMER EXPENDITURE – spending by consumers on goods and services.

NECESSITIES – goods or services whose consumption is seen as essential in order to maintain a minimum standard of living in a society.

LUXURIES – goods and services whose consumption is seen as contributing to a higher standard of living than the minimum.

Interdependence

1 Mr and Mrs Brancelli and their children live in Mexico. He works on a banana plantation, earning £1000 a year.

3 Mr and Mrs Patel and their two children live in the UK. He is a consultant in a hospital, earning £40 000 a year and she is a housewife.

UK

Mexico

Venezuela

2 Mr and Mrs Verdi and their children live in Venezuela. He runs a grocer's shop in the capital city, Caracas, earning £3000 a year. His wife works in a shoe factory, making leather shoes for export, and earns £1000 a year.

4 Mr and Mrs Whittaker and their children also live in the UK. Mr Whittaker works at a factory making fertiliser and insecticides for export, and earns £13 000 a year. Mrs Whittaker is the manageress of a shoe shop, and earns £8000 a year.

S T U D Y P O I N T S

1 Mr Whittaker is made redundant. Give one reason why he might have lost his job. How might the other three families be affected by his redundancy?

2 An earthquake hits Mexico. As a result there is heavy damage to banana plantations. How might this affect Mr Brancelli? How might the other three families be affected?

3 (a) Mr and Mrs Whittaker decide to become self-sufficient: for instance, growing all their own food, making their own clothes, heating their house with firewood from their garden. What would the Whittaker family have to give up as a result?

(b) Would there be any possible benefits?

4 If there were a world catastrophe, such as nuclear war, which of these families is least dependent on others to maintain its standard of living and why?

The Division of Labour

The average household in the UK, according to the government's *Family Expenditure* survey, contains approximately 2.5 people. When people live together, they co-operate in many different ways. One important way in which they co-operate is to share work between themselves. This sharing of work is known as the DIVISION OF LABOUR.

Thirty years ago, division of labour in a household with a husband, wife and two children was usually quite clear. The husband went out to work to earn money for the household. He would also do any 'heavy' jobs round the house, like woodwork, decorating or other DIY activities. He would also be responsible for looking after and driving the family car. The wife would be responsible for cleaning the house, cooking, shopping and bringing up the children. The children would 'work' at school, and when they were older might do some simple tasks like setting the table or cleaning the dishes. Today, with many wives going out to work and with more husbands sharing the household tasks, there isn't such a clear-cut division of labour. But, it is still true that, in most households, some *specialisation* occurs.

Reasons for the Division of Labour

There are a number of reasons why the members of a household specialise in doing certain tasks. The major reason is that by specialisation the household can produce more goods and services with the same number of limited resources. This is because:

- each 'worker' in the household can concentrate on doing what he or she is best at doing; for instance, in one example, a young couple, John and Mary, decided that they would divide the household tasks as follows. John became responsible for cooking, and Mary for gardening, as each showed a particular aptitude for their allotted task.

- the 'worker' can build up an expertise in a particular task which would not be possible if work were shared.

The members of the household can also choose to specialise in what they most enjoy doing.

The Household and the Wider Economy

Members of a household specialise within their household. But the household itself is INTERDEPENDENT with the rest of the economy. The household does not attempt to be totally self-sufficient. It does not grow all its own food, make all its own clothes, build its own furniture or house, for instance. What it does is to buy in many of these goods and services. In *exchange*, the typical household will provide workers to make highly specialised goods and services for other households. The household can then obtain all manner of goods and services – everything from oranges to televisions and foreign holidays – which it would not be able to obtain if it produced in total isolation.

The whole of the modern economy is built upon the division of labour. Each household depends upon millions of other workers all round the world to provide goods and services. That is why households are 'interdependent' and not 'independent' in a modern society. That is also why, if there were a complete breakdown of society (such as might follow a nuclear war), very few people in the UK would be able to survive. Workers have become so specialised that they do not have the skills to be a builder, own food-grower-cum-fuel-gatherer-cum-doctor, etc. What is more, without other workers such as oil drillers and mechanics, very few machines would work and without machines people can produce very little.

This division of labour in industry will be discussed further in Unit 19.

This division of labour in industry will be discussed further in Unit 19.

CHECKPOINTS

1 What is meant by the division of labour?

2 Describe the division of labour in your own household.

3 Would you be better off if you tried to be totally self-sufficient (i.e. if you lived on your own and you produced everything you needed yourself)? Explain your answer.

4 What would a household have to produce in order to be totally self-sufficient? Is it possible, do you think, for a household to be totally self-sufficient in the UK today? Explain your answer.

5 Describe how your household is interdependent with (i.e. depends upon) other households: (a) in your local area; (b) in the UK; and (c) in the world economy.

COURSEWORK SUGGESTION

Observe and record how five different households organise their activities. One of these households should be your own. Analyse the extent to which each member of the household specialises in performing different tasks. Explain why this division of labour takes place. Try to decide whether or not each household is making the most efficient use of its labour. Explain what an 'efficient use' might consist of.

KEY TERMS

DIVISION OF LABOUR – a system whereby workers concentrate on performing a few tasks and then exchange their surplus for other goods and services. The division of labour is an example of *specialisation*.

INTERDEPENDENCE – a situation where one economic unit is economically reliant upon other economic units, for instance for food or raw materials or services.

Exchange

German prisoner-of-war camps consisted normally of 1200 to 2500 people. They were housed in large bungalow huts, 200 prisoners to each hut. Supplies came from two sources. Rations were provided by the Germans. More importantly, Red Cross food parcels were given out containing items such as tinned milk, jam, butter, biscuits, chocolate, sugar and cigarettes.

A complicated system of trade and exchange operated. The cigarette was the standard of value. At the start, people wandered through the bungalows calling their offers – 'cheese for seven' (cigarettes). The hours after a Red Cross parcel issue were chaos. The inconveniences of this system soon led to its replacement. Exchange and Mart notice boards were put up in every bungalow. Under the headings 'name', 'room number', 'wanted' and 'offered', sales and wants were advertised. When a deal went through, it was crossed off the board. Prices became generally known throughout the camp. Although cigarettes were the normal currency, barter deals continued.

Cigarettes performed more or less well the functions of metallic currency or money: as a medium of exchange; as a measure of value; and as a store of value. Cigarettes also shared many of the characteristics of metallic money. They were homogeneous, reasonably durable, and of convenient size for the smallest or, in packets, for the largest transactions.

Prices changed frequently. Part of the problem was that cigarettes were also used for smoking. While the Red Cross issue of 50 or 25 cigarettes per man per week came in regularly, the cigarette currency worked well. But when Red Cross parcels weren't distributed for some reason, prices fell. Then less trade took place and bartering increased. On the other hand, several hundred thousand cigarettes might arrive in the space of a fortnight. Prices would rocket and then begin to fall, slowly at first, but more rapidly as stocks of cigarettes in the camp ran out – until the next big delivery.

(*Source*: Adapted from R. A. Radford, 'The Economic Organisation of POW Camps', *Economica*, vol. XII, November 1945)

S T U D Y   P O I N T S

1 What was a German prisoner-of-war camp?

2 Why did prisoners exchange items from their rations and Red Cross parcels?

3 Why was there no money in the form of notes and coins used in the camps?

4 What is 'barter'? Why was it used in the camps?

5 Why did trading in cigarettes prove more popular than bartering?

6 Why did cigarettes come to be used as money?

7 What problems were there, do you think, in using cigarettes as currency?

Production in the world economy is based upon the division of labour. Workers specialise in producing particular goods and services. What they then do is EXCHANGE these for other goods and services. This unit considers exchange and its importance in the economy.

Barter

Before money came into existence, all exchange was conducted through BARTER. A farmer might want a cow and be ready to pay 20 hens for it. He then had to find a farmer with a cow who might want 20 hens. If he was lucky enough to find one, the two farmers could then barter the cow for the 20 hens. But what if the farmer with the cow didn't want 20 hens, but wanted a horse instead? This was the major problem of barter – it was difficult for one person to find somebody else who was willing to barter exactly what he or she wanted. The result was that trade and exchange didn't form an important part of the economy.

Money

The appearance of money changed this. MONEY is anything that is acceptable to a wide number of people and organisations as payment for goods and services. Money allows a person to sell something – for example, his or her time as a worker – and then to buy something at a later date. Anything which is money has three main jobs or *functions*.

- It is a *medium of exchange* – that means that when buyers and sellers get together to exchange, money is an acceptable means of payment.
- It is a *store of value* – that means that when a seller sells something for money, it will keep its value until it can be spent at a later date.

- It is a *measure of value* – money is used to put a value on goods and services. If a book is priced at £2 and a pair of shoes at £20, then we know that ten books have the same value as one pair of shoes.

In theory, anything can act as money. In the past, everything from cowrie shells, to pigs, to cigarettes have been used. It helps, however, if what acts as money has certain *characteristics* or features. These include:

- *limited supply* – this means that there must be only a limited amount of money available. If it were not limited, it would not have any value. So gold is a good money in this sense, whereas sand would be very poor.
- *divisibility* – it is easier if the money can be broken down into small units. Pigs were not very useful as money, because it is not possible to chop off a small part of the pig to make a payment and keep the pig intact.
- *portability* – it should be easy to carry around.
- *durability* – it should last. Cigarettes, for example, are not a very good form of money, because they deteriorate quickly when passed from person to person.
- *homogeneity* – money of the same value should be the same in size, shape, etc.

Without money, the whole system of the division of labour, specialisation and exchange would collapse. Money is therefore a very important resource in the economy. What constitutes money in a modern economy is considered in Unit 52.

Money must be a medium of exchange, a store and a measure of value.

CHECKPOINTS

1. What is meant by 'barter'? Describe any experiences of barter that you have had. What difficulties did you encounter?
2. Explain why exchange is essential if there is to be a division of labour in the economy.
3. What is the difference between the functions of money and the characteristics of money?
4. Explain why a £1 coin today (a) fulfils the three functions of money and (b) possesses the characteristics of good money.

COURSEWORK SUGGESTION

Examine the use of gold, notes and bank current-account assets as money. Explain why gold was once used as money and why it lost its function to notes and bank current-account assets in the modern industrial world. Analyse the advantages and disadvantages of the use of these three types of money. Evaluate the extent to which notes will cease to be used as money over the next 100 years, as electronic banking becomes a reality.

KEY TERMS

EXCHANGE – the exchange of goods and services for goods (bartering) or for money.

BARTER – the direct exchange of goods and services for other goods and services without using money.

MONEY – anything that is generally acceptable as a means of payment.

The Market

STUDY POINTS

1 What is happening in each of the three photographs?

2 What do you understand by the term 'a market'? Why are all three situations shown in the photographs examples of markets?

3 What influences car owners in their decision (a) to buy petrol rather than other products and (b) to buy petrol at one petrol station rather than another?

4 (a) What will happen to the price of apples, if there is a shortage of apples on the market? Why?
  (b) How might apple producers respond next season to this?

5 What will happen to the production of a particular toy if it proves so popular that supplies are continually running out in the shops? Why?

6 How might a shop react if it had ordered 30 dresses at £19.99 in September, but found that it had only sold 20 of them by 24 December?

7 Who decides what is bought and sold in a market? Is it consumers? Is it producers? Is it the government? Give examples of particular markets in your answer.

- A new hospital is built in Liverpool
- Cadbury's increases its production of chocolate bars
- Consumers buy less butter

Who decides that all this will happen? Who decides what is to be produced and consumed? (Or, as economists might say, who decides how scarce resources are to be allocated?) Economists argue that there are two main ways in which decisions about the allocation of resources are made.

- The *market mechanism* links individual consumers and producers. We will start to consider the workings of the market mechanism in this unit.
- The *state* allocates resources too. This will be considered in Units 53–55.

The Market

A MARKET is a place where goods are bought and sold. In a local street market, shoppers who want to buy goods can meet stall holders who want to sell goods. The market is the place where buyers and sellers meet and goods and services are exchanged. Most markets, though, are not situated in one place like a street market. Consider this statement:

> Iraq's invasion of Kuwait in August 1990 sent the price of oil shooting up to over $40 a barrel. But at the start of the war to free Kuwait in February 1991, the price fell to $20 a barrel.

The oil market is not a visible market like a street market. You cannot pinpoint the oil market to a particular town or city. The oil market here is a worldwide market. Buyers and sellers in the market are linked by telephone and telex. Millions of pounds or dollars will exchange hands in a typical transaction. Markets, in fact, come in all shapes and sizes, from a

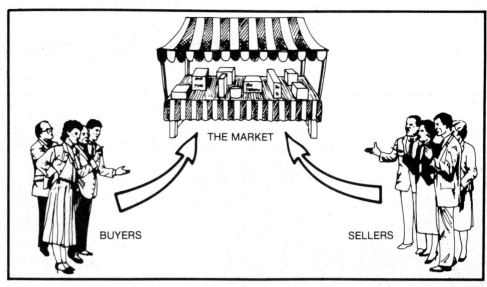

For any market to exist, there must be buyers and sellers.

local market for, say, petrol or potatoes to an international market in, say oil or diamonds.

Price

Read again the extract about oil. Notice the fact that the price of oil went up in August 1990. Buying and selling can only take place when a PRICE is agreed upon for a given *quantity* to be sold. In the case of oil, the price reached over $40 for one barrel of oil. In the market for cassettes, blank cassette tapes might be £9.99 for five tapes. In the textile market, jeans might be £29.99 per pair.

Price is determined (i.e. fixed) by buyers and sellers reacting to each other. In the case of the oil price rise, war meant that oil supplies were threatened. Buyers of oil were afraid that there would be shortages. So sellers of oil were able to put up the price of oil to take advantage of this situation. When shops cannot sell the goods they have on their shelves, what do they do? They reduce the price: for instance, in a sale. The lower prices attract more customers to buy the products. The goods are sold at a lower price.

Conclusion

A market exists whenever buyers wishing to exchange money for a good or service come into contact with sellers wishing to exchange a good or service for money. The price of the good or service and the quantity bought and sold are decided by the actions of the buyers and sellers.

C H E C K P O I N T S

1 What is meant by a 'market' in economics?

2 Give five examples of markets.

3 Why is it not possible for a market to exist where there are only sellers?

4 How are prices fixed in a market?

5 Explain the purpose of a 'sale' in a shop.

C O U R S E W O R K S U G G E S T I O N

Investigate a particular market. It could be a local market or a national or international market. Find out who are the buyers and sellers in the market. Analyse why the market exists and why prices and output are at their present level. Consider the economic consequences if the market were to collapse (i.e. sellers would no longer be willing to sell goods to buyers).

K E Y T E R M S

MARKET – where buyers meet sellers to exchange money for goods and services.

PRICE – the value put on a commodity at the point of exchange.

Data Response Questions
Units 6–9

Unit 6 Patterns of Spending

How spending on motoring changes with income

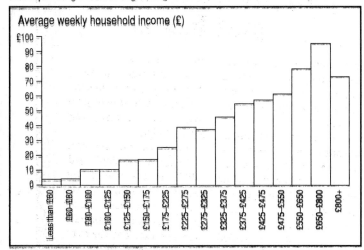

Source: Department of Employment, *Family Expenditure 1990*

1 How much (in £s) did a typical household earning between £80 and £100 a week spend on motoring in 1990?
(1 mark)

2 Approximately what percentage of total expenditure did the average household earning between £175 and £225 spend on motoring in 1990? *(2 marks)*

3 (a) How does spending on motoring change as income changes? *(3 marks)*

(b) Suggest reasons why spending changes in this way. *(9 marks)*

Unit 7 Interdependence

Sales of chocs best bar none

Britons are eating more chocolate than ever – 500 000 tonnes last year, according to a report yesterday.

Despite the recession we would give up most other things before cutting back on chocolate, said Cadbury, the UK's largest manufacturer.

The average couple each spends 93p a week on chocolate and gets through nearly 20lbs of the sweet every year.

Chocolate sales overall last year soared to nearly £2800 million – more than was spent on bread, tea, coffee, crisps, ice cream or breakfast cereals.

'People may be spending less on holidays, new cars and nights out but they are certainly not cutting down on chocolate', said Cadbury.

Source: *Express and Star*, 27 January 1992

1 What happened to chocolate sales in 1991? *(1 mark)*

2 Explain who might have benefited from spending on chocolate (a) in the UK and (b) abroad. *(8 marks)*

3 Who might have lost out because spending on chocolate rose 'despite the recession'? *(6 marks)*

Essay Questions
Units 6–9

1 (a) Explain how you spend your money. *(4 marks)*

(b) Give *four* ways in which the way you spend your money might be different from the way in which a pensioner spends his or her money. *(6 marks)*

(c) Explain, giving *two* examples, what is meant by a 'consumer durable'. *(5 marks)*

(d) Why has spending on necessities, such as food, been declining as a proportion of total expenditure in the UK over the past 20 years? *(5 marks)*

2 The Price household live in their own house in Wapping, London. The father is a print worker, the mother works in a local supermarket and their two children are still at school.

(a) Explain *four* different ways in which this family is dependent upon others in the UK economy. *(8 marks)*

(b) Give *two* ways in which the Price household are interdependent with households in other foreign economies. *(4 marks)*

(c) Why are markets important for the Price household in the way in which they earn money and spend money? *(8 marks)*

Unit 8 Exchange

Funny money

Money comes in something less than billions, as an irritated Milan reader has pointed out to *The Economist*.

Italy has been suffering from chronic shortages of small change for years, but now, he says, the situation is becoming ridiculous. Sweets, and then postage stamps, have for years done duty for small coins. The state autostrada tollgates freely give change in meticulously packed postage stamps which, however, they do not always accept back again in payment from the motorist. Italians can only eat so many gumdrops, and the mail works too dismally for it to be worth posting a letter any more. So Milan has come up with a new substitute: the convertible bus ticket.

At 100 lire apiece, unused tickets have gained wide acceptance at grocers' and small businesses. And, our correspondent adds, at banks. The other day, he walked into a bank, asked for change for a 1,000 lire note and was offered a book of ten bus tickets. One rumour has it that a Milan bank distributes 1m lire worth of tickets daily to its branches to use in lieu of small change. But in Rome and Florence, where bus fares are a paltry 90 lire, the relentless pursuit of small change will persist until more change is minted (the government says not until late 1976) or inflation elevates their bus tickets into a convertible paper currency too. Good news for counterfeiters, bad news for confectioners.

Source: The Economist, 15 November 1975

1 What was being used as money in Italy in 1975, according to the article? *(1 mark)*

2 Why did this situation come about? *(1 mark)*

3 To what extent were the new monies a good medium of exchange? *(3 marks)*

4 What might have happened if the Italian Government had banned the use of the new monies but hadn't minted more small coins to replace them? *(5 marks)*

Unit 9 The Market

Drinkers go home and pubs face axe as £2 pint looms

More and more drinkers are calling time on their local as the price of a pint threatens to spill over the £2 barrier.

The North/South divide means a pint can cost up to twice as much in different parts of the country. Bitter was 86p a pint in a pub in the North West and £1.72 in a London bar.

A gin and tonic varied from 85p in Yorkshire to £1.96 again in London. But it is non-drinkers who are hammered most.

Mineral water at more than £1 a glass is not uncommon, and orange juice works out at a staggering £3.10 a pint.

Colin Brown, research manager for *Which?* said: "With all the will in the world it is difficult to see how anyone can justify such prices, especially when you look at the average store price for orange juice.'

Source: Daily Mirror, 5 March 1992.

1 How do drink prices in pubs vary between different areas of the country? *(2 marks)*

2 Suggest reasons why drink prices vary from region to region. *(4 marks)*

3 Explain why the North West of England and London form
(a) part of the same market for drink and
(b) different markets for drink. *(6 marks)*

4 Why do you think the price of orange juice and mineral water is so expensive in a pub? *(3 marks)*

Demand (1)

Your task is to:
- *formulate a hypothesis*
- test to see whether that *hypothesis* is true.

1 You want to investigate the relationship between the amount bought (or **QUANTITY DEMANDED**) of correction fluid (such as Tippex) and its price. First formulate your hypothesis (i.e. say what you think is likely to be true). Do this by copying out the following:

'*If the price of correction fluid rises, then the quantity of correction fluid will* _____.'

Now fill in the missing words: 'go up', 'stay the same', 'go down'.

2 You now need to interview ten people who you know use correction fluid. Ask them:
- how many bottles of correction fluid they bought over the past year;
- how many bottles they would have bought had the price been (a) half of the price they paid; (b) 1½ times the price paid; (c) twice the price paid; (d) five times the price paid.

3 Now fill in the following chart, Figure 10.1. To do this, first add up the number of bottles of correction fluid that the people you interviewed said they bought or would buy at each price. Then find out the price of a bottle of correction fluid at the moment and fill in each price.

Figure 10.1

	Price (in pence)	Quantity bought
half actual price		
actual price		
1½ times actual price		
2 times actual price		
5 times actual price		

Price (pence)

Number of bottles bought over the past year   **Figure 10.2**

4 Draw a graph, plotting your findings. As shown in Figure 10.2, plot quantity demanded on the *x* axis. On the *y* axis, plot the price. Draw a line showing how many were bought at each price.

5 (a) Is your original hypothesis confirmed or rejected by your findings? Does a rise in the price of correction fluid lead to a rise or fall in the number of bottles bought?
   (b) Why do you think this is the case?

'Sony, the Japanese consumer electronics company, launched the first of the new generation of 8 mm video cameras and recorders to become available in Britain yesterday. It will cost £1100. Sony expects that the UK market for portable video systems will be about 75 000 units, and combined camera-recorders, like Video 8, 48 000.'
(*Source: Financial Times,* 22 March 1985)

Why might 48 000 combined camera-recorders have been sold in Britain in 1985? What has happened to sales of camcorders ten years on now that prices have fallen to around £500? These are questions about what economists call **EFFECTIVE DEMAND** – the quantity of a product that will be bought at any given price.

Economists argue that the lower the price, the more will be demanded. The following extract gives an example of this.

'The Ford Motor Company sold 386 000 cars in the UK in 1991. But it only achieved this level of sales by conducting a price war with its competitors. It offered everything from large discounts to low-cost finance to special fleet deals.'
(*Source:* Adapted from *Financial Times,* 17 February 1992)

By reducing prices, Ford managed to sell more cars. If it had sold them at the normal 'list' price, it would have sold fewer cars. This is because at higher prices some car buyers would have bought other makes of car (Rovers, Vauxhalls, etc.).

Lowering prices, then, will lead to a rise in quantity demanded – an **EXTENSION OF DEMAND**. A rise in prices will lead to a fall in quantity demanded – a **CONTRACTION OF DEMAND**.

A Graphical Analysis

The relationship between the quantity of a product demanded and factors such as price and income can be shown on a graph. Read again the extract from the *Financial Times* about Ford. Then study Figure 10.3.

Figure 10.3

Price per car (£)	Number of cars sold per year
12 000	200 000
10 000	300 000
8 000	400 000
6 000	500 000
4 000	600 000

This table is a crude estimate of the number of cars that Ford would sell at a given average price per car sold. It assumes that all other factors remain the same when prices change.

If these figures are now plotted on a graph, then the result is as shown in Figure 10.4. The line drawn on the graph is known as the DEMAND CURVE (even though in this case the line is a straight line rather than a curve). The demand curve shows how much would

Figure 10.4

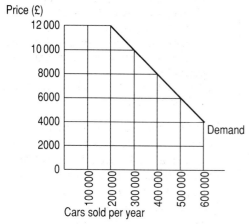

be bought at any given price over a period of time.

So, if Ford sold 250 000 cars a year, it can be seen from the graph that the average price per car sold would have been £11 000. If Ford dropped its average price to £4000, there would be an *extension* of demand to 600 000 cars a year. This is shown by a movement along the curve. If prices now rose to £8000 a year, there would be a *contraction* of demand to 400 000 sales per year, again leading to a movement along the curve from the previous level of demand.

CHECKPOINTS

1 Explain, giving an example, what is meant by 'effective demand'.

2 Give five examples of goods or services you have demanded recently. What price did you pay? How much of the product did you buy?

3 You are thinking of buying a new paperback book at £11.99, but decide in the end not to buy it because it is too expensive. Why is this NOT an example of effective demand?

4 Draw a demand curve from the following data:

Price (£)	Quantity demanded
10	100
8	250
6	400
4	550

Indicate on the curve a contraction of demand from a quantity demanded of 250 units to 100 units.

Figure 10.5

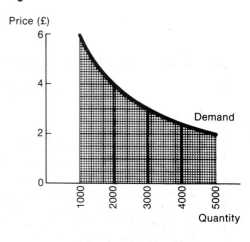

5 From Figure 10.5, how much would be demanded at prices of £4 and £6? What would be the extension in demand, if the price fell from £4 to £2?

COURSEWORK SUGGESTION

This project involves the collection of data over a six-month period. Find out what fruit and vegetables are purchased in your household and where they are commonly purchased. Then, every week, preferably on the same day of the week, note on a record sheet the survey prices in the shops of these fruit and vegetables. On the record sheet, also note down the weekly quantity of each fruit and vegetable purchased by your household. On the basis of the six months' evidence, describe your findings. Draw a demand curve (quantity demanded per week against price) for each fruit and vegetable surveyed. Explain the problems you encountered in gathering your evidence and in analysing it. Try to decide the extent to which the demand curve for fruit and vegetables is downward sloping.

KEY TERMS

EFFECTIVE DEMAND or **DEMAND** – the quantity that a buyer is willing and able to buy over a period of time.

EXTENSION OF DEMAND – the increase in quantity demanded due to a fall in price.

CONTRACTION OF DEMAND – the fall in quantity demanded due to a rise in price.

DEMAND CURVE – the line that shows the relationship between price and quantity demanded over a period of time.

Demand (2)

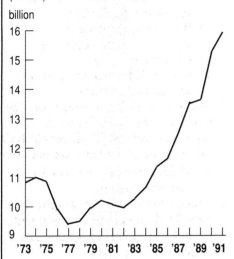

Figure 11.1 Number of letters posted per year (billions)

billion

Source: CSO, *Annual Abstract of Statistics 1984, 1992*

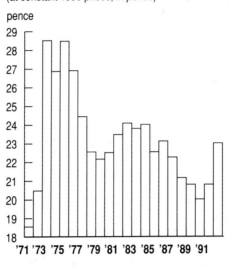

Figure 11.2 Price of a first class stamp (at constant 1990 prices, in pence)

pence

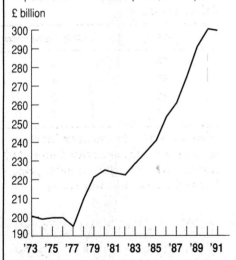

Figure 11.3 Income after tax (real personal disposable income at 1985 prices, billions)

£ billion

Source: CSO, *Economic Trends Annual Supplement*; CSO, *Monthly Digest of Statistics*, April 1992

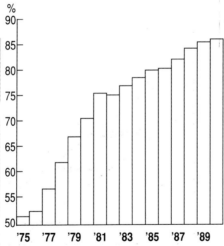

Figure 11.4 Ownership of telephones (% of households with a telephone)

%

Source: CSO, *Annual Abstract of Statistics 1984, 1992*

S T U D Y   P O I N T S

1 Who uses the letter post?

2 Make a list of ten reasons why letters are sent.

3 Look at Figure 11.1. Describe what has happened to the volume of letters sent since 1973.

4 What might have caused this change in demand for letters over time? Consider the evidence in Figures 11.2–11.4. What other factors might be important?

5 What do you think will happen to the demand for letter post in the future?

It was shown in the previous unit that the quantity of a product demanded varied according to the price charged for the product. But price is only one factor that determines demand. Consider Figure 11.5.

In 1981, the average disposable income per person in the UK (at 1985 prices) was £4014. 14.8 million licenses were purchased or demanded (i.e. there were 14.8 million cars on the road in 1981). By 1991, the average disposable income had risen to £5187 and the number of cars on the road had risen to 19.8 million. Economists have found that this relationship of rising income and rising demand is typical for most goods. A good where an increase in income leads to an increase in demand is called a **NORMAL GOOD**. But for some goods, the opposite occurs – as income rises, demand falls. These goods are known as **INFERIOR GOODS**. Possible examples of inferior goods are bread (where people switch to more expensive foods such as meat, as their incomes rise) and bus services (where people switch to cars as their incomes rise).

Other factors, apart from price and income, affect the level of demand for a product. These include:

- *The price of other products.* If, for instance, the price of beef goes up, then consumers are likely to demand more pork.
- *Advertising.* Heavy advertising should increase the demand for a product.
- *Population.* An increase in the population should raise demand for products.
- *Fashion.* Tastes change over time, and as tastes change, so does demand for particular products.

A Graphical Presentation

This can all be shown on a price/quantity graph. Consider Figure 11.6. A downward-sloping demand

Figure 11.5

Year	Income (real personal disposable income per person, UK, £ at 1985 prices)	Quantity demanded (number, in millions, of vehicle licences purchased, private cars UK)
1981	2538	14.8
1991	5187	19.8

(Sources: CSO, Annual Abstract of Statistics; CSO, Economic Trends Annual Supplement)

curve, D, is drawn for cars. What it shows is that as the average price of cars increases, the quantity of cars demanded falls. Assume that 1 million cars a year bought at £10000 each. If the incomes of consumers were to increase, what would happen? At the same price of £10000, consumers would buy more cars. Indeed, at any price more cars would be bought with higher income levels. So the increase in income pushes the demand curve out to the right. In Figure 11.6, it pushes the curve out from D to D'. At a price of £10000, consumers now want to buy 2 million cars, instead of 1 million – so the increase in income must have been fairly large. But this INCREASE IN DEMAND could have been caused by other factors. The price of petrol might have gone down, making motoring cheaper, so that consumers wanted to buy more cars. Or the government might have shut down the whole of British Rail, forcing people to buy more cars to travel.

A FALL IN DEMAND, as shown in Figure 11.7, means that at any given price, less is demanded. So this is shown by a leftward shift in the demand curves from D to D'. A fall in demand could be caused by a fall in consumers' incomes or a fall in the price of competing goods.

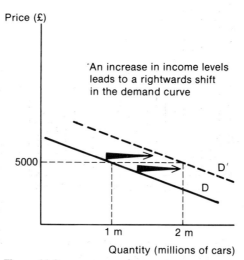

An increase in income levels leads to a rightwards shift in the demand curve

Figure 11.6

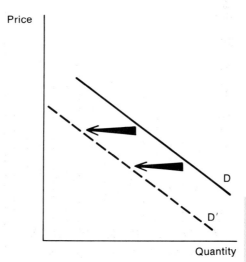

Figure 11.7

CHECKPOINTS

1 Explain carefully how and why the demand for tennis rackets will change:
   (a) if the incomes of all consumers rise by 20%;
   (b) if the price of admittance to tennis courts doubles;
   (c) if exciting matches at Wimbledon are shown on television;
   (d) if there is very poor weather during the summer.

2 Explain carefully how and why the demand for CDs will change:
   (a) if the price of CD players halves;
   (b) if the income of consumers falls;
   (c) if the price of pre-recorded cassettes halves.

3 Using a price/quantity graph, show how the demand curve might shift in each of the four cases described in question 1.

4 Explain, with examples, the difference between a normal good and an inferior good.

5 Draw a demand curve from the following data:

Price (£)	Quantity demanded
20	1
15	3
10	5
5	7

Now assume that incomes increase and, as a result, quantity demanded increases by one unit at each price. Draw the new demand curve.

COURSEWORK SUGGESTION

Construct a sample of ten people of your own age with varying incomes. Ask them to keep a diary of their income and expenditure over a period of one or two weeks. Analyse how they have spent their money, using the standard categories to be found in Unit 6. Classify their income. Explain any link you feel there might be between the income of an individual and his or her spending or saving. Consider the possible impact on demand if these ten people experience a doubling of their incomes.

Supply

Mine owners in Chile cut the wages of miners by 20%.

Petrol prices fall for third time this year.

New technology cuts the cost of making television sets.

Price of video tapes set to fall.

Frost in Brazil wipes out half the coffee crop.

Price of foreign holidays hits all time high.

Increase in tax on petrol.

Pollution threat pushes up the price of organically grown vegetables.

In 1970, the price of oil stood at less than $5 a barrel. The amount of oil known to exist underground stood at 533 billion barrels. By the early 1990s, the price of oil was over $20 a barrel. Known oil reserves had risen to over 1000 billion barrels – and this was despite the fact that 40–50 billion barrels of oil were taken out of the ground each day in the 1970s and 1980s. What had happened was that the large increase in price had encouraged oil companies to find new reserves of oil to sell to households, firms and governments. They went to places like the North Sea or Alaska, which were difficult to work in and until then had not been explored or exploited. On average, the oil men found more new oil than was actually sold in any year in the 1970s and 1980s.

This illustrates a very important principle in economics. As the price of an item rises, more will be supplied to the market. So as the price of oil rose, more oil fields were offered for exploitation. If the price of potatoes rises over a long period, more farmers will grow potatoes and supply them to the market. This relationship is shown in Figure 12.1. At a price of 60p, 150 units per week will be supplied to the market by producers. At a price of £1, producers will want to supply more to the market. The supply curve shows

STUDY POINTS

1 Read the first group of quotes (unshaded). Explain whether
   (a) oil companies,
   (b) manufacturers of video tapes,
   (c) tour operators,
   (d) farmers,
   are likely to raise or cut back on production as a result of each of these news items. These rises or falls are called EXTENSIONS or CONTRACTIONS OF SUPPLY.

2 Now look at the second group of quotes (shaded). Explain which of these:
   (a) is likely to lead to an increase in supply, i.e. where firms are likely to produce more at the same price or might be willing to cut their prices on their existing output;
   (b) is likely to lead to a fall in supply.
   These rises or falls are called INCREASES or DECREASES IN SUPPLY.

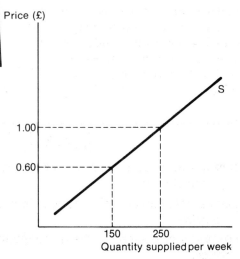

Figure 12.1

that they will want to supply 250 units per week. The definition of the word 'SUPPLY' here is the quantity of a commodity that is offered for sale at any given price over a period of time. As with demand, a change in price affecting quantity supplied is shown by a *movement along* the supply curve and is called an EXTENSION or CONTRACTION OF SUPPLY.

Other Factors Affecting Supply

Consider this:

'Renewed frosts in Brazil over the weekend pushed coffee prices up again.' (Source: *Financial Times*, 14 June 1985)

The weather is an important determinant of the supply of agricultural products like coffee or wheat or rice. Frost in Brazil means that, at any given price, less coffee will be supplied to the market because frost has damaged the crop. So the frost has led to a fall in the supply of coffee to the market.

Other factors affect the supply of coffee too. For instance, coffee supply could be increased, if new higher-yielding plants were developed. Each coffee bush would produce more beans and this would increase the supply of coffee to the market. On the other hand, an increase in wages paid to coffee workers would reduce supply. For any given quantity of coffee beans supplied, growers would now want a higher price to cover the cost of the higher wages. If coffee prices were to remain the same, some coffee growers would no longer be able to make a profit from growing coffee, because of the new higher wages. They would either grow less coffee or stop growing coffee altogether, thus reducing the supply of coffee to the market.

These changes in supply can be shown on a diagram. The frost in Brazil which led to a fall in supply would be shown by a *shift* to the left of the whole supply curve from S to S', as shown in Figure 12.2. If the price, for instance, had been OA, growers would have supplied OC of coffee to the market. The frost has reduced the crop, so at the price of OA, growers are now only prepared to supply OB.

The introduction of higher-yielding coffee bushes, on the other hand, would push the supply curve to the right, as in Figure 12.3. At any given

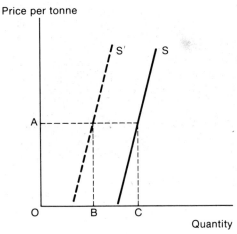

Figure 12.2

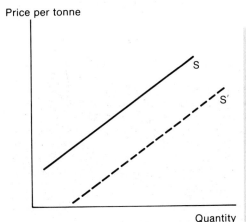

Figure 12.3

price, more coffee will be supplied to the market.

C H E C K P O I N T S

1 Explain using examples, what is meant by 'supply'.

2 What effect would the following have on the supply of cars:
   (a) a fall in the price of cars;
   (b) a fall in wages of car workers;
   (c) the introduction of robots to replace humans so as to reduce costs?

3 What is the difference between an 'extension' of supply and an 'increase' in supply?

4 Draw a supply curve from the following data.

Price (pence)	Quantity supplied
10	4
20	16
30	28
40	40
50	52

What is the quantity supplied at prices of 35p and 45p?

5 Use supply curves to illustrate each of the three cases in question 2 above.

C O U R S E W O R K S U G G E S T I O N

In this project, you are considering the supply of labour by your peer group. Construct a simple questionnaire. From the questionnaire you need to find out who has got a paid job, what the job is and what wage rate is paid. From those who have not got a job, find out why not and what rate of pay would induce them to take on paid employment. Find out from all respondents what their other sources of income are. Ask about 25 of your fellow students to complete the questionnaire. Describe your findings. Construct a supply curve for labour of your group. Analyse what would happen to supply, if wage rates were to increase. Consider the extent to which a cut in wages would affect the supply of labour.

K E Y T E R M S

SUPPLY – the quantity of a commodity that is offered for sale at a price over a period of time.

EXTENSION OF SUPPLY — the increase in quantity supplied, due to an increase in price.

CONTRACTION OF SUPPLY — the fall in quantity supplied, due to a decrease in price.

Price

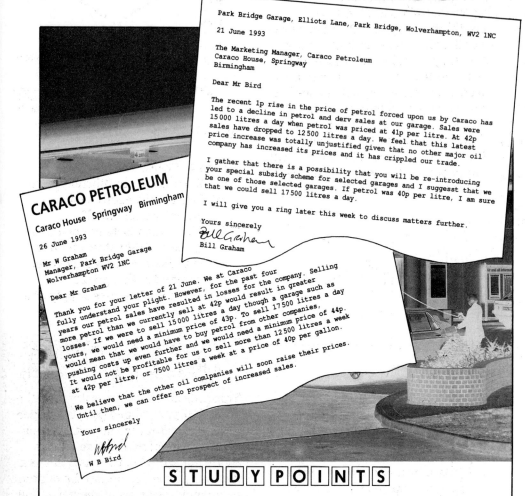

Park Bridge Garage, Elliots Lane, Park Bridge, Wolverhampton, WV2 1NC

21 June 1993

The Marketing Manager, Caraco Petroleum
Caraco House, Springway
Birmingham

Dear Mr Bird

The recent 1p rise in the price of petrol forced upon us by Caraco has led to a decline in petrol and derv sales at our garage. Sales were 15 000 litres a day when petrol was priced at 41p per litre. At 42p sales have dropped to 12 500 litres a day. We feel that this latest price increase was totally unjustified given that no other major oil company has increased its prices and it has crippled our trade.

I gather that there is a possibility that you will be re-introducing your special subsidy scheme for selected garages and I suggest that we be one of those selected garages. If petrol was 40p per litre, I am sure that we could sell 17 500 litres a day.

I will give you a ring later this week to discuss matters further.

Yours sincerely

Bill Graham

CARACO PETROLEUM
Caraco House Springway Birmingham

26 June 1993

Mr W Graham
Manager, Park Bridge Garage
Wolverhampton WV2 1NC

Dear Mr Graham

Thank you for your letter of 21 June. We at Caraco fully understand your plight. However, for the past four years our petrol sales have resulted in losses for the company. Selling more petrol than we currently sell at 42p would result in greater losses. If we were to sell 15 000 litres a day though a garage such as yours, we would need a minimum price of 43p. To sell 17 500 litres a day would mean that we would have to buy petrol from other companies, pushing costs up even further and we would need a minimum price of 44p. It would not be profitable for us to sell more than 12 500 litres a week at 42p per litre, or 7500 litres a week at a price of 40p per gallon.

We believe that the other oil companies will soon raise their prices. Until then, we can offer no prospect of increased sales.

Yours sincerely

W B Bird

S T U D Y   P O I N T S

1 Bill Graham was worried because of falling *demand* for petrol at his garage. As an economist working for Caraco Petroleum, explain:
  (a) how sales have decreased. You may want to plot a demand curve to illustrate your answer
  (b) why demand has fallen. Have motorists stopped buying petrol? Have they switched demand to other petrol stations?

2 How much is Caraco prepared to sell at different prices at Park Bridge Garage? You may want to draw a supply curve to illustrate your answer.

3 Why is Caraco prepared to sell different quantities of petrol at different prices?

4 (a) How much petrol are customers prepared to buy at a price of 40p? How much petrol is Caraco prepared to sell at that price?
  (b) How much petrol are customers prepared to buy at 41p? How much petrol is Caraco prepared to sell at that price?
  (c) How much petrol are customers prepared to buy at 42p, and how much petrol is

Caraco prepared to sell at that price?
  (d) How much petrol are customers prepared to buy at 43p and how much is Caraco prepared to sell at that price?
  (e) How much petrol are customers prepared to buy at 44p and how much is Caraco prepared to sell at that price?
  (f) What is the price at which the amount customers are prepared to buy is equal to the amount Caraco is prepared to sell? (i.e. at what price does demand equal supply? This price is known as the **EQUILIBRIUM PRICE**).

5 Draw a demand and supply curve for petrol at Park Bridge Garage and mark on it the equilibrium price and the equilibrium level of sales.

6 What would happen to the price of petrol if:
  (a) more people bought cars?
  (b) the cost of oil to the oil companies increased?
  (c) the government reduced the taxes on petrol?
  If possible, show the effects of these using a demand and supply diagram.

'Petrol prices will soar to a new record tomorrow when two major companies add 4.5p to the price of a gallon at the pumps. Esso and Shell's retail price of 245p surpasses even the high set during the Gulf War'. (*Source: Express and Star*, 9 June 1992)

What fixes the price that households pay for petrol, or indeed any commodity?

Demand and Supply

Price in a free market is fixed or 'determined' by the forces of demand and supply. Take the price of petrol. If oil companies want to sell more petrol (i.e. if they want to increase the supply of petrol), then they can only do this by persuading motorists to buy more petrol. The easiest way to do this is for the oil companies to drop the price of petrol. If, on the other hand, oil companies reduce the supply of petrol to the market, most motorists would be prepared to pay higher prices to obtain the petrol supplies available, i.e.

● a decrease in demand or an increase in supply will *reduce* prices;

● an increase in demand or a fall in supply will *raise* prices.

A Graphical Analysis

Price determination can be shown by using a demand and supply diagram. In Figure 13.1, a demand and supply curve is drawn for a commodity. At a price of £5, demand will be 250 units

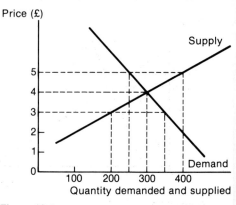

Figure 13.1

but 400 units will be supplied. The result will be that 150 units will be left unsold. The price of £5 is too high for everything produced to be sold. Economists say therefore that EXCESS SUPPLY (i.e. too much supply in relation to demand) exists. If the price is £3, then producers will only want to sell 200 units, but buyers will want to buy 350 units. Many buyers will be disappointed because there will not be enough goods to buy. EXCESS DEMAND (i.e. too much demand in relation to supply) will exist.

Only at a price of £4 will demand exactly equal price. This price is known as the EQUILIBRIUM PRICE or the MARKET CLEARING PRICE. It is the price where the forces of demand and supply are matched so that there is no tendency to change. When there is excess supply, suppliers will not continue forever to produce more than they can sell. They will cut back production, and reduce prices, until supply again equals demand. If there is excess demand, firms will push up prices and expand output to take advantage of the situation where buyers want to buy more.

Changes in Prices

A change in price will come about when either demand or supply changes. For instance, the reason why petrol prices went up in June 1992 was because the price of oil to the oil companies increased. So the oil companies increased the price of petrol at the pumps. This would be shown by an upwards shift in the supply curve for petrol, shown in Figure 13.2. Before the price rise, the market or equilibrium price was 240.5p – that was the price where demand

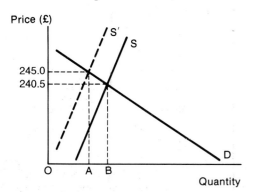

Figure 13.2

equalled supply. After the price rise, the oil companies wanted a higher price to supply the same amount of petrol. So the supply curve shifted upwards from S to S'. A new equilibrium price of £2 was achieved, but the oil companies had to accept that they would not sell as much petrol as before. At 240.5p, motorists were prepared to buy OB of petrol. At 245p they would only buy OA.

Figure 13.3 shows an increase in demand from D to D'. This pushes up the equilibrium price from OA to OB, and increases the equilibrium quantity bought and sold from OE to OF.

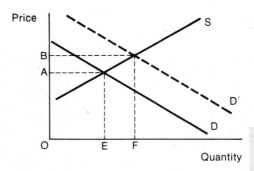

Figure 13.3

CHECKPOINTS

1 What determines the price of a product?
2 Explain how and why the price of beef will change in a free market:
   (a) if the demand for beef increases;
   (b) if the supply of beef decreases;
   (c) if farmers keep more sheep instead of cows;
   (d) if a disease reduces the number of calves born;
   (e) if there is a successful advertising campaign for beef;
   (f) if a report is published linking beef with ill health.
3 In each of the cases (a) to (f) in question 2, draw a demand and supply diagram showing the effect of the change on price and quantity demanded and supplied.

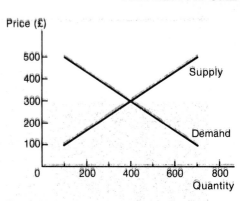

Figure 13.4

4 Look at Figure 13.4.
   (a) What is the equilibrium price?
   (b) What is the equilibrium quantity demanded?
   (c) How much is demanded at a price of £100? How much is supplied? What is the excess demand at this price?
   (d) What is the excess supply at a price of £500?

COURSEWORK SUGGESTION

This project requires research into the change in price of one good or service over a period of time and an analysis of the causes of this change. Take a particular period of time and find out how the price of a commodity or group of commodities has changed over that period. Possibly the best source of data is the Retail Price Index, a detailed breakdown of which can be found in the *Department of Employment Gazette* or *British Labour Statistics: Year Book* (both published by HMSO). Then suggest reasons as to why prices have changed for this commodity, and try to find statistical evidence to support your hypothesis. Evaluate possible future trends in prices. Use demand and supply diagrams wherever possible to support your analysis.

KEY TERMS

EQUILIBRIUM PRICE or MARKET CLEARING PRICE – the price at which demand equals supply.
EXCESS DEMAND – a situation where demand is greater than supply, leading to shortages of commodities.
EXCESS SUPPLY – a situation when supply is greater than demand, leading to a glut of commodities on the market.

Data Response Questions
Units 10–13

Unit 10 Demand (1)

Source: Express and Star, 26 June 1992

1 What is meant in the advertisement by:
   (a) a 'sale'
   (b) a 'massive discount'? *(4 marks)*

2 What is likely to be the effect on demand for furniture at the store as a result of the sale? Use a diagram to illustrate your answer. *(6 marks)*

Unit 11 Demand (2)

Homes gloom continues as prices slump

Government hopes of an upturn in the housing market were dampened today after another big monthly fall in house prices.

Figures for February showed prices down 1.2 per cent on the previous month – the third consecutive fall of more than 1 per cent.

According to the Nationwide building society, the average house now costs £55 308 – about £2300, or 4.1 per cent, less than a year ago.

Experts blame the continued recession and fear of unemployment for the lack of interest in buying.

But Nationwide said it expected new measures, which include waiving stamp duty on transactions up to £250 000 and a buy-back and rental scheme for homes owned by struggling mortgage lenders, would help rebuild confidence.

Source: Express and Star, 2 March 1992

1 What has happened to house prices according to the article? *(3 marks)*

2 Explain why the demand for housing fell in 1991/2. *(6 marks)*

3 How could the 'new measures' mentioned by Nationwide help increase demand again? *(6 marks)*

Essay Questions
Units 10–13

1 The price of a Mars Bar goes down from 20p to 18p.
   (a) What is likely to happen to the consumer demand for Mars Bars? *(2 marks)*
   (b) Explain one other way in which the manufacturers of Mars Bars could change the demand for Mars Bars. *(4 marks)*
   (c) What would you expect to happen to the demand for Mars Bars if the average pocket money of children increased and why? *(4 marks)*
   (d) If the price of other competing chocolate bars went up by an average of 20%, how would you expect the manufacturers of Mars Bars to react and why? *(5 marks)*
   (e) Draw two demand diagrams showing the difference in effect on demand of a fall in price of Mars Bars and a rise in consumer incomes. *(5 marks)*

2 The price of one LP record is £4.99 whilst the price of another is £2.99.
   (a) Suggest *four* reasons why the price of these two records is different. *(8 marks)*
   (b) Explain how and why the price of records might change if more were spent on advertising by record companies. *(4 marks)*
   (c) Using a demand and supply diagram, explain how and why the quantity bought of records might change if the price of record players increased. *(8 marks)*

Unit 12 Supply

All that is gold no longer glisters

The price of gold has fallen to its lowest level for nearly six years. At its peak in 1980, it was priced at more than $800 an ounce. Today it is less than $340.

According to the Gold Fields Minerals Services consultancy group, at least half the world's gold mining capacity is unprofitable at this price.

Most of the uneconomic mines are in South Africa, where large workforces dig to depths of up to 2½ miles to extract the gold from narrow seams.

So far, no big South African gold mine has been forced to close. But many companies have stopped mining uneconomic seams and concentrated on those where gold is more easy to mine.

Employment in South African gold mines has fallen from 505 262 in 1989 to 473 685, the lowest figure since 1980.

If the price continues to fall, there are bound to be a large number of closures of mines in the near future. Mr Harry Oppenheimer, former chairman of the Anglo American Corporation, the world's second largest mining company, said recently that South African gold production could fall by up to 30 per cent by the year 2000 at present prices.

Source: Adapted from the *Financial Times*, 26 March 1992

What happened to the price of gold in the 1980s?

(1 mark)

Explain what effect this price change has had on the gold mining industry. *(4 marks)*

What is likely to happen to the supply of gold in the future? Use a supply diagram to illustrate your answer.

(5 marks)

Unit 13 Price

They've taken TV's millions

– now soccer giants want to fleece fans

Top soccer clubs are getting ready to put the boot in to their working-class fans. For despite a £304 million cash windfall from a television coverage deal, they plan to hike admission fees by as much as *sixty per cent* next season.

The TV money, scored just days ago from BSkyB and the BBC, was meant to equalise the cost of the Taylor safety report, which forces clubs to make their stadiums all-seater by 1994.

But supporters heading for the turnstiles for the start of the new Premier League season will find the price of ground improvements they don't want will be passed on to them.

Club directors also blame the cost of players' wages, transfer fees, signing-on costs and agents' fees for the swinging increases in ticket prices.

Now traditional fans fear they will be left on the sidelines when a new breed of middle-class football followers become the only people who can afford to watch soccer.

Source: *Daily Mirror*, 1 June 1992

1 What is likely to happen to football admission prices in the 1992/3 season?

2 (a) Explain why prices are likely to rise.
(b) Use a demand and supply diagram to illustrate your answer. *(8 marks)*

3 Why will traditional fans 'be left on the sidelines'?

(3 marks)

4 Will the football clubs lose money by putting up prices? Explain your answer. *(3 marks)*

Elasticity (1)

The Cookseys

John Cooksey – aged 40, an English teacher in a comprehensive school;
Sally Cooksey – aged 38, housewife;
Miriam Cooksey – aged 15, still at school;
Mathew Cooksey – aged 13, at school;
Michael Cooksey – aged 11, at school

3 Mayfield Road
lounge, dining room, kitchen,
bathroom, 3 bedrooms.

BUDGET
(Incomings and Outgoings per month)

	£		£
Food and small domestic purchases	340	Take home salary	1140
Mortgage	100	Child Benefit	110
Council Tax	60		
Clothes	60		
Holidays	60		
Car	240		
Pocket Money and Presents	80		
Bills (gas, electric, insurance etc.)	300		
Other	10		
TOTAL	1250		1250

Put yourself in the place of John and Sally Cooksey.

1 Analyse your expenditure by completing the bar graph in Figure 14.1, putting the costliest item first on the left and ending up with the least costly item on the right.

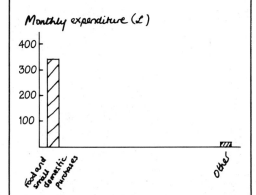

Figure 14.1

2 Building societies put up their interest rates and your monthly mortgage repayment goes up to £120. How will you reallocate your scarce resources as a result? i.e. what item or items of expenditure will you cut to pay for this? Explain the reason for your decision.

3 The cost of food and other small domestic purchases (washing powder, newspapers etc.) goes up by 10% but all other costs remain the same.
  (a) Explain how and why you will reallocate your resources.
  (b) Calculate the price elasticity of demand for food and other small domestic purchases revealed by your decision.
  (c) Calculate too the cross-elasticity of demand for any other categories of expenditure which have changed as a result.

4 More textile imports are allowed into the country and as a result the price of clothes falls by 20%.
  (a) Explain how and why you will reallocate your resources as a result.
  (b) Calculate your price elasticity of demand for clothes.
  (c) Calculate too the cross elasticity of demand for any other categories of expenditure which have changed as a result.

5 Teachers get a pay rise which adds 5% to take home pay.
  (a) Explain how and why you will reallocate your resources.
  (b) Calculate the income elasticity of demand for each of the categories of expenditure on the budget.

- **The price of a packet of crisps goes up by 10%.**
- **Take home pay falls by 5%.**
- **The price of chocolate bars goes up by 20%.**

What effect might any one of the above changes have on the quantity of crisps demanded? Economists measure the responsiveness of changes in quantity demanded to changes in factors such as price, income, price of other goods, etc. by something called ELASTICITY.

Price Elasticity of Demand

For instance, PRICE ELASTICITY OF DEMAND measures the responsiveness of changes in the quantity demanded of a product to changes in its price. The exact formula for price elasticity of demand is:

$$\frac{\text{Percentage change in quantity demanded}}{\text{Percentage change in price}}$$

If the quantity demanded of a good rose by 10% due to a fall in price of 5%, the price elasticity of demand for a product would be $^{10}/_5$ or 2. (To be totally accurate, the answer is −2, since the fall in price of 5% should have been shown by a '−5'. But since changes in price and quantity nearly always move in opposite directions, economists usually do not bother to put in the minus sign.)

Special names are given to various values of price elasticity of demand, as is illustrated below.

If the price elasticity of demand is 0 (i.e. the same amount is demanded, whatever the price), then demand is said to be *perfectly inelastic*. (See Figure 14.2.)

If the price elasticity of demand is between 0 and 1 (i.e. the percentage change in quantity demanded from A to B is smaller than the percentage change in price), then demand is said to be *inelastic*. (See Figure 14.3.)

If the price elasticity of demand is 1 (i.e. the percentage change in quantity demanded is exactly the same as the percentage change in price), then demand is said to be of *unitary elasticity*. (See Figure 14.4.)

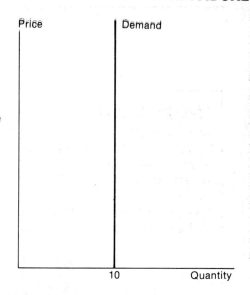

Figure 14.2

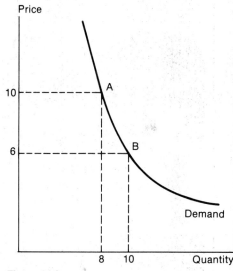

Figure 14.3

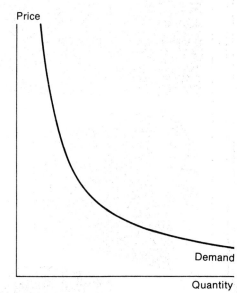

Figure 14.4

If the price elasticity of demand is between 1 and infinity (i.e. the percentage change in quantity demanded from A to B is larger than the percentage change in price), then demand is said to be *elastic*. (See Figure 14.5.)

If the price elasticity of demand is infinite (i.e. purchasers will buy all that is available at the existing price), then demand is said to be *perfectly elastic*. (See Figure 14.6.)

Figure 14.7

Change in quantity demanded:		Change in price (£):		Percentage change in quantity demanded	Percentage change in price	Elasticity
from	to	from	to			
1000	900	2	3	$\frac{100}{1000} \times 100$	$\frac{1}{2} \times 100$	$\frac{1}{5}$
500	200	10	11	$\frac{300}{500} \times 100$	$\frac{1}{10} \times 100$	6
100	20	5	6	$\frac{80}{100} \times 100$	$\frac{1}{5} \times 100$	4
50	40	5	7	$\frac{10}{50} \times 100$	$\frac{2}{5} \times 100$	$\frac{1}{2}$

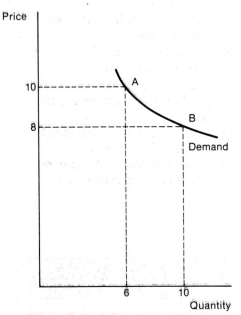

Figure 14.5

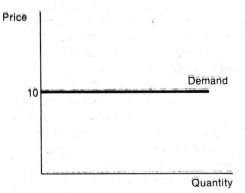

Figure 14.6

To illustrate the concept of price elasticity of demand, consider the market for petrol. Assume that the price of petrol at the pumps increases by 10%. Petrol consumers are unlikely to decrease their consumption of petrol by very much: lorries still need petrol for business, commuters still have to get to work, families will still want to shop at their nearest supermarket. So, in the short term at least, the quantity demanded of petrol is unlikely to fall greatly. If demand fell by, say, 2%, then petrol would have an elasticity of ²/₁₀ or 0.2 (i.e. demand is inelastic). Over a long period, consumers are likely to react to the 10% increase in petrol prices by switching to more fuel-efficient motor vehicles. This will reduce the demand for petrol further. Over a ten-year period, demand might fall by, say, 15%. Then the long-term elasticity of demand for petrol would be ¹⁵/₁₀ or 1.5. Further examples are given in Figure 14.7.

Income Elasticity of Demand

INCOME ELASTICITY OF DEMAND is the relationship between a change in quantity demanded and a change in income. The exact formula for income elasticity is:

$$\frac{\text{Percentage change in quantity demanded}}{\text{Percentage change in income}}$$

For a normal good, an increase in income will lead to an increase in quantity demanded. Income elasticity of demand is therefore positive. For an inferior good, an increase in income will lead to a fall in demand for the good, and so income elasticity is negative. (For a fuller discussion of normal and inferior goods, see Unit 11.)

Cross-elasticity of Demand

CROSS-ELASTICITY OF DEMAND measures the responsiveness of changes in quantity demanded of a product to change in the price of another product. The exact formula for cross-elasticity of demand for product X is:

$$\frac{\text{Percentage change in quantity demanded of product X}}{\text{Percentage change in price of another product}}$$

For instance, if the cross-elasticity of demand for crisps were 2 and the price of chocolate bars went up 10%, then there would be a 20% increase in demand for crisps.

Price Elasticity of Supply

The concept of elasticity is just as applicable to supply. PRICE ELASTICITY OF SUPPLY is the relationship between change in quantity supplied and a change in price. The exact formula for price elasticity of supply is:

$$\frac{\text{Percentage change in quantity supplied}}{\text{Percentage change in price}}$$

Its value is normally positive, because an increase in price is likely to increase the quantity supplied to the market and vice versa. A downward-sloping supply curve, where an increase in price led to a fall in quantity supplied, would obviously have a negative elasticity.

The concept of elasticity is considered further in the next unit.

CHECKPOINTS

1 Explain what is meant by price elasticity of demand. If demand for a good is 'price elastic', what does this mean?

2 How does the income elasticity of demand for a normal good differ from that of an inferior good? Why?

3 Calculate the price elasticity of demand from the following data:

Percentage change in quantity demanded	Percentage change in price	Elasticity
10	20	
5	1	
20	10	
50	30	

4 The following data show how quantity demanded for a good changes as income changes. Calculate the income elasticity of demand for a change in income:
(a) from £100 to £200;
(b) from £200 to £300;
(c) from £300 to £400;
(d) from £100 to £400.

Quantity demanded	Income (£)
10	100
20	200
60	300
180	400

5 For the data in Figure 14.8, calculate the price elasticity of supply for a change in price:
(a) from £10 to £20;
(b) from £20 to £30;
(c) from £30 to £40;
(d) from £40 to £20.

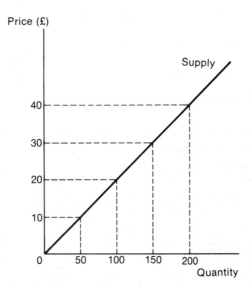

Figure 14.8

6 The cross elasticity of records for pre-recorded cassettes is + ½. Calculate:
(a) the percentage change in demand for records if the price of cassettes went up by 10%;
(b) the percentage change in the price of cassettes that occurred to cause a 10% rise in the demand for records;
(c) the percentage rise in the demand for records if the price of cassettes went up from £5 to £6.

7 What do you think the elasticity values might be in the following cases? Explain your reasoning carefully.
(a) Price elasticity of demand for records.
(b) Price elasticity of demand for tickets to a concert featuring a top British rock group.
(c) Income elasticity of demand for a Mars Bar.
(d) Income elasticity of demand for motorcycles.
(e) Income elasticity of demand for private health care.
(f) Cross-elasticity of demand of Dunlop and Slazenger tennis rackets.
(g) Cross-elasticity of demand of petrol and mini cars.
(h) Cross-elasticity of demand of new houses and large cars.

COURSEWORK SUGGESTION

Keep a record of your spending over a six-month period. Over the same period, make a weekly survey of the prices of ten goods and services that you commonly purchase. Also, keep a summary of changes in your weekly income. Explain the concept of elasticity and estimate the price, income and cross-elasticities of demand for the products you have purchased over the six-month period. Explain the difficulties of measuring elasticity from your data. Consider the extent to which elasticity is a useful tool in economics, given the difficulties of measurement when using actual data.

KEY TERMS

ELASTICITY – the responsiveness of the quantity of a product to a change in the value of a factor determining its quantity. PRICE ELASTICITY OF DEMAND measures the responsiveness of quantity demanded to a change in price; INCOME ELASTICITY OF DEMAND measures the responsiveness of quantity demanded to a change in income; CROSS-ELASTICITY OF DEMAND measures the responsiveness of quantity demanded of one product to the change in price of another product; PRICE ELASTICITY OF SUPPLY measures the responsiveness of quantity supplied to a change in price.

Elasticity (2)

STUDY POINTS

The price of each of the products or services shown in the photographs goes up by 10%.

1 What, in your opinion, is likely to happen to the quantity purchased of the product in percentage terms?

2 For each product, explain why demand is likely to change in the way you have described.

3 What, then, in your opinion, is the price elasticity of demand for each product?

Determinants of Price Elasticity of Demand

'Electricity prices set to rise by 5%.'

How will electricity consumers react to this in the short term? The answer is probably that there will be almost no change in the quantity of electricity demanded – in other words, the demand for electricity is inelastic in the short term. Why is this the case? There are three main reasons:

- Electricity has few good *substitutes*. A **SUBSTITUTE GOOD** is a good that can be used instead of another good; for example, gas is a substitute for electricity, but only under certain conditions. If a householder wishes to run a television or freezer, or have lighting, then electricity is almost the only option. Even those households with electric cookers and heating are unlikely to change hundreds or thousands of pounds of equipment, just because of a 5% rise in running costs. In the longer term, when households do have to replace worn out equipment, they may change to another form of fuel. So in the long run, the demand for electricity will be more elastic than in the short run.

'This wasn't what I expected when you said we'd have a candlelit dinner instead of paying that huge electricity bill.'

- Electricity is seen as a *necessity*. Consumers are likely to cut back on goods and services which they see as luxuries, rather than on cooking or lighting or heating.

- For many households that only use electricity for lighting and running a few appliances like a television, electricity is a very *small part* of their *total spending*. A 5% rise in prices will hardly make them turn off their televisions or not turn on their lights.

In general, demand for a good will tend to be inelastic when there are no good substitutes, where the proportion spent on the product out of total income is relatively small, and where the good is considered a necessity.

Elasticity and Expenditure or Revenue

It has been argued that electricity, at least in the short run, is price inelastic. For instance, with an elasticity of $(-)\frac{1}{2}$, a rise in electricity of 5% would result in a fall in demand for electricity of $2\frac{1}{2}$%. What this means is that total spending on electricity will increase following the price rise, resulting in higher **REVENUE** for the electricity company. On a bill of £100, the price rise would be £5. But the $2\frac{1}{2}$% fall in demand for electricity would mean that the final bill would only come to about £102.50. So if demand is inelastic, a rise in price will lead to a fall in quantity demanded, but overall there will be a rise in expenditure or revenue. On the other hand, a fall in price with inelastic demand will lead to a fall in revenue *and* expenditure.

The opposite is true if demand is elastic. Assume that foreign holidays have an elastic demand and that the

value of that elasticity is $(-)2$. Then a fall in the price of foreign holidays of 10% will raise demand by 20%. That means that total spending by households and total revenue received by the foreign tourist trade will rise. On the other hand, if the price of foreign holidays goes up, the fall in demand for foreign holidays will result in a fall in total spending and revenue.

CHECKPOINTS

1 Explain, giving five examples, what is meant by a 'substitute'.

2 Why is the demand for petrol inelastic, at least in the short term?

3 Explain why a rise in the price of petrol is likely to lead to a rise in expenditure on petrol by motorists and a rise in revenue by garages.

4 What will happen to revenue:
   (a) if prices fall by 10% and elasticity is $(-)3$;
   (b) if prices rise by 20% and elasticity is $(-)2$;
   (c) if prices fall by 50% and elasticity is $(-)\frac{1}{2}$;
   (d) if prices fall by 10% and elasticity is zero.

COURSEWORK SUGGESTION

Examine the expenditure of your household. Draw up a budget which explains how money is spent in the household. Assess the values of price, income and cross-elasticities of demand for each item by asking the decision-makers in your household how they would alter spending, if certain variables changed. (For example, what would happen if household income increased by £10 a week? What would happen if electricity prices went up by 10%? What would happen if food prices went up by 20%?) Explain why certain goods in the family budget have a high price elasticity of demand and others a low price elasticity of demand.

KEY TERMS

SUBSTITUTE GOOD – a good that can be used instead of another good for a particular purpose; for example, gas can be used for electricity for cooking.

(SALES) REVENUE – the sum of money received from the sale of a product. It can be calculated by multiplying the average price received by the total quantity sold.

Saving

John Harris: 19, getting married in three months' time, wants to buy a house.

Sylvia Thistle: 43, married with two teenage children, just inherited £10,000.

Wendy Carrol: 10, at school.

Liz Bertram: 63, retired, husband still alive, children all left home, has saved up £5,000.

How To Open An Account

It's simple – just call into your nearest Halifax office. We will be pleased to provide you with full details of any of the accounts mentioned in this leaflet. You will need proof of identity when opening an account.

West Bromwich Building Society
independent and strong

374 High Street, West Bromwich, West Midlands B70 8LR. Telephone: 021 525 7070

Principal Office:

The Society is a Member of The Building Societies Association. Shares and Deposits in the Society are Trustee Investments.

INTEREST RATES

From 25th May 1992

	GROSS PA	NET PA

TESSA
TESSA (Tax Exempt Special Savings Account) offers tax-free savings for anyone aged 18 years or over. Invest up to £9,000 over 5 years and earn interest free of tax, subject to the Society's terms and conditions and Government regulations detailed in our TESSA leaflet. Minimum deposit: £150.

11.6% TAX FREE Interest paid or credited to the account annually on 31st December

PLUS 1% BONUS Paid on the capital balance remaining at the end of the five year term

180 DAY NOTICE SHARE ACCOUNT
Minimum balance £10,000. 180 days' written notice for withdrawals. However, withdrawals can be made with just 30 days' written notice and 30 days' loss of interest on the amount withdrawn provided at least £25,000 remains in account* Interest credited or paid by cheque each 31st March.

Monthly income option, with interest paid by Bank Transfer, cheque, or transfer to another WBBS account.

	GROSS PA	NET PA
£50,000 and over Interest paid monthly, 10.03% gross, 7.523% net	**10.50%**	7.875%
£10,000 to £49,999 Interest paid monthly, 9.80% gross, 7.350% net	**10.25%**	7.688%

£64,000* FOR YOUR FAMILY IF YOU DIE. £21,000* FOR YOU IF YOU DON'T.

Contrary to popular opinion you don't have to die to cash in on your life assurance.

For just £20 a month Abbey Life has a plan that will insure your life for over £64,000.* Until the age of 60, we can also maintain your policy if you're sick or disabled and we may be able to help if you're made redundant.

But that's not all. The plan will also provide a substantial lump sum on retirement.

Easy Access Saving

INSTANT XTRA PLUS

	GROSS	NET
		5.63%
	7.50%	5.74%
	7.65%	5.93%
£500 +	7.90%	6.38%
£2,500 +	8.50%	6.68%
£5,000 +	8.90%	6.86%
£10,000 +	9.15%	
£25,000 +		
£50,000 +		

You can open an account with £500 and there is no limit to the amount you can invest. Instant withdrawals can be made without losing interest. Interest is added to your account annually on 1st June. A passbook is provided, making it easy to keep track of deposits and withdrawals.

The savings account for 7 to 14 year olds.

Smart 2 Save is especially for 7 to 14 year olds and has been designed to show that saving can be both educational and fun. For an initial deposit of as little as £1, your child will receive a complete kit to help make saving enjoyable. And what's more you will be secure in the knowledge that your child's money is earning 'adult' rates of interest. Smart 2 Save makes real sense for children because:—

• Your child can open an account for as little as £1.

• The opening pack contains:
— A passbook wallet in a choice of 3 exciting colours.
— A wallchart offering a fun way to keep a record of deposits and withdrawals.
— A card that identifies the child as a Smart 2 Saver.
— Information on special offers, exclusive to Smart 2 Save account holders.

'Get the Abbey habit', reads the advertising slogan for the Abbey National Building Society. Building societies are interested in your SAVINGS. Saving takes place when a household or a firm or a government decides not to spend the money available to it. If a household earned £200 after tax, etc. and spent £150, then it must have saved the extra £50.

Why Save?

Saving takes place for a number of reasons. Much saving is for purchases of goods and services in the future. A family might want a car or a new washing machine, so they save to pay for it. People also save for their retirement, when their income from their job will disappear. Saving now will provide an income for the worker when he or she retires. Saving also takes place because savers want to protect themselves against future problems. The car might break down.

STUDY POINTS

1 Why do people save money?

2 Where can they put their savings?

3 What is the link between interest and savings?

4 What type of saving scheme might be suitable for each of the four people above and why?

5 Is it a good thing for people of your age to save and why? To answer this, weigh up the costs and benefits of saving.

6 Find out how many in your group are saving up for something in particular and how many save all the time anyway.

The roof might start to leak. The worker might be made redundant. So households save up to provide themselves with a financial cushion against such events. Third, savers might be attracted by the fact that savings will grow in value over time. For instance, INTEREST is usually paid on savings. Or the value of savings in, say, shares or a house might grow. By not spending now, more goods and services can be bought in the future.

Savings Institutions

Figure 16.1 shows where savers put their money in 1991. Seven per cent went into *bank deposit accounts*. Banks borrow money, some of it from the ordinary person in the street (the personal customer). Bank deposit accounts are designed to attract savers. They give a much higher rate of interest

Figure 16.1 How people saved their money, 1991

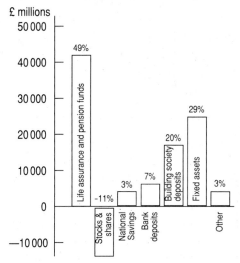

Source: CSO, Financial Statistics, May 1992

than bank current accounts (cheque book accounts) which are designed for people who want to move their money around.

Twenty per cent of new savings in 1991 went into *building society accounts*. Building societies have traditionally borrowed money from savers to lend out again to home buyers in the form of MORTGAGES. Building societies offer a variety of savings accounts. In general, the larger the amount you save with the building society and the longer you promise to keep it with them, the higher the rate of interest on the account.

National Savings attracted 3% of the total. National Savings is run by the government. It borrows money to finance government spending. A number of different National Savings 'products' are on offer. They include National Savings Certificates, Premium Bonds, Income Bonds and two accounts with the National Savings Bank.

Fixed assets, with 29% of the total, is mainly saving in housing. A house is not used up or consumed in the same way as, say, a car. So the amount of new money that a person puts into buying a house is included as part of saving.

The most important type of saving though is *life assurance and pension fund contributions*. Life assurance companies offer savings schemes where a saver promises to pay money at regular intervals to the company (these payments are called PREMIUMS). Then, at the end of say 25 years, the assurance policy of the saver will come to an end (or mature), and the money will be paid back with interest and profits.

Life assurance companies also offer PENSION schemes. Savers pay money to the company, again often on a regular basis, and the company promises to pay them a regular fixed pension when they retire.

Note that in 1991 individuals actually sold about £9 billion more stocks and shares than they bought. Stocks are long-term loans to government and to companies. Shares are shares in companies which can be bought and sold on stock exchanges like the London Stock Exchange. The dissaving in stocks and shares is part of a longer trend. Individuals don't like the large risks involved in saving in stock markets.

CHECKPOINTS

1 What is the difference between consumption and saving?

2 Explain why (a) a 15-year-old, (b) a 25-year-old and (c) a 55-year-old person might save.

3 Have you got any savings at the moment? Where do you keep them? Why do you keep them there?

4 What is the opportunity cost of keeping savings in a building society account?

5 Why do you think that over 75% of new saving is in the form of houses, assurance policies and pension funds?

KEY TERMS

SAVING – income and wealth that is not spent on goods and services.

INTEREST – a sum of money paid as a reward for the loan of money. The INTEREST RATE is the proportion of interest paid in comparison with the size of the loan; it is expressed as a percentage.

MORTGAGE – a loan of money for the purchase of property.

PREMIUM – a sum of money paid regularly for insurance or assurance cover.

PENSION – a sum of money paid at regular intervals when a person has retired.

COURSEWORK SUGGESTION

Describe in detail four different savings schemes. Assess the relative merits of each savings scheme. Analyse why different savers (e.g. a pensioner, a woman at home looking after her family, a young married couple) might decide to choose one saving scheme rather than another. Assess the effects these choices will have on the way resources are used in the economy.

Income, Wealth and Inequality

STUDY POINTS

From Figure 17.1:

1 How much of the total wealth of the UK is owned by the most wealthy 1% of the adult population?

2 If a typical 100 people owned a total of £100, how much would
   (a) the average person own?
   (b) the most wealthy person own?
   (c) the most wealthy 25 people own?
   (d) the least wealthy 50 people own?
   (e) the average person amongst the least wealthy 50 people own?
   (Hint: divide your answer to (d) by 50.)

From Figure 17.2:

3 How much did the top 20% of income earners earn in 1977 and 1988?

4 Which group(s) saw a rise in its share of total income over the period 1977 to 1982?

From Figure 17.3:

5 What happens to benefits received and taxes paid as income rises?

6 What is the largest source of income for the bottom fifth of the population?

7 What is the difference in income between the bottom fifth and top fifth of income earners
   (a) in £s and
   (b) in percentage terms?

From all the Figures:

8 Describe how differences in income and wealth have changed over recent years in the UK.

9 Explain why the most wealthy in the UK are also likely to be among the top income earners.

10 How could the distribution of income and wealth be made more equal? What would be the consequences of this?

Figure 17.1 Concentration of wealth among adult population

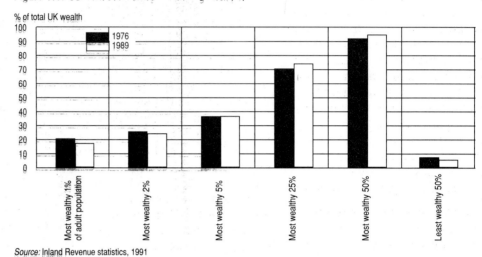

Source: Inland Revenue statistics, 1991

Figure 17.2 Shares of pre-tax income

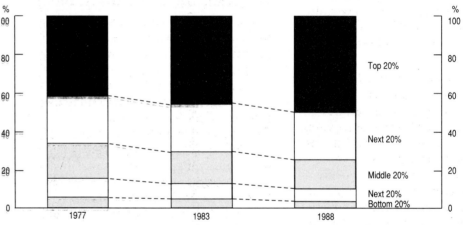

Source: for Figures 17.2–17.3 CSO, *Social Trends*, 1992

Figure 17.3 Distribution of income before and after tax and benefits 1988 (£)

	Income before tax and benefits	Benefits	Tax[1]	Income after tax and benefits
Bottom fifth	1210	3220	200	4230
Next fifth	4440	2790	740	6500
Middle fifth	10 750	1760	1920	10 580
Next fifth	16 260	1080	3220	14 120
Top fifth	27 170	710	5990	23 890

[1] Income tax and National Insurance Contributions

Source: CSO, *Social Trends*, 1992

'Miss J. Lewis, of 16 Hicks Avenue, left £773 000 in her will.'

'Mr B. James is currently the top income earner in the company with a salary of £87 000 a year.'

iss Lewis owned money, property d valuables that amounted to 73 000 at the time of her death. This as the value of her WEALTH. The value a person's wealth (or indeed of the ealth of a company or a country) can e measured *at a point in time* such as December 1995. We are not told w wealthy Mr James is, but he does rn an income of £87 000 over the eriod of a year. INCOME can only be easured *over a period of time*. rious types of wealth give rise to rious types of income. In particular:

HUMAN WEALTH or HUMAN CAPITAL yields EARNED INCOME. Human wealth is the economic value of a person. A person's human wealth can be increased by education, training and work experience. The greater a person's human wealth, the higher should be the income that that worker receives from an employer.

NON-HUMAN WEALTH yields UNEARNED INCOME, such as interest, profit and dividends. Non-human wealth is the value of a person's possessions – money, houses, stocks and shares, building society deposits, etc. By lending or making available money or other assets to other people, an individual can receive an income that is not earned by going out to work.

uman wealth and non-human wealth e unevenly distributed in the UK. igure 17.1 shows how unequally on-human wealth was distributed in the UK in 1989. A mere 1% of the population (that is, one person in every 100) owned nearly one-fifth of the available non-human wealth in the UK. Half the population only owned 6% of the wealth. No figures exist for the value of human wealth in the UK, but it is likely to be as unevenly distributed as non-human wealth.

Figure 17.2 shows how income is distributed before tax and benefits. The bottom fifth of all income earners received a mere 2% of the total income in the UK in 1988. Some people's income had to be increased through benefits such as the state pension and unemployment benefit. These benefits are paid for by taxing the better off. Figure 17.3 shows the distribution of income after taxes and benefits have been taken into consideration. The differences between income earners have been reduced, but there is still a big difference between high- and low-income earners.

Are Inequalities Inevitable?

Does an economy *have* to have inequalities in income and wealth? In practice, every economy produces inequalities, but the degree of inequality is the *choice* of society. For instance, in Britain we could solve the problem of poverty amongst pensioners by doubling the state pension. But that has to be paid for. Is it better to have the higher-paid workers paying more taxes to provide higher pensions? Or is the situation better as it is? This is a difficult choice to make, but it is one that every society has to face.

KEY TERMS

HUMAN WEALTH or HUMAN CAPITAL – the skills and abilities of an individual that enable that person to produce goods and services.

NON-HUMAN WEALTH – the material possessions of an individual, such as money, houses, cars, and stocks and shares.

EARNED INCOME – income derived from working.

UNEARNED INCOME – income derived from non-human wealth, such as interest, rent, profit and dividends.

Production

Types of Production

Yoghurt, tights, boxing gloves, jumbo jets, education and nuclear weapons are just a few of the goods and services produced in the world economy today. Because there is such a wide variety of goods produced, economists tend to split up or *classify* production in various ways. Here are some of them:

- primary, secondary and tertiary production – considered in Unit 48;

- public-sector production and private-sector production – considered in Unit 53;

- production for consumption and production for investment is a distinction made in Unit 22;

- CAPITAL-INTENSIVE PRODUCTION and LABOUR-INTENSIVE PRODUCTION. In some production industries, a great deal of capital (machines, building, etc.) is needed in relation to the number of workers employed. The chemical industry or the motor-vehicle production industry are examples. In other industries, very little capital is needed compared to the number of workers involved. Many industries, such as the tourist industry or the retailing industry, are labour-intensive.

The Chain of Production

Production in a modern economy is a complicated business. Figure 18.1 shows a simple production process. Existing products are combined with machinery, raw materials and labour. A product is then made. For instance, a car manufacturer would need workers, land and other raw materials and machinery to produce a finished car. The manufacturer would also use products purchased from other firms – components such as lights or brakes, or semi-manufactured products such as steel. A CHAIN OF PRODUCTION can be drawn which shows some or all of the links between the factors of production and the consumer. A simple chain is shown in Figure 18.2.

S T U D Y P O I N T S

1 Make a list of all the industries involved in the making and selling of cigarettes.

2 From your list construct a CHAIN OF PRODUCTION. This is a flow chart. At the top put those industries which come first in the production process. At the bottom, put those which are last (in this case, they will be the shops that sell cigarettes). An example of a chain of production for cars is given in Figure 18.2 which accompanies the text for this unit.

3 Why are cigarettes produced in the economy?

4 What would be the effect on other industries if the number of cigarettes smoked per year in Britain declined?

5 Is it desirable that there should be a decline in cigarette smoking in Britain? To answer this, explain;
(a) the social costs (e.g. poor health) and
(b) the social benefits (e.g. employment in the cigarette industry) of cigarette smoking.

The Purpose of Production

What is the purpose of production in society? The ultimate aim of all production should be to create goods and services to satisfy consumer wants. These wants may vary enormously from bread to health care to a cleaner environment. In an economy like that of the UK, households indicate their consumer preferences either through *markets*, by spending money on products for sale, or through the *ballot box* by voting in governments which will spend money on behalf of households. Producers of goods and services should therefore be the servants of consumers. When CONSUMER SOVEREIGNTY exists, consumers tell producers what to produce.

But it is not always the case that production takes place with this in mind.

- Governments and workers may try to produce goods and services which consumers do not demand. The main reasons for this are either to keep wages at too high a level or to keep workers in jobs (both of

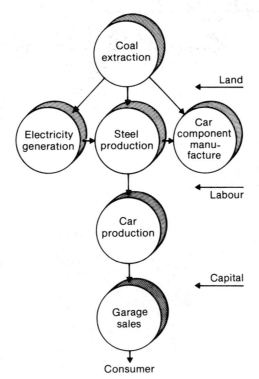

Figure 18.2 A chain of production for cars

these can be seen clearly at work in the Common Agricultural Policy of the EC discussed in Unit 80.) When a factory is closed down, workers often argue against the closure on the grounds that a demand for their product still exists.

- Governments and firms may exploit the market for their own purposes. Firms can sell consumers products which consumers do not really want to buy. Firms can do this, for instance, through advertising, where they try to CREATE a demand for a product. In the EC agriculture industry, farmers have successfully persuaded governments, and

ultimately taxpayers, to pay them to grow far more food than consumers want to buy. 'Mountains' of food are destroyed or fed to animals or sold at rock-bottom prices overseas.

Production just to keep people in jobs is unlikely to be an *efficient* use of scarce resources. Why produce too much butter or too much coal, when the factors of production employed in those industries could be used to produce goods and services that consumers do want?

CHECKPOINTS

1 Construct a chain of production for (a) a pint of milk; (b) a newspaper; (c) a bus ride; (d) a record and (e) any good or service of your choice.

2 What is the purpose of producing goods and services?

3 A farmer produces milk, which is turned into butter. The butter is then bought by the Common Market and eventually sold at a fraction of its cost to Russia.
   (a) Who benefits from this?
   (b) Who loses out?
   (c) Is this an efficient use of resources in the economy?

COURSEWORK SUGGESTION

Take a firm or government organisation that is closing down a production unit in your area. Describe what is being closed, how many workers will be made redundant and what products will cease to be produced. Analyse the effects of this on the local economy in terms of employment, incomes, and the environment, and on the national economy in terms of output, lost tax revenues, and greater government spending (for example, on unemployment benefits). Analyse also why the closure is taking place. Try to decide whether the closure is good or bad overall. Consider, in particular, whether or not the goods and services previously being produced were demanded by consumers.

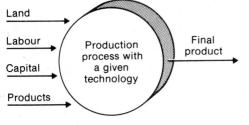

Figure 18.1 The production process

KEY TERMS

CAPITAL-INTENSIVE – an industry or production process where a relatively high amount of capital is used in relation to labour.

LABOUR-INTENSIVE – an industry or production process where a relatively high amount of labour is used relative to capital in production.

CHAIN OF PRODUCTION – shows the various production stages through which a good or service passes before being sold to a consumer.

CONSUMER SOVEREIGNTY – a situation where consumers tell producers what to produce, rather than producers dictating to consumers what they can and cannot buy.

Data Response Questions
Units 14–18

Unit 14 Elasticity (1)

Variation of expenditure with household income

Average weekly household income (£)	Average weekly household expenditure on fuel, light and power (£)
200	11.19
400	12.09
600	14.87

(Adapted from Department of Employment *Family Spending* 1990)

1 How much did the average household earning £200 a week spend on fuel, light and power? *(1 mark)*

2 By how much (a) in money and (b) in percentage terms did expenditure on fuel, light and power increase when incomes increased from £200 to £400? *(2 marks)*

3 Calculate the income elasticity of demand for fuel, light and power for an increase in income:
(a) from £200 to £400;
(b) from £400 to £600. *(4 marks)*

4 Explain why the income elasticity of income changes as income increases. *(3 marks)*

Unit 15 Elasticity (2)

£95-a-second profit BT faces probe on prices

British Telecom today announced profits running at more than £250 million a month, or about £95.50 per second, for the last three months of 1991.

The figures showed a decline in pre-tax profits for the second quarter running after the introduction of stiff new pricing rules in September.

Since September, BT has been forced by its consumer watchdog, Oftel, to restrict price rises to 6.25 per cent below the rate of inflation.

With the Retail Price Index currently running at below 4.5 per cent, the company is obliged to cut its charges.

Source: Express and Star, 30 January 1992

1 What happened to British Telecom profits in the fourth quarter of 1991? *(2 marks)*

2 (a) What is meant by 'price elasticity of demand'?
(b) Explain what your estimate would be of the price elasticity of demand for British Telecom services. *(6 marks)*

3 What effect are the 'stiff new pricing rules' likely to have had on (a) revenues and (b) profits earned by BT? *(7 marks)*

Unit 16 Saving

CHOOSING YOUR PLAN

If you are just starting to save, or want to save small amounts, yet still earn good rates of interest and have instant access to your money, we recommend **First Reserve**

If you can save a minimum of £2,000 and still want instant access, we recommend **Premium Reserve**

If you can save a minimum of £2,000 and can give 3 months notice of a withdrawal in return for even higher levels of interest, we recommend **Crown Reserve**

If you're a tax payer looking for a savings scheme that's tax free and if you are prepared to leave your capital untouched for 5 years, we recommend **TESSA Reserve**

If you want an instant access savings account with a cheque book, and you can start with a minimum of £500, we recommend **Special Reserve**

If you want a choice of the best low-risk and guaranteed insurance bond investments, for income or capital growth, we recommend **Security Plus Service**

If you are prepared to consider a moderate to higher risk to achieve capital growth or income, through unit-trust investments, we recommend **Capital Plus Service**

If you're looking for a highly tax-efficient, limited risk method if investing in stocks and shares, we recommend a **Personal Equity Plan**

If you can invest £20,000 or more, and want an individual service to help make the most of your money, and take the hard work out of arranging your finances, ask at any branch to speak to the Branch Investment Officer, who will tell you more about our **Financial Planning Service**

1 Give two reasons why an individual might be attracted to save with National Westminster Bank. *(2 marks)*

2 Why does a bank like National Westminster Bank offer a variety of savings schemes to its customers? *(6 marks)*

3 How can a bank or building society attract more customers to save with it? *(7 marks)*

Unit 17 Income, Wealth and Inequality

'A fifth of Europe's poorest' in Britain

Over one-fifth of the poorest people in Europe now live in Britain, according to a report published today by the Low Pay Unit.

In the decade 1979–89 the poorest fifth of households saw their annual real disposable income fall by £160, says the unit's report, Poor Britain.

By contrast the real income of the highest tenth of earners went up by £5443.36.

The unit's director Chris Pond said poverty is defined by the European Commission as 'having less than half the average disposable income'.

'Each country is taken separately, and countries like Germany and Belgium have higher disposable incomes than say Portugal or Spain', he said.

In Europe, 50 million people were living in poverty by the mid-1980s by that definition, and about 11 million of them are living in Britain.

The unit also shows that the gap between highest paid and the lowest paid is greater now than in Victorian times.

Mr Pond said the 'greedy 80s' have turned into the 'needy 90s' for millions of people.

Source: Express and Star, 30 March 1992

1 How many people (in millions) were defined as living in poverty in the UK by the Low Pay Unit Report? *(1 mark)*

2 Explain how poverty is defined in the report. *(2 marks)*

3 Suggest reasons why the real disposable income of the bottom fifth of UK households changed between 1979 and 1989. *(6 marks)*

4 How could government reduce the gap between the highest paid and the lowest paid? *(6 marks)*

Unit 18 Production

A teacher delivering education

School textbooks being printed

1 Construct a chain of production for education services showing at least four stages in the production process including those illustrated in the photographs. *(5 marks)*

2 (a) What is meant by a labour intensive industry?
(b) Explain which of the two industries illustrated is the more labour intensive. *(4 marks)*

3 Some schools in the UK have too many classrooms for the number of pupils on roll. What would be the costs and benefits of closing these schools? *(6 marks)*

Essay Questions
Units 14–18

1 British Rail decide to increase all their fares by 20%, whilst the price of petrol and bus fares stay the same.
(a) What effect do you think this will have on the numbers of travellers at peak times during the day when most travellers are people who are going to and from work? *(5 marks)*
(b) What effect do you think this will have on off peak travel when many passengers are shoppers or families going out for the day. *(5 marks)*
(c) To what extent will this increase in fares increase the total revenue from sales of tickets for British Rail? *(10 marks)*

2 Linda Philpott is managing director of a company which she owns. She has savings of £200,000 and is the owner of a block of flats in Mayfair.
(a) Suggest *four* different types of income which she is likely to receive. *(8 marks)*
(b) Distinguish between 'earned income' and 'unearned income'. *(6 marks)*
(c) Which of the different types of income you mentioned in (a) was unearned income? *(2 marks)*
(d) Describe *two* savings schemes which she could have used for her £200,000. *(4 marks)*

The Division of Labour

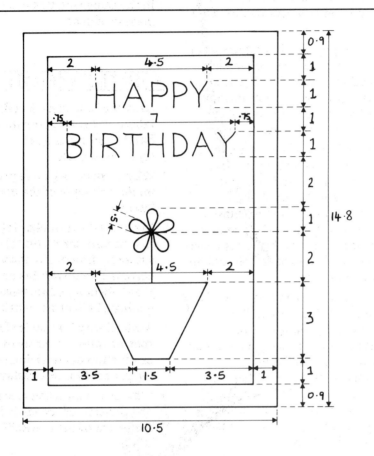

S T U D Y   P O I N T S

- You are going to produce 8 birthday cards.

- Form a team of four workers.

- You will need 4 pencils, 4 rulers, 1 rubber, 8 sheets of A4 paper.

- Spend *five* minutes deciding how you as a team are going to produce the cards.

- All cards must be identical in scale to the card shown above. The figures shown represent measurements in centimetres.

- Do not show any measuring lines. All that should be visible on the card is (a) a border (b) 'Happy Birthday' and (c) a flowerpot with a 5 leaved flower.

- To construct the card, fold the sheet of A4 paper in two from top to bottom. Then fold again from side to side to produce a free standing card. The picture should be drawn on the front of the card.

- On the inside of the card on the right hand sheet, the words 'For my love' in capitals 1 cm high should be written. The message should be centred 5 cm from the top of the page. The team may decide whether or not to

use one or two lines. All cards, however, must be identical.

- The team has *fifteen* minutes to make up to eight cards.

- The aim of the exercise is to produce birthday cards as *efficiently* as possible.

Follow Up

- Describe how your team organised its production.

- In what ways was your organisation (a) efficient, (b) inefficient at producing cards? For instance, did the team produce 8 cards in the time given? Were the cards of good quality? Would it have been possible to produce more cards in less time if the organisation had been different?

- Imagine you worked for a small company which produced hand made cards like this. To what extent would this type of work be satisfying?

- What limited the extent to which work could be divided up between members of the team?

Specialisation and the division of labour have already been discussed in relation to householders in Unit 7. In this unit, we will consider its application in industry and commerce.

Adam Smith, who is often considered to have been the founder of modern-day economics, wrote in his most famous book, *An Inquiry into the Wealth of Nations* (1776), that the division of labour was an important source of efficiency in the economy. To explain the workings of the division of labour, he described a factory making pins:

'One man draws out the wire, another straightens it, a third cuts it, a fourth points it, a fifth grinds it at the top for receiving the head; to make the head requires two or three distinct operations; to put it on is a peculiar business; to whiten the pins is another; it is even a trade by itself to put them into paper; and the important business of making a pin is, in this manner, divided into about eighteen distinct operations.'

If making a pin can be split into eighteen separate processes, each being done by a different worker, then it is obvious that making something as complicated as a car would involve thousands of different processes.

Efficiency

There are several reasons why the division of labour is such an efficient way of producing goods and services. Products can be produced at low cost. This is because specialist workers can be employed who are obviously far quicker and more skilful at their jobs than a worker who tries to do all the tasks by him or herself. A specialist worker is also less likely to lose time moving between jobs. A pin worker who makes and packs pins is going to have to move between a pin-making machine and a packing table. This movement wastes time compared to a situation where workers specialise in each task. Less time and effort are also needed to train workers. Specialist tools can be developed to help with the production of part of the finished product. These tools will also be in far greater use than in a situation where each worker had to have his or her own set of tools, which for most of the time would lie idle.

The division of labour is also efficient because it is only by sharing and co-operating that complex modern products can be created and produced. No individual, for instance, could alone have produced a pocket calculator, or a television set or a modern office block.

But there are also disadvantages in the division of labour.

- Workers may become bored and *alienated* by doing the same job day after day. This is not only unpleasant for the worker, but could lead to poorer work effort and standards.
- Although the division of labour allows more goods to be produced at a cheaper price, these goods tend to be similar mass-produced products. Traditional craft goods, which are individual and pleasing, may disappear.
- Specialisation means that the factors of production may be unemployed, if demand for them declines. If, for instance, a worker has been trained as a steel worker, he may find it difficult to find another job because he lacks the necessary skills

Limitations of the Division of Labour

Although specialisation has many advantages, there is a limit to just how far the division of labour can be taken.

- There are physical limitations as to how far work can be broken up. Adam Smith identified eighteen separate processes in pin-making. It would not have been possible to break it down into more processes.
- The division of labour is limited by exchange. If a farmer wants to specialise in producing wheat, but nobody wants to buy it, then it would not make sense for him to grow wheat. He would do better either growing food he wants to eat himself, or food that can be sold on the open market.
- The division of labour is limited by the extent of the market. It is not possible, for instance, to mass produce Porsche cars, because their high price means that few consumers want to buy them. So Porsche cannot afford to break down its production into as many processes as, say, British Leyland can with its Metro.
- It is not possible for large-scale specialisation to take place, if poor transport means that goods cannot be moved easily from factory to market.
- Consumers may not want to buy mass-produced goods, but may

prefer the individuality that comes from craft products.
- Some products, like hairdressing or tourism, cannot be mass produced in the same way that a car can be mass produced.

C·H·E·C·K·P·O·I·N·T·S

1 Describe how there is a division of labour in (a) a school; (b) a hamburger restaurant; (c) a newsagents.

2 Why do firms organise production on the principle of the division of labour?

3 Explain why a worker (a) on a till in a supermarket and (b) on an assembly line in a factory may become bored with his or her job. What effect may this have on the quality of his or her work?

4 Explain why it is easier for specialisation to occur in the production of television sets than in the production of a restaurant meal.

5 What is meant when it is said that 'the division of labour is limited by the extent of the market'?

C·O·U·R·S·E·W·O·R·K S·U·G·G·E·S·T·I·O·N

Find out the names of all the people who have a job in your school. Give a job description for each worker. Explain how this illustrates the principle of the division of labour at work. Analyse why work is divided up in this way. Consider whether more could be achieved by the school if its scarce resources were allocated in a different way, so that the division of labour were more effective.

The division of labour – tuna fish being cleaned and canned

Economic Resources

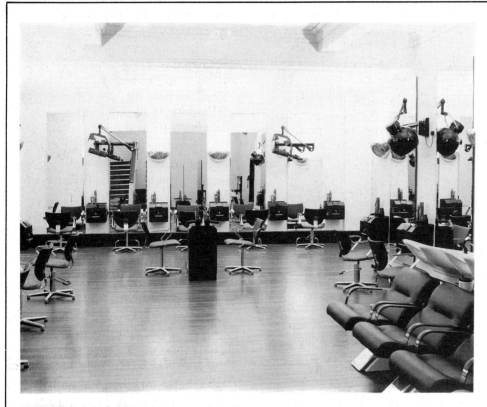

A hairdresser

A blast furnace in a steelworks

Workers in a factory

A farm and farming land

STUDY POINTS

1 Make a list of the factors of production shown in each of the photographs.

2 What factors of production are used to provide you with education?

3 Explain why these factors of production are scarce.

4 To what extent can factors of production be substituted for each other in each of the situations shown in the photographs, e.g. capital for labour in farming?

Types of Resources

Economic resources are scarce. What are these resources? Economists distinguish between three types of resources called the FACTORS OF PRODUCTION. These three factors of production are land, labour and capital.

Land

In 1976, the UK produced the first oil from the North Sea. About 12.2 million tonnes were extracted. By 1991, production was 86.8 million tonnes. This crude oil is an example of what economists call LAND. 'Land' in the economic sense is the natural resources of this planet. It is not only land itself, but also what lies under the land (like coal and gold), what grows naturally on top of the land (like forests and wild animals), what is over the land (like the air), and what is around the land in the seas and oceans (like fish), and under the seas and oceans (like oil). Only one major resource is for the most part free – the air we breathe. The rest are scarce, because there are not enough natural resources in the world to satisfy the demands of consumers, producers, etc.

Labour

LABOUR is the human input into the production process. There are approximately 5 billion people on this planet. Many of these are too young, too old or too ill to work. In the UK, of about 58 million inhabitants only approximately 35 million are of working age (16–64 years for men and 16–59 for women), and of those only

about 26 million have paid jobs. Two important points need to be remembered about labour as a resource:

- Just because a person has not got a paid job, it does not mean that he or she does not produce goods and services. A housewife, a keen gardener and a DIY enthusiast all produce goods and services, but they do not get paid for them.

- Not all labour is of the same quality. Some workers are more productive than others because of the education, training and experience they have received. This is called HUMAN CAPITAL. The greater the human capital of a worker, the more productive he or she will be.

Capital

CAPITAL is a man-made resource. It is the machines, roads, factories, schools and office blocks which human beings have produced in order to produce other goods and services. A modern industrialised economy possesses a large amount of capital, and it is continually increasing. Increases to the *capital stock* of a nation are called *investment*. This capital is sometimes called *physical capital* or *non-human capital* in order to distinguish it from human capital.

Entrepreneurship

Sometimes a fourth factor of production is distinguished. An ENTREPRENEUR is an individual:

- who risks his or her own resources (money in most cases) in a business venture; and

- who organises the business – that is, organises the other three factors of production.

An entrepreneur is a special type of worker. Many economists agree that entrepreneurs should be classed as part of the factor 'labour'.

Labour and capital will be considered in more detail in Units 21 and 22, respectively.

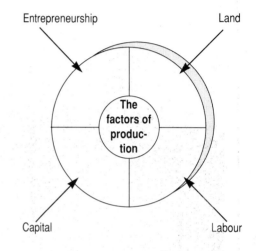

The factors of production

1 What is a 'factor of production'?

2 Which of the factors of production are the following; (a) a factory; (b) a teacher; (c) a road sweeper; (d) a forest; (e) a shoal of fish; (f) a gold mine; (g) a deposit of gold; (h) a business person who owns and runs his/her own business; (i) an MP?

3 Why does the factor 'labour' not include the whole population of the UK?

4 What is the difference between human capital and non-human capital?

5 What is the role of the entrepreneur in the economy?

K E Y   T E R M S

FACTORS OF PRODUCTION – resources of land, labour and capital used to produce goods and services.

LAND – natural resources available for production.

LABOUR – human effort available for production.

CAPITAL – man-made physical goods used to produce other goods and services.

HUMAN CAPITAL – the skills and abilities of workers resulting from investment in education and training.

ENTREPRENEUR – a worker who organises the factors of production and risks his or her capital.

C O U R S E W O R K   S U G G E S T I O N

Identify the factors of production used in your education. Explain how these factors are combined to provide your education. To what extent could these factors be combined more efficiently to produce the same result at a lower cost or a better result for the same cost?

Labour

Figure 21.1 Employment trends in the UK, 1971–91

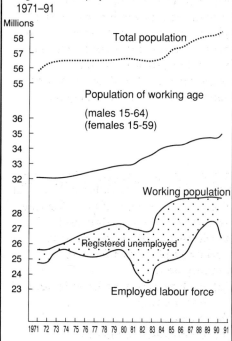

From Figure 21.1:

1 State the population of working age in 1971 and 1991.

2 Describe what has happened to employment over the period 1970 to 1991.

From Figure 21.2:

3 Compare male employment with female employment over the period 1965 to 1991.

From Figure 21.3:

4 What has happened to the educational qualifications of the labour force in the UK over the period 1973/4 to 1988/9? How might this have helped make the labour force more productive?

From Figure 21.4:

5 Describe how the structure of employment has changed in the British economy over the period 1951 to 1991.

From Figure 21.5:

6 Construct a bar chart showing the distribution of employment and unemployment in the UK, putting numbers in millions on the vertical axis and regions along the horizontal axis.

From all the data:

7 Why has the quantity of labour available for production increased in the UK since 1970?

8 Explain what you think will happen to the quality of labour as a factor of production in the future.

9 Give four reasons why there has been a change in the pattern of employment in recent years.

10 In what ways have the changes in the work force in recent years been (a) desirable and (b) undesirable?
Explain your answers carefully.

Figure 21.4 Shares of total civilian employment in the UK, 1951–91

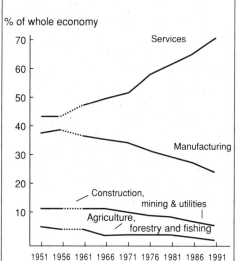

Source: The Treasury, Economic Progress Report, February 1984; Department of Employment, *Employment Gazette*, June 1992

Figure 21.2 Employees in employment – UK mid-year figures

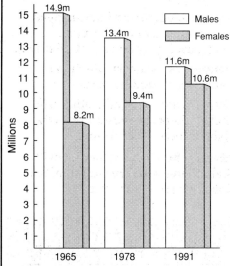

Source: Department of Employment, *Employment Gazette*, June 1992

Figure 21.3 Percentage of school leavers getting two or more GCE 'A' level passes or three or more SCE 'H' grade passes

1973/4	13.0
1977/8	13.2
1988/9	18.2

Source: CSO, *Annual Abstract of Statistics*, 1992

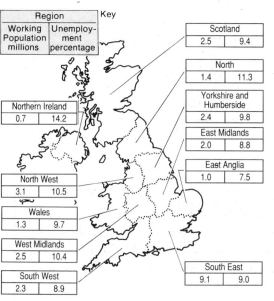

Region		
	Working Population millions	Unemployment percentage

Scotland	
2.5	9.4

North	
1.4	11.3

Yorkshire and Humberside	
2.4	9.8

East Midlands	
2.0	8.8

East Anglia	
1.0	7.5

Northern Ireland	
0.7	14.2

North West	
3.1	10.5

Wales	
1.3	9.7

West Midlands	
2.5	10.4

South West	
2.3	8.9

South East	
9.1	9.0

Figure 21.5 Working population and unemployment by region in the UK, March 1992

Sources: CSO, *Regional Trends*, 1991; Department of Employment, *Employment Gazette*, June 1992

The Quantity of Labour Available for Production

Labour is one of the factors of production. In this unit, we will consider how much of this scarce factor is available for production in the UK and its quality.

Not everybody in the UK is available for work. Figure 21.1 shows that the current population of the UK is over 56 million people. But many of these are either children aged 0–15 or persons of retirement age – 60 years and over for women, and 65 and over for men. The rest – known as the POPULATION OF WORKING AGE – is theoretically available for work.

In practice, many of these do not take on paid work. Young people stay on at school, college or university after the age of 16. Many women leave work to bring up children, as do some men. A smaller number of people are infirm or permanently handicapped, have sufficient income not to work or simply choose not to seek paid employment.

Currently this removes about 6.1 million people from the population of working age. The remaining 28.5 million people form the WORKFORCE – the number of people either in work or seeking work. As can be seen from Figure 21.1, the workforce has tended to rise since 1971.

The single most important reason for this is the growth in the number of women in work. As Figure 21.1 shows, between 1965 and 1991, the number of working women went up by over 2 million.

The growth in the workforce in the 1970s was also due to a rising number of school leavers. But from 1981, the number of 16 year olds in the population went into decline. The number of 16 year olds will only start to increase again in 1995.

Notice that the workforce went down slightly in the early 1980s and again from 1990. This is because the economy was in deep recession in those years. Some unemployed people gave up trying to get a job and simply left the workforce.

Not all members of the workforce have got a job. In 1992, nearly 3 million were registered as unemployed. So the WORKFORCE IN EMPLOYMENT was nearly 3 million less than the total workforce.

The Quality of the Labour Force

The numbers available for work are just one measure of the factor of production called labour. Of equal, if not greater importance is the quality of those workers. The workforce of a poor country like Bangladesh is larger than that of the UK, but it is less productive because the average UK worker has had more education, more training and more experience than the Bangladeshi worker. It is relatively easy to measure the size of the workforce, but it is not possible to give a precise measure of the quality (or *human capital* – a concept explained in Unit 20) of a labour force. One very simple measure of the improvement in the UK's labour force over time is given in Figure 21.3, which shows that the number of people leaving school with 2 or more 'A' levels has increased over time.

Choice

Where are the 24 million or so workers employed in the UK? Figure 21.4 shows what industries these workers are in. Notice the rise in service-sector employment and the fall in manufacturing-sector employment over the last 30 years. The reasons for this trend are explored in more detail in Unit 49. Today, more than half of all workers are in service-sector industry.

Figure 21.5 shows the geographical distribution of the workforce. Notice that the workforce is concentrated particularly in the south of England. Notice also that unemployment is higher in regions outside the south of England. If scarce resources are not to be wasted in the future, industry and jobs will have to be created in those areas, such as Scotland and Northern Ireland, or migration encouraged.

CHECKPOINTS

1 State whether each of the following is part of (i) the population of working age; (ii) the workforce and/or (iii) the workforce in employment:
   (a) each person who lives in your household;
   (b) a teacher;
   (c) a housewife aged 45;
   (d) a pensioner;
   (e) an unemployed steel worker;
   (f) a 15-year-old girl with a paper round;
   (g) an unemployed handicapped worker looking for a job.
   (Note: each *may* be part of all three).

2 Suggest two ways in which the workforce could increase.

3 Explain how your education will help to improve the quality of the labour force in the future.

4 Explain how your schooling will help to improve the quality of the labour force in the future.

COURSEWORK SUGGESTION

Using *Regional Trends* (published by HMSO) and other sources, describe the changes in the labour force in your local area or region in recent years. Analyse why these changes have taken place, and what effect they have had on the prosperity of the region. Discuss further patterns of employment, and whether or not these are likely to bring greater prosperity to the region.

KEY TERMS

POPULATION OF WORKING AGE – all those people between the school-leaving age and the retirement age who are theoretically available for work.

WORKING POPULATION – all those people in paid employment and those who are unemployed.

WORKFORCE IN EMPLOYMENT – all people who are in paid employment.

Capital

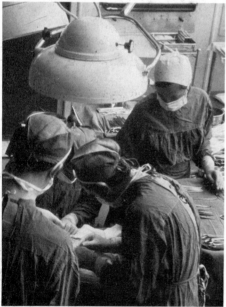

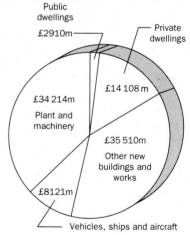

Public
dwellings
£2910m

Private
dwellings

£14 108 m

£34 214m

Plant and
machinery

£35 510m

Other new
buildings and
works

£8121m

Vehicles, ships and aircraft

Figure 22.1 Gross domestic fixed capital
formation, 1991 (£ millions)
Source: CSO, *Monthly Digest of Statistics*, March 1992

S T U D Y P O I N T S

The photographs show different types of *capital*.
Capital is the machinery, factories, tools, offices,
roads, etc., which are used to produce other
goods and services. Figure 22.1 gives statistics
relating to *investment* (called 'Gross Domestic
Fixed Capital Formation') in the UK economy.
Investment is the increase in capital over a
period of time – in this case a year.

1 Make a list of all the different examples of
capital that you can see in the photographs.

2 What goods and services can be produced by
each of the pieces of capital shown in the
photographs?

3 From the pie chart, what was the largest type
of investment in the UK in 1991?

4 How much was invested in new housing in
1991?

5 What do you think is meant by 'other new
buildings'?

6 Why do you think it is important for investment
to increase each year?

7 Investment in public sector dwellings (mainly
council houses) fell in the 1980s. What effect
do you think this had on (a) existing council
house dwellers and (b) on people who wanted
to move into a council house?

8 What do you think is the opportunity cost of
investment in an economy?

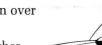

'Industrial investment in Britain should rise by nearly 8% in real terms next year, according to an official survey published yesterday.' (Source: *Financial Times*, 14 December 1984)

Industry needs to update and increase its CAPITAL STOCK. Capital is the machinery, factories, tools, offices, etc. that are used to produce other goods and services. A capital good such as a machine is different from a *consumption good*, because a consumption good is one which, like a chocolate bar, a skirt or an LP record, is bought for the satisfaction or enjoyment that it brings.

Investment in the UK fell by 11% in 1991 and is forecast to fall by 2% in 1992. (*Source:* Adapted from the *Financial Times*, 2 January 1992)

Types of Capital

There are different types of capital. It is very difficult, if not impossible, to measure the capital stock of an economy. It is obviously not possible to add up so many factories, so many machines, so many hospitals, etc. and produce a figure for square metres of capital or tonnes of capital. It is also difficult, if not impossible, to add up the monetary value of the capital stock. For instance, what value would you put on a school building: the cost of replacing it, or the price it would fetch if it was let or sold on the open market? It is, however, possible to calculate how much is spent on investment each year. Figures for UK investment are shown in Figure 22.1. This figure shows that in 1991:

- Approximately 18% of investment was devoted to dwellings (i.e. new housing). A house is a form of capital, because it is used to produce living accommodation over a long period of time.

- Approximately 37% went in other new buildings and works. This category includes investment in factory buildings, office blocks, new school buildings, hospitals, roads and airports.

- Approximately 9% was invested in vehicles, such as lorries and trucks, ships and aircraft, which were all used to produce other goods and services.

- The single largest category of investment (36% of the total) was plant and machinery – everything from a chemical works to a computer to a typewriter. 'Plant' is the term used to describe large fixed machinery, machinery so large that it is the size of a factory unit.

Some of this addition to the capital stock is SOCIAL CAPITAL. This is capital mainly owned by the state and used to produce goods and services that are not, on the whole, sold for money. Examples of social capital are roads, schools, hospitals, sewage works and libraries.

Part of the capital stock is INFRASTRUCTURE. This is the man-made environment – the canals, the railways, etc. (but not, for instance, machinery, vehicles, ships or aircraft).

The Importance of Capital

Capital is essential if a country is to produce the vast quantity of sophisticated goods and services available for consumption today. If an economy is to produce more, it needs to add to that capital – that is, it must invest. The poor investment record of the UK is something that will be returned to in Unit 65.

KEY TERMS

CAPITAL STOCK – the total amount of capital.

INVESTMENT – the addition to the capital stock.

SOCIAL CAPITAL – mainly state-owned capital used to produce goods that are not usually sold via the market mechanism.

INFRASTRUCTURE – the man-made environment.

Data Response Questions
Units 19–22

Unit 19 The Division of Labour

Household division of labour in Great Britain: by marital status (Percentages)

| | Married people[1] | | |
| | Actual allocation of tasks | | |
Household tasks:	Mainly man	Mainly woman	Shared equally
Washing and ironing	1	89	10
Preparation of evening meal	5	77	17
Household cleaning	3	72	24
Household shopping	5	51	44
Evening dishes	17	40	40
Organisation of household money and bills	29	39	32
Repairs of household equipment	82	6	10

[1] 1,209 married respondents.
Source: CSO *Social Trends*

1 What is meant by the 'division of labour'? *(2 marks)*

2 (a) Describe how, according to the data the division of labour is organised in a typical household.
(b) How does this compare with your own household? *(2 marks)*

3 Suggest economic reasons why this division of labour exists in households. *(4 marks)*

4 Would it be more efficient if members of households were to share all tasks equally? *(3 marks)*

Unit 20 Economic Resources

1 Describe in detail what factors of production you think are likely to have been used in the production and sale of this chocolate bar:
(a) at the primary stage;
(b) at the secondary stage;
(c) at the tertiary stage. *(9 marks)*

2 Production of Mars Bars has become capital intensive over the past 20 years. Suggest reasons why this should be so. *(6 marks)*

Unit 21 Labour

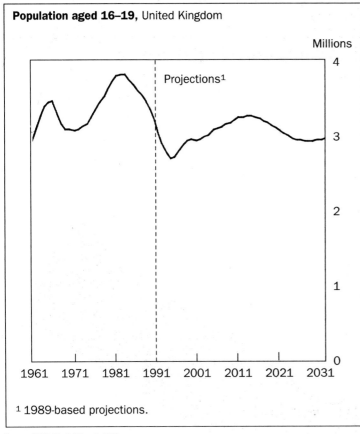

Population aged 16–19, United Kingdom

Millions

Projections[1]

1961 1971 1981 1991 2001 2011 2021 2031

[1] 1989-based projections.

Source: CSO, Social Trends 1992

1 What happened to the number of 16–19 year olds in the population (a) in the 1970s and (b) in the 1980s?
(2 marks)

2 There was a very big rise in youth unemployment in the late 1970s. What does the graph suggest may have been a cause of this? *(3 marks)*

3 What factors will affect the supply of 16–19 year olds to the workforce over the next 10 years? *(5 marks)*

4 Explain what is likely to happen to the demand for university education between now and the year 2031.
(5 marks)

Unit 22 Capital

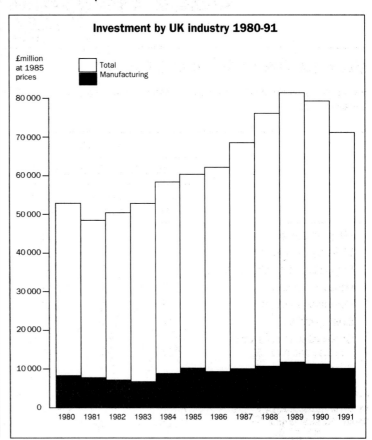

Investment by UK industry 1980-91

£million at 1985 prices

☐ Total
■ Manufacturing

80 000
70 000
60 000
50 000
40 000
30 000
20 000
10 000
0

1980 1981 1982 1983 1984 1985 1986 1987 1988 1989 1990 1991

Sources: CSO, Annual Abstract of Statistics 1992; Monthly Digest of Statistics, April 1992

1 What was the value of total investment in the UK in 1991? *(1 mark)*

2 What happened to manufacturing investment as a proportion of total investment over the period shown?
(2 marks)

3 What effect do you think this trend in manufacturing investment will have had on the competitiveness of UK manufacturing industry? *(7 marks)*

Essay Questions
Units 19–22

1 (a) Describe the main stages in the production of a can of baked beans, starting with the raw materials used and finishing at the point of sale to the consumer.
(6 marks)

(b) Draw a chain of production diagram to illustrate your answer to (a). *(4 marks)*

(c) Give *two* examples of the division of labour in the production of baked beans. *(4 marks)*

(d) What limits the extent to which the division of labour can be applied in this production process? *(4 marks)*

2 (a) Describe the factors of production that would be needed to produce a take-away fish and chip supper.
(8 marks)

(b) What is 'social capital'? Give two examples. *(6 marks)*

(c) Why would it be difficult for consumers to buy fish and chips in Birmingham if there were no social capital in the UK? *(6 marks)*

The Demand for Labour

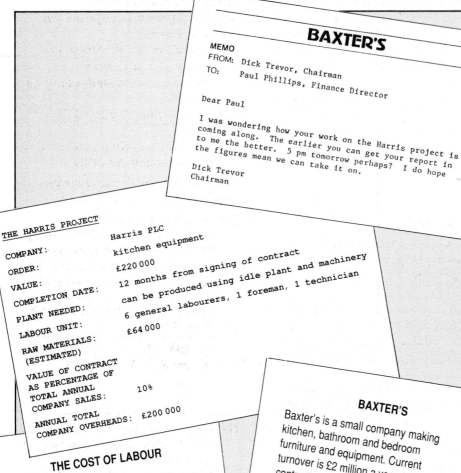

BAXTER'S

MEMO
FROM: Dick Trevor, Chairman
TO: Paul Phillips, Finance Director

Dear Paul

I was wondering how your work on the Harris project is coming along. The earlier you can get your report in to me the better. 5 pm tomorrow perhaps? I do hope the figures mean we can take it on.

Dick Trevor
Chairman

THE HARRIS PROJECT

COMPANY:	Harris PLC
ORDER:	kitchen equipment
VALUE:	£220 000
COMPLETION DATE:	12 months from signing of contract
PLANT NEEDED:	can be produced using idle plant and machinery
LABOUR UNIT:	6 general labourers, 1 foreman, 1 technician
RAW MATERIALS: (ESTIMATED)	£64 000
VALUE OF CONTRACT AS PERCENTAGE OF TOTAL ANNUAL COMPANY SALES:	10%
ANNUAL TOTAL COMPANY OVERHEADS:	£200 000

THE COST OF LABOUR

	Annual Gross Wage
General Labourer	£12 000
Foreman	£14 000
Technician	£14 000

In addition to the gross wage of the worker, the company has to pay 10% of gross wages to the Government in Employers' National Insurance Contributions, and 5% of gross wages to the company pension scheme.

BAXTER'S

Baxter's is a small company making kitchen, bathroom and bedroom furniture and equipment. Current turnover is £2 million a year – the Harris contract would add another £200 000 to that. The company divides its costs of production into overhead costs (costs that are incurred whether anything is produced or not, such as interest on loans, rates, office staff) and variable costs (costs which are incurred due to the fact that a particular contract is undertaken).

'A new £70 million Jumbo repair plant is to be built in Britain, it was announced last night. The hi-tech factory to be owned and operated by British Airways will create more than 1200 highly skilled jobs. The site at Cardiff-Wales Airport beat sites all over the world. Skilled workers employed there will earn at least £17 000 a year.' (*Source:* Adapted from the *Daily Express*, 8 February 1992)

British Airways needs 1200 workers for its new plant near Cardiff – or as economists would say, British Airways has *demanded* more labour. Workers are only demanded by employers because they want to use that labour to produce goods and services. Labour is therefore a DERIVED DEMAND. In the case of British Airways, labour has been demanded because more and more people want to use aeroplanes.

What causes the demand for labour to change? Several factors can be distinguished.

Wage Rates

One factor is the wage rate. The WAGE RATE is the price of labour – how much an employer has to pay a worker to hire him or her for a period of time. If the wage rate falls, it is unlikely that an employer would sack workers. Either the employer will keep the same number as before, or the fall might lead to more workers being taken on. So economists suggest that lower wage rates will lead to employers taking on more workers, whereas higher wage rates will lead to employers taking on fewer workers. This is shown in Figure 23.1. If the wage rate per worker is £200 a week, then the firm will demand or employ 600 workers. If the wage rate went down to £150 a week, then the firm would demand 800 workers. Economists give a number of reasons why the demand curve for labour is downward-sloping:

● One theory, the *marginal revenue productivity theory*, argues that if a firm keeps on employing workers

STUDY POINTS

You are Paul Phillips, Finance Director of Baxter's.

1 Prepare a report arguing whether or not the company ought to take on the Harris contract. In your report you will need to calculate the costs to the company of the contract and compare it to the revenues obtained.

2 The company workforce is awarded a 10% wage rise. Would your decision still be the same and why?

3 If wages went up by 20%, what would you recommend the company to do and why?

4 What determines the number of workers employed by Baxters?

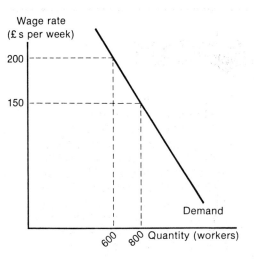

Figure 23.1

with a given quantity of machines, raw materials, etc., then the output per man will eventually start to go down. Each extra worker (or *marginal* worker) will produce less than the last man employed. A firm will only be prepared to pay a worker for the value of what he or she produces. If a worker can add £120 to the value of production, the firm will be prepared to pay that worker up to £120. As the value of the output of each extra worker employed goes down, so will the wage rate the firm is prepared to pay to the last worker it employed. Since workers tend to be paid the same if they are of the same grade, then the more workers a firm employs, the lower will need to be the wages paid to all workers.

- Another theory argues that if a firm is to sell more products, it will need to become more competitive and that means lowering its prices. In order to lower price, the firm will have to reduce costs and that could be done by reducing wage rates. If the firm does sell more products, it will need more workers to produce them. So a fall in wage rates leads to extra demand for labour. One of the reasons why British Airways chose Cardiff as a site to repair jumbo jets is almost certainly because wages are lower in Wales than at, say, Heathrow or Gatwick Airports near London. So the Welsh plant would be more competitive than one built near either of the two main London airports.

- Another argument is that people can be replaced by machines. The higher the wage rate, the more firms will install machines which can replace humans.

Other Factors

The demand for labour is not determined by price alone. The demand for labour is a derived demand. If, say, consumers' incomes went up in the world, more labour in Cardiff would be demanded, because people would travel more. So the level of total or AGGREGATE DEMAND for goods and services in the economy is an important determinant of the demand for labour. For an individual industry, the level of demand for its products is important too. Wage cuts in a firm are not going to help keep workers employed if demand for the goods being produced is falling. Technology, too, is important. Advances in technology can make labour uneconomic at any wage rate. For instance, you cannot make television sets without machinery, even if you pay workers only £10 a week.

As we shall see in Units 58 and 59, what causes firms to demand workers is very important for the debate on the causes of unemployment. Can we solve unemployment by cutting wage rates, or is the solution to expand the demand for goods and services?

CHECKPOINTS

1 Explain what is likely to happen to the number of workers employed by a supermarket chain, if:
   (a) the supermarket opened ten new stores;
   (b) customers bought 10% more goods from the chain;
   (c) the wages of the staff increased by 10%;
   (d) the government put VAT on food;
   (e) the chain installed new computerised cash tills.

2 Explain why the demand for farm workers is a derived demand.

3 (a) On graph paper, draw a demand curve for labour using the following data. (The wage rate goes on the *y*-axis, and the quantity is put on the *x*-axis.)

Wage rate (£ per week)	Quantity demanded
200	10
180	12
160	14
140	16

   (b) How many workers will the firm employ, if the wage rate were £150 a week?
   (c) What is likely to happen to the demand curve, if there is a fall in total spending in the economy?

COURSEWORK SUGGESTION

Arrange to interview the personnel officer of a local firm (or whoever is in charge, or would be aware, of labour recruitment policies in the firm). Before the interview, draw up a questionnaire to help you find out the factors that would influence the hiring or sacking of workers in the firm. From your findings, estimate the price elasticity of demand for labour (i.e. assess the extent to which the level of employment in the firm is dependent upon the level of wage rates). Try to assess the effect of a significant increase in government spending on the level of employment in the firm.

The Supply of Labour

Figure 24.1 Working population in the UK, 1970–91

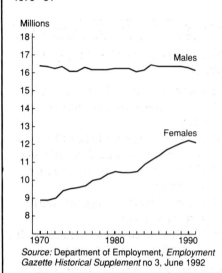

Source: Department of Employment, *Employment Gazette Historical Supplement* no 3, June 1992

Figure 24.2 Average weekly earnings (manual workers in manufacturing and certain industries)

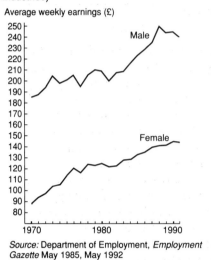

Source: Department of Employment, *Employment Gazette* May 1985, May 1992

Figure 24.3 Possession of labour-saving devices, 1970 and 1990

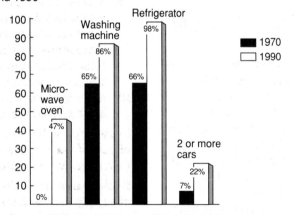

Source: CSO, *Annual Abstract of Statistics 1977;* Department of Employment, Family Spending 1990

STUDY POINTS

1 Describe what has happened to the female working population over the period 1970 to 1991.

2 Why have these changes taken place? In your answer, explain how the benefits of going out to work (such as pay, and availability of new consumer goods like automatic washing machines and videos) have changed since 1970. Explain too how the costs of going out to work (such as time spent on housework like washing and cooking, and looking after children) have altered.

3 Does the evidence in Figures 24.1 and 24.2 support the idea that higher wages increases the number of workers wanting to work? Explain your answer carefully.

4 The Equal Pay Act 1975 stated that women had to be paid the same wage as men doing the same job. What effect do you think this might have had on the number of women wanting a job?

5 What do you expect to happen to the number of women wanting to go out to work in the future? Explain your answer carefully.

In 1970, the working population (the number of people who either had a job or who wanted a job, but were officially registered as unemployed) was about 25 million. In 1991, this had risen to over 28 million. Why had the number of people who wanted to work risen over the period? Or, as economists would say, why had the **SUPPLY OF LABOUR** risen? A number of possible reasons can be put forward.

● The total number of people who could work increased over the period. In 1970, there were 31.7 million people of working age (i.e. men aged between 16 and 64 years, and women aged between 16 and 59). By 1991 this had risen to 34.4 million.

● Wages increased at a faster rate than inflation. The average worker could earn more in 1991 than he or she could in 1970. This is likely to have encouraged more people to look for work.

● Technology in the home changed. Automatic washing machines, dishwashers, freezers, microwave ovens and a host of other appliances meant that women could do their housework in less time. These machines also fell in price relative to earnings, so more people could afford them. Women could go out to work more easily.

● The social climate changed too, with more women looking for jobs, encouraged by the Women's Movement.

These are some of the factors which possibly increased the supply of labour to the whole economy in the 1970s and 1980s.

We can also consider what might affect the supply of labour to an industry like manufacturing industry, or to a particular occupation like teaching. Consider this extract from the mid-1980s which had as it headline 'Low pay hits civil service recruitment':

Figure 24.4

Figure 24.5

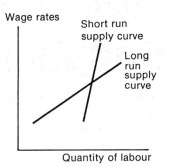

Figure 24.6

'The number of Civil Service vacancies increased by more than 29% last year – but job applications dropped by 2%. (Source: *Financial Times*, 25 April 1985)

Demand for new workers in the civil service increased, but fewer workers wanted those jobs (i.e. the supply of workers to the civil service went down). The article then went on to suggest why this might have been the case. It stated that civil service workers face 'poor' pay levels, lack of promotion prospects, low job interest, poor location and a decline in the standing of civil servants in the community. Workers are preferring to work in other jobs.

Pay, promotion prospects, job interest, etc. add up to what economists call the 'NET ADVANTAGES' OF AN OCCUPATION. If the net advantages increase, then more workers will want that job (i.e. supply will increase). If the net advantages decline, as seemed to be happening in the civil service, then fewer workers will offer themselves for hire in that particular job (i.e. supply will decrease).

A Diagrammatic Representation

The supply of labour can be shown on a diagram like any normal supply curve. It is likely that if wages increase, more workers will want to work in that job. So the supply curve shown in Figure 24.4 is upward sloping.

Figure 24.5 shows an increase in supply from S to S'. What this means is that at any given level of wage rates, more workers will want to work. This shift in supply is what was seen for the whole UK economy between 1970 and 1991. If Figure 24.5 showed an increase in supply for, say, electricians, then this might have come about because the net advantages of being an electrician have increased, or because there are now more people in the working population, or because the net advantages of other occupations such as plumbers have declined. A fall in supply would push the supply curve back, upwards and to the left on the diagram.

The Elasticity of Supply of Workers

Elasticity of supply (explained in Unit 14) is a measure of the responsiveness of changes in quantity supplied to changes in price – in this case, the wage rate. In the short term, the supply of labour to an industry is relatively inelastic. A rise in wage rates will not result in large numbers of workers wanting to become employed in that industry. This is because few workers are likely to have the necessary skills and because workers may see the rise in wages as temporary. Workers do not move jobs every time a small difference in wages between industries occurs. In the long term, however, if the increase in wages is permanent,

and if other wages have not increased by much, then supply is likely to be more elastic – that is, more workers will want to work in that industry compared to the short-run position. This is shown in Figure 24.6.

KEY TERMS

SUPPLY OF LABOUR – the number of people who have a job or who want a job, but are officially registered as unemployed.

NET ADVANTAGES OF AN OCCUPATION – the difference between the private benefit and private cost to a worker of a particular occupation.

The Determination of Wages

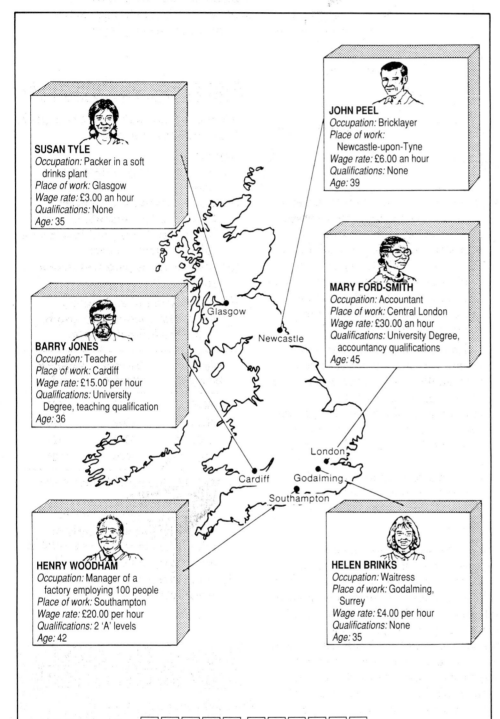

SUSAN TYLE
Occupation: Packer in a soft drinks plant
Place of work: Glasgow
Wage rate: £3.00 an hour
Qualifications: None
Age: 35

JOHN PEEL
Occupation: Bricklayer
Place of work: Newcastle-upon-Tyne
Wage rate: £6.00 an hour
Qualifications: None
Age: 39

BARRY JONES
Occupation: Teacher
Place of work: Cardiff
Wage rate: £15.00 per hour
Qualifications: University Degree, teaching qualification
Age: 36

MARY FORD-SMITH
Occupation: Accountant
Place of work: Central London
Wage rate: £30.00 an hour
Qualifications: University Degree, accountancy qualifications
Age: 45

HENRY WOODHAM
Occupation: Manager of a factory employing 100 people
Place of work: Southampton
Wage rate: £20.00 per hour
Qualifications: 2 'A' levels
Age: 42

HELEN BRINKS
Occupation: Waitress
Place of work: Godalming, Surrey
Wage rate: £4.00 per hour
Qualifications: None
Age: 35

Glasgow
Newcastle
London
Cardiff
Godalming
Southampton

STUDY POINTS

1 Construct a bar graph showing the different wage rates of each worker.

2 Why are these six workers paid different wage rates?

3 Are these workers paid fairly? In your answer explain carefully what you understand by 'fairness' in wages.

4 How would a flat rate wage rise of £3 an hour for all workers affect the allocation of resources in the economy? Would a flat rate rise like this be fairer than a 50% rise for all workers in an economy and why?

Sales assistant required – £3 an hour

Financial Director – up to £50k plus benefits

Fitter needed – £11 200 per annum

Secretary – exceptional opportunity – £160 per week

Librarian post available – salary £9200 to £14 800

Workers are paid different wages. Why is this so? How are wages determined in an economy?

Demand and Supply

Like any price, the price of workers – their wage – is fixed by the forces of demand and supply. If demand for a particular type of worker increases, or the supply falls, then wage rates will rise. If demand falls, or supply rises, then wage rates will fall.

This is shown in Figure 25.1. Assume there is a rise in demand for British textiles. Textile firms will want to take on extra workers – that is, the demand for textile workers will rise from D to D'. At the old equilibrium, where D and S intersected, 100 000 workers had jobs at £150 a week. The increase in demand pushes wage rates up to £200 a week and increases the numbers employed from 100 000 to 120 000.

Difference in Wages

Using the laws of demand and supply, we can now explain why a director is paid more than a textile worker, or a miner more than a cleaner. Wage rates will be higher on average:

- If the job requires special talents, qualifications and experience. Nearly all workers could become machine minders or refuse collectors, so the supply of these workers is very high. Very few workers have the right talents,

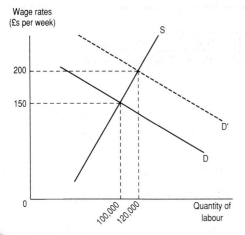

Figure 25.1

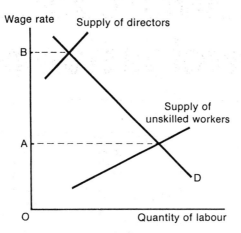

Figure 25.2

is virtually the only source of demand for many workers such as teachers or civil servants. Wages in these situations are fixed not by the laws of demand and supply, but by the relative bargaining strength of the employer and the employees.

qualifications and experience to become directors of companies, so the supply of these workers is very small. As can be seen from Figure 25.2, assuming that the demand for both workers is the same, then the shortage of supply of directors will result in high wages of OB, but unskilled workers will only receive OA.

- If the job is dangerous, unpleasant, or results in long hours of work. Few workers will want to work at the same wage as in safer or more pleasant jobs. So, again, the lower supply will push up wage rates.

Construction workers working on the Dungeness nuclear power plant. Dangerous work!

- If demand for the product that the worker makes is high, thus causing a high demand for workers in the industry. For instance, workers in the electronics industry today are paid more than shipyard workers. In part, this is because the demand for electronic goods is high, whereas the demand for ships is low.

- If the value or MARGINAL REVENUE PRODUCT of one worker is higher than another. The value of the extra output resulting from the employment of a director is greater than the value of the extra output resulting from the employment of an ordinary textile worker. Both this and the last point are shown in Figure 25.1, where the higher demand curve D' causes higher wages.

The above analysis assumes that markets are relatively free, such that there are a large number of buyers and sellers of labour in the market, none of whom are able to influence unduly the wage rate paid. But many labour markets are not free. Trade unions may exist, for instance, which can push wages above the free-market prices. (This is explained further in Unit 27.) Or employers may have immense power. The government, for instance,

KEY POINTS

MARGINAL REVENUE PRODUCT – the addition to revenue gained by employing an extra factor of production such as a worker.

Trade Unions (1)

London steps up jobs fight

BIFU's London Area is stepping up the fight against job cuts in the capital by publishing a job protection guide for members and by calling a major conference on *How to protect your Job* on Saturday April 25.

The guide, also entitled *How to protect your Job* explains what can happen to staff and gives advice on:

✓ Legal rights
✓ Redundancy interviews
✓ Voluntary redundancy pitfalls, State benefits and How to fight redundancy.

Hardest hit

"London has been hardest hit of all by the job cuts now sweeping our industry," said Richard Lynch, Senior London Organiser.

"Over 1,000 jobs are going every month from financial institutions in the capital."

Source: BIFU Report, April 1992, the newspaper of the Banking, Insurance and Finance Union

MSF IN ACTION

Equality gain at General Accident

INSURANCE giant General Accident has conceded that maternity leave will count towards all service-related benefits from April 1 after MSF members took the company to an Industrial Tribunal for sex discrimination.

The company has agreed out-of-court settlements where hearings are pending. Now maternity leave will be treated like sick leave and count towards benefits like pensions, house purchase, and profit sharing.

"It's a pity the company would only move after the threat of legal action," said regional officer Bill McLatchie. "The GA section is grateful to those women in whose name the action was taken and who have notched up another MSF equal rights success."

'Skinflint' gas pay offer rejected

NALGO's gas pay negotiating team flatly rejected a 4 per cent pay offer from British Gas this week.

The tiny 0.1 per cent increase on the April offer was dismissed as "skinflint" by national gas officer Dave Stirzaker.

"British Gas chairman Robert Evans got a 17.6 per cent rise last year and another inflation rate increase this year and yet we are being asked to take a pay cut," he said.

"There is no doubt about the company's ability to pay," he argued. "It has made nearly £1 billion profit each year but they seem to have approached the negotiations on the basis of how little they can get away with."

He said this year's pay round was never going to be easy or straightforward.

"If the members want a decent offer over inflation or simply matching inflation, they must recognise it won't be achieved by negotiation alone," he warned.

Source: NALGO News, no 527, 22 May 1992, the newspaper of the National Association of Local Government Officers

Source: MSF Vol 5, No. 1, 1992, the newspaper of Manufacturing, Science, Finance

- 'Teachers may disrupt exams.'
- 'Cleaners' battle likely to end.'
- 'Postal engineers act over trial manning.'

This sort of headline appears regularly in the news. Many people get the impression that these crises are everyday events for trade unions. In fact, they are most unusual, which is why they get into the news. If trade unions are not all about strikes, what are they about?

The Function of Trade Unions

Trade unions exist to protect the interests of their members. A TRADE UNION is concerned with:

- the level of wages and other forms of remuneration paid to its members;
- promotion prospects and opportunities;
- job security;
- hours of work and other conditions of work;
- health and safety at work;
- dismissal of members;
- benefits paid to workers who are ill, unemployed, retired or injured.

In order to improve the welfare of its members, a trade union needs to negotiate with and put pressure on employers, on other unions and other workers, and on government.

Before trade unions existed, a worker had to negotiate and bargain with an employer on his or her own. Employers were almost always in a more powerful position than workers. In the last resort, an employer could sack a worker and hire another one. The worker who was sacked would probably have found it difficult to get another job. By *combining* in unions, workers could begin to match the power that employers (and government) had over them. COLLECTIVE BARGAINING, where groups of workers

STUDY POINTS

1 Read each of the extracts and summarise them in your own words.

2 Write a short report, using the information contained in the articles as examples, describing the work of trade unions.

3 Would you join a trade union at work? Explain your answer carefully by considering the costs and benefits of union membership.

4 Can trade unions fulfil a useful role in society and what should that role be?

appoint representatives to bargain with the representatives of employers, is an attempt to alter the balance of power in the worker–employer relationship.

Trade Union Membership

Figure 26.1 shows the growth of trade union membership. Today, nearly half of all workers belong to trade unions. Many more workers belong to *professional associations*. These are organisations that perform many of the functions of a trade union, but are not registered as trade unions. They tend to cover better-paid, WHITE-COLLAR WORKERS.

Figure 26.1 Trade union membership

	Membership (millions)			As a percentage of all employees		
	Men	Women	Total	Men	Women	Total
1951	7.7	1.8	9.5	56	25	45
1961	7.9	2.0	9.9	53	24	43
1971	8.4	2.8	11.1	59	32	49
1981	8.4	3.8	12.1	59	38	50
1990	6.2	3.8	10.0	43	32	38

(*Source:* Department of Employment, *Employment Gazette*, April 1992)

Figure 26.1 shows clearly how trade union membership grew in the 1950s, 1960s and 1970s. However, the 1980s saw a dramatic decline in trade union membership. There were two main reasons for this.

Firstly, trade unions were particularly strong in manufacturing industry. But in the 1980s, UK manufacturing industry saw jobs fall from 7.1 million in 1979 to 5 million in 1990. Most of those who lost their jobs will have been trade union members.

Secondly, a Conservative government elected in 1979 under Margaret Thatcher pursued a very strong anti-union policy. Trade unions were blamed for high unemployment, inflation and the loss of competitiveness of British industry. Laws were passed which:

- forced unions wanting to bring their members out on strike to hold a secret ballot first – a majority had to vote in favour to make the strike legal;

- outlawed secondary picketing – this was the practice of workers supporting other striking workers by picketing a place of work which wasn't their own;

- made unions hold secret postal ballots to elect top officials in the union;

- outlawed closed shops – firms and unions could no longer insist that everyone working in a place of work had to join a recognised trade union;

- allowed firms to sue trade unions for damages if they didn't abide by the new laws.

Some workers dropped their union membership as they no longer saw it as relevant to their needs. Firms too which didn't want their workers to belong to trade unions became increasingly aggressive and successful at squeezing out trade unions from the workplace.

Notice, though, that the entire fall in trade union membership between 1981 and 1991 has been caused by a fall in male membership. Female membership has remained the same at 3.8 million. Women workers were far less likely to be employed in manufacturing industry and had a tradition of being less militant than men. The anti-union laws of the 1980s therefore had less impact on women who always had been less likely to go out on strike.

Falling membership has hit unions hard. They depend upon members' subscriptions to pay for the full-time workers employed by the union and for all the other expenses of running a union. The result has been a series of mergers (or amalgamations) between unions to get them back up to a size where they can offer a good cost-effective service to their members.

CHECKPOINTS

1. What is a 'trade union'?
2. Give the names of five different trade unions.
3. Describe three different functions of a trade union (i.e. describe three things a trade union does).
4. Explain why collective bargaining is likely to help a worker obtain higher wages than if he or she had to bargain individually with an employer.
5. Why did trade union membership fall in the 1980s?

COURSEWORK SUGGESTION

Find out about a particular trade union (you could research the NUT or NAS/UWT), either on a national or a local level. Describe its activities. Analyse how it protects the interests of its members. Assess the extent to which it provides positive benefits for (a) its members and (b) the economy as a whole.

KEY TERMS

TRADE UNION – a group of workers who combine to protect their interests.

COLLECTIVE BARGAINING – where the representatives of workers negotiate with the representatives of their employers.

WHITE-COLLAR WORKER – a non-manual worker such as a teacher or a secretary, as opposed to a manual *blue-collar worker*, who works 'with his hands'.

Trade Unions (2)

Company Statistics[1]

| | Actual | | | | Projected |
	1996	1997	1998	1999	2000
Turnover (£ millions)	20	15	25	30	32
Profit (£ millions)	2	−3	1	2	1
Capital employed (£ millions)	40	44	41	45	1000
Number of workers employed	1150	1200	980	1000	47
Average earnings per worker (£)	9990	11 080	11 311	12 000	—
Average pay rise (%)	10	12	2	6.1	—
Inflation rate (%)	5	5	5	6	7

[1]Provided by the company to the unions for the 2000 pay negotiations.

STUDY POINTS

1 Assume you were a full time official of one of the trade unions involved in the dispute which is taking place in 2000. Write a short report explaining the trade union arguments in favour of a pay rise.

2 Can the firm afford to give the workers a pay rise? What is the maximum it could afford to give?

3 What are the economic consequences of a pay rise: (a) for the workers; (b) for the company; (c) for the rest of the economy?

4 What would be the economic consequences of a strike (a) for the workers, (b) for the company, (c) for the rest of the economy?

5 Should the workers accept the 9% offered them by the company? Explain your answer.

Trade unions have always been controversial. But what effects do they have on the economy? Consider this news item:

'Chief union negotiator Mr John Partridge is recommending acceptance of a new improved pay offer at the bus company West Midlands Travel. The new offer freezes pay for three months in return for a taxable lump sum of £250 and an extra day's holiday a year. After three months, a pay increase in line with inflation would be given to cover the next 12 months.' (*Source:* Adapted from the *Express and Star*, 26 June 1992)

The unions have negotiated an improved pay offer for bus workers. Who is going to pay for this pay rise? Different economists give different answers, but it is likely that the pay rise would be paid by one or more of the following:

- *consumers* – West Midlands Travel might put up its fares to passengers to cover the cost of the pay deal;

- *the owners* of West Midlands Travel – the extra wages might be paid for by reducing profits paid to the owners of the company. In this case, unusually for British industry, the owners are some of the workers who bought the company in a management buy out;

- *the workers* – West Midlands Travel might decide that it cannot afford to pay all its workers any more, so it might reduce its workforce;

- *nobody* – because West Midlands Travel would be forced to increase **LABOUR PRODUCTIVITY**. Productivity is defined as output per worker. An increase in wages would force West Midlands Travel to find ways of making workers produce the extra money needed to cover the cost of the increased wage bill.

Trade unionists would argue that increased wages are likely to be paid for by increased productivity and reduced profits. They would argue that workers are always fighting to keep their share of the wealth that their company produces. Without trade unions, profits would be higher and the owners of the company would be richer at the expense of the workers. Others would argue that wage rises hit consumers by forcing firms to push up their prices. This could well lead to inflationary problems in the economy. They would also argue that wage rises cause unemployment. Trade unions, by pushing up wages, leave firms with no alternative but to sack workers. So, they argue, trade union power may be a major cause of unemployment.

A Diagrammatic Analysis

The effect of trade unions on wages and employment can be explained using demand and supply diagrams. In Figure 27.1, the demand for workers by company, such as West Midlands Travel, is given by the line D. The supply curve of workers to the company is given by the line S. The equilibrium level of wage rates is therefore OA and the company will employ OE workers. Now assume that trade unions force the company to pay higher wages, say OB. What this means is that, due to union pressure, the company can't hire any workers at a wage of less than OB. So the supply curve of labour becomes horizontal between B and F. To the right of F, the supply curve becomes upward sloping again – trade unions aren't going to

prevent wages going even higher than OB if market conditions force West Midlands Travel to pay these higher wages. In Figure 27.1 the new equilibrium wage is therefore OB. Note, however, that West Midlands Travel now only wants to employ OC workers, whereas before, at the wage rate of OA, it wanted to employ OE workers. CE workers will therefore lose their jobs. Trade unions have raised wages but at the expense of jobs in the rail industry.

What if the company itself paid for the pay rise out of its profits? This situation is shown in Figure 27.2. Here the company is prepared to employ the same number of workers, whatever the wage rate. It might be prepared to do this, if, for instance, these workers formed only a very small part of the cost of production, but were essential none the less. If, for instance, wages counted for only 1% of the cost of the product, an employer would be unlikely to sack workers if they received a pay rise of 10% rather than 5%. Equally, a company might need an exact number of workers to staff a factory, if it is to produce at all. Here, the choice is between operating the factory or not, irrespective of the wage paid. In both these situations, the demand for labour is perfectly inelastic and is shown in the demand curve D. The company is prepared to employ OC workers, whatever the wage rate. Assume that the factory was profitable at a wage level of OB. Then

if the company can pay lower wages at OA, it will be even more profitable. Trade unions in this situation would be trying to push up wages at the expense of profits.

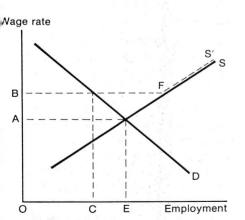

Figure 27.1

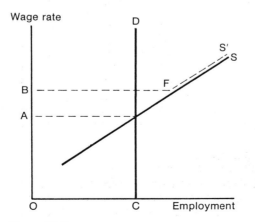

Figure 27.2

KEY TERM

LABOUR PRODUCTIVITY – output per worker.

Data Response Questions
Units 23–27

Unit 23 The Demand for Labour

Pay rises down as age of 'new realism' dawns

Pay rises in service companies fell sharply in the first half of the year to reach their lowest level for almost a decade, new figures showed today.

Settlements averaged 4.4 per cent, around the rate of inflation, compared with 6 per cent in the second half of last year and 7.1 per cent in the first six months of 1991, according to the Confederation of British Industry's pay data-bank.

The CBI said 'realistic' deals were being agreed as the message got through that pay had to match performance.

Since last autumn, low company profits have been reported as an important reason for reduced pay rises as has increased unemployment. Service company settlements are now close to those in manufacturing, where deals averaged 4.3 per cent in the first three months of the year.

CNI director general Sir John Banham said: 'The new realism about pay and performance across the private sector as a whole illustrated by these figures is clearly not a flash in the pan.'

'Wage cost developments now compare more favourably with our overseas competitors.'

Source: Adapted from the Express and Star, 15 June 1992

1 How did pay settlements change in the first half of 1992 according to the article? *(2 marks)*

2 Explain why 'low company profits' and 'increased unemployment' might have affected:
   (a) the number of workers firms want to employ;
   (b) how much they are prepared to pay them. *(8 marks)*

3 What could cause firms to increase their demand for labour? *(5 marks)*

Unit 24 The Supply of Labour

Activity rates	Males aged 60–64	Females aged 55–59
1971	82.9	50.9
1976	80.4	54.3
1981	69.3	53.4
1986	53.8	51.8
1990	54.4	54.9
Projections		
1996	52.5	54.9
2001	51.5	54.9

Source: CSO, Social Trends 1992
Note: an activity rate shows what percentage of the population of a certain age has a job or is unemployed. For instance, reading from the table, in 1971, 82.9 out of every 100 males in the UK aged 60–64 were either in work or were unemployed, but only 50.9 per cent of females aged 55–59 were in work or seeking work.

1 What has happened since 1971 to the proportion of (a) men aged 60–64 and (b) women aged 55–59 who are in work or are unemployed? *(2 marks)*

2 Suggest reasons why this change in male activity rates has occurred. *(6 marks)*

3 Why do you think that there has been a difference between what has happened to male and female activity rates since 1971? *(3 marks)*

4 (a) What has been the effect on the supply of labour in the 1970s and 1980s of these trends in activity rates?

   (b) What is the possible effect on the supply of labour in the 1990s if the projections are correct? *(4 marks)*

Essay Questions
Units 23–27

1 'Nurses are paid far less than pop stars and yet are far more important to people's welfare.'
   (a) Give *three* reasons why workers are paid differently. *(6 marks)*

   (b) Explain why a nurse is paid less than a pop star. *(6 marks)*

   (c) Describe, using a demand and supply diagram, how nurses' pay and the number of nurses employed would change if the Government decided to open 20 new hospitals in the UK. *(8 marks)*

Unit 25 The Determination of Wages

Retail chain raises youth rates by 43%

W. H. Smith, the retail chain, has raised its wage rates for 16 and 17 year olds by up to 43 per cent. It is part of a 10.5 per cent wage deal intended to improve its recruitment of the shrinking number of school-leavers.

The decision by W. H. Smith follows similar upratings of youth wage rates by other retail chains facing difficulties in attracting enough young people up to 1994 as the number of school-leavers fell.

Mr John Ainley, W. H. Smith's retail personnel and training manager, said the company wanted to show it regarded young workers as being valuable. It also wanted to improve its recruitment position.

Multiple retailers including Tesco and J Sainsbury raised their youth wage rates in last year's wage round as part of an effort to make themselves more attractive, particularly in the tight labour markets in the south-east where unemployment is very low.

Source: Adapted from the *Financial Times*, 18 June 1990

1 What is meant by a 'tight labour market'? *(1 mark)*

2 (a) Why did W. H. Smith raise youth wage rates in 1990?
   (b) Use a demand and supply diagram to illustrate your answer. *(8 marks)*

3 Unemployment in the UK roughly doubled between 1990 and 1993 as the economy experienced a severe recession. What effect do you think this had on youth wage rates? *(6 marks)*

2 Jimmy Plant starts work today as a trainee manager at a supermarket.
   (a) Suggest *four* reasons why he might want to join a trade union. *(8 marks)*
   (b) What is a 'shop steward' and how might he help Jimmy Plant and other workers at the supermarket? *(6 marks)*
   (c) Using a demand and supply diagram, explain the possible effects of a 10% pay increase for workers at the supermarket on the number of workers employed by the company. *(6 marks)*

Unit 26 and 27 Trade Unions (1)

Wage freeze at car parts firm

About 700 workers at a big car parts plant in Birmingham have had a pay freeze slapped on them, it was revealed today.

Hourly-paid workers at Hall Green based Magnetti Marelli have started an overtime ban in protest at the move.

Talks were being held between management and unions at the Shaftmoor Lane plant this week in an attempt to avoid a major dispute.

Bob Blakemore, Birmingham East district secretary for the engineering union AEU, said the company had told negotiators it could not afford a pay rise.

He added management had held its position despite unions approaching them to complain, and workers voted to start industrial action last week.

Mr Blakemore added: 'This is not consistent with the three per cent which is being given elsewhere in the industry.' The Fiat-owned company's head of personnel Frank Devine said talks were at a delicate stage and he did not yet want to comment.

Source: Express and Star, 12 February 1992

1 What was the dispute between workers and management at Magnetti Marelli about? *(2 marks)*

2 Suggest why the company had imposed a pay freeze on hourly paid workers. *(3 marks)*

3 What role do you think trade unions played in the dispute? *(5 marks)*

4 Explain whether you think industrial relations would have been better if there had been no trade unions representing workers at the factory. *(5 marks)*

Go for it!

Supervisory and technical staff at Bowater Pipes of Clay Cross, Derbyshire, have won pay rises of between 9 and 11 per cent after threatening to take strike action.

Management originally offered only 7 per cent but upped this amount after staff had voted for one day strikes.

Regional officer Ken Orme said: 'I hope that this MSF group's stand will set a trend elsewhere in the East Midlands. If your case is strong, go for it!'

Source: MSF, Vol 5, 1992, newspaper of the Manufacturing, Science, Finance union

1 What pay award did the union MSF achieve for its members at Bowater Pipes? *(1 mark)*

2 Explain, using a demand and supply diagram, the possible effect on jobs of the pay award. *(6 marks)*

3 What would be the possible gains and losses (a) to companies, (b) to workers and (c) to consumers if this pay award 'set a trend elsewhere in the East Midlands'? *(8 marks)*

Rent, Interest and Profit

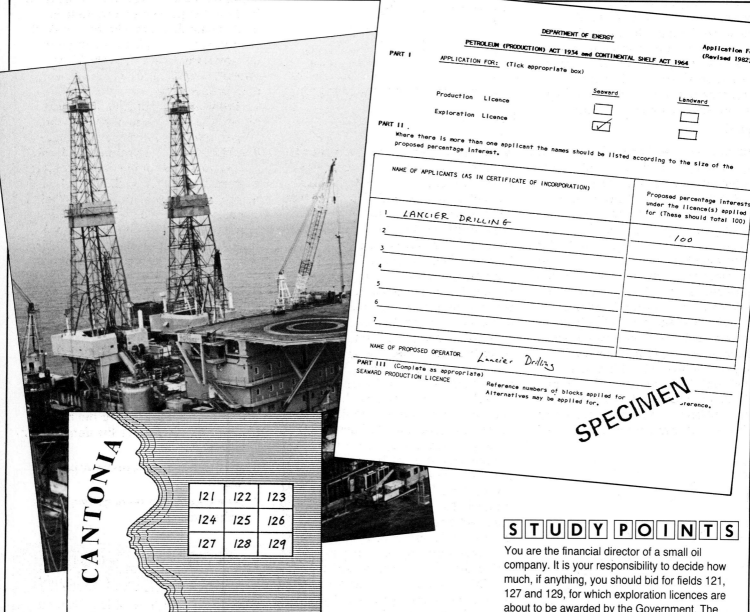

DEPARTMENT OF ENERGY

PETROLEUM (PRODUCTION) ACT 1934 and CONTINENTAL SHELF ACT 1964

Application Form
(Revised 1982)

PART I   APPLICATION FOR: (Tick appropriate box)

Production Licence   Seaward   Landward

Exploration Licence

PART II .
Where there is more than one applicant the names should be listed according to the size of the proposed percentage interest.

NAME OF APPLICANTS (AS IN CERTIFICATE OF INCORPORATION)   Proposed percentage interests under the licence(s) applied for (These should total 100)

1 LANCIER DRILLING   100
2
3
4
5
6
7

NAME OF PROPOSED OPERATOR Lancier Drilling

PART III (Complete as appropriate)
SEAWARD PRODUCTION LICENCE   Reference numbers of blocks applied for
                                  Alternatives may be applied for.

SPECIMEN

CANTONIA

121	122	123
124	125	126
127	128	129

You are the financial director of a small oil company. It is your responsibility to decide how much, if anything, you should bid for fields 121, 127 and 129, for which exploration licences are about to be awarded by the Government. The Government awards the licence to exploit a field to the company which offers the highest amount of money. This must be paid immediately, in full, upon the granting of the licence.

1 What is the cost, excluding the licence, of exploiting each of the fields?

2 What is the revenue likely to be obtained from each field?

3 How much would you be prepared to bid for each of the fields?

4 How much profit would you expect to make after all payments had been made to the factors of production employed?

Field	121	127	129
Likely reserves of oil[1] (millions of barrels)	100	150	200
Price of oil per barrel[2] (£)	20	20	20
Cost of capital[3] (£ millions)	1100	2000	2500
Annual Operating Cost[2], excluding labour (£ millions)	30	40	60
Annual labour costs[2] (£ millions)	10	15	30
Expected life of field (years)	10	10	10

Notes: [1] These figures are for oil which is likely to be recoverable over the lifetime of the field.
[2] At today's prices.
[3] Starting up costs of the field including the cost of exploration and the cost of an oil rig to recover the oil.

Costs

It was shown in Unit 25 how the forces of demand and supply determined how much it cost to hire a worker. In this unit, we will consider the cost or price of hiring the other factors of production. Just as the forces of demand and supply fix the wage paid to a worker, so too do the forces of demand and supply determine what the owners of land, capital and entrepreneurship receive when they hire out their factors of production.

Land

Total land is fixed in supply. There are only so many billion tonnes of coal on this planet, so many hectares of land, etc. But the supply of land for any particular use is not fixed. For instance, the supply of land for building can be increased by reducing the supply of agricultural land, or the land used for recreational activities. Figure 28.1 shows that an increase in the demand for building land from D to D' will raise the price of building land from OA to OB and lead to an extension of supply from OE to OF. The price of hiring land is usually called rent (but, as will be shown in Unit 29, the term 'rent' has come to have a different meaning in economics to the everyday meaning of the word).

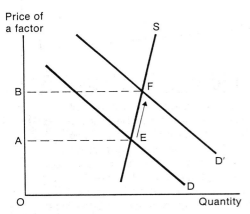

Figure 28.1

Capital

The price of capital, too, is fixed by the forces of demand and supply. In a free market, capital is demanded by business organisations in order to produce goods and services. Of course, a firm does not have to buy capital. It could, instead, save the money it

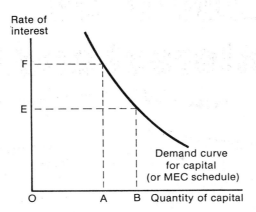

Figure 28.2

would have spent on capital goods by putting it in a bank or in stocks and shares (i.e. it could save the money instead of investing it). The price that a firm pays for its capital is the opportunity cost of the capital – what the firm has to give up in order to invest and hold capital. That price is the rate of interest it could have received if it had saved the money. So the reward to capital is generally considered to be interest.

Capital is supplied to the economy by individuals, business, government, etc. That supply of capital, too, has an opportunity cost. For instance, the household that buys new shares in a company could have used that money for spending or it could have saved the money. Again, the opportunity cost of having capital is the interest that is lost on that money, had it been saved. So the 'price' of capital is the rate of interest. The higher the rate of interest, the more households, firms and governments will choose to supply money to building societies and banks, rather than demand new capital.

This is shown in Figure 28.2. When interest rates are high at OF, the demand for capital, OA, is low. (The demand curve is given the special name of the 'marginal efficiency of capital (MEC) schedule'.) An increase in capital from OA to OB will reduce interest rates by EF.

Entrepreneurship

The reward for entrepreneurship is generally considered to be profit. The entrepreneur risks his or her money or capital in a business and organises the other factors of production. In practice, most output is produced either in the

public sector, where no single person owns and organises production, or in large PLCs (public limited companies) in the private sector, where the shareholders are different people from the directors and managers of the firm. Profit in the private sector, then, is paid to shareholders who have risked their money in buying the capital of the company – that is, profit is the return to capital and not entrepreneurship.

Profit is different from the other rewards to the factors of production. Wages, rent and interest are normally fixed in advance of production. Profit is the amount of money left over after all costs have been paid. For that reason, profit can be negative as well as positive, if cost exceeds revenue. Profit also tends to vary much more than the other payments to the factors of production over a period of time. The role of profits in the economy is discussed in Unit 34.

C H E C K P O I N T S

1 **Explain what determines the hire charge for an acre of farm land.**

2 **What is the opportunity cost of renting an office block?**

3 **Explain why the higher the rate of interest is, the lower the demand for capital will be.**

4 **Why does an entrepreneur earn profit?**

5 **Why can profits be negative, when wages cannot?**

C O U R S E W O R K S U G G E S T I O N

Investigate the prices of land in your locality. One major source of information would be local estate agents. The area under investigation should be large enough to include land used for housing, for industrial purposes, for recreation and for farming. Describe the pattern of land prices and rents. Using demand and supply analysis, explain why land values and rents differ. Consider what would happen to land values and rent, if there were a change in the permitted usage of the land.

Economic Rent, Costs and Profit

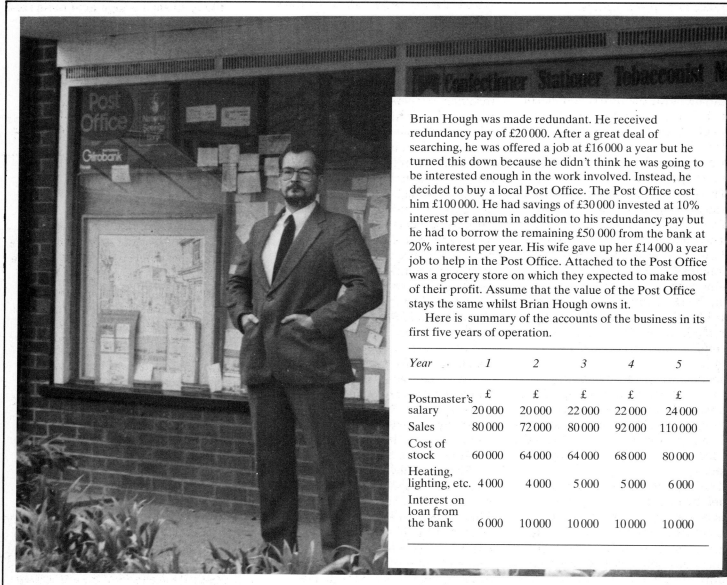

Brian Hough was made redundant. He received redundancy pay of £20 000. After a great deal of searching, he was offered a job at £16 000 a year but he turned this down because he didn't think he was going to be interested enough in the work involved. Instead, he decided to buy a local Post Office. The Post Office cost him £100 000. He had savings of £30 000 invested at 10% interest per annum in addition to his redundancy pay but he had to borrow the remaining £50 000 from the bank at 20% interest per year. His wife gave up her £14 000 a year job to help in the Post Office. Attached to the Post Office was a grocery store on which they expected to make most of their profit. Assume that the value of the Post Office stays the same whilst Brian Hough owns it.

Here is summary of the accounts of the business in its first five years of operation.

Year	1	2	3	4	5
	£	£	£	£	£
Postmaster's salary	20 000	20 000	22 000	22 000	24 000
Sales	80 000	72 000	80 000	92 000	110 000
Cost of stock	60 000	64 000	64 000	68 000	80 000
Heating, lighting, etc.	4 000	4 000	5 000	5 000	6 000
Interest on loan from the bank	6 000	10 000	10 000	10 000	10 000

STUDY POINTS

1 Make a list, in words, of all the costs that Brian Hough faces in running his business. Don't forget to include not only the costs he has to pay directly, but also the hidden opportunity costs of his business such as the pay his wife could have been earning if she weren't employed at the Post Office.

2 Calculate the economic costs of the business in its first five years of operation. Don't forget that 'economic cost' must include the opportunity costs involved.

3 What revenues does the business receive?

4 Calculate the revenue earned by the business in each of its five years of operation.

5 Calculate the economic profit or loss (i.e. revenues minus costs) for each year.

6 How much money did Brian Hough and his wife make with their business in each year? Include not only the postmaster's salary, but also any other earnings or profits they are taking out of the business.

7 If Brian Hough and his wife could have earned £30 000 by working for someone else in year 5, how much more or less did they

earn by working in their Post Office? (This is known as their ECONOMIC RENT.)

8 What effect would a halving of the rate of interest have on (a) the costs of the business and (b) the profits of the business?

9 The Post Office decides to cut all postmasters' pay by 50%. Is the business now making a profit?

10 If the value of the Post Office increased by £10 000 each year, what effect would this have on the profitability of the business.

Economic Rent and Transfer Earnings

The words 'rent', 'cost' and 'profit' have different meanings in ordinary language and in economics. Consider this sentence:

'The rent on the farmland was £5000 a year.'

Rent here is a term used to describe the payment for the hire of a piece of land. This is the ordinary everyday usage of the word. But in economics, the term has come to describe the earnings of any factor of production over and above its transfer earnings.

The **TRANSFER EARNINGS** of a factor are the earnings that a factor could receive in its next best occupation. For instance, assume that a piece of land could be used either as building land, at a rent of £15 000 a year, or as farming land, at a rent of £5000 a year. Then, the transfer earnings of the piece of building land are £5000 a year – what could be earned by renting out the land as farm land instead of building land.

ECONOMIC RENT is any earnings over and above the transfer earnings. So if the rent on the piece of land used for building were £15 000 a year, then the economic rent would be £10 000 – the £15 000 minus the transfer earnings of £5000.

The highest economic rent is earned by factors with very low transfer earnings in comparison to their actual payment. A pop star, for instance, might earn £250 000 a year. His next best job might be as a teacher, earning say £10 000. So with transfer earnings of £10 000, he is earning an economic rent of £240 000. Building land is a good example of high economic rent, because there tends to be a great difference between the rent paid on building land and land for alternative uses.

Economic Cost and Profit

Cost and profit, too, have special meanings in economics. COST includes not only what has to be paid directly, but also the hidden cost of factors that could be used in alternative ways. For instance, consider the businesswoman who works for her own business and who puts in £20 000 to start it off. Her costs will obviously include raw materials, hiring of other workers, etc. But in economics, costs will also include the costs of borrowing that £20 000. The money has an opportunity cost because it could have been lent, say, to a bank and earned interest. The businesswoman must also include a wage for herself, that being the wage that she could have earned in the next best alternative job. So if the businesswoman could have earned £15 000 a year in a job, the economic cost to her business is £15 000 a year.

ECONOMIC PROFIT is the difference between all revenues received and all costs incurred. For instance, if a company earned £30 000 in revenues and paid out £20 000 in costs, then the profit would be £10 000.

Economic profit may well differ from what is ordinarily called 'profit' in the business world by accountants. This is because an accountant considers mainly those revenues and costs that are actual flows of money into and out of the firm. But many costs and benefits are hidden. An economist takes into account all of these costs and revenues, both the accounting costs and revenues as well as these hidden costs and revenues.

KEY TERMS

ECONOMIC RENT – payment to a factor of production over and above its transfer earnings.

TRANSFER EARNINGS – the earnings of a factor in its next best use.

COST – the cost of an activity including not only monetary costs, but also the opportunity cost of factors owned by the producer.

ECONOMIC PROFIT – the difference between all revenues received and all costs incurred.

CHECKPOINTS

1 Explain what is meant by transfer earnings and economic rent.

2 Which of the following workers are likely to earn a high economic rent and why:
(a) a pop star;
(b) an international footballer;
(c) a road sweeper;
(d) a cashier in the supermarket?

3 Copy out and complete the table.

Current earnings (£)	Transfer earnings (£)	Economic rent (£)
10 000	5000	
20 000	8000	
40 000		2000
	6000	0

4 Explain the difference between the ordinary meaning of 'cost' and the economic meaning of 'cost'.

5 You decide to travel by bus into town to do some shopping. Which of the following are the economic costs of this to you and why:
(a) the bus fare;
(b) the petrol used by the bus;
(c) the bus driver's time;
(d) your time spent travelling and shopping;
(e) wear and tear on your shoes;
(f) the money you paid for the goods you bought?

COURSEWORK SUGGESTION

Investigate the market for either pop stars or football players. Find out and describe the earnings of a number of these workers. Explain why they are paid so much. Estimate their transfer earnings. (For instance, what does a football player earn after retirement and in what job? Give specific examples.) Estimate their current economic rent. Should this economic rent be taxed by the government? Put forward arguments for and against this idea.

Factor Mobility

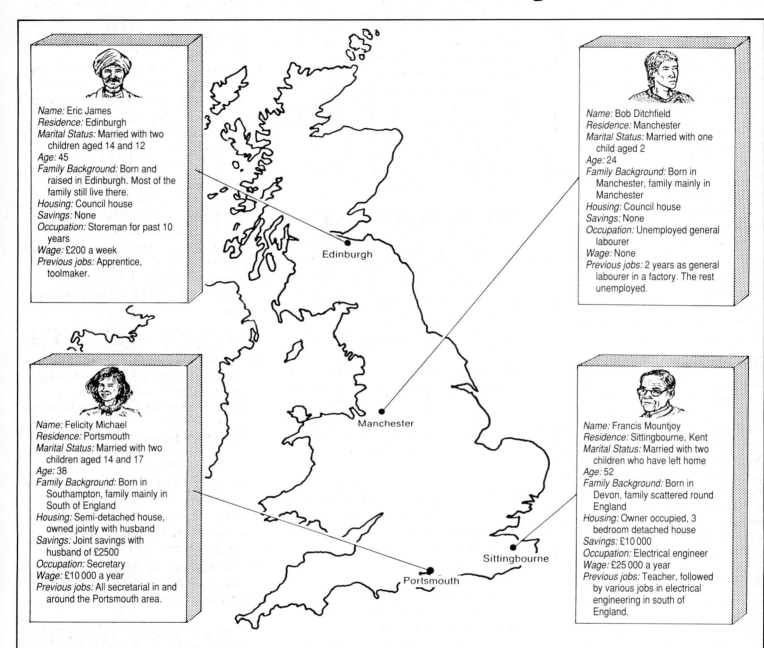

Name: Eric James
Residence: Edinburgh
Marital Status: Married with two children aged 14 and 12
Age: 45
Family Background: Born and raised in Edinburgh. Most of the family still live there.
Housing: Council house
Savings: None
Occupation: Storeman for past 10 years
Wage: £200 a week
Previous jobs: Apprentice, toolmaker.

Name: Bob Ditchfield
Residence: Manchester
Marital Status: Married with one child aged 2
Age: 24
Family Background: Born in Manchester, family mainly in Manchester
Housing: Council house
Savings: None
Occupation: Unemployed general labourer
Wage: None
Previous jobs: 2 years as general labourer in a factory. The rest unemployed.

Name: Felicity Michael
Residence: Portsmouth
Marital Status: Married with two children aged 14 and 17
Age: 38
Family Background: Born in Southampton, family mainly in South of England
Housing: Semi-detached house, owned jointly with husband
Savings: Joint savings with husband of £2500
Occupation: Secretary
Wage: £10 000 a year
Previous jobs: All secretarial in and around the Portsmouth area.

Name: Francis Mountjoy
Residence: Sittingbourne, Kent
Marital Status: Married with two children who have left home
Age: 52
Family Background: Born in Devon, family scattered round England
Housing: Owner occupied, 3 bedroom detached house
Savings: £10 000
Occupation: Electrical engineer
Wage: £25 000 a year
Previous jobs: Teacher, followed by various jobs in electrical engineering in south of England.

Edinburgh · *Manchester* · *Sittingbourne* · *Portsmouth*

STUDY POINTS

1 Eric James is made redundant. There is a vacancy for a storeman in Sittingbourne, Kent. Why is it most unlikely that Eric James would come to work in Sittingbourne?

2 What obstacles are there to Bob Ditchfield finding a job (a) other than a general labourer in Manchester or (b) as a general labourer elsewhere in the UK?

3 If a worker is likely to find it difficult to be offered, or to take a job, in another area of the UK, economists say that that worker is *geographically immobile*. Why is Felicity Michael likely to be geographically immobile? Why is Francis Mountjoy likely to be geographically immobile too?

4 If a worker is likely to find it difficult to change his or her occupation or job, then economists say that the worker is *occupationally immobile*. Why is Francis Mountjoy likely to be occupationally immobile? Why is Felicity Michael likely to be occupationally immobile too?

5 To what extent do you think you are likely to be geographically *mobile* when you are in work? Would you, for instance, consider taking a job in the nearest large town or city to yours? Would you consider moving to a different region of the UK? Would you consider working abroad? Explain your answer carefully.

Specialisation and Exchange

The economy is built upon the principles of specialisation and exchange. Workers, firms, regions and countries specialise in the production of certain goods and services, and exchange them for others. For this type of economy to work efficiently, it is important that the factors of production (land, labour and capital) be *mobile*. If they are not mobile, then workers can become unemployed, firms can go bankrupt, and regions and countries can fail to share in growing world prosperity.

Mobility can be of two types:

- GEOGRAPHICAL MOBILITY describes the movement of a factor of production from one area to another area within a region or within a country or between countries.

- OCCUPATIONAL or VERTICAL MOBILITY describes the movement of a factor between one job and another.

The Mobility of Land

Land is geographically immobile. It is impossible to move land from, say, Glasgow to London to relieve a land shortage in London. Land, however, is occupationally mobile to some extent. Much land has a variety of uses – for agriculture, for recreation, for industry, etc. In the UK, land use is strictly regulated by planning regulations. For instance, it is not possible to develop industry in the Green Belt. This restricts occupational mobility of land.

The Mobility of Capital

Some capital is both geographically and occupationally mobile. A typewriter, or a small lathe, or a computer are such examples. But something like an office block is only occupationally mobile, whereas something like a petro-chemical works is broadly immobile (i.e. it has no alternative use). The fact that much

capital is both geographically and occupationally immobile means that it is difficult to solve the problem of high unemployment in a region quickly and easily. It takes years to build up the capital necessary to provide jobs for everybody who wants them. One of the major problems of an area like north-east England is that it may have plenty of capital in the form of old factory buildings and old machinery, but these remain unemployed, because demand for the goods they were intended to produce has gone and these pieces of capital are immobile (i.e. have no alternative use).

The Mobility of Labour

In theory, labour should be the most mobile of factors. People can move from area to area to work, and can be trained and retrained for new jobs. In practice, labour is geographically immobile because:

- the financial cost of moving from one area to another is high;

- workers, especially those in rented council houses, may not be able to find housing in another area;

- workers are often reluctant to move away from friends, family and their local area, even if they are unemployed;

- there is very little information in one area about job opportunities in another area – for instance, vacancies for unskilled workers in London are not advertised in Aberdeen.

Labour can be occupationally immobile for the following reasons.

- Workers can become over-specialised. Many jobs require long periods of education, training and experience. So a steel worker cannot suddenly become a shop manager or an electrician.

- Workers have different natural

talents. Only a few, for instance, can become professional golfers or university lecturers.

- Institutional barriers, such as laws, qualifications, and trade unions, can prevent workers moving into a particular profession.

- Money (to cover start-up costs) can be a problem for anybody wanting to set up in business by themselves.

- As with geographical mobility, a lack of information can mean that workers don't move from one occupation to another.

Immobility of labour causes unemployment – there may be unemployed workers unable to fill job vacancies because of barriers to mobility. Immobility of labour can also produce differences in wage rates, because the supply of labour may differ between industries and between regions.

CHECKPOINTS

1 In what ways are each of the following workers geographically and occupationally mobile:
   (a) a teacher with her own house in London;
   (b) an unemployed steel worker living in a council house in South Wales;
   (c) a car salesman living in his own house in Wolverhampton?

2 Why is an office block occupationally mobile, but not geographically mobile?

3 Why can the immobility of capital cause unemployment of workers in particular regions?

COURSEWORK SUGGESTION

Using your careers library, find out about two different careers. Describe each job. Compare and contrast the extent of geographical and occupational mobility likely to be open to workers in those occupations. Suggest ways in which geographical and occupational mobility could be improved by the government. Try to assess the costs and benefits of these policies.

KEY TERMS

GEOGRAPHICAL MOBILITY – the movement of a factor of production from area to area.

OCCUPATIONAL or VERTICAL MOBILITY – the movement of a factor of production from industry to industry, or within an industry.

Fixed and Variable Costs

S T U D Y P O I N T S

1 **FIXED COSTS** are costs which do not change however many miles a year Joyce travels. Fixed costs are the same whether she travels 1 mile or 30 000 miles a year. Which of the costs shown in the picture are fixed costs? (Assume that depreciation, servicing and repairs are a fixed cost.)

2 **VARIABLE COSTS** are costs which increase for every extra mile that Joyce travels. Which of the costs are variable costs?

Copy out the grid and record your answers to questions 3 to 9 in it.

Yearly mileage	Total fixed cost	Total variable cost	Total cost	Average cost
10 000				
20 000				
30 000				
40 000				

3 Calculate Joyce's total fixed costs at an annual mileage of 30 000 miles.

4 Calculate Joyce's total fixed costs if she travels (a) 10 000 miles, (b) 20 000 miles, (c) 40 000 miles a year.

5 What are Joyce's variable costs if she travels 30 000 miles?

6 Calculate Joyce's variable costs if she travels (a) 10 000 miles, (b) 20 000 miles and (c) 40 000 miles (assume that costs per mile remain constant).

7 Calculate Joyce's total costs (i.e. total fixed costs plus total variable costs) if she travels 30 000 miles per year.

8 Calculate Joyce's total cost if she travels (a) 10 000 miles, (b) 20 000 miles, (c) 40 000 miles.

9 How much on average did it cost Joyce per mile to run her taxi travelling 30 000 miles over the year? (This is known as the 'average cost'.)

10 How much per mile on average would it have cost Joyce if she had travelled (a) 10 000 miles, (b) 20 000 miles and (c) 40 000 miles over a year?

11 What would be the marginal cost for Joyce travelling an extra mile?

12 The *break even* point is where costs are just equal to the revenue that is earned. So, if Joyce's costs were £10 000 and she received £10 000 in fares, then that would be a break even point for her.
  If she carried 5000 passengers in a year, and travelled 30 000 miles, how much would she have to charge on average per passenger to break even?

13 If Joyce travels 20 000 miles a year, carrying 3000 passengers at an average fare of £3, is she going to make a profit or a loss?

14 Last year, Joyce travelled 30 000 miles and carried 4000 passengers at an average fare of £4. Is she making a profit or a loss? What should she do to improve the situation do you think?

Costs	£
Depreciation on taxi over one year	2300
Tax disc	200
Servicing and repairs	1500
Petrol	3000
Insurance	1000
Wages	12 000
Total costs	£20 000

Joyce Bigford is a taxi driver. She works 40 hours a week, 48 weeks a year irrespective of the number of passengers she carries. For this, she pays herself a wage of £12 000 a year. The costs shown above are based on costs over a year in which Joyce travelled 30 000 miles.

Fixed and Variable Costs

'Jaguar cars are planning to spend more than £1bn throughout the 1990s on product development. They want to bring out 3 new ranges of cars as well as a new engine. At the same time, they must cut the cost of producing a car if they are to be profitable.'

It costs money to make cars. Part of that cost is a **FIXED COST**. This is a cost that stays the same however many cars are produced. Examples of fixed costs include:

- the £1bn to be spent on product development – that cost will remain the same whether Jaguar sells 20 000 or 100 000 of the new model cars per year;

- interest payments on any loans that Jaguar has;

- advertising – again this does not change directly with output.

Fixed costs are often called **OVERHEAD COSTS**. They are the overheads of the business, money which has to paid out whatever the sales.

The rest of Jaguar's costs are VARIABLE COSTS. These costs vary directly with output. The more cars that are produced, the more steel is needed, the more car radios are fitted and the more electricity is used.

The TOTAL COST of production is equal to fixed costs plus variable costs.

Sometimes it is difficult to decide whether a cost is fixed or variable. Overtime by workers is a variable cost because when production is cut, so too is overtime. But what about the basic pay of workers? It is a fixed cost because basic pay has to be paid however much is produced. But workers will be made redundant if output falls far enough. Equally, a rise in output could mean more workers being taken on. So pay could be seen as a variable cost. It isn't always easy to classify costs into fixed and variable. For this reason, some costs are sometimes called semi-variable costs – neither fixed, nor variable but somewhere in between.

Total Average and Marginal Costs

TOTAL COST is the cost of producing all output over a period of time. For instance, Jaguar's total costs in a year might be £1000 million.

The AVERAGE COST is the cost per unit of production. So if Jaguar sells 40 000 cars per year when total costs are £1000 million, the average cost per car will be £25 000 (i.e. £1000 million ÷ 40 000). The formula used here is:

$$\text{Average cost} = \frac{\text{Total cost}}{\text{Quantity produced}}$$

The MARGINAL COST of production is the cost of producing an extra unit. For instance, if the total cost of producing 40 000 Jaguar cars were £1000 million, and the cost of 40 001 cars were £15 000 more than £1000 million, then Jaguar's marginal cost of production would be £15 000.

CHECKPOINTS

1 Explain the difference between fixed and variable costs.

2 Explain which of the following would be a fixed cost and which a variable cost for a car manufacturing firm over the period of one week: (a) a factory building; (b) steel rolls; (c) the basic pay of workers; (d) electricity; (e) car tyres; (f) overtime pay; (g) a robot.

3 What are the fixed costs and variable costs of running a college or school?

4 A firm pays £20 million to produce ten boats. It could have produced nine boats for £17 million. What is: (a) the total cost; (b) the average cost and (c) the marginal cost of producing ten boats?

Product development is a fixed cost

KEY TERMS

FIXED or OVERHEAD COSTS – the costs of production that do not vary with output.

VARIABLE COSTS – the costs of production that vary directly with output.

TOTAL COST – the cost of producing all output. It is equal to total fixed costs plus total variable costs.

AVERAGE COST – the cost per unit of output. It is equal to total cost divided by total output.

MARGINAL COST – the cost of producing an additional unit of output.

COURSEWORK SUGGESTION

Examine the costs of running a household. Obtain a breakdown of the approximate costs of running the household of which you are a member over a period of a year. Compare this with two other households of different sizes. (Size is defined as the number of people in the household and not the size of a house.) Data for this can either be obtained by a survey of two other households or by using figures from the *Family Expenditure* survey (published by HMSO). Which costs are fixed costs (i.e. do not vary according to the number of people living in the household)? Which are variable costs (i.e. costs which do vary with the number of people living there)? Over a period of a year calculate the average cost per person. Estimate the marginal cost by calculating how much it would cost if another person came to live in the household. Compare and contrast the different costs involved in running the three households. Which household has the lowest costs? Why is this so? Try to decide whether or not the household with the lowest costs is allocating its resources in the most efficient way.

Data Response Questions
Units 28–31 and Unit 76

Unit 28 Rent, Interest and Profit

Branson sells Virgin Music

Yesterday, Richard Branson sold Virgin Music for £510 million in cash. He had built the company up from scratch, starting over 20 years ago.

Much of the money will be ploughed into Virgin Airways, started in 1984. The airline company is greedy for cash. Richard Branson wants to run regular services to at least 12 major cities worldwide. To do

that, he needs more planes.

But he is taking an enormous risk. The airline business is extremely competitive. Moreover, Richard Branson is up against British Airways on most routes it wants to run. British Airways has proved to be one of the most successful international airlines over the past five years.

Source: Compiled from various newspaper reports 8 March 1992

1 What business did Richard Branson own according to the article? *(1 mark)*

2 (a) What factors of production would be used in these businesses?
  (b) What rewards would be given to those factors? *(9 marks)*

3 To what extent could Richard Branson be called an 'entrepreneur'? *(5 marks)*

Unit 29 Economic Rent, Costs and Profits

Average house prices in first quarter of 1992

Area	(£)
Greater London	85 290
East Anglia	58 460
North	52 050
Northern Ireland	37 350

Source: Halifax Building Society

1 Compare house prices in England. *(2 marks)*

2 Explain why house prices might vary between regions. *(4 marks)*

3 (a) What is 'economic rent'?
  (b) How and why does the economic rent on houses vary between regions? *(4 marks)*

Unit 30 Factor Mobility

EC unemployment rates

	Average unemployment rate per year %
Belgium	10.7
Denmark	7.6
West Germany	6.0
Greece	7.1
Eire	15.9
Spain	18.5
France	9.3
Italy	9.8
Luxembourg	2.5
Netherlands	10.2
Portugal	7.0
UK	9.7

Source: Commission of the European Communities, European Economy, *Annual Economic Report 1991–2*

1 Describe how unemployment rates vary across the European Community. *(2 marks)*

2 Economic theory suggests that workers will move to find work if they are unemployed. Explain why this might be true. *(5 marks)*

3 Explain four barriers to mobility which exist stopping this evening out of European unemployment between countries. *(8 marks)*

Unit 31 Fixed and Variable Costs

James Meade puts his shirt on mail order

WHEN 35 year-old James Meade left the Coldstream Guards, he decided he wanted to set up in business himself. A year at the London Business School convinced him that mail order was one business he could enter at low cost.

He saw a gap in the shirts market. Made-to-measure shirts start at £40 in the small number of up-market tailors' shops in London. Much of that represents the high cost of rent and rates in the most select areas of the Capital. He argued that they would not be able to cut prices to meet mail order competition from a supplier located in one of London's cheapest areas.

Meade's made-to-measure shirts start in price at £23.50, about half of which represents the cost of buying the shirt from the four shirt manufacturers he buys from. The other half pays for the rent and rates on his premises in Brixton, the advertising in the national press and up-market glossies like 'Harpers and Queen' and 'Country Life', interest on bank loans, postage and packing, V.A.T., wages and sundry expenses.

Source: Financial Times, 7 May 1985

1 Explain the nature of James Meade's business. *(2 marks)*

2 How was he able to attract customers to his business? *(2 marks)*

3 Which of his costs are fixed costs and which are variable costs over a time period of a month? *(4 marks)*

4 What would be the marginal cost to the company of selling an extra shirt? *(1 mark)*

5 If the average cost of selling a shirt is £30 and the company sells 15 000 shirts, what will be the total cost? *(1 mark)*

Essay Questions
Units 28–31

1 Wayne Headly is a 25-year old unemployed, unskilled, general labourer in the building trade who lives in a council house in Liverpool with his wife and two small children.
   (a) Give *four* reasons why he is likely to find it difficult to get a skilled bricklayer's job in London. *(8 marks)*
   (b) Suggest *two* ways in which the Government could help Wayne get this job in London. *(4 marks)*
   (c) Wayne is 'discovered' by a pop manager and starts to earn £200 000 from singing. Explain what is meant by 'economic rent' and illustrate how much economic rent Wayne is now earning. *(8 marks)*

2 Jenny Price runs a shoe repair shop in the centre of town.
   (a) What costs is she likely to face in running her business? *(8 marks)*
   (b) Explain the difference between fixed and variable costs. Which of Jenny's costs are fixed and which are variable? *(6 marks)*
   (c) Why is Jenny likely to be able to experience economies of scale? *(6 marks)*

Unit 76 The Balance of Payments

Japanese investment

The Japanese car company, Nissan, has announced that it is to invest another £200 million in its Primera-producing plant in Sunderland. An additional 600 jobs will be created directly and hundreds more in component companies and in the local community.

Nor is Nissan the only Japanese car company currently investing in Britain. Honda is expanding in Swindon and Toyota is building a factory in Derby.

Over the last 15 years, Japanese firms have ploughed over £16 billion into Britain and created over 30 000 jobs.

Britain, obviously, is a good place to make money.

Source: Daily Express, 20 January 1992

1 How much does Nissan plan to invest in its Sunderland plant according to the article? *(1 mark)*

2 Explain where this investment would be put on the balance of payments account. *(2 marks)*

3 Suggest what effect Japanese investment in Britain might have had on UK:
   (a) visible exports;
   (b) visible imports;
   (c) invisible imports. *(6 marks)*

4 What do you think are (a) the costs and (b) the benefits to the UK of Japanese inward investment in the car industry? *(6 marks)*

This data response question refers to **Unit 76** on *page 190.*

Economies of Scale

John works for a medium-sized chain of small hotels. He currently manages a hotel in Yorkshire, but he wants to leave and set up his own business. To start off, he is thinking of buying a single hotel and then building upon its success to finance future acquisitions.

He has drawn up an outline business plan. In it he compares the likely annual costs of running a single hotel with the costs of the chain of 20 hotels that he works for now. He has assumed that the number of customers using his proposed hotel will be the same as the number currently using each hotel in the chain.

Costs of running the business, £ per year

	John's hotel	Chain of 20 hotels
Food and drink	60 000	900 000
Other consumables (e.g. soap)	2000	30 000
Wages	25 000	660 000
Maintenance	3000	60 000
Heating, lighting, etc.	10 000	200 000
Interest on overdraft	3000	50 000
Laundry	4000	70 000
Advertising and promotion	3000	30 000
Total	**110 000**	**2 000 000**

He estimates that his hotel will cost £400 000, the same price that his chain of hotels would have to pay for an extra hotel.

S T U D Y P O I N T S

1 (a) How much does it cost per year to run (i) the hotel John intends to buy and (ii) the average hotel in the chain of hotels?
   (b) Which is the cheaper to run?

2 Look at the separate costs of running the hotel.
   (a) Which costs are (i) cheaper and (ii) more expensive per hotel for John's proposed hotel compared to the hotel chain?
   (b) For each different type of cost, think of one reason why it might be cheaper to run a single hotel or a hotel in a chain of hotels (e.g. a chain of hotels might get a bigger discount from suppliers on an order for soap because they order larger quantities).

3 Do you think that John will be able to compete with other hotels given the above figures? What strategies does John need to pursue to survive in his new business venture?

Long Run Average Cost

If you bought one car battery, you might pay £40 for it. If a car-maker bought 1 million batteries a year, it would expect to pay a much cheaper price. This is because buying in bulk should be considerably cheaper than buying one at a time. Bulk buying is just one reason why bigger firms can often have lower average costs than small firms.

INTERNAL ECONOMIES OF SCALE occur when long run average costs fall as the size of a firm and its output increase, INTERNAL DISECONOMIES OF SCALE occur when average costs rise when a firm gets bigger and produces more.

Internal Economies of Scale

Consider the figures in Figure 32.1. Note that costs are expressed here not in pounds, but in an index. (Index numbers were explained in Unit 5.)

Figure 33.1

Annual production of diesel engines	Index of costs
1 000	120
5 000	100
50 000	80
100 000	70
200 000	65

Source: G. Rhys, Heavy commercial vehicles: a decade of change. National Westminster Bank Quarterly Review (August 1984)

The figures show that it costs nearly twice as much per diesel engine if only 1000 engines are produced a year than if 200 000 are produced a year. There are a number of reasons for this:

- *Technical economies* arise because greater production allows the use of more efficient methods of production or more efficient machines. In the case of diesel engines, a firm producing 200 000 engines a year will be able to make far more use of the division of labour and buy more specialised machines than a firm that only makes 1000 engines a year.

- *Marketing economies* arise because a large manufacturer can buy in bulk and can therefore get lower prices than the small manufacturer. The cost of selling is also lower, because advertising costs can be spread over a larger number of units sold and specialist salesmen can be employed.

- *Financial economies* arise because a small firm making engines is likely to have to pay higher interest rates on loans. The small firm is also likely to find it more difficult to raise money through selling new shares than a larger diesel engine firm would.

- *Administrative or managerial economies* arise because a large manufacturer can employ specialist staff to manage and supervise production, thus cutting managerial costs per unit. Specialist administrative equipment, like computers, can also be used profitably in large firms.

- *Risk-bearing economies* arise when a large firm sells in more markets and has a wider product range than a smaller company. A larger diesel engine manufacturer may sell in several countries rather than just one and may sell a much wider range of engines than a small manufacturer. This helps spread risks so that if one market does badly (e.g. small diesel engines in the UK), the company has other markets to sell into.

Internal diseconomies of scale arise mainly through problems of management. As a firm grows, management finds it more difficult to organise production efficiently. It is much easier to lose control of costs in a large organisation than in a small organisation. Relations with workers, too, can be worse because there may be little contact between management and workers.

External Economies of Scale

EXTERNAL ECONOMIES arise from the size of the industry rather than the firm. As the industry grows in size and there are more firms in the industry, firms in the industry enjoy lower costs for several reasons.

- Labour costs may be reduced. Firms will be able to draw on a pool of skilled labour, trained by firms and government, thus reducing their own training and living costs.

- The necessary infrastructure is more likely to be present. Roads, gas supplies, etc. are more likely to be laid on, if the industry is large rather than small. This helps reduce costs for individual firms.

- Suppliers for the industry will emerge – specialist firms that make or service machinery, or supply components. Because they specialise, these firms are able to produce goods and services far more cheaply than if the main company attempted to produce them on its own.

K E Y T E R M S

INTERNAL ECONOMIES OF SCALE – reductions in long-run average costs as the scale of production and output of the firm increase.

INTERNAL DISECONOMIES OF SCALE – increases in long-run average costs as the scale of production and output of the firm increase.

EXTERNAL ECONOMIES – falls in long-run average costs for a firm when the industry in which the firm operates in grows in size.

Profits and Revenue

The Peninsular and Oriental Steam Navigation Company (P&O plc)
Group Profit and Loss Account for the year ended 31st December

	1990 £m	1991 £m
Turnover	5036.4	4897.2
Less net operating charges and exceptional items	4770.6	4656.0
Profit before taxation	265.8	241.2
Less tax on profit	73.2	58.7
Less dividends paid to shareholders, minority interest, extraordinary items and employee profit share	37.8	43.9
Retained profit for year	35.4	14.8

Source: P&O, Report and Accounts 1991

'Thorn EMI, the UK music and rentals group, is quitting electrical retailing, which has lost the company about £50m over the past three years. Its chain of about 450 Rumbelows shops, which has not made a profit over the past 6 years, will be converted to rental outlets for consumer electrical goods.'
(*Source: Financial Times*, 1 February 1992)

PROFIT is the difference between **TOTAL REVENUE** and total costs. Thorn EMI had lost £50 million operating its Rumbelow chain of shops between 1989 and 1992. So its profit was negative. The money received by Rumbelows from the sale of electrical equipment such as televisions and hi-fi equipment was less than the money it paid out to buy stock, pay staff, rent shops, etc.

The Importance of Profits

The profit that a company makes is used in three ways.

- Part is kept by the company and used for investment. The company may buy new machinery or re-equip a building. If profits are low, a company may well decide to cut back on investment plans.

- Part is paid to the government in taxes.

- Part is paid out as dividends to the shareholders of the company. The *dividend* is the reward to the owners for having allowed the company to use their money or assets and for the risk which that involves.

Profits act as an indicator. If profits in an industry are too low or even negative, then firms will leave the industry. Thorn EMI decided to pull out of selling electrical goods because they couldn't make a profit.

If, on the other hand, profits are high, then firms will enter the industry. Thorn EMI also owned three chains of rental outlets – Radio Rentals, Multibroadcast and DER. It intended to

STUDY POINTS

1 What was the value of total revenue (i.e. total receipts from sales of tickets, etc.) in 1991 for P&O?

2 What were the total costs of providing services to the public in 1990?

3 Profit is the difference between total revenue and total costs. Explain why profit before tax fell in 1991 compared to 1990.

4 What does P&O do with the profits it makes each year?

5 Suggest why the amount paid in tax by P&O declined between 1990 and 1991.

6 Why did the company pay money to its shareholders in 1990 and 1991?

7 For what do you think the company might use the profit it doesn't pay out to shareholders? (This is its 'retained profit'.)

8 If P&O started to make losses, explain:
(a) why the company would find it difficult to make as large investments as before;
(b) why the company would find it difficult to persuade shareholders to buy new shares in the company.

9 How can profits and losses alter the allocation of resources in the economy over a period of time?

convert some of the Rumbelow shops into these higher profit rental outlets. Even so, profits were not particularly high in TV rentals. Profits were only at 'normal' levels. So Thorn EMI intended only to convert about 200 Rumbelow shops. The other 250 would be sold off.

Profits can also act as an indicator of consumer exploitation. If existing firms can prevent new firms from investing in their industry, they may well be able to keep prices artificially high. Higher prices mean that the company makes bigger profits. Consumers are therefore being *exploited* – being forced to pay more than they might. This will be further discussed in Unit 36.

Revenue

Just as there are different types of costs, so there are different revenues.

- **TOTAL REVENUE** is total receipts from the sale of all products.
- **AVERAGE REVENUE** is the revenue received per unit sold. It is the average price received for the product. It can be calculated by dividing total revenue by quantity sold. If Rumbelows sold 5000 televisions and received £1 million, then total revenue would be £1 million and average revenue, or average price per television would be £200 (£1 million ÷ 5000).
- **MARGINAL REVENUE** is the revenue gained by selling an extra unit of production. If Rumbelows could sell 5000 televisions for £1 million but 6000 televisions for £1.1 million, then the marginal revenue from the sale of the extra 1000 televisions would be £0.1 million.

As sales increase, total revenue should obviously increase too: the more that is sold, the more revenue

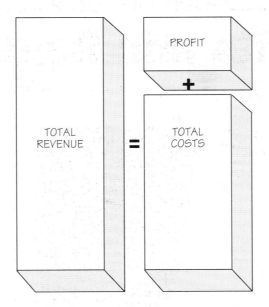

that is gained. But it may well be the case that average revenue would decline as sales increase. This is because a manufacturer may have to give bigger discounts or drop prices to sell more of a product.

CHECKPOINTS

1 Define 'profit'.
2 Calculate the profit earned by a company:
   (a) if revenue were £10 000 and costs were £8000;
   (b) if costs were £2 million and revenue were £2.5 million;
   (c) if revenue were £40 million and costs were £38 000;
   (d) if revenue were £800 million and costs were £900 million.
3 Why would rising costs and falling prices squeeze profits for a company?
4 What would a manufacturing company do with its profits?

5 If profits in the gas supply industry are high in comparison with other industries, what might this indicate?
6 Complete Figure 33.1 and then plot total, average and marginal revenue curves on the graph.

Note: Plot the marginal revenue figures half way between the sales figures. For instance, marginal revenue of £12 should be plotted at ½ on the sales axis, £10 at 1½ and so on.

Figure 33.1

Quantity sold	Total revenue (£ m)	Average revenue (£ m)	Marginal revenue (£ m)
0	0	0	—
			12
1	12		
			10
2		11	
			8
3		10	
			6
4			
			4
5			
			2
6	42		

COURSEWORK SUGGESTION

Find out figures for the relative profitability of different sectors of British industry over a period of time. Examine how the output of these industries has changed over the same period (using data, say from the *Annual Abstract of Statistics* published by HMSO). Analyse the extent to which profitability is linked to changes in output. Try to explain why profits might act as an indicator of how resources should be allocated in the economy. Decide which industries are the growth industries of the future.

KEY TERMS

PROFITS – total revenue minus total costs.

TOTAL REVENUE – total receipts of a company from the sale of production.

AVERAGE REVENUE – average price received per item sold, i.e. the average price received per sale.

MARGINAL REVENUE – the revenue gained from the sale of an extra unit of output.

The Aims of Firms

CRISTARSIN

This drug should provide a complete cure for 'Hymertarsinonosis', the eye disease which afflicts an estimated 20 million people in the developing world and, if left untreated, usually blinds the sufferer within five years of contracting the disease. Preliminary tests strongly indicate that the drug will be marketable.

Key financial statistics are:

Development costs so far	£25 million
Estimated remaining development costs	£10 million
Estimated sales	£53 million per annum for 15 years
Estimated cost of manufacture and marketing	£50 million per annum
Employment – 100 jobs at our Calcutta plant in India	

MOSTARNOL

This drug has been developed to treat a certain type of cancer. An estimated 100 000 people in industrial countries suffer from this disease which causes pain and in severe cases leads to loss of mobility. Preliminary tests indicate that the drug has a 50–70% chance of reaching the stage where it can be put on general sale. Key financial statistics are:

Development costs so far	£35 million
Estimated remaining development costs	£20 million
Estimated sales	£30 million per annum for 15 years
Estimated cost of manufacture and marketing	£20 million per annum
Employment – 30 jobs at our Dundee plant in Scotland	

SOLITOR

This drug should provide a cure for 'Tomirotosis', a disease which attacks the bone structure and in severe cases leads to death. An estimated 20 000 people suffer from the disease in our first world markets. Preliminary tests indicate that there is an 80–90% chance that the drug will reach the final marketing stage. Key financial statistics are:

Development costs so far	£15 million
Estimated remaining development costs	£15 million
Estimated sales	£20 million per annum for 15 years
Estimated cost of manufacture and marketing	£10 million per annum
Employment – 20 jobs at our London plant	

STUDY POINTS

This can either be done on your own in written form or with a small group as a discussion exercise. The company will only develop one of these three products. Your task is to decide which it should be.

1 What are the costs and benefits of each drug (a) to the company and (b) to society?

2 How much profit will each drug yield (a) to the company and (b) to society?

3 What should be the commercial aims of a company manufacturing drugs?

4 Which one of these drugs would you develop and why?

Profit Maximisation

When a household spends money, it aims to get best value for money. That means that it attempts to maximise the *'utility'* or satisfaction from consuming the goods and services purchased. What, then, does a firm aim to do? What are its aims?

To answer this question, we need to know who controls firms and what motivates these decision-makers. The traditional answer is that:

- firms are controlled by their owners, the **SHAREHOLDERS** of the company;

- the shareholders are only interested in making the most money out of the firm. They make money either by receiving a share of the profits – the *dividend* – or by seeing the firm grow in value and therefore seeing the value of their shareholding grow. Growth in size normally means extra investment, much of which will be paid for out of profits made by the company;

- therefore the company, controlled by the shareholders, will attempt to **MAXIMISE PROFITS**.

To see what this might mean in practice, consider a firm that produces highly toxic (i.e. dangerous and poisonous) chemicals as a result of its main manufacturing operations. It has to dispose of the chemicals and can do that in two ways. It can either build a recycling plant, which will make the chemicals safe. Or it can buy a ship and dump the chemicals into the sea. The profit-maximising firms will choose the least costly of these options – where the cost is the **COST TO THE FIRM**. By minimising its costs of disposal, the firm will make the most profit. Therefore if the cost of recycling were £20 million a year, whereas the cost of dumping at sea were £1 million, then the company would choose to dump the chemicals at sea. Note that this might not be the most cost-effective way of disposing of the chemicals from society's point of view. It might be extremely dangerous from an environmental viewpoint to dump highly toxic chemicals at sea. If, as a result of the dumping, £40 million worth of damage is done to the environment, then what was most profitable from the company's viewpoint is highly costly from the viewpoint of society and should be stopped.

Other Aims

Profit maximisation may not, however, be the aim of all firms. For instance, in larger firms, the shareholders are different from the managers and directors of the firm. The managers and directors (i.e. the workers who run the firm) may be far more interested in their own rewards than in the rewards of the shareholders. Directors and managers may be far more interested in receiving big salaries, large company cars and spending time eating expense-paid lunches, than in earning maximum profits for the shareholders. Of course they have to make some profit, otherwise they might lose their jobs. But making enough profit to keep shareholders happy, **PROFIT SATISFICING**, can be very different from making maximum profits, **PROFIT MAXIMISING**.

In other companies, those companies owned by the government, there may be other aims. The government may want its firms to make profits, but it may also want them to keep prices down to help keep down inflation. Or it may want to keep unprofitable factories or works open so that workers do not lose their jobs. Keeping prices down, or unprofitable works open, means less profits over all.

1 What is meant by 'profit maximisation'? Why might a firm aim to maximise profits?

2 A firm could invest in one of the projects in Figure 34.1, all of which involve the same initial investment of £1 million. Which of these should the firm undertake and why?

Figure 34.1

Project	Estimated profit per year (£)	Estimated number of jobs created (+) or lost (−)	Estimated value of exports (£)
A	150 000	+ 600	1 000 000
B	120 000	+ 500	1 200 000
C	160 000	− 100	800 000

3 A firm increases its profits from £30 million to £60 million within a year. Which of the following do you think will benefit and why:
(a) shareholders;
(b) workers;
(c) consumers;
(d) taxpayers?

4 Explain why the fact that the owners of large companies rarely manage them might lead to profit satisficing rather than profit maximising.

5 Why might firms owned by the government not be profit maximisers?

COURSEWORK SUGGESTION

Arrange to visit three companies, preferably of different sizes. You will need to interview a manager who is well acquainted with the overall policy of the company and its finances. Prepare a questionnaire beforehand that asks questions relating to the goals of the firm and the extent to which the company fulfils these goals. After the interviews, prepare a report on your findings. (This should include a copy of the questionnaire, a description of the responses, an analysis of what the questionnaire revealed about the goals of the three firms, and an evaluation of company performance based upon those goals.)

KEY TERMS

PROFIT MAXIMISATION – making the largest profit possible over a period of time.

SHAREHOLDERS – the owners of a company, of whom each owns a part or share of that company.

PROFIT SATISFICING – making enough profit to satisfy the owners of a company.

Competition

QUALITY PLUS

Installation by Specialist Fitters
Guaranteed Prices
Guaranteed Quality
First-class customer and after sales service

For replacement Windows (Hardwood, uPVC and Aluminium) or Double Glazing, you can be sure of Competitive Prices and Standards of Quality & Workmanship often lacking in today's world.

Williams Glazing Ltd
Brodingham, Trest
Tel 46841

THE MARKET

Brodingham is a large town in the South of England. There are three local firms which compete in the window replacement business, Williams Glazing Limited, Harris Double Glazing Company and Dyer's Glazing. Competition comes also from large national firms such as Everest. Williams Glazing averages 120 window/door replacements out of approximately 1000 contracts carried out each year in the town. Competition is fierce.

WILLIAMS GLAZING

COSTS

	£
4 workers	64 000
Rent, rates, etc.	14 000
Advertising and promotion	10 000
Other overheads	6 000
Interest on overdraft	20 000
Materials	248 000

REVENUE

	£
120 jobs at an average of £3000 per job	360 000

S T U D Y P O I N T S

For each of the following situations, prepare a short report explaining how and why Williams ought to react.

1 Dyer's Glazing, the smallest of the firms in the area, cut its prices by approximately 10% three months ago. There is no sign that it is going to raise prices again in the immediate future. Orders at Williams have fallen from about 10 a month to about 8 a month.

2 Harris Double Glazing Company has embarked on a large advertising campaign in the local press, on local radio and through the distribution of leaflets. Estimated cost of the campaign to date is £18 000, about £8000 more than Williams annually spends. Orders at Williams have fallen from about 10 a month to 9 a month since the campaign started.

3 Everest, the national firm of glaziers, has just introduced a new 'wonder window' which, it is claimed, is 20% more effective at retaining heat than existing windows.

4 Harris Double Glazing Company buys Dyer's Glazing.

The Meaning of Competition

'Competition' and 'competitiveness' are words that are frequently heard on the lips of politicians today. **COMPETITION** is felt by many to lead to greater efficiency. Therefore, the more competition there is the better. But what does competition mean? Is it really true that greater competition leads to greater efficiency?

Competition is not something that has a precise meaning, because there are degrees of competition. At one extreme, there is **PERFECT COMPETITION**. In a perfectly competitive industry:

- there are a large number of small producers;

- all these firms produce an identical or **HOMOGENEOUS** product;

- new firms can set up in the industry and existing firms can sell up and leave the industry if they wish – there are no *barriers to entry* or *exit*;

- all firms are able to have access to the same information about techniques of production, likely developments in the industry, etc.

Very few industries are perfectly competitive. Probably the best example of such an industry is farming.

At the other extreme is *monopoly* – a market situation where just one firm produces all the output in the industry. Again, like perfect competition, there are very few examples of monopolies in the real world. In between are various types of **IMPERFECT COMPETITION**. Most industries fall into this category.

The Competitive Process

In a competitive industry, a firm is constantly fighting for its survival, which means successfully selling its products to consumers. The consumer buys those products that give best value for money – value for money means keenest prices, highest quality, latest technology, reliability, etc. If a firm produces goods that are more expensive or lower quality than its competitors, sales decline. Profits will go down too and the company could soon be making a loss. At this point, it will either have to make itself competitive or 'leave the industry' (i.e. stop producing). The successful firm will see its sales and profits climb. This will encourage it to invest, making it even more competitive. It will encourage other firms in the industry to improve their competitiveness to get their share of sales and profits. It will also attract new firms into the industry. This competition serves to keep prices and profits down to a level just high enough to prevent firms from switching their investment into more profitable industries. This level of profits is called NORMAL PROFITS.

Competition can take various forms. In a perfectly competitive industry, firms compete mainly on price. The firm with the lowest price gets the sales. In imperfect competition, since firms sell branded goods, they compete not only on price, but also by advertising and promoting their product and by trying to produce better products than their rivals.

Competition and Efficiency

Consider this extract:

'A holiday price war was launched last night as Britain's biggest travel company Thomson slashed £15 million off the cost of 300 000 summer breaks.' (*Source: Daily Express*, 8 January 1992)

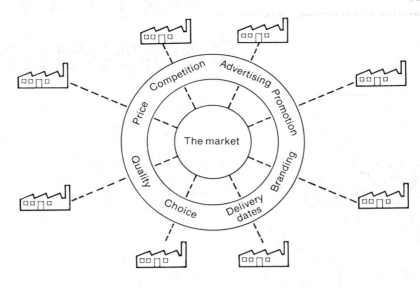

In a competitive market firms compete on price, quality of goods etc. for a share of the market.

Economists would argue that competition in the holiday industry has led to efficiency because:

- prices to consumers are as low as possible (shown by the price war);
- the consumer has a wide range of choice of holidays from different travel agents;
- only those firms offering the best value for money will survive.

However, as we shall see in the next unit, competition does not necessarily lead to the highest level of effciency.

K E Y T E R M S

COMPETITION – a process in which firms or the owners of factors of production offer products for sale in the same market to the same customers.

PERFECT COMPETITION – a situation where there is a large number of buyers and sellers in the market, the sellers offering identical products, and where there are no barriers to entry to or exit from the industry.

HOMOGENEOUS PRODUCT – a product where there are no brands and no differences between individual goods.

IMPERFECT COMPETITION – a situation where a few or a large number of sellers offer branded goods for sale, and where barriers to entry to the market may or may not exist.

NORMAL PROFIT – the level of profit needed to keep a firm from switching its resources into the production of other goods and services.

Monopoly

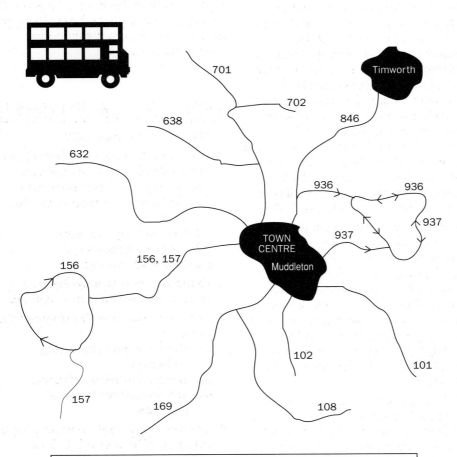

Average bus fare (£)	0.4	0.5	0.6	0.7	0.8	0.9	1.00
Number of passenger journeys (millions)	1.6	1.3	1.1	1.0	0.9	0.7	0.5
Total costs (£ millions)	1.3	1.15	1.0	0.9	0.7	0.5	0.4

S T U D Y P O I N T S

You are the owner and manager of the bus company in Muddleton. You have a monopoly on all your routes shown on the map.

1 You estimate that the number of passengers using your buses will vary according to the figures in the table above. You have also made cost estimates based on the number of passengers carried. What price will you set for your average ticket?

2 The local environmental group says that there are too many people using cars in the town. It would be far better if public transport could carry more people. They lobby you to reduce your fares. Should you reduce them?

3 One of your bus drivers decides to set up in competition with you. He buys a second-hand bus and starts to operate a service on one of your busiest and most profitable routes. What are you going to do about it?

4 You are receiving an average of 40 letters a week complaining about (a) buses being late, (b) buses being too old and uncomfortable and (c) staff being rude to passengers. Explain what you are going to do about each of these complaints.

'Ford's refusal to grant other companies licences to manufacture or sell replacement car body panels is anti-competitive and "clearly adverse to the public interest", the Monopolies and Mergers Commission declared yesterday.' (*Source: Financial Times*, 1 March 1985)

Ford, the motor car company, had refused to allow other companies to manufacture replacement panels for Ford cars. According to the Monopolies and Mergers Commission (the government watchdog which investigates monopolies), this led to:

- higher prices for consumers;
- less INNOVATION (other companies had started the manufacture of part panels to keep down the costs to motorists);
- higher profits for Ford.

Ford, here, was being accused of acting as a MONOPOLIST. A monopolist is a firm that is the only supplier of a product in the market. Ford, by refusing a licence to other manufacturers, was making sure that the only body panels that would fit Ford cars would be made by Ford itself.

Sources of Monopoly Power

A monopolist can prevent competition in the market by preventing new firms from entering the market. Economists say that a monopolist can put up BARRIERS TO ENTRY. A variety of barriers exist:

- *Legal barriers.* This was the source of Ford's monopoly. It had copyright for 15 years over the design of the panels and could legally stop other manufacturers from copying its body panels.
- *Cost barriers.* It may be far too expensive for another firm to set up in the industry. In the car industry, for instance, when it costs £500 million to develop just one car, it is difficult to see a new

mass-production car producer suddenly entering the market.

- *Economies of scale.* These may also be a barrier. Given that the larger the firm, the lower the costs of production are likely to be, then it is possible that just one firm may come to dominate the market. That one firm would be the *natural monopolist*, a term discussed in Unit 43. New entrants would not be able to compete on cost grounds with the natural monopolist.

- *Marketing barriers.* These are barriers such as advertising. A monopolist may develop a very strong brand image for its product so that consumers continue to buy the product, even though better products may appear on the market. (A brand is the name of a company's product, such as 'Persil', 'Mars Bar', or 'Montego'.) Or, a monopolist may make it prohibitively expensive, in terms of advertising costs, for a new firm to launch its product.

Monopoly and Efficiency

As we saw above, Ford was accused, as a monopolist, of pushing up prices, earning excess or ABNORMAL PROFIT, and restricting innovation. Consumers were denied a choice of whom to buy from. The Monopolies and Mergers Commission also accepted evidence that higher prices meant that some car owners preferred not to buy the body panels, but to scrap their cars instead. So higher prices led to lower output of replacement panels. All of these are standard criticisms of monopolies. They all add up to lower efficiency in the economy.

But there is some evidence that a lack of competition can lead to greater

efficiency. This would be the case:

- if economies of scale were very large. Economies of scale mean that as more is produced, so the average cost of producing each item goes down. So long as the saving in production costs is greater than the extra or abnormal profit the monopolist might charge, then monopoly will lead to lower prices for customers. For example, if a monopolist could produce an item at £10 less per item than if several firms were producing smaller quantities, but it charged an extra £6 profit per item, then the consumer would still be £4 better off with monopoly production than if there were competition in the industry.

- if being a monopolist encouraged the company to risk its money in research, investment and new products, in the knowledge that it could sell what it produced at a profit. Ford, for instance, argued that if it did not keep its monopoly on body panels, there would not be enough profit coming in to finance research and development on new products.

- if the high profits earned by a monopolist encouraged other firms to develop totally new products to break the monopoly. On a very small scale, the decision by independent manufacturers to offer part panels, instead of the whole panels initially available from Ford, was an example of innovation in the face of a monopolist.

Overall, it is unclear that competition does lead to greater efficiency than monopoly. It is true that consumers may end up with lower

prices and more choice in the short run. If monopoly encourages research, development, investment and innovation, however, then those short-term gains may be far less important than the long-term gains of higher economic growth resulting from an economy dominated by large monopoly firms.

CHECKPOINTS

1 What is a 'monopolist'?

2 Which of the following industries are controlled by monopolists:
   (a) the rail transport industry;
   (b) the motor car manufacturing industry;
   (c) the banking industry;
   (d) the postal industry?
   Explain your answer.

3 Explain how a monopolist can restrict competition in a market.

4 What barriers to entry do you think exist in:
   (a) the drug manufacturing industry;
   (b) the coal mining industry;
   (c) the market for hospital services?

5 In what ways could a monopoly be: (a) more efficient and (b) less efficient than several firms competing with each other?

COURSEWORK SUGGESTION

Obtain the latest copy of the *Report and Accounts* of British Rail. If possible, also consult past *Report and Accounts* and any other material, such as books or newspaper articles, that refers to the performance of British Rail. Describe the activities of British Rail. Explain in what sense British Rail is a monopolist. Analyse the sources of British Rail's monopoly power. Try to assess whether the privatisation and the split-up of British Rail into several competing firms would lead to an increase in efficiency or not. (This study could be done with any state-sector monopoly.)

KEY TERMS

MONOPOLY – a situation where there is only one seller of goods and services in a market.

BARRIERS TO ENTRY – factors that prevent firms entering a market to compete with existing firms.

ABNORMAL PROFIT – profit earned that is greater than the profit needed to keep a firm producing in a market.

INNOVATION – the development of new products or new techniques of making products.

Data Response Questions
Units 32–36

Unit 32 Economies of Scale

Lloyds bid for Midland Bank

If Lloyds Bank takes over the Midland Bank, will this lead to a reduction in competition and a poorer deal for the consumer?

Lloyds argues that cost cutting will lead to a saving of £700 million over four years. Over 1000 branches out of today's 3745 Lloyds and Midland branches would close. 20 000 staff would have to go.

But, Lloyds argues, service will be better after the merger. Customers wouldn't lose out from the 1000 branch closures because they would be where Lloyds and Midland had branches in the same high street. But in many places, there is only either a Lloyds Bank or a Midland Bank branch. Here, customers would gain.

They would also gain from being offered the best products and services from the ranges currently being offered separately. However, this too would give economies of scale because the new combined bank would offer fewer services than the two banks had offered separately.

Finally, Lloyds claims that the new bank would be better placed to take advantage in information technology. With more customers, it would be possible to use technology developments which would have been too costly for each of the banks on their own.

Source: Adapted from the *Financial Times*, 2 May 1992

1 What is meant by a 'takeover'? *(1 mark)*

2 (a) Explain what is meant by 'economies of scale' and list four different types of economy of scale.
  (b) Explain what economies of scale might result from a Lloyds bank takeover of the Midland. *(10 marks)*

3 Would customers of Lloyds and Midland be better off or worse off as a result of the merger do you think? *(4 marks)*

Essay Questions
Units 32–36

1 (a) What is meant by 'profit'? *(6 marks)*
  (b) What does a firm do with its profits? *(8 marks)*
  (c) How can profits allocate resources in an economy? *(6 marks)*

Unit 33 Profits and Revenue

Vauxhall clocks up £132m in profits

Vauxhall today left its UK car rivals for dead as it unveiled 1991 profits of just over £132 million. Exports more than trebled – mainly to the former East Germany – helping offset the UK sales slump. Even so, the profit was down 45 per cent on the previous year's £239 million.

Compared to its major rivals, the Vauxhall performance was remarkable in a year when new car sales fell by a fifth.

Market leader Ford suffered a record £470 million loss, while even reborn Rover tumbled more than £80 million into the red.

Luton-based Vauxhall, whose best-sellers include the Astra and Cavalier ranges, modestly described the result as "very satisfactory".

Chairman William Ebbert admitted that price-cutting to tempt buyers was a prime factor in the lower profits.

However, he also revealed that last year's turnover of £2.57 billion was the second-highest in the company's history.

Vauxhall's UK sales were down 23 per cent to 248,700, trimming its share of the market a fraction to just under 16 per cent.

The Luton plant achieved a record output though, building 165,000 Cavaliers and Opel Vectras. Overseas sales rocketed from 29,500 to 104,000.

"Without the export boost, our plants would have been on a three-day week," Mr Ebbert said.

Source: Express and Star, 30 April 1992

1 Compare the 1991 profit made at Vauxhall with Ford and Rover profits. *(2 marks)*

2 How was it that Vauxhall's turnover was the 'second highest in the company's history' when it was forced to cut its UK prices in 1991? *(5 marks)*

3 Explain why profits in 1991 fell despite a high turnover. *(5 marks)*

4 Why were overseas markets particularly important to Vauxhall UK in 1991? *(3 marks)*

2 One supermarket chain opens a new branch in a shopping centre where another supermarket chain already has a store.
  (a) Suggest *five* ways in which these two shops might compete for custom. *(10 marks)*
  (b) The two supermarket chains merge to form the largest supermarket chain in Britain. As a result, one of the two stores in the shopping centre is closed. What might be (i) the benefits and (ii) the costs to the consumer of this happening? *(10 marks)*

Unit 34 The Aims of Firms

The choice we must be given

When a state industry is privatised, the customer has the right to expect one of two things to happen: either that industry is exposed to competition, or else the Government controls its profits in such a way as to ensure that the consumers are not ripped off.

In the case of the electricity companies, neither of these two things has happened, with the result that massive profits are being made at the customers' expense.

Yesterday, East Midlands Electricity announced profits of £150 million for last year – a rise of 41 per cent. Though other boards have perhaps not notched up such a large percentage increase, the trend is very much along that same line.

Though the usual story is

trotted out to justify such profits – greater efficiency, and more being ploughed back into the business – the fact remains that such profits are achieved by the simple expedient of charging customers too much. Yet when these boards – together with gas and water – were privatised, the two things that the Government specifically promised were that there would be competition, and that the customer would get a better deal as a result of it.

Neither of these things can be achieved until the customers can choose from which electricity board they buy their power. Only then will the boards be compelled to make their prices competitive, and thus give the customer the better deal the Government promised.

Source: Express and Star, 16 June 1992

1 What has happened to the profits made by electricity companies according to the article? (*2 marks*)

2 Explain why the goal or aim of a privatised electricity company is to maximise profit. (*4 marks*)

3 Discuss whether you think the aim of an electricity, gas, or water company should be to make the most profit for shareholders. To answer this, you must think about what other aims it should possibly have. (*5 marks*)

4 How would competition in the electricity industry help consumers? (*4 marks*)

1 What was meant when one company accused the other of 'trying to monopolise trade'? (*5 marks*)

2 How, according to Metrowest, was West Midlands Travel trying to impose a monopoly on bus travel in the area? (*5 marks*)

3 Why would a bus company want to establish a monopoly on a particular bus route? (*5 marks*)

Unit 35 Competition

Dewhurst butchers rationalises shops

Dewhurst, the biggest UK chain of butchers, is expected to announce today that up to 600 of its 1006 shops will be closed with the loss of 1000 jobs.

The company has been squeezed from two directions. On the one hand, the big grocery chains now account for more than half of all carcase meat sold in the UK, and about 92 per cent of bacon, ham, poultry and other meat products. Shoppers often prefer to buy meat in a supermarket because they don't really know much about what they are buying. But in a butcher's shop,

they have to know exactly what cut of meat they want.

On the other hand, small independent butchers have a competitive edge because they can respond more quickly than larger managed groups to changes in demand. 'Elements like the weather do have an impact on whether people buy stewing steak or barbecue meats,' said Mr John Fuller of the National Federation of Meat Traders. But even small independent butchers are having a hard time. Latest figures showed that the number of registered butchers firms fell by 540 to 13 641 last year.

Source: Adapted from the Financial Times, 8 May 1992

1 How many shops may be closed by Dewhurst, according to the article? (*1 mark*)

2 (a) Explain how competition has forced Dewhurst to close some of its shops.

(b) What part will profit have played in Dewhurst's decision? (*8 marks*)

3 Are consumers likely to be better or worse off as a result of competition in the meat industry? (*6 marks*)

Unit 36 Monopoly

'Bus war' claim as two firms contest routes

A bus war has broken out on Dudley to Wolverhampton and Stourbridge routes, between Cosely-based Metrowest Omnibus Company and West Midlands Travel, it was claimed today. It means two different companies will be running buses along the same route at the same times from Monday 16 February, said a transport boss. Metrowest bosses have accused West Midlands Travel of trying to 'monopolise' trade by forcing smaller companies out of busi-

ness. They claim rival buses have been ignoring timetables in the rush to poach passengers. Mr David Gaymer, a partner in Metrowest, today said: 'We're not worried about the competition because we are confident we give a good service, but we think the public should know what's going on. West Midlands Travel have dropped their fares on the 257 route to compete with our prices. But if they can drop fares on one route they should drop them all.'

Source: Express and Star, 8 February 1992

The Size of Firms

Figure 37.1 Businesses (enterprises) by size of employment, UK manufacturing 1989

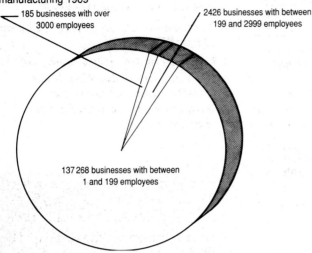

- 185 businesses with over 3000 employees
- 2426 businesses with between 199 and 2999 employees
- 137 268 businesses with between 1 and 199 employees

Figure 37.2 Business (enterprise) size and total employment, UK manufacturing 1989

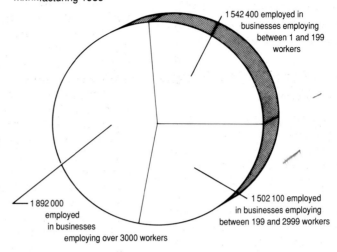

- 1 542 400 employed in businesses employing between 1 and 199 workers
- 1 892 000 employed in businesses employing over 3000 workers
- 1 502 100 employed in businesses employing between 199 and 2999 workers

Figure 37.3 Business (enterprise) size and total output (gross value added at factor cost), UK manufacturing 1989

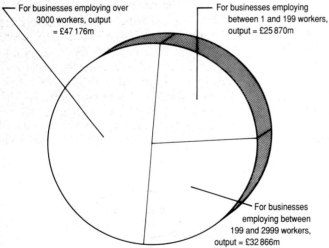

- For businesses employing over 3000 workers, output = £47 176m
- For businesses employing between 1 and 199 workers, output = £25 870m
- For businesses employing between 199 and 2999 workers, output = £32 866m

Source: Figs 38.1–38.3: *Report on the Census of Production*, summary tables; *Business Monitor* PA 1002, 1991

Figure 37.4 Share of the largest 100 businesses (enterprises) in the total output of manufacturers 1909–1989

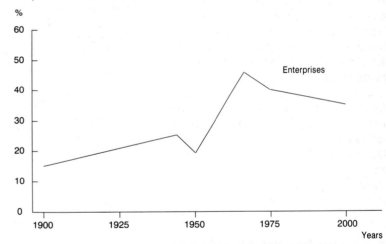

Source: *The Evolution of Giant Firms in Britain*, S. J. Prais, Cambridge University Press; *Business Monitor* summary tables, PA 1002.

S T U D Y P O I N T S

1. Consider Figure 37.1. How many manufacturing businesses employed
   (a) between 1 and 199 workers?
   (b) between 199 and 2999 workers?
   (c) over 3000 workers?

2. Consider Figure 37.2.
   (a) Which size of manufacturing business employed the most workers in the UK in 1989? How many workers did these businesses employ?
   (b) If there were 185 businesses employing 3000 workers and over, how many workers on average did each business employ?

3. Consider Figure 37.3. What was the value of total output in the UK economy in 1987 of all manufacturing firms employing:
   (a) between 1 and 199 workers?
   (b) between 199 and 2999 workers?
   (c) over 3000 workers?
   If there were 185 businesses employing 3000 workers and over, what was the average value of output of each business?

4. Consider Figure 37.4. Describe how the share of total output of the largest 100 manufacturing businesses in the UK has changed over the period 1909 to 1989.

5. If you were employed in manufacturing industry, what size of business would you be most likely to work for?

6. Name 10 manufacturing companies in your area. What size are they? What do they produce?

7. Why do you think most manufacturing companies in your area are small? How do they manage to compete with larger firms?

Firms

Consider Figures 37.1–37.3. They show that nearly all firms in manufacturing industry are small, employing less than 200 workers. Yet these firms produce only a very small part of manufacturing output. 45% of all output is produced by just 185 firms. This unit considers why some firms are small and some are large.

Reasons for the Existence of Large Firms

Large firms enjoy many advantages over small firms. They may enjoy *economies of scale*. Lower costs may mean lower prices and increased competitiveness. Large firms may find it not only cheaper to obtain loans (a financial economy of scale), but also easier to obtain credit and new equity capital than smaller firms. Hence they find it much easier to expand than smaller firms. For these reasons, one would expect to see large firms growing at the expense of small firms. Large firms should be far more competitive than smaller firms and should therefore force smaller firms out of the market. This has happened to some extent. Figure 37.4 shows how the share of total output of the top 50 manufacturing companies has grown in the UK this century. But, as Figure 37.1 shows, there is no shortage of small firms, even if they are producing a smaller proportion of total output than, say, 50 years ago.

Reasons for the Existence of Small Firms

Small firms continue to exist for a number of reasons. First, there is a ready supply of entrepreneurs who want to work for themselves, who see a gap in the market and are prepared to risk their money and time in a venture.

Second, many markets are too small to accommodate large firms. Many markets are localised, perhaps because it is not possible to transport goods cheaply over long distances or because there are special tastes in the local market (e.g. local sausages). Where market demand is small, small firms tend to predominate.

Third, small firms may be more flexible than large firms. They may be willing to supply highly specialised products in small quantities to larger businesses. Large businesses like the speed, flexibility and cheapness of this and buy from small firms.

Fourth, small firms can often pay workers less than larger firms. Unions tend to be weak and there is a history of low pay in small businesses. This helps reduce costs and allows small business to compete.

Fifth, in some industries, optimum production (i.e. where the average cost of production is lowest) is achieved at very low levels of output. This is true of many personal services, such as hairdressing. Without the advantages of lower costs due to economies of scale, there is no reason for firms to grow and outcompete smaller firms.

Lastly, small firms in some industries have combined to share costs such as advertising, research and development. Examples of this are the Spar and Wavy Line chains of independent shops, which pool advertising and other services. Here small businesses can enjoy greater economies of scale than would otherwise be the case.

So small firms will continue to exist, but if past trends are anything to go by, they will produce less as a proportion of total output over time.

CHECKPOINTS

1 Using Figures 37.1–37.4, describe the importance of small firms in the economy.

2 Why might economies of scale give larger firms a competitive advantage over small firms?

3 Account for the continued existence of small firms.

4 Why are hairdressing firms and painting and decorating firms usually small, whereas car manufacturers and banks are usually large?

COURSEWORK SUGGESTION

Arrange to interview the owners of two small firms in your local area. Devise a questionnaire prior to the interview which asks why these small firms are able to exist despite their small size. Also ask whether or not the firms are likely to expand in the future, and why they might want to do this. After the interviews, write up your findings and compare the position of the two firms in your survey. Try to assess the chances of survival and growth for these firms in the future.

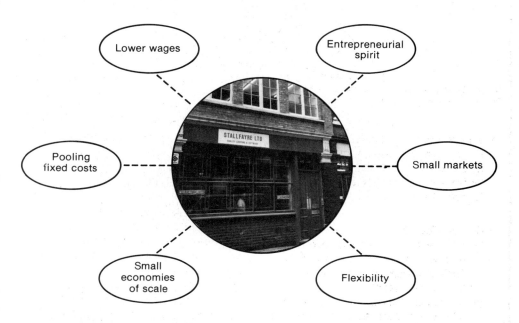

Small firms continue to survive for a variety of reasons.

The Growth of Firms

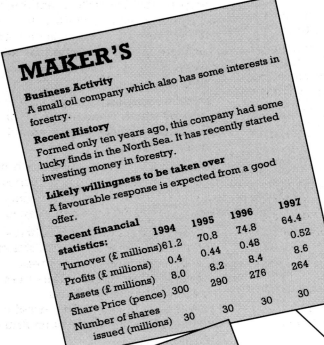

MAKER'S

Business Activity
A small oil company which also has some interests in forestry.

Recent History
Formed only ten years ago, this company had some lucky finds in the North Sea. It has recently started investing money in forestry.

Likely willingness to be taken over
A favourable response is expected from a good offer.

Recent financial statistics:

	1994	1995	1996	1997
Turnover (£ millions)	61.2	70.8	74.8	64.4
Profits (£ millions)	0.4	0.44	0.48	0.52
Assets (£ millions)	8.0	8.2	8.4	8.6
Share Price (pence)	300	290	276	264
Number of shares issued (millions)	30	30	30	30

BAKER'S

Business Activity
Mainly a printing company with a small interest in paper making.

Recent History
Baker's has proved a solid, dependable, if somewhat unexciting company over its 50 year history. It has recently undertaken an ambitious investment programme designed to automate much of its production.

Likely willingness to be taken over
Initial soundings indicate that management and major shareholders would be receptive to a fair offer.

Recent financial statistics:

	1994	1995	1996	1997
Turnover (£ millions)	10.4	11.2	12.6	14.0
Profits (£ millions)	0.2	0.2	0.4	0.44
Assets (£ millions)	2.0	2.2	2.6	3.2
Share Price (pence)	44	48	60	100
Number of shares issued (millions)	5	5	5	5

MILLINER'S

Business Activity
Mainly a book publishing firm but also owns a chain of 30 bookshops nationwide.

Recent History
Founded 153 years ago, this is a well established, old fashioned publishing company. Poor profitability prompted a major change in management three years ago.

Likely willingness to be taken over
Management likely to advise shareholders against almost any offer made.

Recent financial statistics:

	1994	1995	1996	1997
Turnover (£ millions)	20.4	20.6	19.2	19.0
Profits (£ millions)	0.2	0.2	0	−0.4
Assets (£ millions)	6.4	6.6	7.0	7.6
Share Price (pence)	52	44	36	28
Number of shares issued (millions)	10	10	10	10

TAYLOR'S

Business Activity
Mainly a book publishing firm with interests world wide. Also owns a UK national newspaper, magazines and a large newsagent chain in North West England.

Recent History
Started 15 years ago by the dynamic Martin Taylor as a printing company, it grew rapidly in the book publishing field, acquiring several much larger firms. It recently took over the Mixwell newspaper company which owned a national newspaper and a valuable chain of over 100 newsagents.

STUDY POINTS

Taylor's wishes to acquire a small company to expand its interests. It has over £40 million in cash reserves, so price is no object with regard to the three firms described. You are the director of Taylor's.

1 If your company were to take over just one firm, which of the three should it take over? Explain your reasons carefully.

2 What is the opportunity cost of buying any of these firms?

3 What is the maximum price that your company should pay for the chosen company? Explain your reasoning.

Thomas Cook, the British holiday company, is to be taken over by a German charter airline company, LTU, for £200 million. LTU is Germany's second largest airline company. It also owns travel agents and hotels.

Why should a German airline and holiday company want to grow in size by taking over Thomas Cook with its 1600 bureaux in 120 countries? Why should any company want to grow in size? There are a variety of possible reasons.

- Growth could well lead to higher profits and higher share values, simply because more is being sold. LTU will, after all, have a higher turnover after the takeover.

- Growth could take the form of DIVERSIFICATION. This is where a company like LTU moves into a different market from its original activities. Being in two markets reduces *risk*. If one market does badly (like the charter air travel market for LTU), then the firm can fall back on the profits being made in the other market (like Thomas Cook travellers cheques).

- Growth could lead to a reduction in costs. This would arise if growth lead to further economies of scale being exploited. Lower costs could lead to higher profits. With LTU, some cost savings are likely to be made in Germany where Thomas Cook branches could be linked into the LTU chain of travel agents.

- Growth could lead to greater control over the market. The bigger the

share of the market that a company has, the more likely it is to be able to exploit monopoly powers – fixing high prices and earning high profits.

Methods of Growth

There are two main ways in which a firm can grow. *Internal Growth* is achieved by the firm expanding on its own. The firm invests and increases its production and sales. A firm can also grow by taking over or merging with other firms. This is known as growth by AMALGAMATION. A MERGER occurs when two companies of similar size agree to come together to form just one company. A TAKEOVER usually refers to the situation where one firm attempts to buy another firm against the wishes of the directors of the second firm, or where a large company buys a small one. LTU's purchase of Thomas Cook was an example of a large company buying up a smaller company.

When two companies do come together, *integration* is said to take place. There are three major types of integration or merger:

- HORIZONTAL INTEGRATION occurs when two firms producing similar goods and services amalgamate. For instance, LTU's takeover of Thomas Cook is an example of horizontal integration, because both companies are in the travel business.

- VERTICAL INTEGRATION occurs when a company amalgamates either with a company it sells products to (*forward integration*), or with a company it buys products from (*backwards integration*). For instance, there is an element of forward integration in LTU buying Thomas Cook. LTU, the charter

airline, is buying a travel agent which could promote LTU through selling tickets to passengers.

- CONGLOMERATE MERGERS occur when a firm amalgamates with another company that has little or nothing to do with its existing activities. If LTU were to buy a sweet manufacturer or a coal mining company, these would be examples of conglomerate mergers.

A merger could well lead to higher growth and higher profits for the two companies concerned. This need not be the case, however:

- if the amalgamation of the two firms did not result in greater economies of scale than were enjoyed by the two firms producing on their own;

- if diseconomies of scale resulted – for instance, because the two sets of management failed to work well together or because managers from one firm were appointed to positions in the other firm, despite knowing little about the other firm's business.

CHECKPOINTS

1 Explain why a company might want to grow in size.

2 What is the difference between (a) the internal growth of a firm and the external growth; and (b) a merger and a takeover?

3 Explain what type of integration the following represent:
   (a) a brewery merging with a chain of off-licences;
   (b) a furniture maker merging with another furniture maker;
   (c) an oil company merging with a chain of supermarkets;
   (d) a car manufacturer merging with a steel manufacturer.

KEY TERMS

DIVERSIFICATION – Moving into a new and different market.

MERGER, AMALGAMATION or TAKEOVER – a situation where one company is joined to another company.

HORIZONTAL INTEGRATION – the merger of two firms that produce similar goods and services.

VERTICAL INTEGRATION – the merger of one firm with another firm that either supplies it with products or buys from it.

CONGLOMERATE MERGER – a merger between two companies whose markets are unrelated.

COURSEWORK SUGGESTION

Investigate a merger currently in the news. Describe the companies involved. Analyse why the merger is taking place. Evaluate whether the merger will lead to greater efficiency in the economy.

Business Finance

Figure 39.1 Sources of investment funds (£ million) 1987–91

	1987	1988	1989	1990	1991
Retained profit	38 770	39 528	33 839	33 632	37 978
Bank borrowing	12 164	31 812	3 3089	1 8468	—3389
Ordinary shares	13 409	4352	1882	2822	9683
Debenture and preference shares	3590	3586	5648	3403	5051
Other	7601	12 937	27 065	25 537	17112
Total	75 534	92 215	101 523	83 862	66 435

Source: CSO, *Financial Statistics*, May 1992

Figure 39.2 Total output (gross domestic product) of UK economy 1987–91

Gross Domestic Product (£ thousand millions)

Source: CSO, *Monthly Digest of Statistics*, July 1985

S T U D Y P O I N T S

Figure 39.1 shows how companies got money for investment in their businesses to buy anything from factories and offices to machines and computers.

1 What is the most important way in which companies obtain funds for new investment?

2 Describe how companies changed the way in which they got money for new investment between 1987 and 1991.

Figure 39.2 shows the change in gross domestic product, a measure of the total output of the UK economy, between 1987 and 1991.

3 (a) What happened to output between 1987 and 1991?
  (b) How do you think these changes in output

will have affected the profits of UK companies? Does Figure 39.1 give any evidence to support your argument?

(c) How do you think these changes in output will have influenced the amount that companies want to invest? Does Figure 39.1 give any evidence to support your argument?

(d) Suggest a reason why banks paid off more debt than they borrowed in 1991.

4 A government wants to increase investment in the economy. Which of the following measures would most help promote this in your opinion and why? (a) lowering interest rates; (b) making it easier for firms to issue new shares; (c) increasing total spending in the economy.

Financing Investment

In 1992, GPA, the world's largest airline leasing company, issued £1.7 billion worth of new shares. The company, originally Irish, needed the money to buy new aircraft to lease (i.e. hire out) to companies throughout the world.

Firms pay their day-to-day running costs, such as wages or raw material costs, from the revenue or turnover they receive from selling their products. But they also need money to finance investment – perhaps to start up a new product or company or to buy new factories and machinery, or to fund research and development. This unit considers the sources of such money for companies.

Retained Profit

Figure 39.1 shows that the major source of new funds for companies is **RETAINED PROFIT**. This is money that the company has made in profits and instead of being given out to shareholders in dividends, it is kept back by the company for investment. The more profit a company makes, the more funds it has to keep back for investment purposes.

Borrowing Money

The next most important source of funds is borrowing. There are many ways in which a company can borrow money. It can borrow:

- from a *bank*. A company may have a loan, where money is borrowed from the bank and paid back in regular instalments. Or it may have an overdraft, where it borrows money and repays it as and when it wants, through its current account with the bank. The big banks (e.g. Barclays and Lloyds) lend a large amount to British industry. There are also industrial banks, which specialise in lending to industry. Foreign banks also lend money to British industry, often in foreign currencies to finance investment abroad.

- from the *money markets*. Firms can go to a financial centre like London and borrow money from a wide variety of institutions, such as pension funds and insurance companies. One form of such borrowing is DEBENTURES or LOAN STOCK. The company issues certificates in small amounts called debentures or stocks. In return for money, the company promises to pay regular interest and repay the borrowed money at some specified time in the future (the REDEMPTION date). The advantage to the borrower is that these certificates can be sold to another saver, often through stock markets such as the London Stock Exchange, before the time when the stock is due to be repaid or *redeemed*. The new owner then receives interest and the right to be repaid the money originally lent on the redemption date.

- from FINANCE HOUSES and other financial institutions. Firms can buy goods on HIRE PURCHASE or rent them on a LEASING agreement. With hire purchase, the goods are hired and only become the property of the company when the last instalment is paid. Both hire purchase and leasing are really a way of borrowing money, because the company is able to use the goods without having to pay their full cost at the start in order to acquire them. Finance houses are banks that

specialise in providing hire purchase and leasing services.

- from the *government*. The government provides a number of ways in which firms can borrow money cheaply. Recently, the government has been particularly keen to help small firms.

Equity Capital

A company can gain further money by selling new shares in the company. This was what GPA was doing in the extract above. It is known as adding to the EQUITY CAPITAL of the company. This simply means that the value of the company or what it could be sold for increases. For instance, if a company was worth £10 million (i.e. its equity capital was £10 million) and it sold an extra £2 million worth of shares, then the new value of the company would be £12 million. In return for buying the new shares, the new shareholders would be entitled to a share of the profits. The issuing of new share capital will be discussed further in Unit 41.

Grants

Companies can also obtain grants for new investment, mainly from the government and the EC. Firms receiving grants usually receive them for:

- investing in high unemployment areas of the UK;

- investing in new technology;

- restructuring and running down older industries.

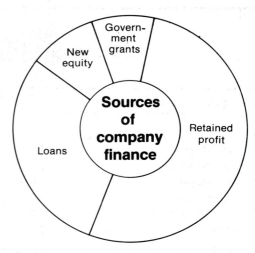

Firms obtain finance for investment from four main sources.

C H E C K P O I N T S

1 **Why do firms need finance?**

2 **What is meant by 'retained profit'? Why is retained profit so important for investment in the UK?**

3 **Compare the different ways of borrowing money for a company.**

4 **What is meant by 'raising new equity'?**

5 **What might a firm receive a grant for?**

C O U R S E W O R K S U G G E S T I O N

Arrange to interview the financial directors (or equivalent) of two local firms, one a small firm, the other a medium to large firm. Draw up a questionnaire that seeks to find out what the sources of finance for the two firms are and what problems they encounter in finding finance for new investment. Also find out whether each company has had to abandon investment plans because of a lack of finance. Describe your findings. Compare and contrast the sources of finance and the difficulties encountered in obtaining finance for the two firms. Discuss whether or not a lack of finance has been a source of lack of investment.

K E Y T E R M S

RETAINED PROFIT – profit not distributed to shareholders, but kept back for investment purposes.

DEBENTURE or LOAN STOCK – a fixed interest security issued by a company in return for a loan of money. The certificate can be sold and resold, if desired.

REDEMPTION – paying back.

FINANCE HOUSE – a bank that specialises in hire-purchase loans.

HIRE PURCHASE – a form of borrowing where the good being purchased is the property of the lender up to the final payment, when it becomes the property of the borrower.

LEASING – renting.

EQUITY – the monetary value of the shareholdings in a firm at a particular moment in time.

Sole Proprietorships and Partnerships

SPENCERS

Name of business: Spencer's

Owner: John Spencer

Activity: Retailing – general hardware

Assets: Stock £15 000, house £70 000, car £4000, cash £14 000, other £40 000

Location: On a parade of small shops in a suburb of Wolverhampton.

Financial statistics for last year:

New stock	74 000	Sales	100 000
Rent, rates	6000		
Other	4000		
Surplus	16 000		
Total	100 000	Total	100 000

History: John Spencer moved into the hardware business after 15 years in the army. The shop has now been established 10 years. Premises are rented. John's wife, Mary, helps out when needed. Trade has always been steady.

S T U D Y   P O I N T S

It has come to the notice of John Spencer that the hardware shop on a similar parade of shops only one mile away is up for sale at a price of £20 000 plus stock. The premises are rented. Last year, the financial statistics for the shop were:

	£		£
New stock	62 000	Sales	80 000
Rent, rates	4000		
Other	4000		
Surplus	10 000		
Total	80 000	Total	80 000

1 If John Spencer were to buy the shop, what would be the implications for him in terms of: (a) staff? (b) total costs of the business? (c) surplus?

2 What is the maximum price he should offer for the business (excluding stock)?

3 Assume that £20 000 worth of stock would be sold with the shop. Where should John Spencer obtain the money from to purchase the business? (Note that Mr. Spencer has a good record with his local bank, but would have to pay 20% interest a year on a loan, and the bank would take his house as security. An older brother lent him the money to start off the business ten years ago, and might be

prepared to lend him money again. An unemployed friend with savings of £8000 would be interested in going into partnership with him.) Explain carefully the reasons for your choice.

4 What would happen if, having bought the business, trade in both shops declined so that the surplus turned into a loss of £20 000 in one year?

Sole Proprietorships

Between 1980 and 1992, the number of people self-employed rose from 2.0 million to 3.1 million at a time when the number of people employed by others fell from 23 million to 22 million. (*Source:* CSO, *Annual Abstract of Statistics 1992*).

There was a big increase in the number of self-employed workers in the 1980s. The self-employed run their own businesses. These businesses are the most common type of BUSINESS ORGANISATION in the UK and are called SOLE PROPRIETORSHIPS.

These are businesses owned by one person only. That person, however, may employ other workers. The owner usually works in the firm and is responsible for its day-to-day running. The owner will receive all the profits made by the firm. He or she is totally responsible for any debts the business runs up. This is known as having UNLIMITED LIABILITY. For instance, if a sole proprietor goes bankrupt owing £150 000, then not only can all the assets of the business be sold – shop or factory, machinery, etc. – but all the proprietor's personal possessions – house, car etc. – can also be sold. Sole proprietorships are common in many service industries, such as hairdressing, retailing (shops) and the tourist industry.

People going into business choose sole proprietorships as a form of business organisation because:

- it is simple to set up, and there is no need to obtain special legal documents;

- the owner can have complete control of the business if he or she wishes;

- there is no legal requirement to publish accounts.

However, the disadvantages include:

- unlimited liability;

- great difficulty in obtaining finance. Many firms are started from moneys raised by the sale or mortgaging of personal possessions, like houses, or money borrowed in the family. Banks are less likely to lend to small firms than large firms, because small firms are far more likely to go bankrupt. Access to finance through the City of London money market is out of the question, because the firm is too small.

- the fact that the firm may find it difficult to compete with larger firms, if larger firms enjoy greater economies of scale.

Partnerships

ORDINARY PARTNERSHIPS are unlimited liability businesses with between two and twenty partners or shareholders. They are commonly found in professions such as medicine, accountancy and the law.

The advantages of a partnership are that:

- it is cheap and easy to form, just requiring a legal contract called a Deed of Partnership;

- having more than one owner should increase the amount of money that can be raised for investment in the business;

- there is no need to disclose publicly the accounts of the business;

- partners who do not work in the business can have *limited liability* (the advantages of which are discussed in Unit 41) – this sort of partnership is known as a *limited partnership*;

- having more partners and more business is likely to help exploit potential economies of scale.

The disadvantages include:

- unlimited liability for ordinary partners;

- twenty partners might still be far too few to exploit economies of scale fully;

- partners have to trust each other, because one partner can sign a contract binding on all partners;

- the partnership lacks continuity, because if one partner leaves, the whole partnership is dissolved and a new one has to be formed by the remaining partners.

C H E C K P O I N T S

1 Explain who (a) owns; (b) controls; and (c) is responsible for any debts in a sole proprietorship and a partnership.

2 Why do sole proprietorships often find it difficult to raise money for investment?

3 Two workers are considering becoming self-employed and setting up their own business. What would be the advantages of them setting up as a partnership rather than setting up as two sole proprietorships?

4 What is the difference between an ordinary partnership and a limited partnership?

C O U R S E W O R K   S U G G E S T I O N

Contact a sole proprietorship or a partnership. Describe the business by stating who owns it, who runs it, what it produces and sells, who is responsible for profits and losses, and how the business is financed. Describe, too, how it was initially started. Analyse the success of the business and the problems facing it. Assess the extent to which these problems could be overcome and success increased, if the business were to become larger and perhaps change its form of organisation.

K E Y   T E R M S

BUSINESS ORGANISATION – an organisation established with the purpose of producing and selling goods and services.

SOLE PROPRIETORSHIP – a one-person business with unlimited liability.

UNLIMITED LIABILITY – a legal obligation on the owners of a business organisation to pay all debts of the business. Even their own personal wealth may be claimed.

ORDINARY PARTNERSHIP – an unlimited liability business where between two and twenty partners own, control and finance the business.

Joint-stock Companies

Bellows

Name of company:	Bellow's
Legal status:	Private Limited Company
Business activity:	Holiday tour operator
Value of company:	estimated £18 million
Shareholders:	Donald Bellow (30%) his wife, Nancy Bellow (30%) his son, Robert Bellow (15%) his son, David Bellow (15%) John Phillips, the financial director (10%) who is not a member of the Bellow family
Main financial statistics for last year:	Turnover £34 million, profits £2.8 million, borrowing £8 million

Norweb, the Manchester-based regional electricity company, yesterday announced pre-tax profits up by 96 per cent to £137.9m for the year to 31 March 1992. 'This year's results demonstrate that high quality customer service and profits can, and must, go hand in hand,' said Ken Harvey, Norweb's chairman. (*Source: Financial Times*, 17 June 1992)

Norweb is an example of a public limited company (PLC), one of the two types of JOINT-STOCK COMPANY. Joint-stock companies are the most important form of business organisation in the UK. There are more sole proprietorships and partnerships, but joint-stock companies are bigger and produce a larger proportion of total output.

Joint-stock companies are owned by shareholders. By law, there must be at least two shareholders in the company. These shareholders elect a board of directors and a chairman. In the extract, it mentioned that Mr Ken Harvey was the chairman of Norweb. The Board of Directors appoint managers to run the day-to-day business of the company. At least some of the directors are likely to work full-time for the company, but others may be part-time directors. Shareholders, unless they also happen to be directors and managers, do not have a direct say in how the company is run. As was mentioned in Unit 34, this could result in the interests of shareholders and managers conflicting.

There are two types of joint-stock company:

- A PRIVATE LIMITED COMPANY is usually the smaller of the two types. It can range from a small family business, with just a few shareholders, to much larger companies. The shares of the company are not freely available for purchase by the general public.

- A PUBLIC LIMITED COMPANY is a company whose shares must be freely available for purchase by the

STUDY POINTS

The board of Bellow's is meeting today to consider a £6 million expansion plan. Based mainly in London and the South East, it is proposed that new travel agents should be set up in the South West and the Midlands. It is estimated that profits would increase by £0.5 million per annum. Finance for the expansion can only come from one of two sources. A bank loan would cost 17% per annum in interest. Or the company could go public. The professional fees for a flotation would be £600 000. It is likely that a successful flotation would require existing shareholders to sell some of their shares, so that the Bellow family would own no more than 60% of the shareholding.

1 What would be the cost to the company of borrowing the money?

2 Why might their bankers be reluctant to lend them the £6 million?

3 What would be the cost to the company if new shares were issued?

4 What would be the implications for the existing shareholders of a share flotation in terms of (a) dividends, (b) control of the company, (c) the ability of shareholders to sell their shares?

5 Should the board decide against the expansion plan, borrow the money or go public and issue new equity?

general public on a stock exchange like the London Stock Exchange. The company must have £50 000 worth of capital when it is formed.

Finance

Joint-stock companies are in a much better position than sole proprietorships or partnerships to raise money for expansion. The larger the company, the greater the number of sources of finance. Not only can these companies borrow relatively easily from banks, finance houses, etc., but PLCs have the additional advantage of access to stock exchanges. They can issue debentures. They can also issue two types of shares in the company:

● *preference shares* – shares which carry a fixed rate of dividend (say 5%), a dividend which must be paid before ordinary shareholders receive their dividends;

● *ordinary shares* – shares where the dividend earned varies according to the amount of profit made: if the company makes a large profit, dividends should be high and vice versa.

If a company votes to raise money through the issue of new equity, it will offer shares for sale to the public, probably acting through a bank or merchant bank. Once the shares have been sold, they will become tradable on a stock exchange. Shareholders can sell their shares, if they want to. This makes the share in PLCs far more attractive than those in a private limited company, where there is no open market for the shares.

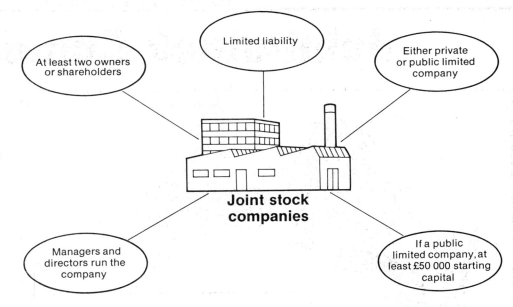

Joint stock companies

- Limited liability
- At least two owners or shareholders
- Either private or public limited company
- Managers and directors run the company
- If a public limited company, at least £50 000 starting capital

Advantages and Disadvantages

Joint-stock companies have advantages in that:

● they have access to wider sources of capital than sole proprietorships and partnerships – this is particularly true of PLCs;

● because they tend to be larger, they can enjoy economies of scale;

● shareholders have LIMITED LIABILITY.

They also have disadvantages, in that:

● accounts have to be made available to the public;

● it is very expensive to form a PLC;

● the original founders of the company are likely to lose control of it, as their shareholding is diluted and this may discourage owners of firms from going public.

C H E C K P O I N T S

1 What is a joint-stock company?

2 Explain the difference between a shareholder, a director and a manager of a company.

3 What are the advantages and disadvantages of a private limited company rather than a partnership as a form of business organisation?

4 How can a public limited company raise money for expansion?

5 Explain the difference between a preference and an ordinary share.

C O U R S E W O R K S U G G E S T I O N

Investigate the activities of a large public limited company which has a factory, offices, shops and other premises in your locality. Write to the headquarters of the company and obtain a copy of its *Company Report and Accounts*. Request any other material which might be of help to your project. In a written report, describe and analyse the structure of the company, its activities and how those activities are financed. Consider to what extent the shareholders do control and should control the company.

K E Y T E R M S

JOINT-STOCK COMPANY – a company that has an independent legal existence from its shareholders and where shareholders have limited liability.

PRIVATE LIMITED COMPANY – any joint-stock company that is not a public limited company.

PUBLIC LIMITED COMPANY – a joint-stock company that must have £50 000 capital when founded, and must allow its shares to be traded freely (e.g. on a stock exchange).

LIMITED LIABILITY – a legal safeguard that allows shareholders to be liable for their company's debts only up to and including the value of their shareholding.

Co-operatives

The Mondragon Co-operatives

Mondragon is a town in the Basque region of Spain. In 1956, inspired by a Catholic Priest, workers set up a workers co-operative. It was called ULGOR and produced washing machines and refrigerators.

Organisation

• Each worker must be a member of the co-op, with one vote.
• Policy decisions of the co-op are taken democratically through a general meeting, or through a board of the company which has been elected.
• Managers carry out the decisions of the co-op.
• The ratio between the highest and lowest wages is 3:1.
• Workers can only get their share of the profits made when they retire. Before then, the profit is reinvested to expand the co-op and create jobs.
• If workers do have to lose their jobs, they get 80% of their wages paid to them whilst they are looking for similar work. But unemployment is unlikely to last long because other expanding co-ops will take on these workers.

The Co-operatives Today

Today there are

• 85 manufacturing co-operatives;
• 6 co-operative banks;
• 6 farming co-operatives;
• 14 housing co-ops;
• 43 co-op schools and colleges;
• a social security and pensions co-op;
• a medical and hospital services co-op;
• a consumer co-op.

Setting up a Co-operative

At the heart of the co-operatives is the Caja Laboral Popular (CLP). This is the bank controlled by the co-operatives. For a proposed new co-operative, the CLP will:

• make a feasibility study, help design and develop the factory and train or supply a manager;
• provide 75% of the cost of setting up a new co-op in the form of a ten year loan at cheap interest rates. 12.5% of the cost is a low interest loan from the government. The final 12.5% comes from the workers. It averages £2600 per worker. It can be paid over two years from wages interest free or over five years as a loan from the bank.

Where The Profits Go

'70% to the workers themselves in proportio to their wages'

'20% to co-ops collected reserves'

'10% to a social fund to benefit the local community'

Statistics

85 manufacturing companies:

• have sales of £525 million;
• have 18 000 worker owners;
• vary in size from 20 to 3400 workers with an average of 200.

Assume you are a worker member of the Caja Laboral Popular, the co-op bank. You have been asked to prepare a report on the setting up of a new co-op to make plastic bottles. It is proposed that the co-op should start off with 25 worker employees. It will cost £1 million to set up the co-op. A manager worker will be appointed at a salary of £18 000 per year. You will need to include the following in your report.

S T U D Y P O I N T S

1 What will be the role of Caja Laboral Popular in setting up the co-operative?

2 How will the government help the co-operative?

3 What will be the role of the worker in the co-operative: (a) in providing money to set up the co-operative; (b) in making decisions about the running of the co-operative; (c) in benefiting from the profits of the company?

4 What will be the role of the manager of the co-operative?

5 How will the local economy and the local community benefit from the setting up of the co-operative?

6 Why would you expect the workers of the co-operative to work hard and act responsibly? Would you expect workers, for instance, to go on strike?

Types of Co-operatives

The word 'co-operative' comes from the verb 'to co-operate', which means to join together to do something. CO-OPERATIVES differ from ordinary companies in that the main aim of the company is not necessarily to make as much profit as possible for the shareholders. There are two main types of co-operative in the UK; producer co-operatives and consumer co-operatives.

Producer Co-operatives

Producer co-operatives are businesses owned by some or all of the workers in the firm. The aim of the co-operative movement is to run the business for the sake of the workers and not for the shareholders, who may have nothing to do with the firm except own shares. The workers have to provide any money or financial capital to set up the business. They then have to find some way of making decisions – for instance, by appointing managers or, if a company is small, by voting on important issues. They also have to decide how to distribute the profits of the co-operative, although these will almost certainly go to the workers, since they are the shareholders of the company. Workers do have the advantage under law of having limited liability.

The main advantage of a worker or producer co-operative should be that there is no conflict of interest between workers and shareholders, since workers are the shareholders. So there should be no strikes, and workers should have a strong incentive to work. Worker co-operatives are extremely rare in the UK. This is because:

- workers find it difficult to raise enough money to set up and then finance the growth of firms;
- workers often lack the necessary management experience to make a company successful.

Probably the most successful example of worker co-operatives is in the Mondrian region of Spain, where there are a number of very successful co-operatives, ranging from a bank to the largest washing-machine manufacturer in Spain.

Consumer Co-operatives

Consumer or retail co-operatives are co-operatives set up with the aim of helping consumers. The first such co-operative in the UK was set up in 1844 in Rochdale by 28 weavers, who wanted to sell food more cheaply than in the local shops.

> *Some of the Original Rochdale Principles*
>
> 1. Voluntary and open membership.
> 2. Democratic control – one man, one vote.
> 3. Payment of fixed interest on capital.
> 4. Surplus allocated in proportion to members' purchases – the dividend.
> 5. Education facilities for members and workers.

The co-operatives are owned by members of the general public, who can own between £1 and £5000 of shares. Interest is paid on the shares. Unlike limited companies, shares can only be sold back to the co-operative, and each shareholder (or 'member') is only entitled to one vote at shareholders' meetings, however many shares are held. Shareholders elect a management committee (like the board of directors in a PLC), who in turn appoint paid full-time managers to run the co-operative society on a day-to-day basis. Profits are distributed not to shareholders, but to shoppers, according to how much they spend at the co-op. Many co-ops now pay this in the form of stamps. Co-operatives finance their investment mainly through retained profits and loans of various sorts.

The co-operative ideal has to a great extent diminished over the past twenty years. Co-operatives have found that larger PLCs, such as Sainsbury's, have been able to exploit economies of scale and often sell produce more cheaply and in greater variety. If co-operatives can no longer guarantee to have the cheapest produce, what is their role in the economy? Co-operatives have responded in part by joining together in larger and larger societies, to exploit the economies of scale needed to reduce prices. However, in 1992 there were 65 co-operative societies in Britain, many of which are very small. As they get larger, they lose their local roots, and it becomes more difficult to maintain the original aim of having shops controlled by the people who shop there. It is difficult to see how co-operatives are going to be very different from other companies in the future.

CHECKPOINTS

1 Explain how a typical producer co-operative is owned, financed and controlled.

2 Explain the role of the shareholder, the consumer and the management committee in a typical retail co-operative society.

3 In what ways does a typical retail co-operative society differ from a public limited company?

4 Why have retail co-operatives to some extent lost their traditional role in the economy?

COURSEWORK SUGGESTION

Write to your local retail co-operative society and ask for its latest *Report and Accounts*, together with any other material which might be of help to you. Describe and analyse the ownership, finance, control, location and activities of the society. Try to assess the extent to which the co-operative aim is being upheld by the society in your local economy.

KEY TERMS

CO-OPERATIVES – firms that exist either for the benefit of their worker-owners (*worker* or *producer co-operatives*), or for the customers they sell to (*consumer* or *retail co-operatives*).

Data Response Questions
Units 37–42

Unit 37 The Size of Firms

Mail market in shirts

Lexi Douglas and Henrietta Nettlefold started Sparklers', their mail order business, in 1986. They sell shirts designed for women. But instead of making them in non-breathing synthetic fibres as do most women's blouse makers, they make them in high quality men's shirting material.

They sell mainly through mail order, advertising in the national press and *Good Housekeeping* magazine. Their mailing list has been built up to 30 000 and they expect 13 per cent of those customers to place an order when mail shots are sent out. This is very good for the mail order business, although it is down in the recession from 21 per cent just three years ago.

20 per cent of their sales are generated from stalls at charity functions. Sparklers' pays a table fee and 10 to 15 per cent of its takings during the day to that charity.

Last year, they bought the small, family owned garment manufacturer which had been making up their shirts under contract. It cost them £5000–£10 000 but has yearly sales of £120 000.

The business is run from the homes of the two founders. Apart from the garment manufacturer, the company has no business premises. The only staff member is a woman who works in the Douglas house despatching order forms and shirts. The garment manufacturer employs 7 workers and another 10 out-workers.

Lexi Douglas knows that competition is likely to be fiercer in the future. But, she says, 'I think the growth of mail order is a good thing because it is changing buying habits. I think a lot of people are getting fed up with shopping.'

Source: Adapted from the *Financial Times*, 15 February 1992

1 What does the company described in the article sell?
(1 mark)

2 Who, do you think, are they in competition with?
(4 marks)

3 How can a small company like this survive when there are far larger businesses in the industry? *(6 marks)*

4 Suggest why the two founders of the business decided to buy the garment manufacturer. *(4 marks)*

Unit 38 The Growth of Firms

The tough path to world leadership in music

Thorn EMI yesterday announced that it was buying the Virgin Record Group for £510 million. Richard Branson owns 80 per cent of Virgin.

The deal will bring to Thorn artistes like the Rolling Stones, Phil Collins, Genesis and UB40 as well as Fine Young Cannibals, Tears for Fears and the Pet Shop Boys.

It will transform Thorn from being the world's fourth largest recorded music group, with a market share of about 14 per cent, to being one of the three top companies alongside Polygram and Time Warner, the market leaders.

Thorn is not buying any physical assets. Virgin Music had no manufacturing plants or distribution facilities. The £510 million price tag is for the recording rights to Virgin's past issues, and the hope that existing successful Virgin artistes will renew their contracts with Thorn rather than look elsewhere.

Some say that the price is far too high. But Thorn believes that Virgin, which made little profit last year, can be turned into a big money spinner. Profits can be raised in three ways. Firstly, Virgin product prices can be raised to the level of those charged by Thorn. Secondly, Thorn will become the sole manufacturer and distributor of Virgin records as and when existing contracts with other firms expire. There will thus be gains from economies of scale. Thirdly, Virgin artistes who don't sell well and are therefore unprofitable will be dropped far more quickly than under existing Virgin management.

By making it to the top, Thorn can now afford to pay the huge fees demanded by world-class artistes essential to the survival of an established recording company today. It is therefore in a safer position than it was just two days ago.

Source: Adapted from the *Financial Times*, 7 March 1992

1 Describe what Thorn is buying from Richard Branson which is worth £510 million. *(3 marks)*

2 What type of takeover or merger is taking place? *(1 mark)*

3 Explain in detail two reasons why Thorn wishes to buy Virgin Music. *(8 marks)*

4 Suggest why Thorn has bought Virgin Music rather than, say, a clothing manufacturer or a chain of petrol stations.
(3 marks)

Unit 39 Business Finance

BUSINESS FINANCE

Whatever your business, the chances are that you will need to borrow money at some point; to start up, ease the cash flow or buy equipment. Whatever your requirements, there's a NatWest lending scheme to suit you. Amongst the most popular forms of borrowing are the Business Start-Up Loan and Overdraft.

Business Start-Up Loan
The first 12 months of any business can be a difficult time. To give you a head start, our Business Start-Up Loan gives you a preferential rate of interest, below our normal rate for a Business Development loan. No matter how volatile the economic situation becomes, the interest stays fixed at the rate agreed when you first took out the loan. You can apply to borrow any sum from £1000 up to £15000 – repayable over up to ten years. A Capital Repayment Holiday facility is also available over the first six months of the loan.

Business Development Loan
You may require additional finance to expand your business, to purchase an asset (for example, a van or an item of equipment) or simply to provide working capital. The Business Development Loan can be used for these and virtually any other business purpose. With its fixed interest rate, fixed term and fixed monthly repayments, the costs are known at the outset, thus making budgeting easy. You can borrow any amount between £2000 and £250000, covering repayments over a period of between 1 and 20 years.

To ease your repayments for up to the first two years, you can also request a Capital Repayment Holiday on sums over £15000. This means during that period you only pay the interest on your loan; which can be particularly helpful when you are investing in an asset which doesn't immediately generate full income.

Business Overdraft
For day-to-day expenditure, the Business Overdraft can provide flexibility and versatility. We agree the borrowing limit and the interest rate and you then control the amount you borrow within that limit and, as interest is calculated daily, you are only charged on the amount you have borrowed.

Loan Protection Insurance
When taking out either the Business Development or Business Start-Up Loan we also recommend that you take out insurance to protect the loan. The NatWest Development Loan Protector provides cover to meet loan repayments in case of accident or serious illness and, in the event of death, full repayment of the loan.

Source: National Westminster Bank. Information correct at the time of going to press.

1 How much can a new business borrow as a loan from National Westminster in its first year? *(1 mark)*

2 (a) Describe the difference between a loan and an overdraft.
  (b) Explain whether it is better for a firm to use a loan or an overdraft to finance: (i) the buying of a new machine; (ii) build-up of stock for sale at Christmas; (iii) late payment for goods by a customer. *(8 marks)*

3 What is the cost to a company of borrowing money from a bank compared to issuing new equity capital to finance investment? *(6 marks)*

Unit 42 Co-operatives

Profit fall at Co-op brings call for change

The Co-op, Britain's biggest retailer, last year saw trading profits fall 1.3 per cent to £173 million on sales up 6.6 per cent to £7.3 billion.

The Co-op held on to its 7.8 per cent slice of the food market, but its total retail market share dropped to 4.6 per cent from last year's 4.7 per cent. Just under two-thirds of Co-op sales are in food while about 14 per cent are non-food through its department stores. The Co-op is Britain's biggest undertaker and a strong force in retail travel.

Profit margins – profits as a proportion of sales – fell to 2.6 per cent. A 2.5 per cent level is seen as the minimum safe level for any co-operative retailer. The most efficient societies achieve 6 per cent.

In the South East, the Co-op is being severely squeezed by competitors like J. Sainsbury. It simply doesn't have the money for development that the other big chains have. For instance, land for a new 6 acre superstore in the South East is likely to cost £25 million, compared to just £1 million in some other parts of the country.

But the Co-op will never be fully commercial. It is committed to retain shopping facilities in local communities where the big chains won't operate. Stopping the fall in market share, providing modern shopping facilities of a standard with competitors and maintaining community shopping is going to be a very difficult task to achieve in the 1990s.

Source: Adapted from the *Financial Times,* 26 May 1992

1 Describe what the Co-op sells. *(2 marks)*

2 What happened to profits and profit margins at the Co-op in 1991? *(2 marks)*

3 What are the problems that the Co-op faces in the 1990s? *(6 marks)*

4 Why do you think that the Co-op has been more successful in its undertaking business than in its food business? *(5 marks)*

Data Response Questions for **Units 40** and **41** can be found on *page 220.*

Essay Questions
Units 37–42

1 Two chocolate confectionery manufacturers merge to form one company.
  (a) Suggest four reasons why this might have happened. *(8 marks)*
  (b) What type of merger is this? *(2 marks)*
  (c) What might be the effects of this merger for (i) consumers and (ii) the workers of the two companies? *(5 marks)*

2 'Workers trying to set up in business often find that the most important obstacle is the finance to start the business.'
  (a) Describe where a woman wanting to set up a small engineering firm could raise the money to start it. *(5 marks)*
  (b) What form of business organisation might she choose for her firm and why? *(5 marks)*
  (c) Why do small businesses find it difficult to obtain finance? *(5 marks)*

Nationalisation and Privatisation

THE PRIVATISATION OF BRITISH RAIL

RAILTRACK

Railtrack will remain a public sector company. It will own the track, signalling and other infrastructure. It will charge companies for running trains over its tracks.

BRITISH RAIL

British Rail will own and run passenger trains over the track owned by Railtrack. It will have to pay Railtrack for the hire of the railway lines.

If a private company shows an interest in running a passenger service, British Rail will have to compete with the private company to win the contract for the service.

PRIVATE COMPANIES

Any private company will be able to offer to run a particular passenger service (e.g. London to Brighton, or London to Glasgow). The government will then invite British Rail and other companies to make a competing bid. The company which offers the highest amount of money to the government for providing a good quality service will be awarded the franchise to run the route. On loss-making routes, the winning bid will be the one which offers to run the service for the least subsidy. The private company may choose to hire trains and carriages from British Rail. Franchises will be awarded for a limited period – e.g. five years. At the end of it, companies will have to bid again for the route.

STATIONS

Railway stations will be sold off or hired out to the highest bidder wherever possible. Private companies might be interested in stations because they can use them to sell goods and services (everything from tights to coffee) to passengers.

FREIGHT

Freight will be completely sold to private companies.

STUDY POINTS

1 Make a list of things which you think make a railway service a good service (e.g. trains run on time).

2 From what you know about British Rail today, do you think that British Rail provides a good service?

3 Look at how British Rail is to be privatised.

(a) In what ways might privatisation lead to a better deal for (i) passengers and (ii) taxpayers (who provide subsidies of £500–£1000 million per year to the railways)?

(b) How would BR workers be affected?

Nationalisation

In 1945, a Labour government came to power promising to NATIONALISE key industries in the economy. This means that it promised to buy these industries from the private sector and run them as state-owned companies. It nationalised gas and electricity (most of which were already owned by government anyway), coal, the railways, the steel industry and what is now British Airways.

It did this for the following reasons.

- One nationalised industry is able to exploit economies of scale far better than several smaller firms competing against each other. This will reduce costs and therefore prices to consumers.

- Consumers are often exploited by private monopolies. Monopolies will charge as high a price to consumers as possible in order to maximise profits. They can also get away with providing a poor service because there is no competition.

- Nationalisation of the basic industries, such as coal and steel, helps the government control the economy more easily.

- Nationalisation improves economic performance. Many private sector companies, like the railways, were seen as poorly run by incompetent managers. There was not enough investment. Nationalisation would make them far more efficient.

- Nationalisation would create companies owned by the people. The people would benefit through lower prices and a share of the profits. The companies would also take into account social costs and benefits, not just those costs and benefits relevant for making a profit.

Privatisation

In 1979, the Conservative Party gained power under Margaret Thatcher. She said the nationalised industries were inefficient. They would be far more efficient if they were sold back to the private sector. Those who favoured PRIVATISATION put forward the following arguments.

- Nationalisation often leads to higher costs and higher prices for consumers. This is because nationalised industries lack any real competition. Without the pressures of competition, workers and managers allow costs to rise.

- Privatisation leads to more *choice*. Nationalised industries only provide a narrow range of choice between products for consumers. Having competing firms provides far greater choice and that choice benefits the consumer.

- Privatisation leads to improved *quality* in goods and services.

- Private firms are much more sensitive to the demands of consumers than nationalised industries, which can sell anything because they are monopolists. Private firms are far more likely to innovate and develop new desirable products than nationalised industries.

Between 1979 and 1992, the government privatised companies such as British Aerospace (1981), Sealink Ferries (1984), Jaguar Cars (1984), British Telecom (1984), British Gas (1986), British Airways (1987), Rolls Royce (1987), British Steel (1988), British Leyland (1988), the water boards (1989) and the electricity industry (1990 and 1991). The government now intends to sell off British Coal and as much of British Rail as it can.

The major issue today is whether the government was right to privatise companies which have become monopolies. This will be considered in Unit 44.

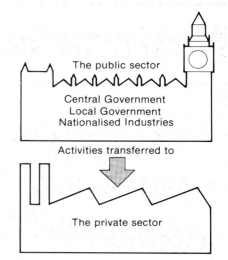

The public sector
Central Government
Local Government
Nationalised Industries

Activities transferred to

The private sector

Privatisation means selling nationalised industries to the private sector and replacing government provided goods and services by private sector provision.

CHECKPOINTS

1 What companies were nationalised between 1945 and 1951?

2 What arguments were put forward in favour of nationalisation?

3 What arguments were put forward in favour of privatisation?

4 Assume that the Post Office were to be privatised. What benefits might this bring for the consumer? What might be the costs?

COURSEWORK SUGGESTION

Find out about the privatisation of any one company. Describe the activities of the company before privatisation. How was the company privatised? Describe the activity of the company since privatisation. Analyse the changes that have occurred so far as the consumer is concerned. Try to decide whether or not the consumer has benefited from privatisation.

KEY TERMS

NATIONALISATION – the taking into state ownership of private sector firms.

PRIVATISATION – the sale of government-owned firms to the private sector.

The Control of Monopolies

Brittel is a private telephone company operating in a country where there are two other major competing telephone companies. It has 40 per cent of both the household and commercial (industry and commerce) markets for telecommunications.

Dimtel is a state-owned telephone monopoly. It has no competition in its country.

Technotel is a private telephone company. It has a near 100% per cent monopoly in the household market. In the commercial market, it has one small competitor which currently has 10 per cent of the market.

Protel is a state-owned telephone company. It has no competition in its country.

Figure 44.1 Selected statistics for previous year   £ billions

	Brittel	Dimtel	Technotel	Protel
Profits (£ billions)	1.2	0.8	3.0	—2.8
Capital employed (£ billions)	12.0	16.0	15.0	56.0
Number of employees	150 000	200 000	200 000	500 000
Income per line (£)	50	35	70	40
Average cost per minute of call (pence)				
local off peak households	1.0	1.5	2.5	free
local peak time households	2.0	2.5	5.5	5.5
local peak time industry	2.0	2.0	3.5	4.5
long distance off peak households	6.0	6.5	8.0	6.5
international peak time all users	50	55	65	55
Average time taken (days) to:				
clear fault business user	0.5	1.0	3.0	2.0
clear fault household user	1.0	3.0	6.0	2.5
install new telephone business user	5	20	30	5
install new telephone household user	6	40	70	7
Investment in new equipment, etc. (£ billions)	1.3	0.4	1.5	7.0

Privatisation

During the 1980s, the government privatised a large number of state-owned companies. Most were already in industries where there was competition. The Rover Group for instance was in the fiercely competitive car market. British Steel, although virtually a monopoly producer of steel in the UK, faced fierce competition from foreign steel producers.

However, some companies were privatised as monopolies. These were British Telecom, British Gas, the water boards and the electricity boards. What policies should the government adopt to control these and other existing private sector monopolies?

The Monopolies and Mergers Commission

In 1948, the government passed an Act of Parliament which created the Monopolies and Mergers Commission (MMC). This is a group of experts whose job it is to investigate monopoly situations. The Secretary of State for Industry, a government minister, and the Office of Fair Trading, a government department responsible for ensuring fair trading in the UK, can refer a company or an industry to the MMC. It will then look into the

S T U D Y   P O I N T S

You are a financial reporter writing for the leading newspaper in the country where Technotel is the telephone company. Write an article discussing whether or not Technotel is exploiting its monopoly position. Then discuss whether and how Technotel should be prevented by its government from exploiting consumers. Structure your report round the following.

1 Study the data carefully and think about whether Technotel is (a) making a reasonable profit; (b) charging reasonable prices to its customers; (c) providing a good service now; (d) likely to provide a good service in the future.

2 Think of ways in which a government could control a private sector company (e.g. by fixing maximim profits, fixing maximum prices or introducing competition). Which is the best way to ensure that there is an efficient supply of telephone services in your country and why?

situation and produce a report.

In the report, it makes recommendations. Sometimes, it says that there is no evidence of companies exploiting their consumers. But in other cases, it will find that consumers are suffering. It will make recommendations such as:

- prices should be lowered;
- the monopoly company should be split up or forced to sell off some of its parts;
- the monopolist should allow competition into its market;
- unfair trade practices, such as forcing customers to buy one product from the monopoly if they want to buy another, should be abandoned.

Usually, the recommendations are accepted by the government which then makes sure the monopolist complies with the recommendations.

The Privatised Monopolies

In the 1980s, the government privatised four industries, often called *utilities* because they are so important to every consumer. These were the telecommunications industry, gas, electricity and water.

British Telecom, British Gas, and the area water boards were privatised as a whole. They were not broken up so that different parts could compete with each other. This was because they were examples of NATURAL MONOPOLIES. Natural monopolies occur where one firm operating on its own in the market still cannot fully exploit economies of scale. For instance, it would obviously be more costly to have a system where two or three water pipes belonging to different companies ran to each house and households could choose which company's water to use. It is far cheaper to have a monopoly water board run one pipe to each house.

With electricity, the industry was broken up. Regional distribution boards and the national grid were privatised as a monopoly. But electricity generation – the power stations – were broken up between three companies.

Controlling the Privatised Monopolies

Each of the four privatised utilities was given a regulator when it was privatised. These were:

- Oftel for British Telecom;
- Ofgas for British Gas;
- Ofwat for the water industry;
- Offer for the electricity industry.

These regulatory bodies have different powers. But they all have a brief to protect the consumer from being exploited by the monopolist.

The most important way they do this is by fixing maximum prices for the monopoly companies. Price increases are limited by an 'RPI' formula. The RPI (retail price index) is a measure of inflation throughout the economy. So, in 1993:

- British Telecom couldn't increase prices by more than the RPI minus 7.5% per year (e.g. if inflation were 5%, British Telecom would have to have to cut prices by 1%);
- British Gas price increases are limited to RPI minus 5%;
- electricity prices are complicated but the area electricity boards aren't allowed to increase their prices to households by more than the RPI;
- water charges differ from area to area, but the average yearly increase allowed is RPI plus 5.4%.

The price formula is fixed by the regulator in advance and is reviewed every three or four years. Where prices have to fall below the rate of inflation, the industry is expected to reduce its costs mainly through the introduction of new technology. Where they rise above the rate of inflation, as with water, it is because the companies are expected to have to make substantial investments without this leading to lower costs.

The regulator also monitors standards in the industry and advises whether the industry could be made more competitive. British Gas, for instance, was forced to agree in 1992 to allow substantial competition into the gas market for industrial users.

The RPI pricing formula is designed to prevent exploitation of the consumer. At the same time, it encourages the companies to become more efficient. If they cut costs by more than the regulator thinks possible, then they can keep the difference as extra profit.

However, some economists think that the pricing formulae have been too generous to the companies. They have turned in billions of pounds of profits in recent years. They argue that prices should fall much more. The companies disagree of course!

C H E C K P O I N T S

1 What does the Monopolies and Mergers Commission do?

2 Which are the four privatised monopolies?

3 How are the privatised monopolies prevented from exploiting the consumer?

4 Would it be better for consumers if the four monopolies were taken back into government ownership? Explain your reasons.

C O U R S E W O R K S U G G E S T I O N

Look at any one of the four major privatised utilities. Describe the structure of the industry. Find out about prices and profits. Explain how the industry is regulated. Discuss whether or not the consumer is being exploited.

K E Y T E R M S

NATURAL MONOPOLY – a monopoly situation that arises because only one firm can fully exploit all the economies of scale existing in the industry.

The Location of Industry

The company

Wilsons is a medium sized company in the light engineering industry. Established for over 150 years at its site in Wimbledon in London, it has outgrown its factory premises and is seeking a new location. Four sites have been proposed. One is just half a mile away. The others are in other parts of the country. Much of the firm's business is done with firms in the South of England and on the Continent. Moving to another area of the country would increase transport costs, both for raw materials and for transport of finished products. These increased costs are likely to be offset by cheaper labour costs and site costs.

Financial statistics (£ million estimated)

	Glasgow	Washington	Cardiff	Wimbledon
Cost of site, premises and new machinery	7.2	7.0	9.2	15.6
Financial cost of moving	1.4	1.4	1.4	0.4
Change in transport costs (per year)	+0.5	+0.4	+0.2	0
Change in labour costs (per year)	−0.6	−0.6	−0.5	0
Change in other costs (per year)	−0.2	−0.2	−0.2	0

Report on staff reaction to a move

Last month, a detailed questionnaire was circulated to all salaried staff, and Grade III and above, manual workers, concerning the proposed move. It is obvious that there will be strong resistance to any move away from Wimbledon and that the company stands to lose many of its key personnel. This could impose severe costs to the company, especially if suitable staff cannot be recruited in the new location.

Glasgow
Renovated premises in the industrial heartland of Glasgow. The factory building is 10% larger than required and adjoining land would allow a doubling of capacity if needed.

Washington New Town
New purpose-built premises on an industrial park with enough land to increase production potentially by 50%.

Cardiff
New purpose-built premises on an industrial park with enough land to increase production by a potential 20%.

Wimbledon
An existing factory with no further room for expansion.

STUDY POINT

1 Which of the four sites should the board of Wilsons choose to move to? Write a 200 word report explaining your decision.

£200 million is a great deal of money
to spend on a shopping and leisure
centre. Why are the property
developers prepared to spend this
amount? Why are they looking at
Essex? And what is the significance of
the M25?

Businesses locate themselves in a
particular area for a variety of reasons,
which include:

- *Proximity to their markets.* Essex is
a large centre of population and is
next to an even larger centre –
London. The building of the M25
motorway means that shoppers can
travel longer distances more
quickly, so they will be attracted to
a large shopping centre near the
motorway. The new shopping
centre will, itself, attract firms
making goods for sale there. This is
because their transport costs will be
lower compared with firms situated
in, say, Glasgow. They will also be
able to see more quickly and easily
the sorts of products that people in
Essex want to buy. Some firms, like
hairdressers, will have no option
but to set up near their market.

- *Proximity to raw materials.* Some
industries, like coal mining, have to
be sited where there are raw
materials. Others, like the steel
industry, are sited near their raw
materials, because the cost of
transporting raw materials is high.

- *Availability of suitable labour.*
Building a shopping complex in
Essex will not be worth while if
there are no workers available to
work in the complex. There is
unlikely to be a problem in this
case. But firms do locate themselves
on the basis of being able to get the
right workers in an area. One of the
reasons why many micro-chip firms
have located themselves along the
M4 motorway is because most of the

key workers in this still small
industry live in the area.

- *Cost.* Building a complex in Essex
will not be cheap, but the land will
certainly be cheaper than if the
developers wanted to build the
shopping centre in central London.
The costs of land, of buildings, of
training workers, etc. will all play a
part in the decision of a firm as to
where to locate.

- *External economies of scale.* (These
were discussed in Unit 32.) If an
industry has grown up in an area
such that the infrastructure, the
labour force and the suppliers are
now better suited than in other
areas, then that will attract other
firms in that industry to the area.

- *Inertia.* Firms, especially small
ones, dislike moving. So a firm
based in London will tend to stay in
London, even if costs are cheaper
in, say, Glasgow. This is known as
industrial inertia. It helps to
explain, in part, why firms continue
to grow in the south of England,
despite the very high costs of
staying in the region.

- *Other factors.* These include climate
(one of the main reasons for the
growth of the cotton industry in
Lancashire was the wet climate,

which helped in the manufacture of
cotton) and safety (nuclear power
stations cannot be sited near large
centres of population).

- *Government policy.* The
government has attempted to alter
the location of industry through its
regional policy (this will be
discussed in Unit 71).

The geographical location of industry is
discussed further in Unit 66.

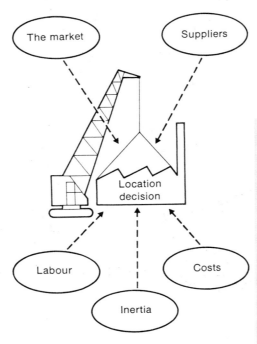

A business has to take into account many factors
when deciding where to locate new premises.

The Social Costs of Production

Global Warming

Over the past 200 years, there has been a big increase in 'greenhouse gases' in the atmosphere. These are gases, like carbon dioxide, which trap heat from the earth and prevent it escaping into space (like glass traps heat inside a greenhouse). World temperatures over the next 50 years are predicted to rise by between 1° and 3° centigrade. This will cause enormous economic costs as sea levels rise and climate changes impact on agriculture.

The increase is linked to the growth of industry and consumption in recent times. Consumers and industry produce greenhouse gases as a by-product of their activities. Twenty per cent of emissions of greenhouse gases in the UK, for instance, come from electricity power stations. We have also been chopping down the world's forests to collect timber or to turn the land into agricultural land. Trees absorb carbon dioxide. The fewer trees there are, the less gas is taken out of the atmosphere.

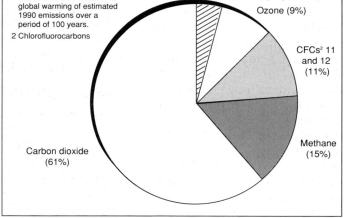

Figure 46.1 Relative contribution[1] to the greenhouse effect of various gases

1 Based on the contribution to global warming of estimated 1990 emissions over a period of 100 years.
2 Chlorofluorocarbons

Nitrous oxide (4%)
Ozone (9%)
CFCs[2] 11 and 12 (11%)
Methane (15%)
Carbon dioxide (61%)

Source: CSO, *Social Trends* 1992

Figure 46.2 Where the gases came from: UK emissions 1989

Carbon dioxide	%
Power stations	33
Other industry	23
Road transport	19
Domestic	14
Other	11

Methane	%
Deep mined coal	27
Cattle	23
Landfill sites	21
Sheep	10
Gas leakages from pipes	10
Other	9

Source: CSO, *Social Trends* 1992

Figure 46.3 World deforestation

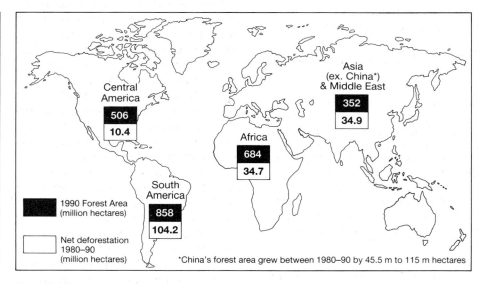

Central America
506
10.4

Asia (ex. China*) & Middle East
352
34.9

Africa
684
34.7

South America
858
104.2

■ 1990 Forest Area (million hectares)

□ Net deforestation 1980–90 (million hectares)

*China's forest area grew between 1980–90 by 45.5 m to 115 m hectares

Source: World Resources Institute, 1990; *Financial Times*, 12 February 1992

STUDY POINTS

Look at Figure 46.1

1 Which gas contributes most to global warming?

2 Which greenhouse gas also is helping to destroy the ozone layer?

Look at Figure 46.2

3 Why do coal-fired electricity power stations contribute so much to greenhouse gas emissions in the UK?

4 Why does (a) driving a car and (b) drinking milk contribute to the greenhouse effect?

Look at Figure 46.3

5 Why do you think, looking at the map, that ecologists are very worried about the destruction of the Brazilian rain forest?

Consider all the data

6 (a) How could global warming be reduced or stopped?
   (b) What would be the economic cost of these measures?

7 What would be the economic costs if nothing were done about global warming?

Costs and Benefits

In Unit 3, a distinction was made between *private* costs and benefits and *social* costs and benefits. Private costs and benefits are the costs and benefits paid and received by the individual, firm, area, country, etc. which engages in a particular activity. Take, for instance, a firm making cars. Its private costs are the money costs it has to pay for raw materials, components, workers, etc. The social costs and benefits of an activity, however, are all the costs and benefits paid and received. The firm making cars, for instance, might cause a noise problem for residents in the area of the factory. This is not a private cost for the company, because it does not have to pay anything. But it is a social cost, because local residents have to bear this cost of production.

The difference between social costs and benefits and private costs and benefits is known as an EXTERNALITY – i.e. private costs + externalities = social costs. Of what interest is this to economists and indeed to anybody?

Misallocation of Resources

Consider this extract:

'The European Court's Advocate General declared today that the UK was breaking Community Law. It had failed to meet strict EC purity standards for drinking water. The Friends of the Earth said that 12 million people in the UK received water which contained one or more pesticides above the legal EC limit. Nitrates were a particular problem too.'
(*Source:* Adapted from the *Express and Star,* 21 January 1992)

Farmers in the UK use large quantities of nitrates and pesticides to improve their crop yields. But some of the chemicals used leach out from the soil into rivers. Some liquid waste is dumped into rivers too.

There is much controversy about the effects of these chemicals on humans. The water companies say that all UK drinking water is safe to drink and can cause no ill effects. But we know that pollution in rivers kills wildlife and plantlife. Could it be affecting people's health too?

The EC has decided, by imposing strict drinking water standards, that there is currently a misallocation of resources. Too much pollution, an externality, is being created and not enough resources are being used to clear up the problem.

Policy Options

Negative externalities lead to a misallocation of resources. So what should the government do?

Traditionally, governments have responded by placing limits or bans on activities. In the UK, a number of agencies including the National Rivers Authority, have the power to limit pollution by producers. If a firm exceeds a given limit, it can be taken to court and fined.

Economists, though, favour market solutions particularly using taxes and subsidies. A limit on how much pollution a firm can create doesn't give any incentive to that firm to reduce pollution below the limit.

But this would be different if pollution were taxed according to how much was being produced. For instance, think what would happen if the government imposed a 50% tax on nitrates used by farmers. Nitrate pollution would be cut because farmers would have an incentive to reduce their use of nitrate fertilisers.

The money raised in taxes would equal the cost to society of the pollution. The money could then be used to compensate the people who suffer as a result of the pollution. Or it could be used to reduce the effects of the pollution. In the case of farm nitrates, the money could be given to the water companies to clean up the water before it is sent into homes for drinking.

C H E C K P O I N T S

1 Using an example, explain what is meant by an 'externality'.

2 A garage seeks to set up on waste ground opposite a row of houses. What externalities might the garage produce for local residents?

3 The Central Electricity Generating Board decide to build a nuclear power station on the coast of East Anglia. What externalities might this power station produce?

4 Why need a company not take into account the externalities it produces when making its decisions?

5 Find out why car exhaust emissions damage the environment. Why would a tax on petrol reduce the externality created?

6 A firm dumps waste into a river which then seriously pollutes that river. Do you think it should (a) be stopped from dumping any waste into the river OR (b) be made to pay to clean up the pollution it has created? Give reasons for your answer.

C O U R S E W O R K S U G G E S T I O N

Examine a local environmental issue. Describe the background to the issue. Analyse the private costs and benefits and the social costs and benefits involved. Try to decide how the issue should be resolved in order to maximise the level of social profit.

K E Y   T E R M

EXTERNALITY – social costs minus private costs, i.e. that part of costs that is not borne by the individual consumer, producer, etc. whose activities have given rise to it.

Data Response Questions
Units 43–46

Unit 43 Nationalisation and Privatisation

Competitive bids urged for fire services

Local authorities should sell off their fire services to private companies, a report out today urges.

The Adam Smith Institute argues that the fire service at the moment is inefficient. Costs are constantly rising. There is little innovative use of equipment or manpower. Managers find it difficult to deploy staff as they want to because of old-fashioned working practices.

The report states that local authorities should be free to buy in the cheapest fire service subject to minimum quality constraints. That way they would get best value for money for the taxpayer.

Source: Adapted from the *Financial Times*, 18 September 1989

1 Explain the arguments put forward by the Adam Smith Institute in favour of privatising the fire service. *(6 marks)*

2 Who might gain and how would they gain from privatisation of the fire services? *(6 marks)*

3 What arguments can you think of against the proposal in the report? *(3 marks)*

Questions for Unit 44

1 What is the role of Ofgas? *(4 marks)*

2 Explain why British Gas had to cut its prices in May 1992. *(4 marks)*

3 (a) Why did British Gas not want to reduce prices in May?
   (b) Give one other reason why British Gas may have wanted to keep prices at a higher level. *(4 marks)*

4 Why does British Gas need a regulator when a company like ICI or Ford UK doesn't have one? *(3 marks)*

Unit 44 The Control of Monopolies

Climbdown on gas bills 'still not enough'

Gas bills are to be cut by 3 per cent, after British Gas caved in to the threat of legal action to stop it 'ripping off' customers.

Eighteen million homes and small businesses will benefit from the victory by the Government watchdog Ofgas.

It will mean a saving of about £13 a year for a typical family and boost Chancellor Norman Lamont's battle against inflation.

The climbdown came only days after consumers' champion Sir James McKinnon, head of the regulatory body set up to protect customers when the business was privatised in 1986, read the riot act.

But last night he made it clear that he was still not satisfied and intends to get even more money back for customers.

In the commons, Mr Major welcomed the news, saying it illustrated very clearly the benefits of properly regulated privatisation.

On hold

There is no doubt that the victory for consumers blows a hole through claims by Labour opponents of State industry sell-offs that the official regulators would have no teeth.

Lorry driver's son Sir James, 63, who climbed the career ladder as a chartered accountant, warned that the price-cut announcement by British Gas boss Bob Evans meant that the threat of legal action had been put on hold – not abandoned.

Yesterday's decision to cut tariffs by 3 per cent from July 1 was the 'minimum acceptable', Sir James declared. He added: 'Customers can be assured that any attempt by the monopolist to overcharge will be stamped on.'

The Ofgas chief was furious in March when Mr Evans, whose salary last year rose by 17.6 per cent to £435,000, including an £84,500 bonus, said the industry would merely be freezing its prices from April 1 – not reducing them.

There was public outrage because, with inflation falling, the index-linked system under which British Gas fixes its tariffs could have meant a reduction of 2p a therm – the gas consumption unit. And though down on last year because of the mild winter, gas profits were still £932million for the first three months of 1992.

It prompted the outburst from Sir James: 'British Gas cannot get away with ripping off customers!' Weeks went by, but the only response from Mr Evans was to attack what he called 'the creeping power' of watchdogs.

Last Wednesday, his patience expended, the Ofgas chief issued his 'give way or be sued' warning. Yesterday's cut represents a drop of only 1.7p a therm, hence the warning that legal action is still possible. And Sir James is also unhappy that the cuts are not being backdated to April 1.

Sheepish

British Gas claimed sheepishly that a price reduction had been on the cards anyway, without the legal threat. Finance director Barry Reynolds insisted that the company had been intent on maintaining 'a degree of stability', rather than moving tariffs continuously up and down.

But Ian Powe, of the non-statutory Gas Consumers' Council, commented acidly: 'A reduction of this size can only mean that British Gas either got its sums wrong or decided to hoodwink its customers.'

Source: Daily Mail, 15 May 1992

Unit 45 The Location of Industry

SOUTH KESTEVEN LINCOLNSHIRE

'Tis my delight!

☐ LOW RENTS ☐ LOW RVs ☐
☐ START-UP GRANTS ☐
☐ SETTLED SKILLED LABOUR ☐
☐ A1 LOCATION ☐

Contact Chief Executive's Dept for up-to-date
advice on **Grantham (0476) 591591**

Note: RV stands for 'Rateable Value', the value on which business rates are assessed.

1 Which area of the country is trying to attract businesses in
the advertisement? *(1 mark)*

2 What attraction does the area offer? *(4 marks)*

3 Explain whether or not any of the following companies
would be attracted to the area:
  (a) a computer sales company which has strong business
  in London as well as Yorkshire and Tyneside:
  (b) a large car manufacturer based in the West Midlands
  wanting to build a new plant;
  (c) an international hotel company wanting to build a
  new hotel. *(10 marks)*

Unit 46 The Social Costs of Production

New Euro tax threat to price of petrol

A new EC energy tax to counter global warming could push up the price of a gallon of petrol by 4p and diesel by 5p.

The European Commission today urged EC governments to back the proposals and off-set the impact on consumers by cutting tax elsewhere.

The commission agreed to propose an energy tax to reduce harmful emissions of carbon dioxide. But the measure would take effect only if other industrialised countries followed suit.

The decision to propose a directive, rather than a recom-mendation, was taken by the 17 EC commissioners.

Ambitious

A final decision on the contro-versial tax on fossil fuels and other non-renewable energy sources must be taken by the 12 European Community governments.

The plans are the most ambitious and far-reaching in the EC's campaign against environmental pollution.

Britain has expressed reservations about the idea.

It has warned that although such a tax would produce some switching from coal to gas, there is still too much uncertainty about how much carbon dioxide the EC will be producing by the end of the century.

Source: Express and Star, 13 May 1992

1 (a) What environmental problem does the burning of
  petrol lead to?
  (b) Why is this an example of an externality? *(5 marks)*

2 (a) How is the European Community planning to deal
  with the problem?
  (b) Use a demand and supply curve diagram to show why
  the consumption of petrol will be changed. *(8 marks)*

3 Why might the measure proposed have little impact on
the problem? *(3 marks)*

Essay Questions
Units 43–46

1 'The Government plans to sell off the whole of the railway
industry to the private sector.'
  (a) Give four reasons why the Government might want to
  sell off the railway industry. *(8 marks)*
  (b) How might the consumer be affected by this privatisation? *(6 marks)*
  (c) How could the industry be privatised without creating
  a private sector monopoly? *(6 marks)*

2 (a) Give five reasons why a firm making cars might decide
  to open a new factory in one place rather than another.
  (10 marks)
  (b) What would the costs and benefits be to the local
  economy of the establishment of such a factory in the
  area?
  (10 marks)

National Income

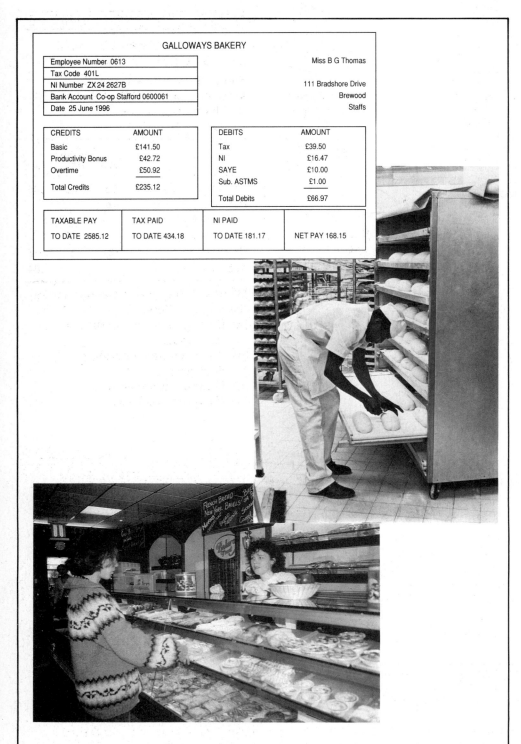

GALLOWAYS BAKERY

Employee Number 0613
Tax Code 401L
NI Number ZX 24 2627B
Bank Account Co-op Stafford 0600061
Date 25 June 1996

Miss B G Thomas

111 Bradshore Drive
Brewood
Staffs

CREDITS	AMOUNT	DEBITS	AMOUNT
Basic	£141.50	Tax	£39.50
Productivity Bonus	£42.72	NI	£16.47
Overtime	£50.92	SAYE	£10.00
		Sub. ASTMS	£1.00
Total Credits	£235.12		
		Total Debits	£66.97

TAXABLE PAY	TAX PAID	NI PAID	
TO DATE 2585.12	TO DATE 434.18	TO DATE 181.17	NET PAY 168.15

STUDY POINTS

1 What is the link between these three illustrations?

2 Use these illustrations to show how money flows round the economy.

3 Construct a circular flow diagram showing the transactions in the three illustrations.

4 What would be the effect if the Government imposed a 10% tax on the sale of bread?

'GNP to rise by 3% next year.'

GNP or gross national product is a measure of *national income*. It measures the value of the goods and services produced over a period of time by an economy, which must also equal what is spent and earned in the economy as a whole.

National income can be measured in a number of different ways:

- **GROSS DOMESTIC PRODUCT** (GDP). This is the value of all the goods and services produced over a period of time within a country.

- **GROSS NATIONAL PRODUCT** (GNP) is GDP plus what is called 'net property income from abroad'. The citizens and organisations of one country may own assets such as firms or land in another country or may have lent money to another country. These assets will earn interest, profits and dividends, which can then be brought back to the home country to spend, and so they are part of the income of that country. UK *net property income from abroad* is the difference between income earned abroad and what the UK has to pay to foreigners who own assets in the UK.

- **NATIONAL INCOME** is GNP minus an allowance for *depreciation*. Over a period of time, the value of the existing stock of capital in an economy – the machines, buildings, etc. – declines through wear and tear. So depreciation needs to be taken away from the gross income of the economy to get at the true value of what the country has earned after allowing for the wear and tear of the nation's stock of physical wealth.

The Circular Flow of Income

The **CIRCULAR FLOW OF INCOME** is a way of showing how income circulates in the economy. Figure 48.1 shows a simple economy with no government sector and no foreign trade. There are only households and firms in the economy. Households spend money on goods and services produced by firms. What households spend must equal exactly the value of what firms have produced for sale – i.e. national expenditure must equal national output. Households get the money to buy these goods and services by supplying the factors of production they own to firms. Households earn their income by working for firms, hiring out the land and the machines they own, etc. So income must equal expenditure. Hence:

National Income = National Expenditure
= National Output.

In the real economy, this is still true. Matters are complicated, however, because there is a government sector and there is foreign trade. In Figure 47.1, it was assumed that households spent all their income on the output produced by firms, and that firms produced only goods and services for consumers. In Figure 47.2, this assumption is relaxed.

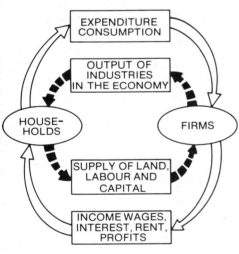

Figure 47.1

- Money is added to the circular flow, because firms – as well as producing goods for consumers – also *invest*. Governments spend money on public expenditure programmes and foreigners buy exports. Investment, government (public) spending and exports are known as *injections* into the circular flow of income.

- Money leaks out of the circular flow because both households and firms have to pay taxes to the government; money is spent on imports (i.e. goods and services not produced by UK firms); and firms and households do not spend all their income, but save some of it. Savings, taxes and imports are known as *leakages* or *withdrawals* from the circular flow.

At any point in time, money going into the circular flow must equal the money leaving it – i.e. injections must equal withdrawals. But the amount of money going round the circular flow of income can and does change over time. National income tends to grow.

Figure 47.2

What this might mean to the ordinary citizen is discussed in Unit 64.

1 **What is the difference between GDP, GNP and national income?**

2 **Figure 47.3 shows national accounts. Copy out the table and fill in the missing figures.**
   Figure 47.3

		£ billion	
	1995	1996	1997
Gross domestic product	100	102	105
Net property income from abroad	+4		
Gross national product		107	
Depreciation	−6	−5	−7
National income			104

3 **What will happen to the income in the circular flow:**
   (a) **if investment expenditure increases;**
   (b) **if government spending declines;**
   (c) **if saving increases;**
   (d) **if exports decline?**

Consider a small part of the circular flow of income. Take your household and the employers for whom members of your household work. Show to whom money is paid from your household (e.g. your local shop). Try to show how those firms pass on that money to other firms or back to households. Find out how the employers receive money to pay for the wages, salaries, interest, etc. earned by your household. Show how the government and the foreign sector fit in to all this. Explain why the circular flow of income in the real world is much more complex than the simple textbook model. Try to assess the extent to which income tax cuts by the government might help to increase income in the circular flow and create jobs.

NATIONAL INCOME – the value of income, output and expenditure of an economy over a period of time.

GROSS NATIONAL PRODUCT – the value of national income, not including the value of wear and tear (or *depreciation*) on the capital stock of the economy.

GROSS DOMESTIC PRODUCT – the value of all goods and services produced within an economy over a period of time.

CIRCULAR FLOW OF INCOME – a term used to describe the flow of money round the economy as it passes between consumers and producers.

Output

Figure 48.1 The change in the composition of output, 1750 to the present day

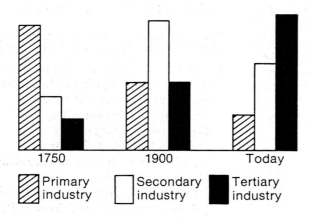

Primary industry | Secondary industry | Tertiary industry

Figure 48.2 Value of national output by industry (value added, gross domestic product at factor cost), 1979 and 1991

	1979 £bn	1991 £bn
Agriculture, forestry and fishing	3677	7102
Energy and water supply	13838	24334
Manufacturing	48714	106995
Construction	10617	36085
Distribution, hotels and catering, repairs	22863	70151
Transport and communication	13203	34031
Banking, finance, insurance, business services and leasing	20776	87260
Ownership of dwellings	10307	30719
Public administration, national defence and compulsory social security	11438	31524
Education and health services	12377	45143
Other services	9224	30983
Total	178797	504327

Source: CSO, *United Kingdom National Accounts* 1992

Figure 48.3 The rise in spending: 1991 consumers' spending as a percentage of 1979

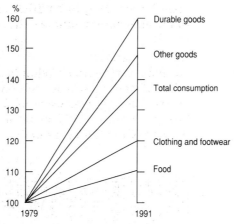

Source: CSO, *Economic Trends Annual Supplement 1992; Monthly Digest of Statistics,* April 1992

Figure 48.4 Stagnant manufacturing output: output 1991 as a percentage of 1979

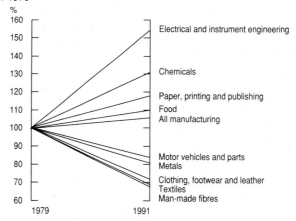

Source: CSO, *Annual Abstract of Statistics* 1990; *Monthly Digest of Statistics,* April 1992

S T U D Y   P O I N T S

Read the section on 'Primary, Secondary and Tertiary Industry' in the text. Look at Figure 48.1

1 How has the composition of output in the UK economy changed?

Look at Figure 48.2

2 Make a list of primary, secondary and tertiary industries.

3 Estimate the proportion of total output in the economy in 1991 produced by each of the three sectors of industry.

4 How has the output of each of the sectors changed in size between 1979 and 1991?

Look at Figure 48.3

5 Why might you expect from Figure 48.3 that manufacturing output should have gone up over the period?

Look at Figure 48.4

6 How has output in manufacturing industry changed between 1979 and 1991?

7 What are the likely effects on jobs and incomes in the UK of the changes in output in manufacturing shown in Figure 48.4?

Primary, Secondary and Tertiary Industry

The factors of production – land, labour and capital – are combined to produce goods and services. Choices have to be made about what to produce. What do the economic decision-makers in the UK economy choose to produce?

The value of total production in the economy is known as total OUTPUT. This can be measured by calculating the value of production in the three sectors of the economy.

- The PRIMARY sector of the economy is where raw materials (i.e. the factor of production called land) are being mined, grown, collected or cut down. Coal mining, agriculture and North Sea oil production are the three most important primary industries in the UK.

- The SECONDARY or *manufacturing* sector of the economy turns raw materials into goods – everything from steel bars and tanks to flower pots and yoghurt.

- The TERTIARY or *service* sector of the economy produces services ranging from education to prisons to tourism to defence.

Changes Over Time

The economy changes over time. The UK economy has developed in a broadly similar way to other developed economies round the world. Three hundred years ago, it was still an economy that was essentially agricultural. The primary sector of the economy was the most important wealth-creating sector of the economy.

Then came the Industrial Revolution, which started about 200 years ago. A series of important inventions led to the development of new manufactured products and new cheaper ways of producing those products. People moved to towns and cities to work in the new factories. Manufacturing became the most important sector of the economy. During the twentieth century, it has been the tertiary or service sector of the economy that has seen the fastest growth. With rising incomes, consumers spend a larger and larger proportion of their incomes on services such as health, education and financial services. This process is shown in Figures 48.1–48.2.

Deindustrialisation

Manufacturing industry may have been shrinking as a *proportion* of total output, but the demand for manufactured goods has grown as household incomes have increased. Figure 48.3 shows how spending on a variety of manufactured goods has risen in the UK.

Yet Figure 48.4 shows that total manufacturing output has hardly grown in the 1980s. Indeed, total manufacturing output in 1991 was slightly lower than in 1973. Whilst some industries have performed well, others have suffered very badly.

The fall in manufacturing output in the UK is a very worrying trend. It is known as DEINDUSTRIALISATION – losing industry. It is worrying because less industry means fewer jobs. Between 1973 and 1979, over half a million jobs were lost in manufacturing industry. But between 1979 and 1991, nearly 2.5 million jobs were lost. It is also worrying because less industry means lower income. While foreign countries grow better off, partly by selling their products to the UK, Britons see their incomes growing at a much slower pace. It is worrying too because the extra imports of manufactures give the UK balance of payments problems which will be discussed in Unit 78.

CHECKPOINTS

1. State whether each of the following are examples of primary industry, secondary industry or tertiary industry: (a) hairdressing; (b) copper mining; (c) car manufacturing; (d) farming; (e) education; (f) financial services; (g) steel; (h) forestry; (i) oil extraction; (j) garage selling petrol; (k) oil processing; (l) British Rail; (m) health.

2. Which is the fastest-growing sector of the UK economy at the moment and why?

3. Assume you were given £50 for your birthday. What would you spend this money on? Which sectors of the economy would benefit as a result?

4. What is meant by 'deindustrialisation'? What is the effect of deindustrialisation on (a) workers; (b) consumers; (c) foreign firms; and (d) the total income of the UK economy?

COURSEWORK SUGGESTION

Examine the industrial base of your local economy. *Either* try to find out figures for the output of different industries in your local area by contacting the local council, or borough; *or* use figures from *Regional Trends* (published by HMSO) for your local region. Describe how the output of different sectors of the local economy has changed over time. Analyse why this has taken place. Try to assess whether or not these changes have been beneficial for the local economy.

KEY TERMS

OUTPUT – that which is produced by the factors of production.

PRIMARY INDUSTRY – industry that extracts raw materials from the earth, such as coal, fish or wheat.

SECONDARY INDUSTRY – industry that processes primary products into manufactured goods.

TERTIARY INDUSTRY – industry that provides a service, such as banking, hairdressing or retailing.

DEINDUSTRIALISATION – the process whereby an economy loses established industries, which are not replaced by new industries.

The Standard of Living

Figure 49.1 Annual income per person in the UK (personal disposable income per capita at 1985 prices)

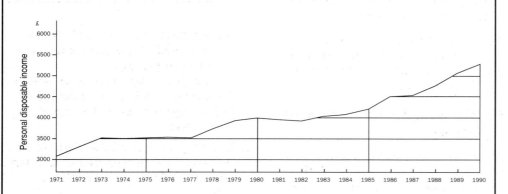

Source: CSO, *Economic Trends*, May 1992

Figure 49.2 Housing standards (GB)

Percentage of households lacking sole use of	1971	1989/90
Fixed bath/shower	12	2
WC inside building	13	2

Figure 49.3 Availability of durable goods

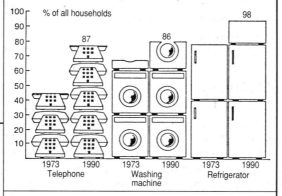

Figure 49.4 Holidays: number taken each year by adult residents of Great Britain

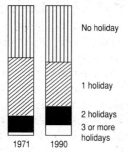

No holiday

1 holiday

2 holidays

3 or more holidays

1971 1990

Note: A holiday is defined as a period of 4 or more nights away from home which is considered by the respondent to be a holiday.

Source: Figures 49.1–49.5: CSO, *Social Trends*, 1992

Figure 49.5 Unemployment, UK

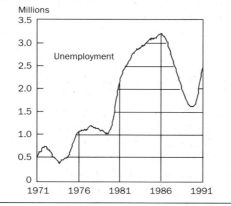

Is the UK better off today than it was 20 or 50 or 200 years ago? How is the UK doing compared to countries such as France, the USA or Japan? These are important questions and they relate to the measurement of a country's **STANDARD OF LIVING**. There is no precise measure of a country's standard of living, but economists produce a variety of statistics which help provide answers.

National Income

The set of statistics most commonly linked to measurement of the standard of living is national income. At first sight, this makes a lot of sense. If your income were to go up by £10 a week, surely your standard of living would improve? Unfortunately, the answer is 'not necessarily'. National income statistics have a number of important limitations.

- National income statistics only measure the value of goods and services sold, or incomes actually paid in the economy. Much 'expenditure' and 'income' goes unrecorded. Housewives, for instance, produce goods and services, but they do not receive a wage for that. DIY is another example. If you pay a decorator to paint your house, that will be recorded as part of national income. If you do it yourself, it will not be recorded. The end product – a painted house – is the same, however. Changes in the amount of unrecorded output, expenditure and income can have a very important effect on the standard of living, but they will not show up on national income statistics.

- National income statistics measure the value of income, including the inflation element. This inflation element must be taken out of the statistic if any sensible comparison is to be made.

- National income may grow, but that does not necessarily mean that

STUDY POINTS

1 Take each of the pieces of data in turn and explain what changes have taken place since the early 1970s.

2 Have these changes resulted in an improvement or a deterioration in people's standard of living on average? Explain your answer carefully.

3 If you were to analyse how standards of living have changed over time, what other figures might you want to consider apart from those shown above?

4 What do you expect to happen to living standards over the next fifteen years and why?

everybody will be better off. Some groups in society may be a great deal better off, and others may actually be worse off. National income only shows how the economy *as a whole* is doing.

- Income may grow, but so too may population. So it is far better to consider income per head of the population if any comparison is to be made.

- National income statistics do not show any improvements in the quality of products. National income may stay the same over time, but if the quality of products is rising, then the standard of living should be improving too.

- Goods and services may be produced, but they do not necessarily help increase the standard of living of the population. Cigarettes, for instance, arguably lead to a lowering of the standard of living for smokers and non-smokers, but they are included in national income.

- The social costs of production – pollution, stress, crime, etc. – are not recorded as part of national income, yet they need to be included in a measure of the standard of living.

Consumption and Ownership Statistics

An alternative way of judging living standards is to consider consumption and ownership patterns. This is particularly useful in developing countries, where national income figures are even less reliable as a measure of the standard of living than in developed countries. Consumption and ownership statistics might include:

- the number of households that own a cooker, television set, refrigerator, car etc;

- the number of patients there are per doctor;
- the number of children per thousand of the population who die each year;
- the average food intake per person;
- the proportion of the population that can read or write.

These statistics should give an indication of what proportion of the population is enjoying a minimum standard of living.

Social and Environmental Statistics

A further way of judging living standards is to look at social and environmental indicators, such as:

- the crime rate;
- whether there are free elections in the country;
- the amount of pollution there is in the country;
- the suicide rate.

Conclusions

By considering these different measures, it is possible to have some idea of how standards of living have changed over time, but it is not possible to come up with a precise measure. Ultimately, any answer must be based on a value judgement of how to weigh all the different components that go to make up a country's standard of living.

C H E C K P O I N T S

1 From the figures in Figure 49.6, calculate for the period 1990–2000:
   (a) the change in national income (at current prices) in pounds;
   (b) the percentage change in national income (at current prices);

Figure 49.6

Year	1990	2000
National income (£ million)	9000	11000
Population (million)	9	10
Price level (1990 = 100)	100	110

   (c) the change in national income per head of the population (at current prices);
   (d) the percentage change in prices.
To what extent has the standard of living improved over the period 1990–2000?

2 Does a growth in DIY activity in an economy indicate an increase in the standard of living or a decline? Why?

3 Why might an increase in (a) cigarette consumption; (b) butter consumption; (c) consumption of alcoholic drink lead to a rise in national income, but a decline in the standard of living?

4 Why are social and environmental factors important in the standard of living of a population?

C O U R S E W O R K   S U G G E S T I O N

Compare changes in the standard of living for the UK economy with that of a particular individual or household. Interview an older person or persons, such as your grandparents. Ask them questions about the standard of living as they remember it in a particular year (e.g. 1950) and their standard of living today. Gather statistics from sources such as the *Annual Abstract of Statistics, Social Trends* and *Economic Trends Annual Supplement* (all published by HMSO). Social history books of the period might be of help, too. Compare the way in which living standards have changed for the person you have interviewed and for the nation as a whole. Try to assess the extent to which both are better off now than in the past.

K E Y   T E R M

STANDARD OF LIVING – how well off an individual or a nation is at a point in time. One important, but imperfect measure of the standard of living is the level of national income.

The Financial System of the UK

BARCLAYS PERSONAL OVERDRAFTS
More help when you need it.

20% off

SALE FINAL WE...

BARCLAYS CONNECT
The cheque you don't have to write.

AnyBank
Holding Branch

BARCLAYS CONNECT

VISA

539 7864 5389 1004 CLASSIC

10/88 EXPIRES END 10/92 CV
TURNER
99-93 10763210

Lloyds Bank

VALUE COVER
HOME CONTENTS
INSURANCE

INTRODUCING BARCLAYS TESSA

Tax Exempt Special Savings Account – TESSA for short, is a rare opportunity to save and not pay a single penny in tax!

When you save with a Barclays TESSA for five years, all the interest earned on your money is paid to you entirely free of tax.

Who can save with a Barclays TESSA?
Anyone who's saving or about to start saving
Especially anyone who's paying tax.
Putting some money by for a child's educ...
Home improvement...
Retirement? A specia...
– maybe even th...
honeymoon? Or...
security that sav...
A Barclays T...
good sense.

The tax benefits are so good that th...
allows only one account per pers...
be aged 18 or over. Although joi...
allowed, both you and your pa...
Barclays TESSA and benefit...

Several ways to save.
Barclays TESSA is a ver...
to save.
You can save by trans...
up to the permitted...
Barclays TESSA.
Or you may prefer...
You choose whe...
monthly, quarter...
free to make a...
add to your s...

...CLAYS CAPPED RATE MORTGAGE

Take advantage of Barclays Capped Rate mortgag...
8.99% Capped until 30th June 1993. See A...
This is guaranteed as the maximum rate you w...
the end of June 1993.
If our variable Barclays mortgage rate falls belo...
rate during that period, you will automatic...
paying the lower rate, there is no deferred in...
about.
We will offer you a choice at the end of th...
of taking a fixed rate, or alternatively s...
...lays Mortgage Rate.

THE BARCLAYS
BANK ACC%UNT
Three options and no transaction charges.

+ + + Y%U'RE
BETTER %FF
TALKING T%
BARCLAYS

High-street Institutions

Most adults in the UK today have a bank or building society account of some sort. This was not true 50 years ago. The growth of *financial institutions*, such as banks, has come about because the increase in real incomes has meant that customers have demanded more and more sophisticated financial services.

Banks, building societies and other financial institutions are *financial intermediaries*. What this means is that they specialise in acting as go-betweens amongst customers. Customers fall into three main categories: ordinary people ('personal customers'), firms and government. There are three main services which these go-betweens supply:

- as *borrowers*, they enable customers to keep money in a safe place, and to earn interest on their savings;
- as *lenders*, they enable customers to borrow money to finance spending;
- as *transferrers of money*, they enable customers to pay bills, and get money from place to place and from customer to customer.

Most financial institutions aim to make a profit. They do this by charging for transfers of money and by lending out money at higher rates of interest than those at which they borrow.

Probably the most important high-street financial institutions are BANKS. They borrow money from customers either through *current accounts*, which pay customers little or no interest, but do give them facilities for issuing cheques and other ways of transferring money; or through *deposit accounts* which give higher rates of interest on savings. They lend to customers through loans or overdrafts. Customers use their bank to transfer money through the *cheque* system.

Some banks, often called *secondary banks* or *finance houses,* specialise in providing credit loans and hire-purchase agreements. They also accept savings and many provide a limited cheque system.

Building societies specialise in providing loans for property (mortgages). Almost all the money to finance these loans is borrowed from ordinary customers through their branch network. Many building societies now offer cheque book accounts like current accounts at banks.

The London Money Markets

Very large borrowers, such as governments and financial institutions, themselves borrow and lend money on the LONDON MONEY MARKETS. For instance, Barclays Bank may borrow £200 million from other banks and use this money to lend to the government. Or the Halifax Building Society may have borrowed £50 million more from customers than it can lend in mortgages. Rather than let that £50 million do nothing, it will lend the money on the London money markets to earn interest.

Some of the main institutions in the London money markets are:

- *The Bank of England.* Owned by the government, it is responsible for policing the money markets and making sure that banks and other institutions act properly. It is responsible for the implementation of monetary policy (discussed in Unit 70). It is the government's banker, and is responsible for handling the government's revenue and spending as well as its borrowing. It is responsible for issuing new notes and coins. As the bank to other banks, it is the 'lender of the last resort', willing to lend money to the banking system to prevent banks going bankrupt.

- DISCOUNT HOUSES. These are specialist institutions that borrow money for as short a period as 24 hours and lend it out to governments and other financial institutions on a slightly broader basis. They hold a crucial role in London, because they are the only institutions allowed to borrow money from the Bank of England in its role as lender of the last resort.

- The STOCK EXCHANGE. This is probably the most famous institution in the City of London, although it is not the most important. It is a market for the buying and selling of stocks and shares. It is important for the government, because the government borrows a great deal of money by issuing stocks. It is also important for companies since the existence of a market for second-hand shares allows companies to issue new shares more easily.

C H E C K P O I N T S

1 What is a 'financial intermediary'?

2 Why would a firm use a bank?

3 Compare the activities of finance houses and building societies.

4 What are the functions of the Bank of England?

5 How do you think a discount house makes a profit?

6 What is the role of the Stock Exchange?

C O U R S E W O R K   S U G G E S T I O N

Research one financial institution. Describe its activities. Assess the role that it plays in the economy. Try to evaluate the extent to which it secures a better allocation of resources in the economy.

K E Y   T E R M S

BANK – a financial institution that specialises in borrowing, lending and transferring money.

LONDON MONEY MARKETS – the term used to describe the market for money borrowed and lent by and between banks, finance houses, discount houses, the Bank of England and other financial institutions.

DISCOUNT HOUSES – financial institutions that borrow and lend at very short notice on the London money markets.

THE STOCK EXCHANGE – a market for new and second-hand government stock and for second-hand shares.

The Creation of Credit

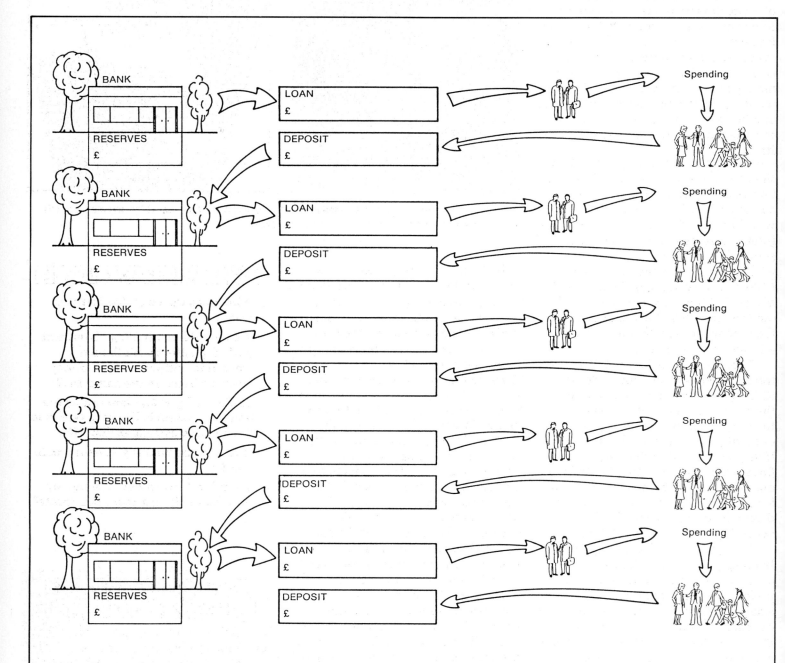

S T U D Y P O I N T S

Assume that there is only one bank in the economy. Any money which the bank lends out is eventually redeposited in the bank by other customers. The government of the country has ordered that the bank must keep a fixed percentage of its total deposits in the form of notes and coins. A customer enters the bank and opens an account with £100 worth of notes and coins.

1 Copy out the diagram above and fill in the £ figures, assuming that the bank has to keep 50% of its deposits in cash. If the process carries on until the bank can lend out no more money, how much cash will it have in its vaults? How much money will it have lent out in total? How much money will the bank have deposited with it?

2 What would your answers be to Task 1 if instead of keeping 50% of deposits in notes and coins the bank has to keep: (a) 25% and (b) 10%.

Credit Creation

How much money have you got in the bank? How much money does the bank have available to repay you and all the other customers it has borrowed from? It may come as a surprise to know that for every £1 deposited in a bank, the average bank has only got about 1p in cash. If everybody wanted his or her money back at the same time, the bank would go bankrupt, however big it was and however well run it was. Why is this the case and of what importance is it?

Imagine a customer depositing £100 in notes into a bank account. The bank knows from past experience that the customer is unlikely to want to withdraw that £100 in total in the near future. Assume that past experience shows that on average only £1 is withdrawn on any one day for every £100 deposited with the bank. That means that the bank can safely lend out the other £99. It earns interest on the money lent and therefore it makes a profit on the transaction.

Therefore £99 is lent out. What will the borrowers of that money do with it? They may well spend it, and then the firms or individuals who receive the money are likely to redeposit part or all of that money in a bank account. If they deposit all of the £99, the bank finds itself again in a position to lend out more money, because it need only keep 1% of the £99 to satisfy customer demands for repayment. So the bank keeps 99p and lends out £98.01.

This process of depositing and lending goes on for as long as customers have too much cash and prefer to deposit it in the bank. In our example, the bank ends up with deposits of £100 + £99 + £98.01 + £97.03 + £96.06 + £95.10 + . . . which added up comes to no less than £10 000. This process is what is known as CREDIT CREATION. Banks have the power to increase the amount of bank money (not by the manufacture of notes and coins of course, because

only the Bank of England and the Royal Mint can do that) in circulation.

It is important to realise that when it is said that banks can create money, it is not their own money they are creating. They are creating money for their customers to borrow and lend. If the banks did not lend money, then their lenders could not spend it, and so other customers could not receive money to put back into the banks.

It is also important to realise that banks can only create a limited amount of money. The limits to this creation are fixed by the sorts of assets that banks have to keep when they borrow new money from their customers. For instance, if the banks have to keep £1 in every £100 deposited in the form of notes and coins in order to satisfy the day-to-day cash needs of their customers, then they cannot borrow £10 000 million from their customers and only have £10 million in cash. If they only have £10 million in cash, then they can only borrow a maximum of £1000 million from their customers. Any more and they are threatened with bankruptcy, if they cannot repay customers their money on a day-to-day basis.

Two ways in which money is created – the Royal Mint coining money and banks lending money which will be redeposited as new money with the banking system.

CHECKPOINTS

1 What does the term 'bankruptcy' mean?

2 Why would any bank go bankrupt, if all depositors with the bank wanted to withdraw their money from the bank on the same day?

3 Explain why £1000 lent out by the banking system is likely to return to the banking system as deposits.

4 How can the banking system create credit?

5 What limits the amount of money that the banking system can create?

COURSEWORK SUGGESTION

Using figures from the latest copy of the *Bank of England Quarterly Bulletin*, describe the balance sheet of the UK clearing banks. From textbooks or other material, find out what legal requirements exist for the clearing banks to hold particular types of assets. From this, explain what limits there are to the banking system's ability to create credit.

KEY TERMS

CREDIT CREATION – the ability of the banking system to create new deposits and loans, and hence to increase the money supply.

Data Response Questions
Units 47–51

Unit 47 National Income

National Income 1990 (£ billions)

Gross domestic product	550.6
Net property income from abroad	4.0
Capital depreciation	61.0

Source: CSO, United Kingdom National Accounts, 1991

1 Calculate (a) gross national product, and (b) national income in 1990. *(2 marks)*

2 Explain what is measured by gross domestic product. *(3 marks)*

3 (a) What is meant by capital depreciation?
   (b) Why should it be subtracted from the nation's gross income to measure better the value of its income? *(5 marks)*

Unit 48 Output

Percentage shares of output in the industrialised countries of the world

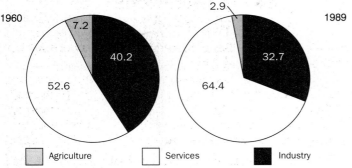

1960: 7.2, 40.2, 52.6
1989: 2.9, 32.7, 64.4

Agriculture Services Industry

Source: The Treasury, Economic Briefing, November 1991

1 Describe how the shares of primary, secondary and tertiary industry have changed between 1960 and 1989 in the world's industrialised economies. *(4 marks)*

2 Outline four reasons why this change has occurred. *(8 marks)*

3 Do you think it is likely that service industries will carry on increasing as a percentage of total output? *(3 marks)*

Unit 49 The Standard of Living

Is society becoming richer and richer?

Most people believe that the gross national product – the national income – provides a good measure of changes in our economic performance. But if we are to decide whether people are better off now than, say 30, 50 or 100 years ago we must look at other more powerful measures of change.

National income is a poor measure of changes in standards of living for a number of reasons. For instance, over the past 30 years national income has risen due to the fact that more women have gone out to work. But the loss of services produced in the home as a result has not been deducted from national income because they were never included in the first place.

Or take defence spending. Does rising spending on defence indicate that the country is better off or in fact that it is worse off because we feel more threatened by other countries?

National income also includes those expenditures needed to help us work – motorways, cars, buses to transport goods and people, banks to provide finance for business, inspectors and equipment to control pollution. But these don't add to our standards of living. They are part of the cost of producing.

Our industrial society is becoming richer and richer, but isn't it true that pre-industrial society was just as well off and catered better for man's basic spiritual and biological needs?

Adapted from The Guardian, 19 December 1984

1 What is meant by:
   (a) 'national income';
   (b) 'standard of living'? *(4 marks)*

2 Explain in your words why, in the author's opinion, national income is not a good measure of the standard of living. *(2 marks)*

3 Describe two ways in which people might have been better off in a pre-industrial society than today. Describe two ways in which they might have been worse off. *(4 marks)*

Unit 51 The Financial System of the UK

NatWest cuts 4000 jobs as profits dive

National Westminster Bank yesterday announced that it had had to write off nearly £2 billion in bad debts in 1991. Profits plunged by £400 million to £110 million.

In the late 1980s, NatWest had expanded lending to small businesses. Now, with company collapses running at record levels, NatWest has lost enormous sums of money. Over 40 per cent of the bad debt was accounted for by lending to small businesses under £50 000. Nearly one-third of the losses were against individual customer loans. The company also lost £300 million in the USA, much of it on prop-erty loans. Losses of £83 million in Australia were due to a number of big company failures.

The branch banking operation, the American and Australian divisions and merchant banking arm County NatWest, all made losses. But the group was hauled out of the red by other subsidiaries including Coutts, Ulster Bank and the insurance and mortgage divisions.

NatWest closed 130 branches in 1991 and cut 6400 jobs from its 102 000 strong workforce. NatWest said it would be forced to cut another 4000 jobs in 1992.

Source: Adapted from the *Guardian*, 26 February 1992

1 What services does a bank, like National Westminster offer? Give examples from the article to illustrate your answer.   (8 marks)

2 Why do you think NatWest cut staff in 1991 and 1992?
                                                          (4 marks)

3 How can a bank avoid having bad debts?   *(3 marks)*

Unit 51 The Creation of Credit

Run on the Middlewhich Bank

The Middlewhich Bank had to close its doors today as depositors continued to withdraw funds from the troubled bank. Rumours that the bank might have had debts running to hundreds of millions of pounds as a result of lending to small North Sea oil exploration companies prompted the bank's small depositors to remove their savings from the bank. Unless an aid package is forthcoming from some of the major banks or from the Bank of England, the Middlewhich is likely to have to declare itself bankrupt within the next few days.

1 What problems face the Middlewhich Bank?   *(3 marks)*

2 Why has the Middlewhich Bank not got enough cash to repay all its depositors immediately?   *(3 marks)*

3 Using the Middlewhich Bank as an example, explain briefly the process of credit creation by banks.   *(4 marks)*

Essay Questions
Units 47–51

1 'Service output grew faster than manufacturing output in the 12 months to December'.
  (a) Explain, giving *four* examples, what is meant by 'manufacturing' industry.   *(6 marks)*
  (b) What is 'service output'?   *(4 marks)*
  (c) What factors have led to a faster growing service sector in the UK economy in recent years?   *(10 marks)*

2 (a) Describe *three* services that a bank offers to its customers.   *(9 marks)*
  (b) What does a bank do with the money that its customers lend to it?   *(6 marks)*
  (c) Explain *two* ways in which the commercial banks have dealings with the Bank of England.   *(5 marks)*

The Money Supply and the Rate of Interest

PREFERENCE SHARES

CERTIFICATE No.	TRANSFER No.	DATE	NUMBER OF PREFERENCE SHARES
A 2112	T 21121	7 SEPTEMBER 1993	**600**
			OF £1 EACH

International Ferries Group Plc
(Incorporated in England under the Companies Acts 1948 to 1981, No. 1810102)

This is to Certify that the undermentioned is/are the Registered Holder(s) of the number of 5 per cent Redeemable Non-Cumulative Preference Shares of £1 each fully paid in the above Company stated below, subject to the Memorandum and Articles of Association of the Company.
A summary of the rights of the Preference Shares is printed overleaf.

HOLDER(S)

NUMBER OF PREFERENCE SHARES

ALAIN GEORGE ANDERTON ESQ
8 BROMLEY GARDENS
CODSALL
WOLVERHAMPTON
STAFFS   WV8 1BB

**SIX HUNDRED SHARES

MRS MARIE-NICOLE ANDERTON

Given under the Securities Seal of the Company

002146

Lloyds Bank Limited
EXCHANGE BRANCH
EXCHANGE BUILDINGS LIVERPOOL L2 3UP
30-93-13

19___

11-24

PAY

OR ORDER

Z DAVIS

⑂259825⑂ 30⑂9313⑂ 0112542⑂

Midshires Building Society

High Return Account

bank giro credit ⑆

	Notes	£50	
Paid in by		£20	
Address		£10	
		£5	
		£1	
	Coins	£1	
		50p	
Destination Branch Code number		20p	
Bank		Silver	
		Bronze	
	Total Cash £		
Branch where account is held	Cheques, etc		
	No of Cheques	£	
A/c			
Cash	Fee	Account (Block Letters) & A/c No	
Cheques etc			
£	NWB1450 Rev May 81-1 Please do not write or mark below this line		

⑂ 70

STUDY POINTS

1 If something is to be called 'money' what distinguishes it from items which are not money? (Or as economists would ask, what are the *functions* of money?)

2 Which of the items shown in the illustrations could be called 'money' and why? To help you answer this question draw up a grid with 4 vertical columns and 6 horizontal divisions. In the left-hand column list the 6 different items shown above. Above each of the other columns write a *function* of money. Fill in the grid by giving a mark out of 3 for how well each item fulfills each function. For instance, if you think that notes and coins are a very good medium of exchange, you would record a 3 in the appropriate section of the grid.

3 What would be the costs to the economy if there were no money in circulation?

Assets other than Money

It was argued in Unit 8 that money had to be able to fulfil three functions: it had to be a medium of exchange, a measure of value and a store of value. In the UK today, money is often thought to be notes and coins. But notes and coins form only a very small part of the MONEY SUPPLY – the total stock of money in the economy. This is because there are other assets, apart from notes and coins, that act as money.

Current Accounts

Far more important than notes and coins is money deposited in current accounts at banks and building societies. A current account is one where the customer is able to deposit and withdraw money without giving any notice. If a customer has £20 000 in a current account and wishes to withdraw it all in cash, the bank has to release the money immediately. Current account holders are given a *cheque book*, and they can use cheques to withdraw money from their account. Money in a current account is money because:

- it is a medium of exchange – cheques are acceptable means of payment for most transactions;
- it is a measure of value just like notes and coins;
- it is a store of value – money put into a current account can be used at a later date to purchase goods and services.

Note that cheques themselves are *not* money – it is the money behind the cheque in the current account that counts as money.

Money in deposit or savings accounts at banks or building societies can also be counted as money. A deposit account is aimed at savers. Interest is paid on money in the account, but notice of withdrawal from the account often has to be given if the saver is not to lose interest. Deposit money is not a direct medium of exchange like current account money because no cheque service is provided. But the money is easily available to change into either current account money or notes and coins. Deposit money is also a good measure of value and store of value. So deposit money performs the functions of money almost as well as notes and coins and current account assets. So, too, do a variety of other assets, including deposits in the National Savings Bank.

Therefore the question 'what is money?' is not easy to answer. What we find is that a variety of assets, ranging from notes and coins through to bank accounts and building society accounts through to other financial assets, perform the functions of money to varying degrees. The government currently calculates four important different measures of the money supply. These, roughly defined, are:

- MO, which consists mainly of notes and coins;
- M2, which is notes and coins plus money in cheque book current accounts at banks and building societies;
- M4, which is most assets in M2 plus money in deposit and savings accounts with banks and building societies;
- M5, which is M4 plus various forms of very short-term saving in the City of London.

The Money Supply and the Rate of Interest

If an individual, company or government wishes to obtain extra money, it can do so by borrowing that money. The price it has to pay for that is interest on the loan. So the price of money is the rate of interest. Like any price, if the supply of money increases, then the price or the rate of interest will go down. This is because, with more money to lend, the banks have to lower their rates of interest to encourage more customers to borrow. If, on the other hand, the supply of money decreases, then interest rates will go up. This important relationship will be discussed further in Unit 68.

C H E C K P O I N T S

1 What are the functions of money?

2 Explain why notes and coins perform the functions of money.

3 Why is money in current accounts at banks considered to be money?

4 Explain why gold no longer performs the functions of money in the British economy today.

5 Why are credit cards not money?

6 Explain the difference between M0 and M4.

7 What would you expect to happen to the rate of interest, if the money supply increased? Why?

C O U R S E W O R K S U G G E S T I O N

Using statistics from past issues of the *Bank of England Quarterly Bulletin* (published by the Bank of England) and *Financial Statistics* (published by HMSO), examine changes in the various definitions of the money supply since the mid-1960s. Describe the different measures of money supply. Analyse their change over time. Evaluate the extent to which assets used in broader measures of the money supply, such as M5, can really be seen as money.

K E Y T E R M S

MONEY SUPPLY – the total stock of money available in the economy at a point in time. Because there are various assets that act as money or near-money, there are a number of different definitions of the money supply, including M0, M2, M4 and M5.

Public Expenditure (1)

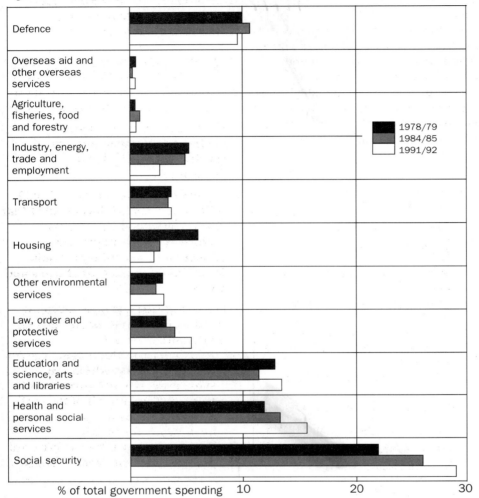

Figure 53.1 Change in government spending, 1978/79 to 1991/92

Categories (top to bottom): Defence; Overseas aid and other overseas services; Agriculture, fisheries, food and forestry; Industry, energy, trade and employment; Transport; Housing; Other environmental services; Law, order and protective services; Education and science, arts and libraries; Health and personal social services; Social security

Legend: 1978/79, 1984/85, 1991/92

% of total government spending   10   20   30

Source: HM Treasury, *Public Expenditure Analysis to 1994–95*, The 'Brown Book', (Cm 1920)

STUDY POINTS

1 Which was the costliest public expenditure programme in 1991/92? Which was the least costly?
2 If total public expenditure was £200 billion in 1991/92, how much would the social security programme have cost?
3 Which public expenditure programme would include spending on:
   (a) nurses' pay
   (b) school textbooks
   (c) a police van
   (d) a new motorway
   (e) YT
   (f) repairs on a flat
   (g) unemployment benefit
   (h) a public park?
4 What have been the benefits, if any, of the change in defence spending over the period 1978/79 to 1991/92? What has been the opportunity cost of this change?
5 What has happened to the percentage spent on education over the period? Why might this have happened?
6 Which public expenditure programmes have increased their share of the total budget over the period 1978/79 to 1991/92? Explain why there might have been this increase.
7 If the government could increase public expenditure by £1000 million, what should it spend the money on and why?
8 If the government had to cut public spending by £1000 million, what should it cut and why?

Public and Private Sectors

The **PUBLIC SECTOR** is that sector of the economy owned and controlled by the 'state' or by 'government'. The **PRIVATE SECTOR**, by contrast, is the part of the economy directly owned and controlled by private individuals. The public sector is made up of four main parts:

- *Central government* – run by Parliament sitting in Westminster. The Prime Minister is the most important single figure here.
- *Local government* – counties, boroughs, parishes, etc. Local government is controlled by local councillors.
- *Nationalised industries* – companies owned in whole or in part by the government, such as British Rail or British Coal.
- *Other bodies* – such as the BBC, which are public bodies, but are not directly owned or controlled by central or local governments.

Public-sector nationalised industries and the private sector both, for the most part, allocate resources via the market mechanism (this was discussed in Units 9–13). In the market place, goods and services are offered for sale and are then purchased by buyers who demand those goods and services. Consumers with no money to spend will not be allocated goods and services. The more money an individual has, the more goods and services he or she is able to buy.

Public Expenditure

Most public-sector goods and services are not allocated in this way. They are allocated on the basis of *need*. Figure 53.2 gives a breakdown of **PUBLIC EXPENDITURE** – spending by local and central government. Taking health as an example, everybody in the UK is entitled to receive 'free' medical treatment. It is free in the sense that the consumer does not have to pay for it when he or she receives medical treatment (although there are a few exceptions to this, such as prescription charges). But the citizen does pay for it through the taxes that he or she pays.

In this system, it is the government that decides how to allocate resources. It has to decide, for example, whether to spend £1 million on treating old people or £1 million on heart transplants; £100 million on strike aircraft or £100 million on nuclear submarines. Under this system, individual consumers cannot buy themselves better defence or better

roads in the way that they can buy better cars or better houses, if they have the money. They can influence how governments spend money, but they do this through political means – such as voting for a particular party in an election – rather than economic means.

The government has to make very hard choices. Like an ordinary citizen, it would prefer to be able to spend more and more money – a policy which would be certain to make it popular with the electorate. But for many reasons discussed elsewhere in this book, it cannot do that. Every

pound spent in one way has an opportunity cost – (i.e. some other item which could have been bought with that pound, but which now cannot be bought). In other words, the government is faced with exactly the same problems as the individual – how best to allocate the scarce resources at its disposal.

C H E C K P O I N T S

1 Explain the difference between the public sector and the private sector.

2 Name five services offered by central government and five services offered by local government.

3 A government has an extra £1000 million to spend. It has decided that it will spend it either on new motorways or on improving education in secondary schools. What would you advise it to do and why?

4 Here are three goods or services: (i) education; (ii) prescriptions for medicines; (iii) coal.

(a) Which of these three items are free to the consumer, which are subsidised (i.e. the government pays part, but not all, of the cost), and which does the consumer have to pay for in full?

(b) Who has to pay if the government provides services free of charge to the consumer?

Figure 53.2 Breakdown of public expenditure

Programme	Main responsibility	Examples of spending
Defence	Central government	Army, navy and air forces
Overseas aid and overseas services	Central government	Foreign aid to poor countries Contributions to EC
Agriculture, fisheries, food and forestry	Central government	Financial help to farmers, fishermen and foresters
Industry, energy, trade and employment	Central government	Investment grants, training schemes such as Youth Training
Transport	Local government	Roads, subsidies for bus and rail services
Housing	Local government	Council housing – repairs, renovation and new building
Other environmental services	Central and local government	Parks, sports centres, refuse collection
Law, order and protective services	Local government	Police, firemen, ambulances, prisons
Education and science	Central and local government	Universities, FE colleges, schools, scientific research
Arts and libraries	Central and local government	Subsidies to theatres, libraries
Health and personal social services	Central and local government	National Health Service Social Services departments
Social security	Central government	Unemployment benefits, pensions, Family support
Government lending to nationalised industries	Central government	Lending to British Rail, British Coal
Other	Central and local government	Help for Scotland, Wales, Northern Ireland Civil servants

Note: Central government pays for a large part of local government spending by providing grants to local authorities.

K E Y T E R M S

PUBLIC SECTOR – the sector of the economy owned and controlled by the state or government.

PRIVATE SECTOR – the sector of the economy owned and controlled by private individuals and organisations.

PUBLIC EXPENDITURE – spending by the government on programmes such as defence and social security.

C O U R S E W O R K S U G G E S T I O N

Describe the changes in government expenditure over the past ten years. Analyse why expenditure has changed – both total expenditure and expenditure on particular programmes. Analyse also the impact of these changes on particular groups in society, such as workers, the sick, school pupils and taxpayers. Consider whether the government has made the right changes in public spending. A good source of statistics and facts is past copies of the *Economic Briefing* (published by the Treasury)

Public Expenditure (2)

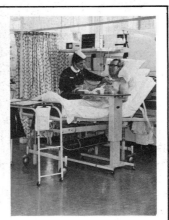

STUDY POINTS

All these photographs are examples of public expenditure.

1 Identify which services are provided in each case.

2 Which of these services would the private sector *not* provide if the government did not: i.e. which services would never be produced by a private firm and then sold to customers? Why is this the case?

3 (a) Which services can be and are provided by the private sector?

(b) Give examples of private sector firms and institutions which provide these services in the UK or abroad.

(c) Are these services better provided by the public sector or by the private sector? List all the arguments for and against in each case.

Public Goods

The government plays a very important role in the economy. Nearly half of all income generated in the UK is spent by the government, and the government is the single most important employer in the country. Why should the public sector be so large? Why should the government provide education and roads, but not televisions and apples?

One reason is that the market mechanism – where goods and services are bought and sold for money – cannot provide certain important goods and services. Look at Figure 54.1.

Figure 54.1

Year	Average prison population
1980	43 109
1985	46 278
1990	45 636

Source: CSO, *Annual Abstract of Statistics*, 1992

The number of people sent to prison has been rising in recent years. How are these extra prison places to be provided and who is going to pay for them? The market mechanism will not provide them. For example, if you are robbed, would you then pay the £26 000 it cost in 1991 to keep a person in prison for a year? If you would not pay, who would? The only sensible way is for the government to take a small amount of money from each citizen in taxes to pay for a service which few or no individuals would pay for themselves.

A prison is an example of a **PUBLIC GOOD**. Other examples are the army, the police, lighthouses and the judiciary (judges, magistrates, etc.). Public goods have two essential features:

● Once the good is provided, it benefits everybody. For instance, the benefit you get from the prison service doesn't fall because others benefit too. But with a non-public good, like an apple, if you eat it, no-one else can eat it and benefit.

- It is impossible to prevent somebody benefiting from the good, once it has been provided. For instance, once the defence of the UK has been provided, an individual citizen cannot fail to benefit from that provision.

An ordinary private good is different. If a consumer buys a television, that television set will not benefit everybody in the country – it will only benefit the owner and the people he or she allows to watch the set. So the owner can prevent others from enjoying the benefits of the set.

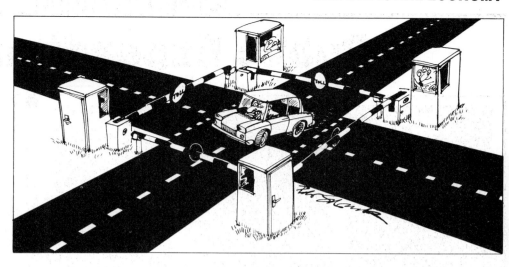

Merit Goods

Public goods, such as defence and law and order, account for only a small part of total public spending. Another important justification for government spending is that otherwise the market would not provide enough of a particular good or service. Take education, for example. If everybody in the UK is to prosper in the future, it is essential that the country should have a well-educated work force. It is also important that citizens are educated to play a responsible role in society. People who cannot read and write, or who cannot use numbers, or who do not understand basic economic issues are going to be a drain on society rather than an asset. But what if all parents had to pay for their children's education and all schools were private? Many parents would not be able to afford or might not want to afford to send their children to school. Fewer children would receive a proper education. Not only would those children be harmed, but everybody else in society would be affected indirectly for the worse.

Products that free market forces would underprovide are known as MERIT GOODS. Examples are roads (imagine the consequences of paying a

toll for each section of road you want to use), health services (what if people were walking the streets with contagious diseases, because they could not afford treatment?), and education.

Equity, Efficiency and Control

There are three other important reasons why governments spend money.

- *Equity* – government spending is used to help those in need in society, such as the old, the sick and the unemployed. This aspect is covered in Unit 72. (Note that the word 'equity' has other meanings, including the one explained in Unit 39.)

- *Efficiency* – the government may be able to provide better-quality goods and services at a cheaper price than the private sector. This was considered in Unit 43.

- *Control* – the government may use public spending to improve the general state of the economy. Reducing unemployment, lowering inflation and eliminating externalists are a few examples. This is considered in Units 67–71.

CHECKPOINTS

1 What is the difference between a public good and a merit good?
2 Why is a lighthouse an example of a public good?
3 Why is government spending on vaccinating all children against diphtheria an example of a merit good?
4 Why is it better for the government to provide a network of 'free' roads rather than for the private sector to provide it?
5 How are 'free' services such as education and health paid for? How is private education and private health care paid for?
6 Explain why governments provide goods and services.

COURSEWORK SUGGESTION

Describe the way in which a merit good, such as education or health services, is provided in the public sector and in the private sector. Describe what services are offered and their quality, who supplies these services, and how they are paid for. Analyse what would happen if all these services were provided by just the private sector or just the public sector. Consider the advantages and disadvantages of these options.

KEY TERMS

PUBLIC GOOD – a good that has to be provided by government. Once provided, it is impossible to prevent others from benefiting equally.

MERIT GOOD – a good that would be under-consumed, if left to free market forces.

Taxation

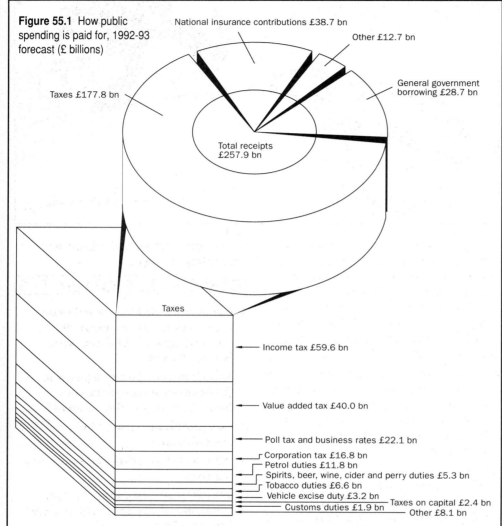

Figure 55.1 How public spending is paid for, 1992-93 forecast (£ billions)

National insurance contributions £38.7 bn

Other £12.7 bn

General government borrowing £28.7 bn

Taxes £177.8 bn

Total receipts £257.9 bn

Taxes

Income tax £59.6 bn

Value added tax £40.0 bn

Poll tax and business rates £22.1 bn

Corporation tax £16.8 bn

Petrol duties £11.8 bn

Spirits, beer, wine, cider and perry duties £5.3 bn

Tobacco duties £6.6 bn

Vehicle excise duty £3.2 bn

Customs duties £1.9 bn

Taxes on capital £2.4 bn

Other £8.1 bn

Source: HM Treasury, *Financial Statement and Budget Report 1992–93*, House of Commons No 319 (The 'Red Book')

STUDY POINTS

Look at Figure 55.1

1 How much did the government expect to raise in taxes in 1992/93?

2 What proportion or percentage was this of total receipts?

3 If there were 57.8 million inhabitants of the UK in that year, how much on average did each man, woman and child pay in tax?

4 What was the largest tax in terms of revenue?

5 Which taxes do you pay while in education?

6 Which additional taxes are people likely to pay when they start working?

7 What does the government do with its taxes and other income?

8 The government wishes to cut taxes. How could it raise the money to do this?

9 If the government were to cut taxes by £10 billion, would this lead to an increase in welfare in the economy? To answer this, consider the costs and benefits to society of such a move.

Why Tax?

A tax is a levy paid by citizens and organisations to their government. There are several reasons why the government imposes taxes:

- To raise money to pay for public expenditure. Figure 55.1 shows that most public spending is paid for by taxes. The rest is paid for by royalties on North Sea oil; national insurance contributions; 'other' sources, such as profits from nationalised industries or rents from council houses; and government borrowing.

- To affect economic behaviour. For instance, taxes on cigarettes discourage smoking. Taxes on petrol encourage motorists to economise on fuel.

- To help redistribute income between different individuals and between different sectors of the economy. This is considered further in Unit 72.

- To help control the economy. This is considered further in Units 67–72.

The Main Taxes in the UK

Taxes are either direct or indirect. A DIRECT TAX is a tax levied directly on an individual or organisation. Today, direct taxes are mainly taxes on income or wealth although the poll tax was a direct tax too. An INDIRECT TAX is a tax on a good or service. All major taxes except the Council Tax are paid to central government. Local authorities also get the money collected by central government from business rates. The main taxes in the UK and their importance in terms of revenue are shown in Figure 55.1.

- *Income tax* is the most important tax in the UK. It is a direct tax on a person's income. An individual is allowed to earn a certain sum free of tax; this is called TAX ALLOWANCE. A single person is allowed, for instance, to earn about £4000 a year free of tax (1992–93 figures). Money earned on top of the allowance is taxed at 20% for the first £2000 of income and then at 25% on the rest. Any income over £24 000 of taxable earnings (gross income minus tax allowances) is taxed at 40%. Hence, the TAX RATE on the last pound earned varies from 20% to 40%.

- *Value added tax* (VAT) is an indirect tax levied on most goods and services at a rate of 17.5%. If an item were priced at £117.50, then £17.50 of that would be VAT and £100.00 the cost of the good. Some important items are zero-rated. (i.e. there is no VAT charged on them). These include food, children's clothes, books, newspapers and public transport such as buses, coaches and rail services.

- The *Council Tax* is an indirect tax on property. How much you pay is linked to the value of your house. It replaces the highly unpopular poll tax, which was a flat-rate tax on every adult.

- *Business rates* are again an indirect tax on property. They are paid by businesses.

- *Corporation tax* is a direct tax on the profits of companies.

- *Duties* on petrol, drink and tobacco are indirect taxes. They are taxes on top of the VAT you pay when you buy these goods. Unlike VAT, they are calculated on quantity rather than value. For instance, the duty on a bottle of wine is the same whether it costs £2 or £200. This compares with VAT, where VAT on a £200 bottle would be one hundred times as much as on a £2 bottle.

- *Vehicle excise duty* is the indirect tax which is paid each year by car owners. You show you have paid the tax by displaying a tax disk on the windscreen.

- *Taxes on capital* are direct taxes.

Capital gains tax is a tax mainly on profits made when stocks and shares are sold at higher prices than they were bought for. Inheritance tax is a tax on money left by people who die. If your uncle were to die leaving £1 million, then tax would have to be paid on that.

- *Customs duties* are an indirect tax on goods coming into the country from outside the European Community. The money raised in this tax is given to the EC to help finance its spending.

- *National insurance contributions*. There is some debate about whether these are taxes or not. All other taxes are paid into one fund (known as the 'Consolidated Fund') and used to pay for public spending. National insurance contributions, however, are paid into the national insurance fund and used only to pay for national insurance benefits (such as state pensions and unemployment benefits) and a small part of the National Health Service. National insurance contributions are paid by workers and their employers, and are calculated as a percentage of wages.

C H E C K P O I N T S

1 Explain the difference between (a) taxation and government borrowing; and (b) direct and indirect taxes.

2 Which taxes (a) do you pay and (b) do other members of your household pay at the moment?

3 Compare how income tax and VAT are calculated.

4 What is (a) an allowance and (b) a tax rate?

5 Which taxes are paid to (a) local government and (b) the European Community?

6 Explain why governments impose taxes.

C O U R S E W O R K   S U G G E S T I O N

Find out and describe in detail how taxes have changed over the past ten years. Explain why they have changed. Assess whether or not these changes have been desirable, and whether or not a different structure of taxation might have been more beneficial. Useful sources of statistics would be past copies of the *Economic Progress Report* (published by the Treasury) and the *Annual Abstract of Statistics* (published by HMSO).

K E Y   T E R M S

DIRECT TAX – a tax levied directly on an individual or organisation.

INDIRECT TAXES – a tax levied on a good or service.

TAX RATE – the percentage paid in tax.

TAX ALLOWANCE – a sum on which no tax is paid.

Data Response Questions
Units 52–55

Unit 52 The Money Supply and the Rate of Interest

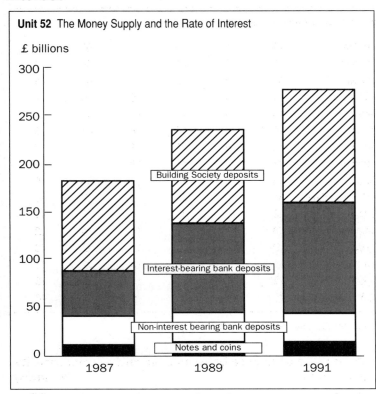

Unit 52 The Money Supply and the Rate of Interest

£ billions

- Building Society deposits
- Interest-bearing bank deposits
- Non-interest bearing bank deposits
- Notes and coins

1987 1989 1991

Source: CSO, *Financial Statistics*, May 1992

1 List *three* different types of money. *(3 marks)*

2 How has the make-up of the money supply M4 changed between the last quarter of 1987 and the last quarter of 1991? *(3 marks)*

3 Discuss *two* factors which might have led to this change in the composition of M4. *(4 marks)*

4 Explain whether you think that notes and coins will eventually disappear from the money supply. *(5 marks)*

Unit 53 Public Expenditure (1)

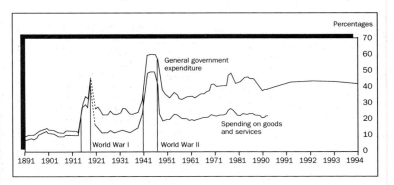

Source: CSO, *Social Trends*, 1992

1 What percentage of national income (measured by GDP) was spent by government in (a) 1900 (b) 1930 (c) 1960 (d) 1990? *(2 marks)*

2 GDP in 1980 was approximately £200 billion. What was the approximate total value of government spending in £bn in that year? *(2 marks)*

3 Why did government spending as a proportion of GDP rise so much between 1915 and 1918, and 1940 and 1945? *(2 marks)*

4 (a) What happened to government spending as a proportion of GDP in the 1980s?
(b) Discuss the costs and benefits of this to the ordinary citizen of the UK. *(9 marks)*

Essay Questions
Units 52–55

1 (a) Describe *four* ways (apart from education) in which government spends money in your local area. *(8 marks)*

(b) Explain how you and the rest of society will benefit from the education you have received so far. *(8 marks)*

(c) To what extent can education be described as a public good? *(4 marks)*

2 (a) Name one tax which you pay at the moment and describe how much you pay in that tax. *(5 marks)*

(b) Name one tax which people are likely to start paying once they start full-time work and describe how much they are likely to pay in that tax. *(6 marks)*

(c) Give *three* reasons why government raises taxes. *(9 marks)*

Unit 54 Public Expenditure (2)

Big leisure price rises in pipeline

Big price rises were today in the pipeline for Wolverhampton families who use council-run leisure outlets. They will hit swimming, hire of sports halls and outdoor playing facilities, the use of Aldersley stadium, and the cost of borrowing equipment.

The increases, which will push up charges by an average of nearly 13 per cent, are aimed at boosting income as part of a £15 million savings package ordered by the authority's Labour leaders.

If approved, the increases will bring in an extra £82 600 next year.

At the same time, the committee will be asked to chop the subsidy for staging classical music concerts at council-owned venues to £18 000 compared with £42 000 this year.

Leisure services director, Mr Derrick Anderson, admits in a report that the massive cutback will effectively destroy what he called the subscriber base for classical music in the town.

Most of the subsidy will be swallowed up by just three performances, and he says that a drastic re-appraisal of their policy for promoting the concerts is needed.

Source: Express and Star, 13 February 1992

1 How much money does Wolverhampton hope to save by its increases in charges and cuts in subsidies for leisure services? *(2 marks)*

2 Who is likely (a) to lose out and (b) to gain from the increased charges at council-run leisure outlets? *(6 marks)*

3 Discuss whether councils like Wolverhampton should subsidise classical music concerts. *(5 marks)*

Unit 55 Taxation

Taxes and social security contributions as a percentage of gross national product at factor cost

	Percentage and rank					
	1979		1984		1989	
Including social security contributions						
Sweden	49	1	50	1	57	1
Denmark	45	5	48	4	50	2
Norway	48	2	48	3	47	3
Netherlands	46	4	46	5	46	4
Belgium	46	3	48	2	45	5
France	40	8	45	6	44	6
Austria	42	6	43	7	41	7
Germany	41	7	41	8	41	8
Italy	29	15	35	11	38	9
United Kingdom	34	9	38	9	37	10
Finland	33	10	35	10	37	11
Canada	30	12	32	14	34	12
Greece	29	13	33	12	32	13
Switzerland	31	11	32	13	32	14
Japan	25	16	28	16	31	15
USA	29	14	28	15	30	16

Source: CSO, Economic Trends, February 1992

1 What is the difference between a tax and a social security contribution? *(2 marks)*

2 What percentage of national income (measured by GDP at market prices) was paid in taxes and social security contributions in Italy in (a) 1979 and (b) 1989? *(2 marks)*

3 (a) How did the UK compare with other countries in the proportion of tax paid in 1989?
   (b) How did the UK's position change over the 1980s? *(4 marks)*

4 Discuss whether the UK would be better off if it increased its taxes to the level of some of her other EC partners such as Germany or Denmark. *(7 marks)*

Unemployment

Bill Phillips, aged 62, forced to take early retirement but would still like to have a job.

Harry Cole, aged 45, general labourer, out of work now for four years.

Jill Butterworth, aged 52, in part-time work but would like a full-time job.

Helen Briggs, aged 24, physically handicapped in a wheelchair, unemployed but wants a job.

Mary Roberts, aged 35, children now at school, not actively looking for work at the moment, but would like a job if jobs were easily available.

Jane Onslow, aged 17, on a YT placement.

STUDY POINTS

1 Look carefully at the details for each person. Giving as many arguments as possible, explain whether or not you think they should be classified as 'unemployed'.

2 (a) How does the government count the number of people unemployed?

(b) Explain which of these people would officially be counted as unemployed in the UK.

COURSEWORK SUGGESTION

Find out the unemployment figures for your local area or region, both past and present. Try to break down the overall unemployment figure by industry and by duration. Present your findings using graphs, etc. Compare your findings with the national picture. Analyse why the local economy differs from or is the same as the national average. Try to predict likely future trends in unemployment in your area.

This sort of newspaper headline was common as the economy went into recession from 1990. In the early 1950s and early 1960s, unemployment averaged a little over 300 000. In 1993, it was nearly ten times that level. But what do we mean by 'unemployment'?

Measuring Unemployment

Measuring the level of unemployment is not easy. In the UK, it is measured monthly by the numbers of workers registering for benefits at the Department of Social Security (DSS). Before 1983, it was measured by the number of jobless signing on at Jobcentres, the government 'job shops'.

There is an alternative count of the unemployed in the UK. Once a year, the Department of Employment compiles the Labour Force Survey. This is a survey of 60 000 households in the UK. It finds out about people's occupation and pay, etc., but it also finds out who is unemployed. The unemployment figures from the Labour Force Survey are different from those taken from the DSS count.

One reason is that some unemployed people want a job but aren't eligible to claim unemployment benefits. So they don't get included on the DSS count. They form part of the HIDDEN UNEMPLOYED.

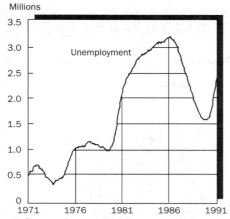

Others who are hidden unemployed and who are not measured in either government count are:

- those on various government training training schemes like Youth Training;

- youngsters who stay on at school or college because they can't get a job but would take a job if offered;

- workers forced to take early retirement when the less attractive alternative would have been compulsory redundancy but who would have preferred to stay working.

Types of Unemployment

Unemployment can be broken down into four main types.

- FRICTIONAL UNEMPLOYMENT will always be present in an economy. It is short-term unemployment caused because many workers who change jobs do not immediately go from one job to the next. They spend a week or a few weeks unemployed. Unemployment up to 8 weeks should be considered frictional unemployment.

- SEASONAL UNEMPLOYMENT is unemployment caused by changes in demand for workers at different times of the year. For instance, workers in the tourist trade and building trade might be laid off in winter.

- CYCLICAL UNEMPLOYMENT occurs when workers and factories lie idle because there is insufficient spending in the economy to make use of all the factors of production. When economists say that the economy is in 'recession' or is in a 'slump', they are saying that the resulting unemployment is cyclical.

- STRUCTURAL UNEMPLOYMENT occurs when firms and industries are run down and no new industry steps in to take up the workers made unemployed. Many manufacturing industries, such as shipbuilding and textiles, have been in decline in the UK for a long time. Because declining industries are located in certain regions of the UK, structural unemployment is often the cause of regional unemployment.

CHECKPOINTS

1 The television newsreader announces that last month 2 976 322 people were unemployed. How is this figure arrived at? Is it an accurate measure of unemployment?

2 Are young people on Youth Training part of the unemployed? Explain your answer carefully.

3 What type of unemployment does each of the following represent:
   (a) a hotel worker who is laid off during the winter;
   (b) a steel works which is closing permanently where the workers are made redundant;
   (c) a worker who spends two weeks unemployed before getting another job;
   (d) a car worker who is laid off because orders for new cars drop;
   (e) a textile worker who is made redundant in an area of existing high unemployment?

4 To what extent is unemployment in the UK today frictional and seasonal?

KEY TERMS

UNEMPLOYMENT – lacking a job while seeking employment. The number of unemployed is measured in the UK by a count of those unemployed who are receiving DSS benefits.

HIDDEN or CONCEALED UNEMPLOYMENT – workers who are unemployed, but who are not counted as unemployed in the official statistics (e.g. young people on Youth Training).

FRICTIONAL UNEMPLOYMENT – short-duration unemployment caused as workers move from one job to another.

SEASONAL UNEMPLOYMENT – unemployment caused by changes in demand for workers at different times of the year (e.g. in the building industry, fewer workers are employed in the winter months).

STRUCTURAL UNEMPLOYMENT – unemployment caused by insufficient capital (e.g. factories, offices, machines) in the economy.

CYCLICAL UNEMPLOYMENT – unemployment caused by a lack of demand for goods and services in the economy.

Unemployment – Its Consequences

STUDY POINTS

1 (a) Write down *three* points which the father is making about unemployment or the unemployed.
  (b) Are his opinions right or wrong do you think? Explain your reasoning carefully.

2 What are the costs of unemployment to:
  (a) an unemployed person like the boy in the cartoon
  (b) a taxpayer like the father
  (c) the economy as a whole, like the British economy?

3 What would be (a) the costs and (b) the benefits to (i) the unemployed, (ii) taxpayers, (iii) other workers, of a rise in unemployment benefit of £2 a week?

4 Should unemployment benefit be raised today? Explain your answer carefully.

5 The father said that 'if you try, you'll get a job'. Do you think that any worker who has not got a job after eight weeks of being unemployed should have his or her unemployment pay stopped? In your answer, explain the costs and benefits of such a proposal.

- 'The greatest evil of our times'
- 'A great social scourge'
- 'A drain on the nation'

These are some of the phrases used to describe unemployment in Britain today. Why is unemployment so terrible?

The Cost to the Unemployed

The main losers from unemployment are the unemployed themselves. Unemployment is a major cause of poverty. Benefit levels in the UK are high enough to prevent the unemployed from dying of physical hardship, but they do little more. Very few of the unemployed are better off on the dole than in work. So the unemployed are deprived of spending power that they would otherwise have, if they were in employment.

A loss of earnings is only one aspect of the problem of unemployment. Social problems, such as heavy drinking, drug abuse and suicide, arise because the unemployed suffer psychologically. Many feel they ought to be working. They feel rejected by society, because nobody wants to employ them. They feel guilty and demeaned by receiving state hand-outs. Many end up feeling that they are to blame for their position. It is these feelings that blight the lives of many unemployed and that add to the already high cost arising from the loss of earnings.

The Cost to Those in Work

The main burden of unemployment falls on the unemployed, but those in work pay a heavy price too. One major way in which those in work have to pay for unemployment is through higher taxes. The unemployed receive benefits. In 1992, this amounted to about £3000 per unemployed person per year. More important though, the unemployed pay far less tax than they would if they were in work – an average of about £5000 less per worker. Remember that workers not only pay income tax but also national insurance contributions. Employers too have to pay national insurance contributions for each worker employed. Then the

government loses VAT and excise duties because the unemployed spend so much less. Companies make less profit and so corporation tax receipts fall. The unemployed also pay reduced local authority taxes.

Those in work, too, may lose out because high unemployment is likely to be associated with a lack of opportunity to work. Employment prospects and wage prospects will be much better in a full-employment, booming economy rather than in an economy where over 3 million people are unemployed. Those in work may also be harmed by social factors. Unemployment, as has been argued above, causes problems of illness, drink, drugs, etc. Increases in crime are linked to unemployment. Those in work have to suffer from these problems of society.

The Cost to the Economy

There is a major cost on a 'macro-economic' level too. The *opportunity cost* of, say, 3 million unemployed is what could be produce just £8000 worth of goods and services. The opportunity cost of unemployment is a staggering £24 000 million, or about £415 for every man, woman and child in the UK. In practice, for every two people officially unemployed, there is likely to be another person who forms part of the hidden unemployed. Also, £8000 is likely to be a low figure for the amount that each unemployed worker would produce. If each unemployed worker produced as much as the average worker, then he or she could produce £17 000 or £18 000 worth of goods and services. With 4½ million unemployed at £18 000, the cost of lost output would be £81 billion, or about £1400 per person in the UK. Whether the figure is £24 billion or £81 billion, or something in between, it is obvious that high unemployment represents a vast waste of *scarce resources* in the economy.

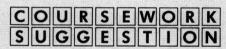

CHECKPOINTS

1 What are (a) the social costs and (b) the economic costs of unemployment to
   (i) the unemployed; and
   (ii) those in work?

2 What is the opportunity cost of unemployment to the economy as a whole?

3 Calculate the lost output in the economy in each of the following cases:

Number unemployed (millions)	Value of output that each worker could produce on average (£)
3.5	5000
3.75	6000
4.5	4000
5.0	9000

COURSEWORK SUGGESTION

This involves conducting a survey. Contact five unemployed workers who are willing to take part in your survey. Draw up a list of questions concerning the cost of unemployment to an individual person (both social costs and economic costs). Interview each of the five workers. Write up your findings. Explain whether or not you think your sample was representative of the unemployed in the UK today. Decide how important it is that these workers should be found jobs.

Unemployment – Its Causes (1)

'Jobs come from customers and nowhere else.'[1]

'Jobs are created when businesses produce goods and services that people want at prices they can afford.'[1]

'The biggest single cause of our high unemployment is the failure of our job market.'[1]

'We all should hang our heads in shame for treating would-be wealth creators with contempt.'[2]

'The Government will reduce the deterrent to taking on workers, by extending to two years in all firms the qualifying period for the right to claim unfair dismissal.'[1]

'Workers have added to unemployment by demanding pay rises which far outstrip productivity, and unions by organising crippling strikes.'[2]

'The Chancellor said that the link between pay and jobs was well established, as with the link between high levels of taxation and sluggish economic performance.'[3]

'Our major competitors have paid themselves less, improved their productivity far more, and consequently priced Britain out of the job market.'[2]

'A family man on average earnings might just as well be on the dole. Millions of people are still caught in the "why work" trap. This produces a lack of incentive to work.'[4]

'The biggest sufferers from excessive wage rises are the unemployed.'[1]

Sources: 1 Department of Employment, *Employment News*, number 129, March 1985
2 *Daily Express*, 29 March, 1985
3 *Express and Star*, 26 June, 1985
4 *Daily Express*, 24 April, 1985

STUDY POINTS

1 What, according to the quotes, are the causes of unemployment?

2 Assume you were the Government. If these were the causes of unemployment, what measures would you take to reduce unemployment?

The Labour Market

There are two major schools of thought on the causes of unemployment. In this unit, we will consider what is called the 'neo-classical' viewpoint. This viewpoint broadly argues that unemployment is caused by problems in the *labour market*.

The labour market is the market where workers offer themselves for work (workers are *supplied* onto the market) and where employers hire them (workers are *demanded* by employers). Neo-classical economists argue that the market for labour is no different from, say, the market for bananas or the market for clothes. The forces of demand and supply fix a price for labour and this is called the *wage rate*. The same forces also determine how much labour will be bought and sold at any one time. In 1993, for instance, about 25 million people had a job. The problem arises when the number of people who have a job at the existing wage rate (25 million in 1993) is less than the number of people who want a job (about 28 million in 1993). It is then that unemployment occurs (about 3 million in 1993).

In the market for bananas, if bananas are not being bought, then the sellers of bananas have to reduce their prices or not sell their bananas. So too, if workers cannot find a job, it is because wages are too high. Workers have 'priced themselves out of jobs'. Two organisations can be blamed for this.

- The *trade unions* are to blame, because they have forced wages up so that firms cannot afford to take on as many workers as they would if wages were lower.

- The *government* itself is also to blame, because of various Acts of Parliament which keep wages too high. Government wages councils have the power, for instance, to fix minimum wages for a large number of low-paid workers and to fine employers who do not pay these wages. The Equal Pay Act also led to many women losing their jobs.

But this neo-classical view does not see unemployment being caused only by high wages, which lead to a lack of demand for workers by employers. Workers themselves, it is argued, refuse work, because welfare benefits for the unemployed are so high that many workers are better off on the dole than working.

Excessively high wages, welfare benefits and taxes thus cause unemployment. But we know that in a country like West Germany, wages, benefits and taxes are even higher, yet unemployment is much lower. This is because West Germany is a successful economy. In the past, it has created more jobs than the UK because:

- Inflation has been lower. German goods have not been priced out of markets.

- On average, Germans pay higher taxes than UK citizens, but Germans have been taxed less on the last (or marginal) pound earned than Britons. This encourages Germans to work harder and new firms to be created by the self employed. (However, since 1988, UK tax rates on income have fallen below German levels, giving UK workers a competitive advantage at the moment.)

- Banks have been more sympathetic to small businesses and their proprietors' demands for financing.

- Investment has been higher because firms have been able to earn higher profits. Higher investment leads to more jobs in the long term.

- There is less government 'red tape', which pushes up labour costs.

To put it another way, the West German economy has been more *competitive* than the UK economy. So now it can afford to pay its workers more, without pushing up unemployment.

To sum up, British industry would *demand* more workers, if wages were lower and if industry were more competitive in international markets. Workers would be prepared to *supply*

more labour at lower wage rates, if welfare benefits were cut. The solution to unemployment is to free the labour market of the barriers – like trade union power, government wage-fixing and welfare benefits – which prevent wages from falling and clearing the labour market of unemployment.

A Diagrammatic Analysis

Figure 58.1 shows the market for labour. With a wage rate of OE, employers want to employ OA workers, but OC workers want a job. So unemployment of AC occurs. If wage rates declined to OF, then full employment would result because:

- employers would take on AB extra workers;

- BC workers would decide that wages were not high enough and would stop looking for a job.

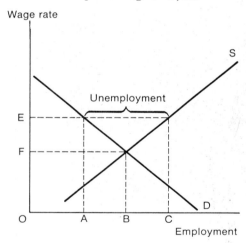

Figure 58.1

Figure 58.2 shows what happens when either trade unions push up wage rates or governments increase welfare benefits for the unemployed. Workers are now only prepared to work for higher wage rates, thus pushing the supply curve for labour from S to S'. The resulting increase in wage rates of EF causes unemployment of AC. Workers could be paid wage rates of OE without unemployment occurring, if the British economy became more competitive. This would increase orders for British goods so that, at any given wage rate, employers would want to employ more workers – i.e. the demand curve would shift to the right. Full employment would be restored, if the new demand curve passed through the point G.

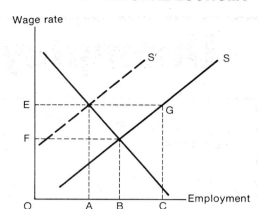

Figure 58.2

1. A firm employs 100 workers at an average wage of £100 per week. Why might the firm be willing to take on more workers, if the average wage were only £80?

2. Explain what is meant when it is said that workers have 'priced themselves out of work'.

3. Joan Williams is a housewife. Why might a 20% reduction in average wages discourage her from taking on paid employment?

4. Draw a demand and supply diagram and show why unemployment might be caused by too high real wage rates.

5. How do unions force up wages? Does this create unemployment?

6. Why might an increase in the competitiveness of the UK economy reduce unemployment?

You are going to investigate the theory that unemployment benefits cause unemployment. Find out the levels of unemployment benefit, social security benefits, etc. that those out of work can claim. Then, by looking at the local newspaper or by going to your local Jobcentre, find out the rates of pay for different jobs. What sort of workers might be discouraged from taking a job at existing levels of benefits? What would be the costs and benefits to workers, employers and the economy as a whole, if the government were to abolish unemployment benefits?

Unemployment – Its Causes (2)

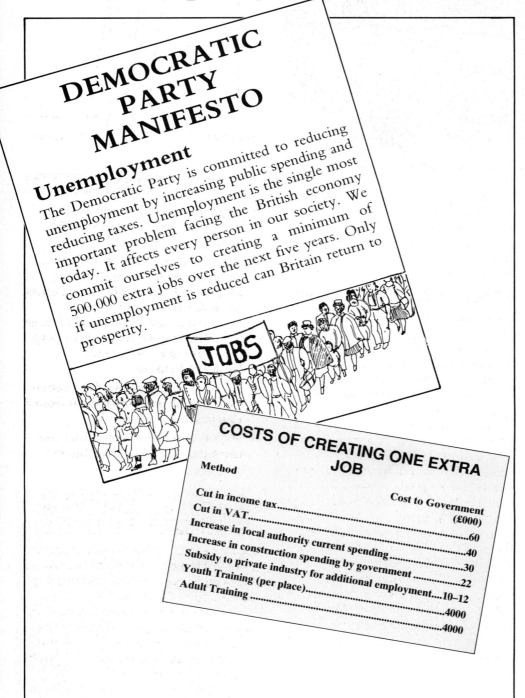

DEMOCRATIC PARTY MANIFESTO

Unemployment

The Democratic Party is committed to reducing unemployment by increasing public spending and reducing taxes. Unemployment is the single most important problem facing the British economy today. It affects every person in our society. We commit ourselves to creating a minimum of 500,000 extra jobs over the next five years. Only if unemployment is reduced can Britain return to prosperity.

COSTS OF CREATING ONE EXTRA JOB

Method	Cost to Government (£000)
Cut in income tax	60
Cut in VAT	40
Increase in local authority current spending	30
Increase in construction spending by government	22
Subsidy to private industry for additional employment	10–12
Youth Training (per place)	4000
Adult Training	4000

- 'Michelin to cut 2600 tyre jobs.'
- 'Shell to axe 1000 refinery jobs.'
- 'BSC to close plate mill with loss of 250 jobs.'

Such headlines have become so common in the UK that they rarely make the front page of national newspapers. In the previous unit, we saw that 'neo-classical' economists argue that jobs are lost because wages and benefits are too high, and because industry does not have enough incentives to create new jobs. There is, however, an alternative theory, which is often called 'Keynesian' after John Maynard Keynes, an economist who worked between the two world wars. Keynesian economists argue that unemployment is caused mainly by a lack of demand for goods and services in the economy.

Jobs and Spending

Money spent on new housing would directly create jobs for workers ranging from plumbers to bricklayers to kitchen-makers. But job creation would not stop there. Jobs would be created in other industries too as construction workers spent their wages and bought everything from bread to petrol to furniture.

Keynesians argue that this is just an example of a wider principle. They argue that jobs will only be created if there is more spending in the economy. Consumers need to spend more. Firms need to spend more on up-to-date factories, machines and offices. Governments need to spend more on everything from hospitals to education. Foreigners need to spend more on British goods.

Keynesians blame the lack of spending for the recession of the early 1990s. It was caused by a number of factors.

- Consumers saving a much bigger proportion of their incomes – meaning lower spending in the economy.
- Government putting up interest rates

STUDY POINTS

You are a member of the newly elected Democratic Party Government.

1 How do you intend to cut unemployment by 500 000 as promised in your Party Manifesto?

2 What will be the cost of these policies? How will you pay for them?

3 What do you think will be the effect of your decisions on (a) imports coming into the country, (b) inflation, (c) the economic prosperity of those in work, (d) interest rates?

Keynesians see the way forward for the UK through highly paid workers using sophisticated machines.

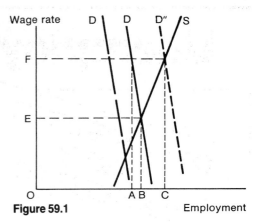

Figure 59.1

between 1988 and 1990 to very high levels which cut borrowing by both consumers and firms and thus cut spending.

- Firms cutting spending on investment because of high interest rates and falls in profits.
- Foreigners buying too few British goods because most major world economies were in recession too.

Jobs and Investment

Spending more money will not necessarily create many jobs. This is because much of the increase will be spent on goods imported from abroad, and some of the extra spending will trigger off a rise in prices (inflation) as companies see the chance to make bigger profits. Britain today has too few factories and offices to employ everybody who wants a job. Even when the economy was in boom in the late 1980s, unemployment only fell to 1.6 million. So much of Britain's unemployment is structural.

Keynesians argue that the only way to get round this is for the extra spending to be concentrated on investment – producing more factories, more offices, better roads, more education. Only increased investment in people and industry will create work places. It will also make Britain more competitive abroad.

A Diagrammatic Treatment

Keynesian ideas can be shown diagrammatically, as in Figure 59.1. The demand and supply of labour are both inelastic. Keynesians argue that increasing or decreasing wage rates would have little effect either on an employer's demand for labour or a worker's supply of labour. Employers need workers to produce or else they would have to shut down, and workers need a job to earn a living. The figure shows that a massive cut in wages from OF to OE would be needed to get rid of unemployment of AC. What is more, reducing wages might push the demand curve D to the left to D′, as workers could not afford to buy so many goods as before, and more workers would be put out of work. The solution to unemployment is to increase spending, and thereby increase the demand for workers from D to D″.

Data Response Questions
Units 56–59

Unit 56 Unemployment

2.7m on dole as jobless at 4-year high

A huge rise in unemployment announced today means that almost 2.7 million people are now out of work.

Employment Secretary Gilian Shephard said the increase was 'clearly disappointing'.

Labour spokesman Tony Blair said the figures were 'disastrous'.

The dole queue has now lengthened every month over the past two years. The number out of work is the highest for more than four-and-a-half years.

The rise came as a big blow after last month's comparatively small increase of 7800.

But Mrs Shephard said there were still grounds for cautious optimism on the economy, with clear signs of increasing confidence among consumers and businesses.

However, the government is resigned to unemployment rising for some time, accepting that the jobless figures will be one of the last economic indicators to show improvement.

Today's official figures show that in April unemployment rose by 42 600 to 2 695 300.

Source: Express and Star, 14 May 1992

1 What, according to the article, was happening to unemployment? *(3 marks)*

2 What was the official level of unemployment in (a) March 1992 and (b) February 1992? *(2 marks)*

3 How could increased 'confidence among consumers and businesses' affect the level of unemployment in the future? *(5 marks)*

Unit 57 Unemployment – Its Consequences

From nouveau riche to nouveau poor

THE RECESSION swept through the ranks of white collar and middle class workers like a virus, taking away job security and presenting a new breed of unemployed with the harsh realities of life on state benefit.

It is a life they are not prepared for. It is not simply a question of means testing, or claim forms that can appear complicated, or bleak benefit offices, but the feeling of hopelessness and even shame that can accompany the process.

For people claiming benefit for the first time these feelings can be overwhelming.

Couple them with another stumbling block, such as lack of understanding over the procedure or a harassed, overworked DSS official and they may simply not play.

The "nouveau" unemployed may have little or no idea what they are entitled to, or how to go about finding out. Men who see their role as providing adequately for a family can be reluctant to claim Family Credit, geared to low earners.

Source: Express and Star, 1 June 1992

1 Why does unemployment go up in a recession? *(2 marks)*

2 What problems do the newly unemployed face, according to the article? *(5 marks)*

3 Explain how (a) unemployed workers and (b) taxpayers lose money as a result of unemployment. *(3 marks)*

Unit 58 Unemployment – Its Causes (1)

Minimum wage 'to cost 57 000 jobs'

Fifty-seven thousand jobs could be lost in the West Midlands if Labour's minimum wage policy is introduced, claims a regional survey today.

The survey, by Business Schools at Warwick and Wolverhampton, says that 3 per cent of firms quizzed claimed they would be forced to close if a minimum wage were introduced.

However, just over 50 per cent said Labour's plan would not influence their levels of employment.

The authors of the report admit that the findings give an 'upper estimate' of job losses. This is because the survey only looks at 'first round' effects.

'Where a firm predicted it would go out of business, we assumed that all jobs were lost. However, in many cases either new or existing firms will take over that firm's market and will require more labour.'

Because the impact of that change cannot be estimated, it has been ignored for the purposes of the survey.

Source: Adapted from the Express and Star, 15 January 1992

1 What is meant by a 'minimum wage'? *(3 marks)*

2 (a) Explain why a minimum wage might lead an increase in unemployment.

(b) Draw a demand and supply diagram to show the unemployment effect. *(8 marks)*

3 Why could it be the case that the introduction of a minimum wage will lead to no job losses at all? *(4 marks)*

Unit 59 Unemployment – Its Causes (2)

Give us a job

The line of hope zig-zags for 200 yards around the concrete-clad building – a shuffling, slow-moving symbol of what has happened to a town that once had everything going for it.

Jobs are what they are after. Jobs in a place that only three years ago boasted an unemployment figure so low that it was officially rated zero.

This is Crawley, West Sussex, where, in the first two days of this week, more than 2000 people have queued from breakfast till long after dark for the chance of work at a new shopping centre due to open in April with a staff of 2500.

Local unemployment has rocketed to an unheard-of 4.8 per cent as the recession bites hard. 'And we know we're one of the lucky towns,' admits Job Centre manager Jack Harris.

Alf Peglar, leader of Crawley Council, said: 'This town was once so affluent that we sold more council houses than any other council in England. Now we're near the top of the table for the number of repossessions.'

People don't have the money to pay their mortgages. And they don't have the money because they don't have a job.

Source: Adapted from the Daily Mirror, 15 January 1992

1 How did unemployment change in Crawley between 1989 and 1992 according to the article? *(1 mark)*

2 Explain what caused this change in unemployment. *(3 marks)*

3 (a) Why does unemployment lead to house repossessions?

(b) Why might the problem of house repossessions lead to even more unemployment? *(7 marks)*

4 Why might rising unemployment in Crawley lead to some of those taken on at the new shopping centre losing their jobs? *(4 marks)*

Essay Questions
Units 56–59

1 'Unemployment last month was 3 456 702 according to official government statistics.'
(a) How is unemployment measured by the government? *(4 marks)*
(b) What are the costs of unemployment to the unemployed worker? *(8 marks)*
(c) What are the costs of unemployment to the government and the taxpayer? *(8 marks)*

2 'A 3% fall in real wages could result in an extra 250 000 jobs being created in the economy.'
(a) What is meant by a '3% fall in . . . wages'? *(4 marks)*
(b) Explain why a firm might be willing to take on more workers if it could pay each worker less for working the same time. *(8 marks)*
(c) The government cuts the real wages of all its workers by 3%. Suggest two reasons why this would not result in an extra 250 000 jobs being created in Britain. *(8 marks)*

Inflation

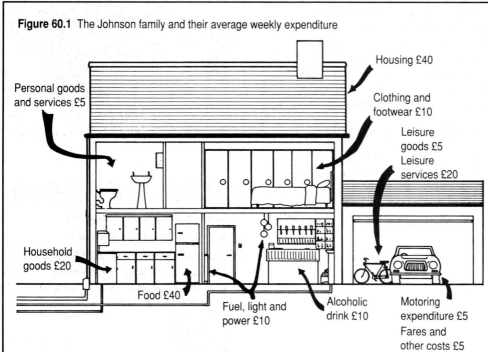

Figure 60.1 The Johnson family and their average weekly expenditure

Housing £40

Clothing and footwear £10

Leisure goods £5
Leisure services £20

Personal goods and services £5

Household goods £20

Food £40

Fuel, light and power £10

Alcoholic drink £10

Motoring expenditure £5
Fares and other costs £5

Note: definition of the less obvious categories as follows:

- household goods include furniture, kitchen appliances like cookers, and small items such as toilet paper and bleach;
- household services are services such as insuring the contents of the house, postage, telephone and dry cleaning;
- personal goods and services include

handbags, watches, jewellery, medicines, cosmetics and hairdressing;
- leisure goods include television sets, books, newspapers, magazines and gardening items like seeds and plants;
- leisure services are services such as cinema and theatre, video rental and holidays.

STUDY POINTS

1 How much a week does the Johnson family spend?

2 The price of food goes up by 10%. How much would the family need to spend extra in £s to buy the same amount of goods and services as before?

3 How much extra would they need in terms of a percentage of their total expenditure?

4 The price of alcoholic drink goes up by 20%. How much extra would the family need to spend (a) in £s and (b) in percentage of total expenditure to buy the same basket of goods as before?

5 The percentage increase in total expenditure that you have calculated in questions 3 and 4 is the rate of inflation for the Johnson family. What is the rate of inflation for them if the price of food went up by 20%?

6 The price of food goes up 10% and the price of transport and vehicles by 20%. How much extra would the family need to spend (a) in £s and (b) in percentage to maintain their real spending? What has been the Johnsons' rate of inflation?

7 Food prices increase 10%, household goods 20% and leisure services by 40%. What is the inflation rate for the Johnson family?

'Annual inflation rose to 4.3 per cent last month. The increase from 4 per cent in March was blamed on higher taxes on drink, petrol and tobacco announced in the Budget as well as more expensive clothing.' (*Source:* Adapted from the *Express and Star*, 15 May 1992)

What is inflation and how is it measured?

A Definition of Inflation

INFLATION is a *general* rise in prices. In the above extract, it is said that prices or the COST OF LIVING rose by 4.3% compared to a year ago. What that means is that on average what would have cost £100 a year ago would cost £104.30 today. Notice that inflation takes places over a period of time. Inflation rates are most commonly calculated on a monthly or yearly basis.

Inflation Over Time

Figure 60.2 shows how inflation has changed over time in the UK. Inflation was not considered a major problem in the UK in the 1950s and early 1960s, but from the mid-1960s it became an important issue. The high inflation of the 1970s led to the control of inflation becoming the most important priority of government in the early 1980s.

How Inflation is Measured

The prices of different goods do not go up by the same percentage over a period of time. For instance, the increase in the price level mentioned in the extract above was caused by increases in taxes and the price of clothing. In the same month, food prices and housing costs actually fell. So the measure of inflation has to average out these price increases and price falls.

Inflation in the UK is measured by the RETAIL PRICE INDEX (RPI). It is calculated in the following way.

- The government finds out the typical spending pattern of a British household. It does this by asking about 7000 households each year to record all their spending over a two-week period. The findings are then averaged out and the spending of the typical or average household is calculated.

- Each month, the government attempts to collect about 75 000 prices of some 600 different items up and down the country. The average price of each of the 600 items is calculated.

- The average inflation rate can then be calculated. Each individual price rise (or fall) is weighted according to how important it is in the typical household's budget. For instance, food represents about 20% or one-fifth of household spending. Therefore, a 10% rise in the price of food would raise average prices by 10% × ⅕ or 2%. Household goods represents about 10% or ¹/₁₀ of average household spending. So a 15% price rise in household goods would add 15% × ¹/₁₀ or 1.5% to the retail price index. Because of this process of weighting, the retail price index is a WEIGHTED INDEX.

- An index number is then given to the level of prices. This is done by calling the level of prices in one year '100' and comparing how prices have changed before and after that 'base' point. Index numbers were discussed more fully in Unit 5.

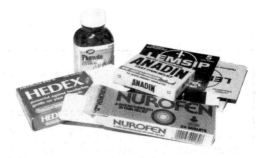

The price of a prescription rose 19 times from 1971 to 1992. This is part of a general increase in prices over the period.

1 What is meant by inflation?

2 How is inflation measured?

3 Calculate how much a £100 basket of goods bought by the average household, would cost if the retail price index went up:
   (a) by 10%;
   (b) by 15%;
   (c) by 3%;
   (d) from 100 to 110;
   (e) from 100 to 120;
   (f) from 200 to 210;
   (g) from 50 to 60.

4 Why would a 10% increase in the price of petrol, all other prices remaining constant, *not* lead to a rise in the retail price index of 10%?

5 Why is your personal cost of living index almost certainly different from the retail price index?

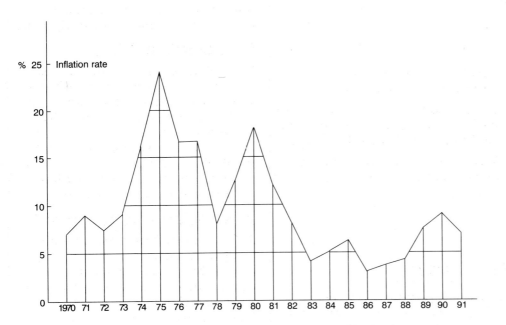

Figure 60.2 UK Inflation rate, 1970–91

Source: CSO, Economic Trends, 1992

COURSEWORK SUGGESTION

Describe how prices have changed in the UK over a period of time. Describe how the retail price index is calculated. Analyse what components of the retail price index have risen faster than other components, and how this has affected the cost of living. Assess how different households (pensioner households, one-parent households) have fared over time with rising inflation. What are price levels likely to be in the years 2000 and 2050?

KEY TERMS

INFLATION – a general rise in prices.

RETAIL PRICE INDEX – the measure of the level of prices in the UK.

WEIGHTED INDEX – an index constructed by giving each component of the index a different importance or *weight*.

COST OF LIVING – the money cost of buying a typical basket of goods and services.

The Costs of Inflation

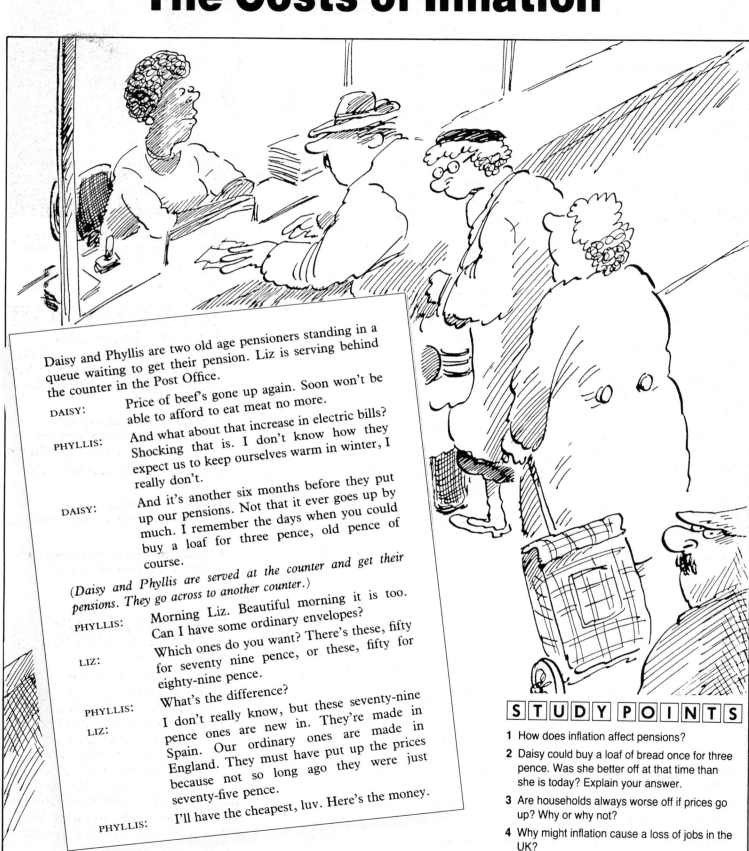

Daisy and Phyllis are two old age pensioners standing in a queue waiting to get their pension. Liz is serving behind the counter in the Post Office.

DAISY: Price of beef's gone up again. Soon won't be able to afford to eat meat no more.

PHYLLIS: And what about that increase in electric bills? Shocking that is. I don't know how they expect us to keep ourselves warm in winter, I really don't.

DAISY: And it's another six months before they put up our pensions. Not that it ever goes up by much. I remember the days when you could buy a loaf for three pence, old pence of course.

(Daisy and Phyllis are served at the counter and get their pensions. They go across to another counter.)

PHYLLIS: Morning Liz. Beautiful morning it is too. Can I have some ordinary envelopes?

LIZ: Which ones do you want? There's these, fifty for seventy nine pence, or these, fifty for eighty-nine pence.

PHYLLIS: What's the difference?

LIZ: I don't really know, but these seventy-nine pence ones are new in. They're made in Spain. Our ordinary ones are made in England. They must have put up the prices because not so long ago they were just seventy-five pence.

PHYLLIS: I'll have the cheapest, luv. Here's the money.

STUDY POINTS

1 How does inflation affect pensions?

2 Daisy could buy a loaf of bread once for three pence. Was she better off at that time than she is today? Explain your answer.

3 Are households always worse off if prices go up? Why or why not?

4 Why might inflation cause a loss of jobs in the UK?

'Inflation up and worse is still to come', reads a newspaper headline. Why is inflation bad and why is a higher rate of inflation worse than a lower rate of inflation? Would a fall in prices be desirable?

The Erosion of Values

One reason why inflation is generally considered to be undesirable is because inflation reduces the PURCHASING POWER OF MONEY – i.e. the value of what can be bought with a sum of money. In 1945, for instance, £1 would have bought 16 pints of beer. Fifty years later, that same £1 would only have bought just over ½ pint of beer. Rising prices is not a major problem for many people, because their wages go up even more quickly than prices, leaving them better off. But other people do suffer.

'Millions of people who retire on a decent pension are robbed by inflation. At the present inflation rate of five per cent, anyone retiring on a pension of £115 a week now will find its value sinking to less than £71 in ten years' time.'

The pensioners referred to here are pensioners on FIXED PENSIONS – pensions that stay the same from the moment a worker retires. As prices go up, the pensioner can buy less and less with his or her money. The higher the rate of inflation, the more quickly will the real value of the pension go down.

Pensioners are one group who suffer from inflation. Other groups include:

- workers who find it difficult to get pay increases in line with inflation;
- savers who find that the interest rate on their savings is lower than the inflation rate, so that the value of their savings goes down.

The problem of erosion of values can, to a great extent, be solved by INDEX LINKING – increasing pensions, wages, savings, etc. in line with the retail price index. Most welfare benefits are already index linked in the UK, as are state pensions.

Uncertainty

Inflation is also a cost to the economy, because of the *uncertainty* it creates. High inflation means that people find it difficult to keep track of what is the right price to pay for a good. Firms do not know how much they will be able to sell their products for in two years' time. Nor do they know how much it will cost to produce the good. Savers do not know how much their savings will be worth in 20 or 40 years' time. People, firms and governments go to great lengths to avoid uncertainties in their activities – they take out insurance, sign long-term contracts, etc. It is not surprising that they dislike inflation, which creates so much uncertainty about the future.

Inflation imposes costs on producers and consumers. Producers have to increase prices regularly. They have to calculate the new prices and then issue new price lists. Restaurants for instance have to print new menus – hence 'menu costs'. Consumers and producers also have to spend more time shopping around to get lowest prices – 'shoe leather costs'.

Unemployment

Some economists argue that inflation causes unemployment. High inflation prices British goods out of foreign markets and encourages imports leading to a loss of British jobs. Other economists argue that the only way to keep inflation low is to keep unemployment high. If unemployment comes down, workers are in a better position to get big pay rises which lead to higher prices.

Pensions have to be increased each year by at least the rate of inflation if pensioners are to be able to buy as much as before.

CHECKPOINTS

1 A pensioner retires on a fixed pension of £10 000 a year in 1995. Ten years later, in 2005, prices have doubled. What is the effect of this on the pensioner?

2 Explain why (a) savers and (b) non-unionised workers are particularly vulnerable to inflation.

3 Why do ordinary people not like inflation?

4 Why does inflation create uncertainty? Why is uncertainty an economic cost?

5 Explain the possible link between inflation and unemployment.

COURSEWORK SUGGESTION

Conduct a survey on the costs of inflation to individuals. Interview a pensioner with an occupational pension, a man or woman at home looking after a young family, a businessman and a manual worker. Ask them questions which will reveal the perceived and the actual costs of inflation to these individuals. Analyse your findings and try to assess the extent to which inflation is a cost to society.

KEY TERMS

PURCHASING POWER OF MONEY – what goods and services can be bought with a fixed sum of money.

FIXED PENSION – a pension that remains the same in monetary terms, even when the cost of living increases.

INDEX LINKING – a rise (in pensions, wages, savings, etc.) in line with the retail price index.

The Causes of Inflation (1)

John T. Mayne and Henry Field Junior were the only two survivors of a plane crash on a desert island in the Pacific Ocean ten years ago.

Luckily for them, they escaped the wreck with their wallets intact. Being good upright capitalists, they decided that competition and free market forces should rule their dealings. They both had exactly three hundred dollars in their wallets.

John was a great fisherman and set up a firm catching fish. Henry was a farmer and decided to set up a business growing wheat. Each became self sufficient in all commodities apart from wheat and fish.

When it came to fixing prices, John sold 1 fish for a dollar, whilst Henry sold a measure of wheat for two dollars. Each year John sold 300 fish whilst Henry sold 150 measures of wheat.

One day, Henry and John's world was turned upside down by the arrival of George Rex, or GR for short, in his pleasure cruiser. He decided he liked the island so much that he would stay there for a year.

But he did want some fish and wheat – 150 fish and 75 measures of wheat to be precise. Henry and John were producing as much as they could already, but each saw an opportunity to up the price of their products. They knew GR had $600 in his wallet.

STUDY POINTS

Before GR arrived:

1 What was the value (in dollars) of all the output sold in the desert island economy p.a.?

2 What was the total money supply?

After GR arrived:

3 What is the total money supply in the economy now?

4 Half of that money will be used by GR and Henry to buy fish from John. What is the highest price that John can now charge for each fish?

5 Half the money will be used by GR and John to buy wheat from Henry. What is the highest price that Henry can now charge for each measure of wheat?

6 What has happened to prices in the economy as a result of the increase in the money supply?

7 Are Henry and John better off or worse off than before? Explain your answer.

Inflation is a general rise in the price level. In this unit, we will consider what might cause the level of prices in an economy to rise over time. There are three main views or explanations. One, the view covered in this unit, is *monetarist*. Monetarists are economists, politicians, businessmen, etc. who believe that there is a definite link between inflation and the rate of growth of the money supply. The term 'monetarist' has also come to be associated with a whole range of other beliefs, including the belief that free market forces and as little government intervention as possible in the economy will lead to greater efficiency. The other two theories of inflation, covered in the next unit, are *Keynesian*. Keynesian economists believe that, in general, free market forces often lead to a very inefficient allocation of resources and that therefore the state needs to intervene strongly in the economy.

The Monetarist View

Monetarists argue that the only cause of inflation is excessive increases in the money supply. To understand their basic idea, consider this example. In an economy, £1000 worth of notes and coins circulate. Notes and coins are the only form of money. The only good which money buys is red socks. Each year, 2000 pairs of red socks are produced and they are all sold. Once sold, these red socks are never resold. It is obvious that the price of a pair of red socks will be 50p (£1000 ÷ 2000). Now assume that the government prints a further £1000, so that the total money supply is now £2000. The government spends its £1000 on red socks. Then the price of red socks will rise to £1 per pair (£2000 ÷ 2000). Two things have happened as a result of the doubling of the money supply:

- Prices have doubled.
- There has been a redistribution of purchasing power, in this case in favour of the government. This is shown by the fact that the government can buy 1000 pairs of red socks, which previously were bought by the private sector.

The redistribution effects of inflation were discussed in Unit 60. Here, we want to consider the link between money supply and the price level. There would have been no inflation, if the output of socks had doubled along with the money supply. Prices would have remained at 50p per pair.

Monetarists argue that what is true in this simple example is true of the real world. They argue that inflation is caused by increases in the money supply over and above increases in the output of the economy. So, if the money supply rose by 10% and output rose by 3%, then approximately 7% inflation could be expected.

The Evidence

The evidence to support this view of inflation is difficult to interpret for a number of reasons.

- As was shown in Unit 52, there is no clear definition of 'the money supply'. Different measures of the money supply can move in different directions at the same time, so it is often difficult to say whether the rate of growth of the money supply is increasing or decreasing.

- Most monetarists argue that an increase in the money supply leads to higher inflation over a period of time of several years. So inflation in, say, 1998 will be the result of increases in the money supply over the period 1995–8 and possibly before. It is thus very difficult to pinpoint the exact rise in the money supply that led to a particular rise in prices.

CHECKPOINTS

1 **What is the monetarist view of the cause of inflation?**

2 **On monetarist assumptions, fill in the missing figures in Figure 62.1 (all figures will be approximate).**
Figure 62.1

Growth in the money supply (%)	Growth in output (%)	Change in prices (%)
10	0	
8	2	
14		13
	4	4

3 **Explain why it is difficult to prove or disprove the monetarist theory of inflation.**

COURSEWORK SUGGESTION

Describe the pattern of inflation over the past twenty years. Statistics can be obtained from sources such as *Economic Trends Annual Supplement* and the *Annual Abstract of Statistics* (both published by HMSO). Discuss changes in the money supply (figures are available from the same sources). Investigate the extent to which there is any link between changes in the money supply and changes in inflation.

The Causes of Inflation (2)

Figure 63.1 Inflation rate, UK, 1970–1991

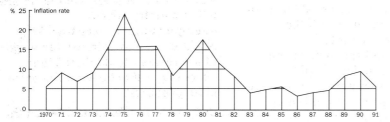

Figure 63.2 Percentage change in import prices, UK, 1970–1991

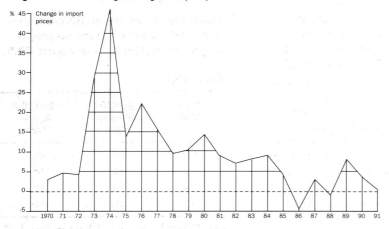

Figure 63.3 Percentage increase in average earnings, UK, 1970–1991

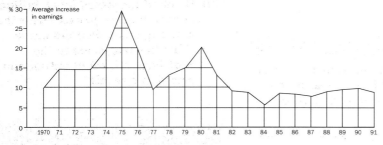

Note: 1970–76 figures are for increases in basic weekly wages of manual workers

Source: Figures 63.1–63.3: CSO, *Economic Trends*, 1992

S T U D Y P O I N T S

Consider the graphs above.

1 What was the highest annual rate of inflation over the period 1970 to 1991 and in what year did it occur?

2 What was the lowest annual rate of inflation and when did it occur?

3 What is an 'import'?

4 Explain why an increase in import prices can lead to an increase in inflation.

5 If a firm gives a pay increase to its workers, why may it well attempt to increase the prices of its products to customers? Why does this lead to inflation?

6 Look carefully at all three graphs. Do they show, in your opinion, that changes in import prices and pay inceases for workers lead to increases in the rate of inflation?

The monetarist view of inflation was explained in Unit 62. But it is not the only explanation of what causes inflation. Another group of economists called Keynesian economists (after John Maynard Keynes, a famous economist who died in 1946) believe that inflation is caused either by a rise in costs or by a rise in demand.

Cost–Push Inflation

Some Keynesians argue that inflation is caused by increases in costs. This is known as the COST–PUSH view. A firm faces a number of major costs:

- The major one is often the cost of labour;

- Equally important can be the cost of goods and services purchased from other firms. At least some of these goods and services will be imported from abroad;

- Taxes are yet another cost.

Cost–push economists argue that most firms set prices by calculating how much it costs to make a product, and then adding a MARK-UP to provide a profit. For instance, it may cost £100 to produce a bicycle. The firm will add a 10% mark-up as its profit and sell the bicycle for £110. This method of pricing is known as COST-PLUS PRICING. Obviously, any increase in costs or profits will increase prices. So the argument is that inflation is caused by increases in costs.

What is more, inflation can become permanent if a WAGE–PRICE SPIRAL is set up. This occurs when an initial increase in prices prompts workers to ask for higher pay rises. These higher wages add to firms' costs and so to even higher prices. This sets off further demands for wage increases, and so it goes on.

There is no doubt that inflation in Britain increased sharply on the two occasions in the 1970s (in 1973/4 and 1978/9) when oil prices shot up. But if the cost–push view of inflation is correct, it needs to be shown that this rise in oil prices increased inflation over a period of time and did not just push up prices on a once-and-for-all basis. Whether this happened is not clear from the evidence available.

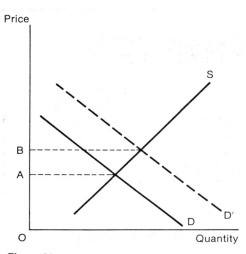

Price

S

B
A

D   D'

O   Quantity

Figure 63.4

Demand–pull Inflation

The other main Keynesian theory of inflation is the DEMAND–PULL theory. In a normal market, if demand increases, so do prices. This is shown in Figure 63.4. Here, an increase in demand from D to D′ leads to an increase in prices from OA to OB. Some economists argue that the same is true of the whole economy. If consumers try to spend more on consumer goods, or firms try to invest more, or foreigners want to buy more exports, or governments want to increase public spending, then inflation is likely to result.

How much inflation will result depends upon how large the increase in demand is and also on how near the economy is to FULL EMPLOYMENT. Full employment is defined as that level of employment where all available

factors of production are fully employed – i.e. no unemployment exists. If the economy is well below full employment, then firms can take on more workers, buy more machines, etc. to produce more goods and services when demand increases. So an increase in demand here should not lead to much inflation. But if the economy is near to or at full employment, then firms will not be able to employ extra factors of production, and therefore they will not be able to produce more goods and services. Thus, an increase in demand at full employment will lead to inflation, but not increased output.

Demand–pull economists argue that inflation could well increase again, if demand rose substantially today, even though there are 3 million people unemployed. It is claimed that this is because, although there are plenty of workers available, there is not enough capital in Britain to produce a large increase in goods and services. Because Britain has failed to invest enough over the past ten or fifteen years, there is a shortage of capital. So an increase in demand today could well spark off a rise in demand–pull inflation.

C H E C K P O I N T S

1 A firm gives its workers a 10% pay rise. Why might the prices of the firm's products go up as a result?

2 The prices of imported goods, including raw materials, goes up by 20%. Why might this lead to an increase in the price of British goods?

3 A firm wants to take on more workers, but it is situated in an area of the country where unemployment is very low. Why might it have to increase the wages of its workers to do this? What effect might this have on the price of its products?

4 Explain the difference between the cost–push view of inflation and the demand–pull view.

5 Draw aggregate (total) demand and aggregate supply curves on graph paper, using the data in Figure 63.5.

Figure 63.5

Price level (£)	Aggregate demand (£bn)	Aggregate supply (£bn)
10	60	45
12	55	55
14	50	60
16	45	60

(a) What is the equilibrium level of output and prices?

(b) Demand increased by £5 billion at each level of prices. Draw the new aggregate demand curve. What has happened to the equilibrium level of output and prices as a result?

K E Y   T E R M S

COST–PUSH INFLATION – the view that inflation is caused by increases in costs to producers, such as higher wages, higher import prices or higher profit levels.

COST–PLUS PRICING – this occurs when a producer fixes the price of a product by calculating its cost and adding a profit mark-up.

MARK-UP – the percentage that a producer adds to the cost of a product to arrive at the final price.

WAGE–PRICE SPIRAL – a process by which increases in wages lead to increases in prices, which in turn lead to increases in wages and so on.

DEMAND–PULL INFLATION – the view that inflation is caused by more demand in the whole economy than can be supplied at existing prices.

FULL EMPLOYMENT – the level of employment where all factors of production in the economy are fully utilised.

C O U R S E W O R K   S U G G E S T I O N

Arrange to interview the finanancial directors (or whoever is responsible for pricing products) of several firms. Draw up a questionnaire beforehand which asks how the firm prices its products. For instance, does it rigidly use a cost-plus mark-up system or are prices set independently of costs? Describe your findings. Compare and contrast the different pricing methods used. Try to decide the extent to which your evidence supports a cost–push view or a demand–pull view of inflation.

Economic Growth

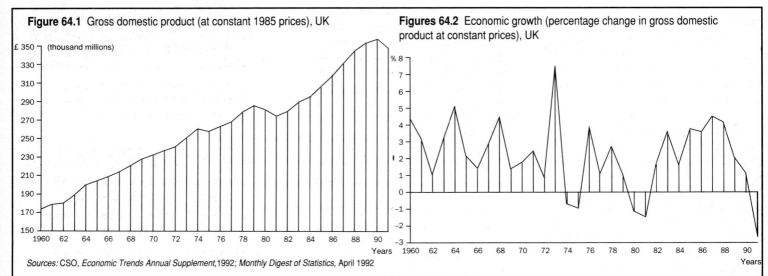

Figure 64.1 Gross domestic product (at constant 1985 prices), UK

£ 350 (thousand millions)

Sources: CSO, *Economic Trends Annual Supplement*,1992; *Monthly Digest of Statistics*, April 1992

Figures 64.2 Economic growth (percentage change in gross domestic product at constant prices), UK

Sources: CSO, *Economic Trends Annual Supplement*, 1992; *Monthly Digest of Statistics*, April 1992

Figures 64.3 Average annual change in real GDP, 1960–1990

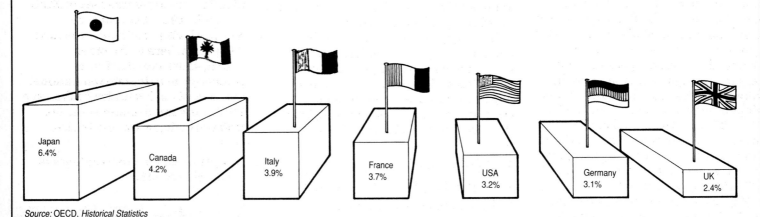

Japan 6.4%
Canada 4.2%
Italy 3.9%
France 3.7%
USA 3.2%
Germany 3.1%
UK 2.4%

Source: OECD, *Historical Statistics*

STUDY POINTS

Consider Figure 64.1

1 What is meant by 'gross domestic product'? (Use the index at the back of the book to find the definition if you do not know.)

2 What was the value of gross domestic product (a) in 1960 and (b) in 1991 in the UK?

3 By how much did gross domestic product increase between 1960 and 1991 (a) in £s and (b) in percentage terms?

4 In what ways might this increase in gross domestic product improve the standard of living of the average Briton?

Consider Figure 64.2

5 In what year did gross domestic product grow the most in percentage terms?

6 In what years did gross domestic product go down compared to the previous year?

7 Why is a high rate of growth in gross domestic product generally considered to be better than a low rate of economic growth?

Consider Figure 64.3

8 Which country had the fastest average annual rate of economic growth between 1960 and 1990? Which country had the lowest?

9 Assume that Japan and the UK both had GDPs of £100 in 1960. Use your calculator to find out how much their GDPs would be in 1990.

10 Does it matter that the UK had a low growth rate compared to other countries over the period 1960 to 1990? To answer this, consider the costs and the benefits of economic growth.

The Chancellor of the Exchequer said in his 1992 budget speech:

> '(Last year), GDP fell by 2½ per cent . . . I expect growth in this year to be about 1 per cent.'

When the Chancellor talked about ECONOMIC GROWTH he was referring to growth in national income. Normally national income rises each year, but in 1991, in a severe recession, national income actually fell by 2½%.

Figure 64.1 shows how national income has grown in real terms (i.e. after inflation has been taken out of the figures) over the period 1960–91. The measure of national income used is gross domestic product or GDP (explained in Unit 47). In almost every year, GDP has been higher than in the previous year, so that by 1991 GDP was double what it was in 1960.

Figure 64.2 shows the rate of growth of GDP over the same period. Growth averaged about 2½% – in some years it was less, in some years more. Notice that the figures tend to go up and down in a regular pattern. This is known as the TRADE CYCLE. On average, the economy goes into *boom* (i.e. there is high economic growth) every five years. So the economy was going through a boom in 1963, 1968, 1973, 1979 and 1988. But between these booms were RECESSIONS – periods of low growth. The economy was going through a recession in 1962, 1966, 1971, 1975, 1980 and 1991.

Figure 64.3 shows that since 1960 the UK economy has grown, but it has not grown as fast as its rivals in the world economy. Does this matter?

Growth: Desirable or Not?

Britain's low growth rate is a matter of grave concern. In 1950, the UK was almost the most affluent country in Europe and indeed the world. The average British citizen could spend more money than his or her French, German, Spanish or African counterpart. By 1992, this had changed considerably. Britain now has one of the lowest incomes per head in Western Europe; for instance, the average Briton has less money to spend than the average French or German citizen. The basic economic problem is that human wants exceed what can be produced. If Britain fails to grow as fast as other countries, then this problem will become relatively more difficult than in those other countries.

However, a failure to grow quickly is not necessarily bad. We saw in Unit 49 that national income is not the same as the standard of living in an economy. Growth will lead to a lowering of the standard of living, if the advantages of having extra output are more than outweighed by the costs of that output, such as greater pollution, greater stress on workers, etc. Today organisations like the Friends of the Earth argue that the advantages of being able to consume more goods and services through economic growth are far outweighed by the cost of this production. These include:

- global warming,
- destruction of the ozone layer,
- extinction of many species,
- degradation of agricultural land,
- the exhaustion of non-renewable resources like oil.

They predict that by the time you want to draw your pension, the world's economy will have ceased to exist.

Nuclear power can help us meet our energy requirements and achieve growth; but many people are worried about safety.

CHECKPOINTS

1 Giving an example, explain what is meant by economic growth.

2 Explain the difference between a 'boom' and a 'recession'.

3 Why does low economic growth present a problem for a national economy?

4 Suppose two countries had identical national incomes of £100 billion in 1985. One country averaged 2% growth over the next 25 years, whereas the other averaged 3% growth. Use a calculator to calculate the national incomes of each country in the year 2010. How much better off is the faster-growing economy in that year?

5 List the possible disadvantages of economic growth.

COURSEWORK SUGGESTION

Consider your local economy (village, town, city or region in which you live). Gather as many statistics as you can to show how that economy has changed over the past 25 years. Useful sources might be your local town hall, central library, and government statistics such as *Regional Trends* (published by HMSO). Evaluate the extent to which economic growth has resulted in an improvement in the standard of living for the local population. What might be the costs and benefits of a high-growth local economy in the future, as opposed to a low or zero-growth economy?

KEY TERMS

ECONOMIC GROWTH – an increase in national income over a period of time.

TRADE CYCLE – changes in a nation's level of economic activity.

RECESSION – a period of higher than average unemployment and lower than average growth.

The Causes of Economic Growth

Figure 65.1 Average rate of economic growth 1980–91 (% change in real GDP)

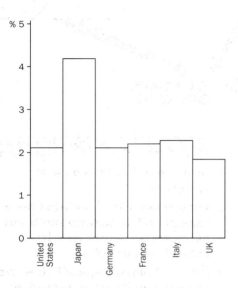

Figure 65.2 Investment as a percentage of national income 1980–91 (gross fixed capital formation % yearly average of GDP at market prices)

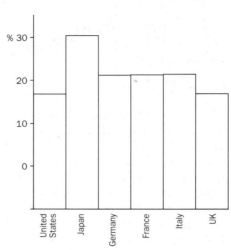

Figure 65.3 Growth in manufacturing and industrial production (% annual change)

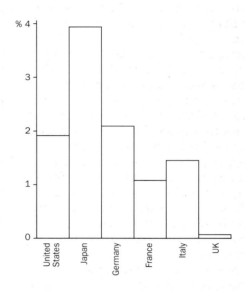

Figure 65.4 Research and Development investment (% of domestic industrial production)

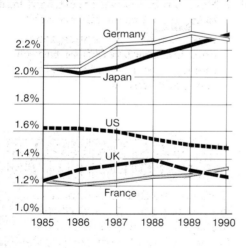

Source: OECD, CSO, Sciteb Analysis

Figure 65.5 Defence spending (total defence spending as a proportion of GDP)

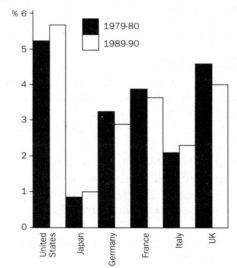

Source: OECD, Eurostat

Figure 65.6 Labour costs 1990

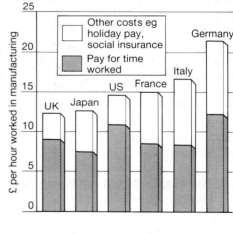

Source: US Bureau of Labour Statistics

STUDY POINTS

Write a report about the UK's growth performance.

- How did the UK grow in the 1980 compared to other world economies?

- What could have caused this? Look at the data given above. How might these variables be linked to economic growth? Do they help explain the UK's growth record? What other information would you need to make your report?

- How could the UK improve its growth performance over the next ten years?

The Factors of Production

Some 10 000 years ago, world output was extremely small. It consisted mainly of food, simple shelter, wood and other simple necessities of life. Today, the output of just one small economy, that of the UK, is well over £600 billion a year. How has this transformation taken place? What are the likely sources of economic growth in the future?

Long-term growth is generated mainly by increasing the quantity and quality of the factors of production in an economy. Some countries have grown because of their rich resources of *land*. As we have seen, 'land' includes not only land itself, but all natural resources. Saudi Arabia, for instance, has grown because it has been able to exploit its oil reserves. The UK, too, is rich in many natural resources. North Sea oil alone contributed up to 2–3% a year in the 1980s to the national income of the UK.

Not all countries possess rich natural resources. But *labour* too, can be an important source of growth. A country is likely to produce more if it has more workers. An increasing population is therefore likely to boost growth, but of course that may not mean that income per head of the population is growing. The main sources of growth per head of the population are:

- an increase in the quality of the workforce;
- a better utilisation of the population.

Increasing the quality of the workforce, through better education, training and experience, increases the value of *human capital* (explained in Unit 20) in the economy and makes workers more productive. Making better use of workers would involve moving workers into more productive industries or bringing into the workforce more women who had wanted to work, but were denied the opportunity by legal, economic and social pressures.

Increasing the stock of *capital* and making more efficient use of it is another important source of growth. Equipping workers with better

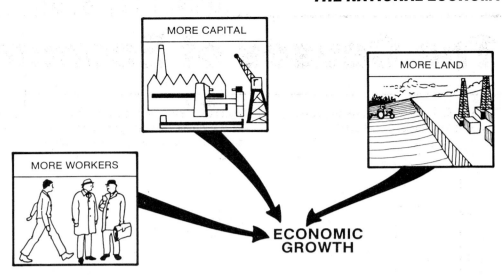

MORE CAPITAL

MORE LAND

MORE WORKERS

ECONOMIC GROWTH

machines is likely to make those workers more productive – each worker will be able to produce more in the same time. It is perhaps not surprising that Japan, with one of the highest growth rates in the post-war period, should also have one of the best investment records. But investment in itself is not enough to produce growth. If Britain today invested large sums in declining industries, such as shipbuilding and steel making, then that investment would be largely wasted. Since 1945, Japan has not only invested, but has invested in the industries of the future.

Efficiency

Growth can also be stimulated, if more efficient ways are found of combining all the factors of production. For instance, the economy could produce more goods and services:

- if the employment of factors of production like labour were increased. If 1 million unemployed workers were back in work, producing just £5000 of output each, that would add £5000 million to output;
- if there were fewer strikes. These strikes are usually caused by the conflict of interest between the owners of capital who want to earn more profit by paying workers less, and workers who want higher wages;
- if workers and managers worked harder to get the most out of the limited resources available.

Data Response Questions
Units 60–65

Unit 60 Inflation

THE PRICE OF PASSING YEARS

	Average prices*	
	1945	1991
1 loaf of bread	1.88p	58p
Packet of 10 cigarettes	4.38p	100p
1 pint of beer	6.25p	130p
1 gallon of petrol	9.75p	203p
Average three-bedroom house	£5625	£60 534

*Decimal value

	Average weekly earnings	Average hours worked**	Average hourly earnings**
1945	£6.07	49.7	12.21p
1991	£255.60	45.1	£5.67

**including overtime

£1 in 1945 is now worth in 1991 in real terms only 5.9p; in other words, to have the same purchasing power as £1 in 1945 you would need £16.84 in your pocket.

Source: Daily Express, 8 May, 1992; CSO Annual Abstract of Statistics 1992; Economic Trends Annual Supplement

1 What was the price of 2 pints of beer in 1945 and 1991?
(1 mark)

2 Calculate how many times the price of a gallon of petrol has risen over the period 1945 to 1991. *(1 mark)*

3 Which of the goods mentioned in the data has gone up most in price in percentage terms? *(1 mark)*

4 A worker earned £10 a week in 1945. How much would he have had to earn in 1991 to buy the same basket of goods and services? *(1 mark)*

5 Explain whether or not the average manual worker could buy more goods and services in 1991 than in 1945.
(3 marks)

6 Why would a 10% rise in the price of petrol not add 10% to the general price level? *(3 marks)*

Unit 61 The Costs of Inflation

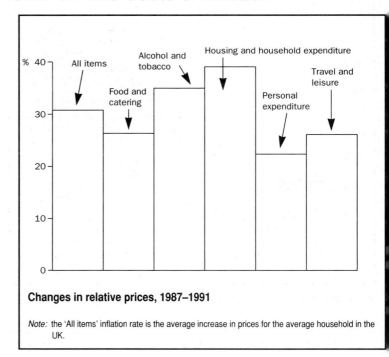

Changes in relative prices, 1987–1991

Note: the 'All items' inflation rate is the average increase in prices for the average household in the UK.

1 By how much did average prices in the UK increase between 1987 and 1991? *(1 mark)*

2 Which prices went up by more than the average?
(2 marks)

3 Pensioners spent a larger proportion than the average household on food between 1987 and 1991.

(a) How might this have affected the rise in average prices faced by pensioners? *(2 marks)*

(b) How might this have affected their standard of living if their pensions went up in line with the all-items measure of inflation? *(6 marks)*

The Data Response Question for **Units 62 and 63** can be found on page 221.

Unit 64 Economic Growth

Output of the whole economy, manufacturing and service industries 1979–91

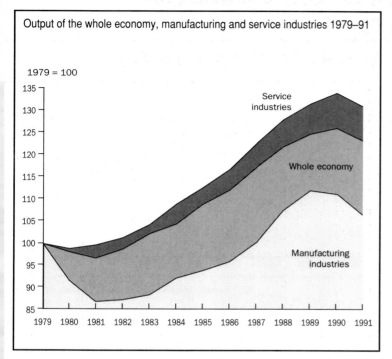

1979 = 100

Source: CSO, Economic Trends Annual Supplement; CSO, Monthly Digest of Statistics

1 Describe how the output for the whole economy has grown between 1979 and 1991. *(3 marks)*

2 (a) Compare how output in manufacturing has changed with that of service industries.
(b) Which sector has contributed most towards economic growth between 1979 and 1991? *(4 marks)*

3 What are the possible (a) advantages and (b) disadvantages of relatively slow growth in Britain's manufacturing industry? *(8 marks)*

Unit 65 The Causes of Economic Growth

Use the Budget to create jobs, Lamont urged

The Chancellor of the Exchequer, Norman Lamont, was today urged to spend billions in next month's Budget in a bid to create half a million jobs and training places.

The call was made by the TUC which told Mr Lamont the country was 'crying out' for more jobs and better public services.

The main proposals in the TUC's budget submission are:
• A £2 billion public investment programme to improve housing, schools, hospitals and transport.
• £1 billion for training schemes, including a temporary work scheme.
• Reforms of unemployment benefits, costing £800 million, to improve sick pay, extend payments and provide loans to help the jobless find more work.

The TUC estimates that the measures would create 250 000 new jobs and 250 000 extra places on training schemes along with other special measures.

Source: Express and Star, 3 February 1992

1 What do the letters 'TUC' stand for? *(1 mark)*

2 Why do you think the TUC is interested in public investment, training schemes and unemployment benefits? *(3 marks)*

3 How would the TUC's proposals if carried out raise the rate of economic growth in the UK? *(8 marks)*

4 What other policies could the government pursue if it wanted to raise the rate of economic growth? *(3 marks)*

Essay Questions
Units 60–65

1 (a) What is meant by 'inflation'? *(4 marks)*
(b) Describe *two* possible causes of inflation in Britain today. *(8 marks)*
(c) Explain the view that inflation causes unemployment. *(8 marks)*

2 'Growth in national income of the UK slowed to 1.4% last year.'
(a) Suggest *two* reasons why a slow down in the UK's rate of growth of national income is bad for people in Britain. *(6 marks)*
(b) How could growth in national income be increased in the future? *(8 marks)*
(c) To what extent does growth in national income always lead to an increase in economic welfare? *(10 marks)*

Regional Inequalities

Figure 66.1 Regional inequalities, 1989–1991

Region	Unemploy-ment rate (%) 1991	Gross domestic product per head (£) 1989	Average gross weekly earnings: men (£) 1990	Percentage of households with telephone 1989–90	Infant (0–1) mortality (deaths per 1000 live births) 1989	Percentage of workforce holding a degree or equivalent 1990
South East	6.9	9086	344.4	91.5	8.1	13.4
South West	6.4	7187	277.3	89.5	7.9	8.3
East Anglia	5.8	7460	281.1	91.1	6.4	8.7
West Midlands	8.6	6898	269.3	85.4	9.9	7.2
East Midlands	7.5	7131	269.7	88.1	8.3	8.5
Yorkshire and Humberside	8.7	6649	266.9	84.1	8.8	7.0
North	10.4	6522	265.2	80.3	8.4	6.5
North West	9.4	6898	274.7	84.4	8.6	8.2
Scotland	8.7	7021	276.4	82.4	8.7	8.0
Wales	8.7	6372	258.6	82.3	8.0	7.2
Northern Ireland	13.7	5758	253.5	73.4	6.9	8.2

Sources: CSO, *Employment Gazette*, May 1992; *Family Spending 1990*: *Regional Trends,* 1991

Figure 66.2 Specialisation by region in the UK 1990

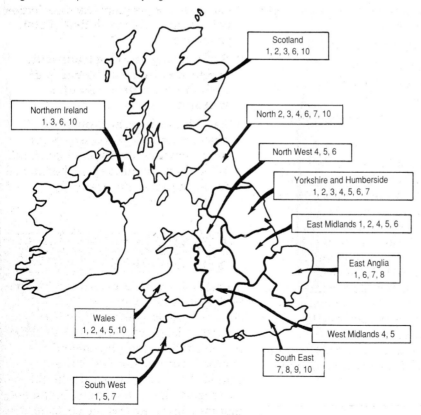

Scotland
1, 2, 3, 6, 10

Northern Ireland
1, 3, 6, 10

North 2, 3, 4, 6, 7, 10

North West 4, 5, 6

Yorkshire and Humberside
1, 2, 3, 4, 5, 6, 7

East Midlands 1, 2, 4, 5, 6

East Anglia
1, 6, 7, 8

West Midlands 4, 5

Wales
1, 2, 4, 5, 10

South East
7, 8, 9, 10

South West
1, 5, 7

KEY

1 Agriculture, forestry, fishing
2 Energy and water supply
3 Construction

MANUFACTURING

4 Metals, minerals and chemicals
5 Metal goods, engineering and vehicle industries
6 Other manufacturing

SERVICES

7 Distribution, hotels and catering, repairs
8 Transport and communication
9 Banking, finance, insurance, business services and leasing
10 Public administration and other services

The map shows those regions which have more than the national average percentage of their labour forces employed in a particular sector of industry

Source: CSO, *Regional Trends,* 1991

STUDY POINTS

1 Prepare a report on your region. Compare its living standards with other regions.

2 Assess what employment opportunities there are in your region compared to other regions.

3 Evaluate the prospects for your region, remembering that service industries are growing at a much faster rate than manufacturing industry at the moment.

Indicators of Affluence

The UK can be divided into two areas. The South, made up of the South East, East Anglia and the South West, has been relatively well off since the Second World War. The North, made up of the rest of the regions of the UK, has not been as well off.

Figure 66.1 shows six different measures of affluence for each region of the UK. The three southern regions clearly come out as being more affluent than the rest of the UK. Why should this be so?

Causes

One fundamental reason for this inequality between regions is the location of industry. The South of England has come to have more and better industry than the rest of the UK. This was not always the case. One hundred years ago, the prosperous areas of Britain were in the North. This was where the new industries of the time – manufacturing industries such as steel, textiles, shipbuilding and engineering – had based themselves. The prosperous parts of the UK were situated on the west coast – e.g. Bristol, Liverpool and Glasgow – because our major trading partners were North America and the British colonies. During the twentieth century, manufacturing industry has been in slow decline, as has been shown in Unit 48. Much of the 'new' manufacturing industry, such as motor manufacturing and light engineering, has tended to establish itself in the Midlands and the South. This has left the rest of the UK with declining industries and rising unemployment.

The prosperity of the South was further increased by the growth of service industries in the UK economy. London, the capital of the UK, became a centre for banking and other financial services. It was also the seat of government and this created many new jobs. The South was, and still is, the most important centre of

Liverpool was one of the UK's most prosperous cities in the nineteenth century.

population in the UK. Service industries tend to set up where people live and buy those services. A last important factor has been the growth of trade with Europe and the relative decline in trade with North America and the colonies. This has meant that industry has been attracted to the South to cut down on transport and other costs in its trade with the Continent. The current distribution of jobs, by industry, in the UK is shown in Figure 66.2.

The South has become increasingly prosperous because:

- new industry creates new jobs;
- which creates income;
- which creates a demand for goods and services;
- which creates new industry and jobs.

Regions outside the South suffered particularly during the recession of 1980–81. One million manufacturing jobs were lost between 1979 and 1981. But in the late 1980s, the recovery in the North was relatively strong. More importantly, the recession which began in 1990 particularly hit service industries – concentrated in the South. For the first time in over 80 years, the North suffered relatively less than the South in a recession.

Whether areas such as Scotland and Wales will continue to catch up with the South in the 1990s is difficult to say. However, trends in employment are more hopeful in regions outside the South than they have been for a very long time.

C H E C K P O I N T S

1 In what ways are regions of the UK unequal in an economic sense?

2 Compare the geographical distribution of industry today with that of 100 years ago.

3 Explain why growing trade with Western Europe has helped pull industry towards the South of England.

4 Land is cheaper, buildings are cheaper and workers' wages are lower outside the South of England. Why, then, is industry still attracted to setting up in the South?

C O U R S E W O R K S U G G E S T I O N

Compare the region you live in either with Northern Ireland, or the south-east of England, whichever provides the greater contrast. Describe the industry in each region and compare various indices of the standard of living. Explain why the two regions have developed in the way that they have. Assess the costs and benefits of bringing the poorer regions up to the standards of affluence (i.e. wealth) of the richer regions.

K E Y T E R M

REGIONAL PROBLEM – the fact that different regions of the UK have different employment rates, and therefore different standards of living.

Government Economic Policy

City sees year-end inflation at 8.25%

ECHO AND STAR

PRICES UP AGAIN

UK's current account deficit widens as imports rise sharply

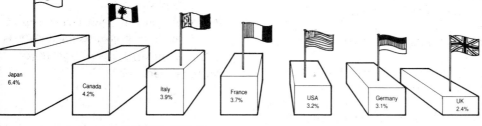

Average annual change in real GDP, 1960–90

Japan 6.4% | Canada 4.2% | Italy 3.9% | France 3.7% | USA 3.2% | Germany 3.1% | UK 2.4%

STUDY POINTS

1 Look at the photographs and the statistics. What economic problems facing the British economy are suggested by them?

2 The government has a responsibility to ensure that the economy is developing in as desirable a direction as possible. Traditionally, four major areas of responsibility have been singled out: the maintenance of a low level of unemployment, price stability (which in practice means low levels of inflation), high economic growth and a balance on foreign

trade (i.e. making sure that the UK is paying its way in the world by at least exporting as much as she imports). Explain why (a) high levels of unemployment (b) high levels of inflation and (c) low levels of economic growth can affect you in a negative way?

3 If a government had to choose between a doubling of inflation and a doubling of unemployment, which do you think it ought to choose and why? In order to answer this, consider the costs and benefits of each alternative.

Government Economic Policy

In 1988, unemployment was falling and UK national income was growing fast. But inflation was going up too and the country was importing more than it was exporting.

In 1992, unemployment was rising and national income was increasing only slowly. But inflation was low and the gap between imports and exports was narrowing.

Was the economy in better shape in 1988 or 1992? Unemployment, economic growth, inflation and the current balance (the gap between exports and imports) are the four key economic indicators in the economy. What can a government hope to achieve?

Unemployment

In the 1950s and 1960s, unemployment varied between 200000 and 600000. The 1970s saw unemployment climb to over 1.5 million. Then in the early 1980s unemployment rose to 3.5 million before falling back to 1.5 million in 1990. Since then it has gone back up towards the 3 million level. So the best the government could hope for in the long term at the moment is perhaps 2 million unemployed and it might be stuck at worst with 3 million.

Inflation

Since 1945, annual inflation rates have grown from 0% in 1958 to 24.8% in 1975. Today, the government has to keep inflation down to the inflation rate of our main competitors in the European Community. If British inflation rates are higher than, say, Germany's then British firms find that they are undercut in prices by German firms. We would lose jobs and income to our European partners. So inflation today has to be kept to a few per cent.

Growth

At worst, the British economy has had negative growth. In 1974–5, 1980–81 and 1991–2 the UK produced less than it had in previous years. At best, growth in output has been between 3 and 5%. On average though since 1945, the British economy has grown about 2.5% per year; 2.5% per year seems to be about the most we can grow without triggering off more inflation.

The Current Balance

The UK has to pay its way in the world by selling as much abroad (exports) as it buys from foreign producers (imports). If imports are greater than exports, the UK either has to run down its foreign savings to pay for this or it has to borrow. In the long term, it cannot borrow forever as countries like Brazil and Poland found out in the 1980s. Exports minus imports is called the current balance. If the current balance is positive or 'in the black', then exports are greater than imports and all is well. If the current balance is negative or 'in the red', then imports are greater than exports and Britain could be faced with problems in the future. So the government needs to aim to at least make imports equal to exports in the long term.

Conflicts of Objective

The past 50 years' history of the UK suggests that any government faces

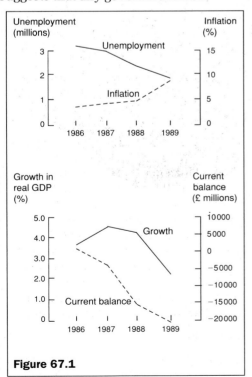

Figure 67.1

economic problems in the short term.

Look at Figure 67.1. This shows what happened to the economy between 1986 and 1989. This period was called the 'Lawson boom', after the Chancellor of the Exchequer of the time, Nigel Lawson. In a boom economy, output grows very fast, as it did in the late 1980s. This means that firms need to take on extra workers to keep up with the extra demand. So unemployment falls. Between 1986 and 1989 unemployment nearly halved.

But fast increases in output have a cost. Extra output means extra income for workers. They spend part of their extra money on goods from abroad. Imports go up so the current account position gets worse. In 1989, the current account deficit rose to over £20 billion, a huge figure.

Workers are also in a much better position to get higher wage increases. So you get cost–push inflation. Firms can pass on increases in costs in the form of higher prices because consumers have more money to spend. So you get demand–pull inflation. This higher inflation appeared in the UK in 1988 and 1989.

The government realised in 1988 that the economy was growing too fast and that inflation would be a problem if it didn't do something. So it doubled interest rates in the economy. This slowly hit spending in the economy because people and firms borrowed less.

Figure 67.2 shows what happened. The economy went into recession. Growth fell and was negative in 1990 and 1991. Unemployment began to climb again. But fewer imports were bought so the current account deficit was cut. Inflation too fell.

So UK governments seem to have to accept that there is a trade-off between lower unemployment and higher growth on the one hand and lower inflation and a better current account balance on the other.

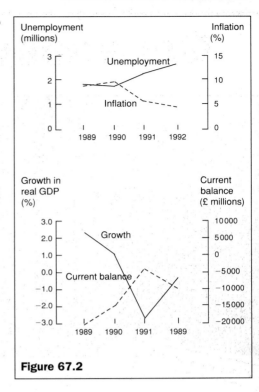

Figure 67.2

1 What are the four major economic policy objectives of the present government?

2 Why, according to Keynesians, is it difficult for an economy to have:
   (a) low unemployment and low inflation;
   (b) low unemployment *and* a good balance of payments situation?

3 What is meant by a 'trade-off' of policy objectives?

C O U R S E W O R K
S U G G E S T I O N

Describe and analyse the present government's economic objectives. Consider the extent to which those economic objectives are in conflict. Research material for this can be obtained from past copies of the *Economic Briefing* (published by the Treasury) and from newspaper articles.

Monetary Policy

Government keeps interest rates high as money supply keeps growing at too fast a rate

Banks eager to lend money to personal customers. Interest rate cut expected

Money supply growth sparks off renewed fears of inflation

Companies call for lower interest rates to help reduce costs and increase price competitiveness

Building company gone into liquidation. The company blames "too high mortgage rates" which have caused a slump in demand for new houses

Credit card companies report less spending since interest rates were increased

Increased money supply explains the recent reduction in interest rates

Company defers investment plan due to "too high interest rates"

Pound falls on foreign exchange markets. Government steps in to stop the fall by increasing interest rates

Mortgage rates up again as Government increases interest rates

STUDY POINTS

1 Write a report explaining why the money supply and the rate of interest are important in an economy. In your report, make use of each of the examples above. Structure your report round the following:

(a) Explain the link between the rate of interest and the level of spending in the economy.

(b) Explain the possible link between the money supply and inflation.

(c) Explain the link between the value of the pound and the exchange rate.

(d) What is the relationship between the rate of interest (which is the price which has to be paid if money is borrowed) and the supply of money? If you have any difficulty in answering this, go back to Units 12 and 13 which discuss supply and price.

MONETARY POLICY is government policy with regard to the level of interest rates and the growth of the money supply.

There are a large number of different interest rates in the economy. For instance, there are mortgage interest rates, credit card interest rates, bank rates and interest rates on long-term government borrowing. The UK government has, however, traditionally tried to influence one key rate in the economy – the bank base rate. This is the central interest rate of the big banks like Lloyds and Barclays. They charge above their base rate to customers who borrow money from them and give interest below base rate to their savers.

The money supply, as was explained in Unit 52, is made up not just of notes and coins but of bank deposits and building society deposits too. It was also explained in Unit 52 that the money supply and the rate of interest are linked. Increases in the money supply, all other things remaining the same, will lead to a fall in interest rates. On the other hand, a fall in the money supply will lead to a rise in interest rates.

Reasons for Controlling the Money Supply

There are three main reasons why a government might want to control the money supply and interest rates.

- As was explained in Unit 62, monetarists believe that inflation is caused by excessive increases in the money supply. Controlling the money supply is therefore the key to controlling inflation.

- Many economists believe that changing interest rates will affect the level of total spending or aggregate demand in the economy. If interest rates go up, consumers will borrow less because the repayments on loans will be larger. Firms too will be hit by higher repayments on existing loans and will cut back on investment spending. Falling interest rates will have the opposite effect – consumption and investment will tend to rise. Increased aggregate demand will then lead to a boost in growth and a reduction in unemployment.

- Interest rates are a key weapon to stabilise the value of the pound against other foreign currencies in the Exchange Rate Mechanism (ERM). If interest rates in London go up, more foreigners will want to save their money in London rather than New York, Paris or Tokyo. So they buy more pounds than before to invest in the London money markets. This greater demand for the pound pushes the value of the pound up. On the other hand, a fall in interest rates creates selling pressure on the pound, so the pound tends to weaken.

Techniques of Monetary Policy

Governments tend to operate monetary policy through their central banks. The central bank of the UK is the Bank of England.

In theory, the Bank of England has a number of different ways in which to influence the money supply and the rate of interest. One way is called OPEN MARKET OPERATIONS. Here the Bank of England either borrows more money than it needs to finance the PSBR (government borrowing) or it repays money owed by government to the rest of the economy. Borrowing more money than is needed is called OVERFUNDING. The Bank of England

borrowing money and then not spending it reduces the money supply. It also therefore pushes up the rate of interest as explained in Unit 52. Equally, if the Bank of England pays back some of its previous borrowing, this increases the money in circulation in the economy.

Another technique is for the Bank of England to issue MONETARY DIRECTIVES. Directives were used a lot in the 1950s, 1960s and 1970s. The Bank of England would order the banks not to lend out more than a certain amount. Or the Bank of England would place a limit on the growth of deposits of the banks. Restricting lending or borrowing by the banks should help restrict the growth in the money supply. However, banks became increasingly able to get round these regulations, for instance by borrowing and lending in Europe or the United States.

FUNDING is the name given to the process of changing short-term government borrowing to long-term government borrowing. The effects of funding depend upon the particular rules of the banking system. One effect is likely to be a rise in long-term interest rates and a fall in short-term interest rates, as the demand from the government for short- and long-term funds changes.

Today, the Bank of England operates its monetary policy by influencing interest rates. It does this by using open market operations – buying and selling stocks – in one key money market in the economy called

the discount market. The rate of interest in the discount market fixes bank base rates. Remember, bank base rate is the interest rate which fixes the rate of interest which banks charge to borrowers and pay to savers. This then influences most other interest rates in the economy. Fixing interest rates also gives the Bank of England some control over the rate of growth of the money supply because the interest rate and the money supply are linked.

C H E C K P O I N T S

1 Give 5 different interest rates in the UK.

2 Why might a government want to control the money supply?

3 What is the difference between open market operations and funding?

4 Explain how the Bank of England controls interest rates today.

5 Use a diagram to explain how changes in the rate of interest can affect the money supply.

C O U R S E W O R K S U G G E S T I O N

Take any three-month period. Describe what has happened to interest rates and the money supply over that period. Analyse why changes have occurred, particularly looking at the effect of the control of monetary variables exerted by the Bank of England. Consider the extent to which monetary policy has been effective over the period. This project will require a thorough reading of the financial press (particularly the *Financial Times*) over the period.

K E Y T E R M S

MONETARY POLICY – government policy with regard to the money supply and interest rates.

OPEN MARKET OPERATIONS – the buying and selling of government securities by the Bank of England in order to influence the stock of money in the economy.

OVERFUNDING – a form of open market operations where the Bank of England sells more government stock than is needed to finance the PSBR.

MONETARY DIRECTIVES – instructions from the Bank of England to the banks to restrict the growth of borrowing and lending.

FUNDING – the substitution of long-term government debt for short-term government debt.

Fiscal Policy

STUDY POINTS

1 Read the article carefully and then study the statistics. You have to prepare a report for the Opposition on the likely effects of the Chancellor's measures. In particular, you need to consider the effects on:

(a) unemployment;
(b) inflation;
(c) the balance of payments;
(d) the rate of economic growth.

Once you have prepared your report, you may want to discuss what actually happened after March 1972.

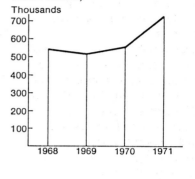

Figure 69.1 Unemployment (excluding school leavers)

£1,211m tax cuts in 72–73

The main features of the Chancellor's budget are:

- total tax cuts of £1,211m. By far the single most important item in this is a cut in income tax which should mean that every taxpayer pays £1 a week less in tax.
- increased help to companies which invest. Companies will be able to pay less tax if they undertake investment. Total cost to the Government is estimated at £200m a year.
- increased help for Britain's high unemployment regions (the "Development Areas"). Companies investing in these areas will be able to get back 20% of the cost of any investment made.
- overall, the Chancellor's measures will lead to tax cuts and extra government spending of an estimated £1,391 million a year.

The Chancellor, Mr Anthony Barber, said that the purpose of his Budget was "To revitalise British industry so that it can open up the new frontiers of Europe. To achieve a rate of growth twice as fast as in the past decade. To secure a growing prosperity which can be sustained into the foreseeable future and which will benefit all our people."

He claimed that the UK now had "the most powerful combination of national and regional investment incentives since the war".

The estimated effect of the budget will be to add another 2% to national output (taking into account direct and multiplier effects), 1½% of which is attributed to income tax cuts.

The Chancellor said that his budget was not "inimical" to the fight against inflation. He pointed out that business had repeatedly claimed that a faster growth of output was, via the effect on productivity and profitability, one of the most effective means of restraining price increases.

Adapted from the Financial Times, 22 March 1972.

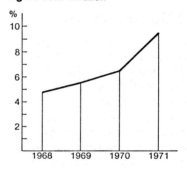

Figure 69.2 Inflation

Figure 69.3 Growth (in GDP at constant prices)

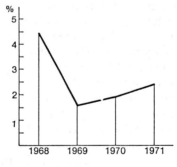

Figure 69.4 Current balance on the balance of payments

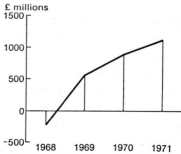

Source, Figures 69.1–69.4: CSO, *Economic Trends Annual Supplement*, 1985

Fiscal Policy

Governments spend money on everything from defence to education. To pay for most of this, they raise money in taxes.

If government spending (or public spending) is more than government revenues (mainly taxes), then government has to borrow money. In the UK, government borrowing is called the PUBLIC SECTOR BORROWING REQUIREMENT or PSBR.

But occasionally, as between 1987 and 1990, government revenues are more than government spending. So the government can pay back some of its debt. When this happens, the government is said to have a PUBLIC SECTOR DEBT REPAYMENT or PSDR.

FISCAL POLICY is government policy with regard to public spending, taxation and borrowing.

Demand Management

Government spending is part of total spending or aggregate demand in the economy. So it would seem likely that a rise in public spending will lead to a rise in aggregate demand.

Equally, a cut in taxes will affect total spending. If the government cut income tax, workers would have more money in their pockets. They would then spend more. This would increase aggregate demand.

In most years, the UK government spends more than it receives. So it has to borrow money, i.e. it has a public sector borrowing requirement or PSBR. Increasing government spending or lowering taxes will increase the amount the government has to borrow.

So an increase in government borrowing (the PSBR) will lead to more spending in the economy. A fall in government borrowing (less government spending or higher taxes) will lead to a lower level of aggregate demand.

Governments can therefore manage the level of aggregate demand in the economy in the short term. It can produce booms and recessions by changing its fiscal policy.

The size of the effect of changes in the PSBR is disputed by economists. Some economists argue that the MULTIPLIER EFFECT – the ratio of the change in national income to a change in public spending – is over 1. An extra £1000 million of public spending will increase national income by over £1000 million. Other ecomomists say the effect is quite small and even zero in the longer term. Extra public spending will have to be paid for by extra taxes or extra borrowing. More public spending CROWDS OUT private sector spending. This view argues that governments can't use their spending and taxes to manage demand in the economy.

Policy Objectives

Changing the level of aggregate demand affects the four key policy objectives of government. More spending in the economy resulting from increased government borrowing (higher public spending or lower taxes) will have the following effects.

- Unemployment will fall as more jobs are created.

- There will be higher economic growth because national income will rise as a result of the increase in spending.

- Inflation will increase because higher demand will allow firms to push up prices.

- The current account on the balance of payments will get worse because part of the extra spending in the economy will go on imported goods.

Equally, if the government tightens its fiscal policy by borrowing less, this will tend in the short term to put the economy into recession – raising unemployment, lowering growth, but reducing inflation and the current account deficit.

Other Effects of Fiscal Policy

Fiscal policy can also affect the supply side of the economy and the distribution of income and wealth. These aspects will be considered in Units 70, 71 and 72.

CHECKPOINTS

1 What is the difference between the PSBR and the PSDR?

2 Explain how a rise in taxes could cut aggregate demand in the economy.

3 The government increases its spending on new motorway building. What will be the effect on:
   (a) motorway construction firms;
   (b) companies that make building materials such as cement;
   (c) motorway construction workers;
   (d) unemployed workers in areas around the new motorways;
   (e) shows in the motorway areas;
   (f) firms that are not directly involved in motorway construction?

4 How do your answers to question 3 illustrate the 'multiplier effect' of an increase in government spending?

COURSEWORK SUGGESTION

Find out how the government changed taxes and government spending in its last budget. Analyse the effect this will have on aggregate demand. Evaluate the extent to which it will help with the problems of unemployment, growth, inflation and the balance of payments.

KEY TERMS

PUBLIC SECTOR BORROWING REQUIREMENT (PSBR) – government borrowing when government spending is greater than government revenues such as taxes.

PUBLIC SECTOR DEBT REPAYMENT (PSDR) – repayment of government debt when government receipts are greater than government spending.

FISCAL POLICY – government policy with regard to public expenditure, taxation and borrowing.

MULTIPLIER EFFECT – the theory that extra government spending will lead to further increase in spending in the rest of the economy.

CROWDING OUT – the belief that extra government spending leads to less spending by the private sector.

Data Response Questions
Units 66–69

Unit 66 Regional Inequalities

Jobs crisis spotlighted by survey

High unemployment, poor housing and health care and rising crime are rife in a deprived Wolverhampton area earmarked for a £37.5 million Government facelift, a report has revealed.

A survey prepared by the West Midlands Enterprise Board on the Low Hill and Whitmore Reans areas pinpoints a varied number of problems facing residents.

The survey was presented to yesterday's meeting of the City Challenge Partnership Board, which is overseeing the five-year rejuvenation programme.

It reveals:
• One in five residents in the City Challenge area is unemployed, with over a third of the total classed as long-term unemployed.
• Only one in seven people obtains five or more GCSE passes, twice as bad as the national average. Thirty per cent of residents have no formal qualifications.
• Sub-standard health care,

with high waiting lists and a low number of GPs per head of population.
• A high crime rate, with one in eight homes broken into last year, 900 cars stolen and a further 600 driven away.
• A lack of nursery facilities and a shortage of child-minders.

Dr Ian Pearson from the West Midlands Enterprise Board, presenting the report, said that some housing was also in grave need of improvement.

He added: "The City Challenge area has extremely poor health standards. Over one in six say they are in poor health, and there is a low health awareness.

"Over the area, burglary is very much a major issue. Over 90 per cent of people said that it was the most important crime issue."

Board member Dr Kevin Kelleher of Wolverhampton Health Authority said that the lack of education and training was the most significant aspect of the survey.

Source: Express and Star, 3 June 1992

1 Outline *three* of the problems faced by the Low Hill and Whitmore Reans areas of Wolverhampton. (*6 marks*)

2 Suggest reasons why an area becomes 'deprived'. (*5 marks*)

3 What policies can the government pursue to improve local deprivation? (*4 marks*)

Unit 67 Government Economic Policy

Business leaders stay cool on praise

Norman Lamont's low-key Budget was today damned with faint praise by the West Midlands' business community.

Accountants Coopers and Lybrands' senior Birmingham tax partner, John Mills, described it as 'a budget for recovery, but one with a small "r"'.

Regional TUC secretary Sid Platt described Mr Lamont's measures as a 'do-nothing strategy, which will not help most West Midlands' firms'. He was angry that nothing was done for the unemployed, or for the hundreds of thousands

of workers who had hoped for more cash to be pumped into training schemes. It would also do nothing for the current account deficit.

Mr Edward Roberts, chairman of the regional CBI, described the Chancellor's measures as a 'careful Budget'.

He said they would 'continue the important fight against inflation'.

This would provide the essential base for the future success of West Midlands' industry and help maintain its competitiveness against foreign imports.

Source: Adapted from the Express and Star, 11 March 1992

1 What should be the major goals of government policy according to the people interviewed about the Budget? (*6 marks*)

2 Which of these goals is the most important today in your opinion and why? (*5 marks*)

3 To what extent can the government achieve all of its goals at the same time? (*4 marks*)

Unit 68 Monetary Policy

Base rates cut to 4-year low of 10%

The UK government yesterday cut interest rates to their lowest level for four years in an effort to help the economy out of recession.

Commercial bank base rates fell from 10.5 per cent to 10 per cent – after the Bank of England reduced its short-term money market rates.

The move was widely welcomed by industry. The Institute of Directors said that it would be the 'best possible stimulus' for a revival.

However, Sir John Banham, director-general of the Confederation of British Industry, said that interest rates were still too high. He said that, while the government's action would 'provide a useful boost to business confidence', high real interest rates were damaging prospects for many companies, particularly those in the manufacturing sector.

Some building societies immediately cut their mortgage rates which should help stimulate consumer spending.

On the currency markets, the pound fell slightly due to selling pressure against the pound. However, the pound stayed comfortably near its central rate in the Exchange Rate Mechanism.

Source: Adapted from the *Financial Times*, 6 May 1992

1 How did the Bank of England change its monetary policy according to the article? *(1 mark)*

2 (a) What are the possible effects of the cut in interest rates mentioned in the article?
   (b) What other effects might there be on the economy? *(8 marks)*

3 Explain how the Bank of England succeeded in getting building societies to cut their interest rates. *(3 marks)*

4 Explain the likely effect on the money supply of the cut in interest rates. *(3 marks)*

Unit 69 Fiscal Policy

Labour promises
Today, millions of people fear losing their jobs, their homes or their business. The new Labour government's National Recovery Programme will start to remove that fear with immediate action on investment, jobs and training. It will combat recession now and build sustained and sustainable recovery for the future.

We will provide enhanced capital allowances to encourage companies immediately to bring forward manufacturing investment in new machinery and plant, innovation and design. They will last for a limited period.

We will introduce an investment tax incentive tailored to meet the special needs of small businesses.

We will immediately begin the phased release of receipts from the sale of council houses, land and property to allow local authorities to build new homes and improve old ones.

Housing investment will generate jobs. We will also establish a work programme, combining three days a week work for the unemployed.

Over the next 22 months, additional resources of at least £600 million will be available for investment in education.

Over the next 22 months, additional resources of at least £1 billion will be available for investment in the National Health Service.

Source: Extracts from the Labour Party Election Manifesto 1992

1 Describe *two* of the measures proposed by the Labour Party in its election manifesto. *(2 marks)*

2 Explain what effect the Labour Party proposals, if put into action, might have on the economy. *(8 marks)*

3 Why might the increased spending proposed have a multiplier effect throughout the whole economy?

(3 marks)

4 What might be the opportunity cost of *one* of these proposals put forward? *(2 marks)*

Essay Questions
Units 66–69

1 'The Government in its budget increased income tax.'
   (a) Suggest *three* reasons why the government might have decided to increase taxes in its budget. *(9 marks)*
   (b) Explain why this increase in income tax could lead to unemployment in the economy. *(6 marks)*
   (c) To what extent would a rise in unemployment help reduce inflation? *(5 marks)*

2 (a) Describe *three* types of money in the UK. Explain why they are money. *(9 marks)*
   (b) How might a government attempt to control the growth of the money supply in the UK? *(6 marks)*
   (c) Why might the government want to control the rate of growth of the money supply? *(5 marks)*

Supply-Side Policies

Tracey Garfield

Age 21. Single. Living with parents. Unemployed. No qualifications. Last job, checkout assistant at a London Tesco supermarket. Dismissed for persistent lateness four weeks ago.

Susan Bromley

Age 35. Married with two children aged 6 and 10. Secretary to the Managing Director before leaving work to bring up her children. For the past year, a part-time worker stacking shelves at Sainsbury's on an evening shift.

Gary Hart

Age 27. Married with three children. Unemployed. No qualifications. Dole money £90 per week. Last job one year ago working for a building firm in Glasgow.

Brian Golding

Age 32. Married with three children. Currently a toolmaker in an engineering company.

Julian Smith-Harcourt

Age 50. Married with two children at university. Managing director of a company with a turnover of £20 million per year. Salary £120 000 per annum plus benefits.

Clare Holden

Age 37. Recently divorced with two children to look after aged 10 and 8. With a university degree and six years' experience of working as a designer in a clothing manufacturer. Hasn't been employed since having the children.

Supply-Side Policies

SUPPLY-SIDE POLICIES are government policies aimed at increasing total supply in the economy. This means trying to get more people into work, particularly the unemployed, and getting existing workers to work harder. It also means getting land into more productive use as well as increasing the amount of capital – machines, factories, offices, etc. – in the economy. Increasing total supply should lead to more output and higher levels of economic growth.

Some supply-side policies are *fiscal* policies – policies which change taxation and government spending. Others change laws which regulate the way in which production takes place.

Labour Policies

INCOME TAX RATES Some economists argue that high income tax rates make workers less willing to work. Since 1979, the government has made it a high priority to reduce the rate of income tax. The top rate of income tax paid by very high income earners has been reduced from 83 to 40%. The basic rate of tax has been reduced from 33 to 25%.

Lowering income tax rates is most likely to be an incentive to people who have some control over how much they earn. This is likely to include the self-employed, business owners and part-time workers with domestic responsibilities.

TRADE UNIONS Trade unions are organisations which try to protect the interests of their members. They fight for higher wages and better working conditions. They also tend to fight change because change can lead to redundancies, workers being downgraded or being asked to undertake more responsible work without extra pay.

Some economists argue that trade unions can damage the economy. Too high pay means that firms become uncompetitive leading to unemployment. The same is true if management can change working practices to suit the changing needs of the firm. Since 1979, the power of trade unions has been reduced in the UK through a number of different laws such as making it more difficult for workers to strike. This, it is claimed, has increased labour 'flexibility'.

LEGAL RESTRICTIONS ON THE USE OF LABOUR During the nineteenth century, laws were passed which limited the use of labour. For instance, it was made illegal for women to work underground in coal mines. Workers under 18 could only work a maximum 48 hour week and no more than nine hours a day. By 1989, the government thought that much of this legislation was out of date and reduced labour flexibility. So in the Employment Act of that year it abolished many of these restrictions.

TRAINING Many economists believe that education and training standards in Britain are low compared to industrial competitors such as Japan and Germany. Too many young people leave school at 16 and too few workers receive high quality training in work. Since 1979, the government has introduced the National Curriculum

into schools. It has established over 100 Training and Enterprise Councils (TECs) in local areas to organise training in the UK. In the 1990s, there is also a new national system of vocational qualifications – National Vocational Qualifications or NVQs – which sets standards of quality in training.

STATE BENEFITS Welfare benefits protect the unemployed and the sick. But they also act as a disincentive to work. Why get a job if you can get more money on the dole? During the 1980s, state welfare benefits were cut so that the unemployed became worse off. Extra benefits were also given to those unemployed starting up their own businesses or to those on low pay to encourage people to work.

Capital

Supply-side economists believe that competition is the most effective way to make the economy efficient. They argue that the best way to get firms to invest efficiently is to remove restrictions on free markets.

For instance, during the 1980s, the government relaxed regulations and laws in the financial services market. The Building Societies Act 1986 gave building societies the power to provide many services that banks were already providing. 'Big Bang' in 1986 introduced competition into the stock market.

In 1979, the government abolished exchange controls. These limited the ability of British firms to invest abroad. British firms are today free to invest anywhere in the world.

Government grants to industry were cut during the 1980s. These had been used to favour firms moving to areas of high unemployment or industries which were either in trouble (like ship-building) or were seen as the industries of the future (like semi-conductors). Supply-side economists said that governments had a very poor record of helping industry to grow. Much of the

money granted was wasted on firms or industries which ultimately were failures.

Government 'red tape' was reduced too. Planning controls, VAT regulations and labour laws were just some of the areas where government tried to get rid of red tape and help industry by making things simpler.

Privatisation was seen as an important way of increasing the efficiency of industry and stimulating investment. This was discussed in Unit 43.

Inner cities have become a major problem over the past 20 years. The government has attempted to regenerate inner city areas by encouraging private industry to work with government to provide jobs and housing in the inner city. Enterprise Zones were created where taxes were lower for businesses and red tape reduced. Development corporations were established for some areas which had some government money to stimulate the regeneration of a particular area like the London Docklands.

Entrepreneurship

Entrepreneurs – risk-takers in industry – are seen as crucial to the success of a free market economy by supply-side economists. They provide new ideas and the competition for existing firms needed to stimulate economic progress. Cuts in income taxes, less government red tape, making it easier to borrow money or acquire share capital were some of the ways that the government attempted to help entrepreneurs in the 1980s.

CHECKPOINTS

1 Explain how (a) training workers, (b) cutting unemployment benefit, (c) reducing the basic rate of income tax and (d) reducing the ability of trade unionists to strike would increase the amount or value of work in the economy.

2 Why should increasing competition help improve the efficiency of British industry?

3 How could an increased supply of entrepreneurs benefit the whole economy?

KEY TERMS

SUPPLY-SIDE ECONOMICS – the study of how changes in the total supply of goods and services and the factors of production affect variables such as national income and employment.

Regional Policy

GLASGOW

Population 1992: *695 630*

Projected 2000: *631 205*

Geography: *Situated on the west coast of Scotland. A rejuvenated city centre is surrounded by housing estates built in the 1950s, 1960s and 1970s. Many of these housing estates have poor reputations with tenants experiencing very high levels of social deprivation. Housing stock is often poor. Crime and drug addiction is high.*

Communications: *Motorway links to the north west of England, Birmingham and London. High speed rail link to London. International airport.*

EMPLOYMENT BY SECTOR

Primary	
Manufacturing	5702
Construction	57 443
Services	24 558
	262 182
Total	
	349 885

Over the past ten years, employment in manufacturing has fallen from 100 000 to 57 000.

UNEMPLOYMENT

The unemployment rate is 15.5%. Male unemployment is higher at 21.6%. Manufacturing industry, such as shipbuilding, is still declining. New jobs created tend to be in service-sector industries. This pattern of development favours female labour. The unemployed male workforce tends to be unskilled.

RECENT JOB GAINS

In the past six years, a number of major employers have set up in Glasgow. The government has moved to or established in Glasgow a regional passport office, the Census Office, DSS Remote Payments Office, the Criminal Injuries Compensation Board and Ministry of Defence Pensions. Tourism has been a big growth area with an estimated 22 000 people now employed directly in the tourist industry.

GOVERNMENT HELP

The area has Development Area status. In the 1980s, the city benefited from a £350m EC grant for urban renewal.

STUDY POINTS

You have been appointed by Glasgow City Council to evaluate Glasgow's economic problems and to put forward proposals which will deal with them. In your report, you must:

1 Describe the problems that Glasgow faces.

2 Evaluate what help is already being given to help combat these problems.

3 Suggest what the City Council could do to alleviate the situation.

4 Point out the opportunity costs of your proposals.

'Between 1982–83 and 1989–90, £5.5bn was spent on regional assistance.' (*Source:* CSO, *Regional Trends*)

In Unit 66, it was shown that there are very large economic differences between the various regions of the UK. The South of England is relatively more affluent than the rest of the UK. In Unit 48, it was argued that a major cause of this was the growth of industry in the South at the expense of the rest of the UK. Governments since the 1930s have attempted to narrow this gap between the regions through **REGIONAL POLICY**. As the above quote states, £5.5 bn was spent between 1982/3 and 1989/90 alone. What can governments do about this problem and how effective have actual policies been?

Demand-side Policies

One way of tackling high unemployment and low incomes in a region would be to increase demand for goods and services in that region. More spending would result in more jobs and higher wages, as more labour is demanded. This policy, however, has not been attempted in the UK, simply because an increase in spending in a region is likely to benefit other regions far more, as consumers buy goods produced elsewhere in Britain or abroad. So traditional Keynesian policies of increasing demand in the economy are unlikely to help the problem regions.

Supply-side Policies

What governments, both Keynesian and monetarist, have attempted to do instead, is to implement supply-side policies. This means creating new work places (jobs) through additional investment. Firms need to be attracted to the problem regions to invest there, rather than not investing at all or investing in the more prosperous regions of the UK. This will increase the supply of goods and services produced in the problem regions, helping to reduce unemployment and raise incomes.

Since the 1930s, governments have offered a variety of incentives to businesses. In 1992, these included:

- Grants of 15% on new buildings, machinery and equipment, with a minimum of £3000 per work place (i.e. job) created to a maximum of £10 000 per work place. For instance, if a businessman invested £5 million and created 120 jobs, then the firm would get 15% of £5 million (i.e. £750 000 of that) back from the government in grants. The maximum grant the firm would get for creating 120 jobs would be 120 × £10 000 (i.e. £1 200 000), and the minimum grant would be 120 × £3000 (i.e. £360 000). The grants can only be obtained if a company invests in the worst unemployment areas in Britain, which the government has called DEVELOPMENT AREAS. These Development Areas are shown on Figure 71.1.

- Additional grants of money, if the government feels that these are needed to create jobs. They are available in both Development Areas and Intermediate Areas. INTERMEDIATE AREAS are areas where unemployment is high, but not as high as in Development Areas.

- Cheap rents on government-built factories in Development and Intermediate areas.

- Training grants for workers, again in both Development and Intermediate Areas.

Success Or Failure?

Far less is spent today in real terms by the government on regional policy

Figure 71.1 UK Development Areas

than in the 1960s. Governments have cut back on public spending and regional policy has suffered. What is more, governments are less hopeful of curing unemployment today in, say, Glasgow, when the whole of the economy is suffering high unemployment, than 20 years ago when the economy was mostly at full employment.

It was stated at the start that £5.5 bn was spent on regional policy between 1982–3 and 1989–90. Was regional policy effective? The answer is probably yes. If there had been no regional policy, unemployment in areas such as Wales and Scotland would probably have been even higher. Government grants do help create jobs. But those grants have an opportunity cost. The government has to decide

whether creating jobs in Glasgow is more important than building hospitals in Kent or spending more on defence.

CHECKPOINTS

1 Why is regional policy necessary in the UK?
2 How would a cut in taxes for all people living in Liverpool:
   (a) affect jobs for those in Liverpool;
   (b) affect the rest of the UK?
3 Explain what incentives are offered to businesses to create jobs in the problem regions of the UK.
4 Calculate the amount of grant that a company setting up in a Development Area would automatically be entitled to receive in the following cases:

Value of investment in new factories and equipment (£)	Number of jobs created	Grant (£)
100 000	4	
5 000 000	20	
200 000	10	

5 Why does regional policy have an opportunity cost?

COURSEWORK SUGGESTION

Arrange to interview several firms that have recently established themselves in a Development Area of the UK. Prepare a detailed questionnaire which assesses why the firms set up in those areas and the influence that regional incentives had upon their decisions. Write a report describing your findings. Compare and contrast the reasons for the firms' decisions. Try to evaluate the extent to which the complete abolition of regional incentives would lead to less investment in Development Areas.

KEY TERMS

REGIONAL POLICY – government policy that attempts to readjust regional economic imbalances.
DEVELOPMENT AREAS – areas of the UK designated by the government as eligible for regional assistance because of their high unemployment.
INTERMEDIATE AREAS – areas of less high unemployment, but still eligible for some regional assistance.

The Redistribution of Income

How income is redistributed through taxes and benefits, 1988

	£ per year				
	Quintile groups of households ranked by disposable income				
	Bottom fifth	Next fifth	Middle fifth	Next fifth	Top fifth
Average per household (£ per year)					
Earnings of main earner	740	3090	7400	10 830	19 500
Earnings of others in the household	90	470	1940	3830	6200
Other income	390	880	1410	1590	3570
Total original income	1210	4440	10 750	16 260	29 170
+state benefits in cash	3220	2790	1760	1080	710
Gross income	4430	7240	12 500	17 340	29 880
− direct taxes such as income tax	670	1220	2450	3790	6690
Disposable income	3760	6020	10 050	13 540	23 190
− indirect taxes such as VAT	1080	1470	2410	2900	3710
Post-tax income	2680	4540	7650	10 640	19 480
+benefits in kind					
Education	790	790	960	810	420
National Health Service	1120	1060	980	820	720
Housing subsidy	100	100	50	30	10
Travel subsidies	40	50	50	50	70
School meals and welfare milk	60	20	20	10	10
Final income	4800	6570	9700	12 360	20 700

Source: CSO, Social Trends 1992

Note: each figure is rounded to the nearest £10, so the Final income does not always tally.

Look at the table. At the top, you will notice 'quintile groups'. Imagine that there are ten students in your economic group. We can rank order them by income. First comes the person with the highest income, last the person with lowest income. We can then split the ten students into five groups – quintile groups. The two lowest income earners go in the bottom group, and so on until the two highest earners go in the highest group.

In this table, the collectors of the statistics have split UK households into five equal groups, rank ordered by the disposable income of each household. The bottom fifth are those with the lowest incomes, the top fifth those with the highest.

S T U D Y   P O I N T S

1 The bottom fifth of households get most of their disposable income from state benefits. Which quintile group pays most in taxes so that these benefits can be given?

2 The table indicates that the top fifth of households (a) are the wealthiest, (b) live in the largest houses, (c) send fewest children to state schools, (d) use private medicine the most and (e) travel the most. What evidence is there in the table to support this?

3 Show which group is least affected by the 'Robin Hood' act of the state taking from the rich to give to the poor.

The Welfare State

It was shown in Unit 17 that large differences in income and wealth exist between individuals in the UK. If the government did not intervene, some individuals would die of malnutrition or poor health, simply because they did not have the income to buy essential goods and services. The young, the old, the sick, the handicapped and the unemployed would be most vulnerable.

To prevent this from happening, all Western European democracies have established some form of welfare provision. In the UK, this has come to be called the WELFARE STATE. The welfare state was established after the Second World War and it was based upon the recommendations of the Beveridge Report, which was published in 1942. Lord Beveridge argued that five main problems faced the country:

- *want*, which could be overcome by the existing national insurance scheme and by a social security system;
- *disease*, which could be overcome by the setting up of a free National Health Service;
- *ignorance*, which could be attacked by more and better schooling;
- *squalor*, which could be avoided by more and better housing;
- *idleness* (i.e. unemployment), which could be tackled by greater government control of industry.

Forty years after the setting up of the welfare state, we know that poverty, disease, squalor and unemployment are still with us. But it is almost certainly true that, without the welfare state, differences between the rich and the poor would be much greater, and the poor would be much poorer.

The welfare state was created by the Labour government of 1945–51. This photograph shows Aneurin Bevan, Minister for Health, marking the site of one of the first National Health Clinics in the UK.

Public Spending and Taxation

Income and wealth are redistributed by the government through its spending and through taxes. Spending on welfare programmes tends to benefit the poor more than the rich. Spending on social security benefits is for the most part used to raise the income levels of the poorer sections of society. Income support, for instance, can only be claimed by people on low incomes. Spending on health, education and housing helps the poor, because they are supplied with services that they would not otherwise be able to afford.

This spending is paid for through taxes. The government redistributes income by making higher-income earners pay more in tax than they receive from government spending and by using that surplus to pay for benefits to poorer people in society. Some taxes are PROGRESSIVE – the higher the income, the higher the proportion or percentage that is paid in tax. Income tax is progressive. A worker earning £6000 a year might pay 10% of total income in income tax. A worker earning £30 000 might pay 30%. (Note, however, that a tax where the higher the income the more that is paid in tax is not necessarily a progressive tax. A worker earning £6000 a year might pay £600 in tax. A worker earning £30 000 might pay £601. This is *not* a progressive tax, because the percentage paid in tax has declined dramatically as income increases.) UK taxes that are generally considered to be progressive are income tax, capital gains tax and inheritance tax.

Not all taxes are progressive. Some are PROPORTIONAL, where the percentage paid in tax stays the same as income changes. Others are REGRESSIVE – the percentage paid in tax actually falls as income rises. Examples of taxes that are generally considered to be proportional or regressive are excise duties, VAT and local authority rates.

By spending on programmes to help the poor and paying for them by raising taxes on the better off, the government is able to ensure a more equal distribution of income and wealth. 'More equal' does not of course mean that it is more desirable or fairer. Some people argue that the present system is unfair because it takes from individuals who have earned money to give to others who have done nothing to deserve these benefits. Others argue that the system does not go far enough in helping the disadvantaged in society and that present inequalities are unacceptable. This, of course, is a debate about how scarce resources are allocated in an economy. Society has to choose between different degrees of inequality, and such choices are always difficult to make.

KEY TERMS

The **WELFARE STATE** – the system that ensures that every member of the population receives adequate food, shelter, health care and education.

PROGRESSIVE TAX – a tax where the higher the income of the taxpayer, the larger the percentage of total income paid in tax.

PROPORTIONAL TAX – a tax where the percentage of total income paid in tax remains the same at different income levels.

REGRESSIVE TAX – a tax where higher-income earners pay a lower proportion of their income in tax compared to lower-income earners.

Data Response Questions

Units 70–72

Unit 70 Supply-Side Policies

IMF urges cut-off point for benefit

The IMF has urged the UK to cut the length of time during which unemployment benefit is paid. It said that a cut would help reduce unemployment.

Basic unemployment benefit, currently £41.40 a week, is paid in Britain for up to a year, but after that individuals who have no savings can claim indefinite income support at only a slightly lower weekly rate.

Mr Tony Blair, for the opposition Labour Party, was critical of the IMF recommendation. He said: 'It would be wrong to think that a cut in the period of unemployment benefit would, of itself, bring lower unemployment.'

The IMF says that action is needed to increase the responsiveness of British wages to market conditions and to promote labour mobility.

It also suggests 'increasing training programmes and improving the functioning of labour exchanges' to prevent a rise in unemployment.

Source: Adapted from the *Financial Times*, 25 April 1991

1 List the three proposals put forward by the IMF. *(3 marks)*

2 Why might a cut in unemployment benefit (a) 'promote labour mobility' and (b) 'increase the responsiveness of British wages to market conditions'? *(6 marks)*

3 How might (a) 'increasing training programmes' and (b) 'improving the functioning of labour exchanges' reduce unemployment? *(6 marks)*

Unit 71 Regional Policy

New life for the urban wasteland of inner cities

Derelict inner city areas are earmarked for revival under a plan to be unveiled this summer.

The Government intends to 'bring to life' 150,000 acres of urban wasteland, providing jobs, homes and new opportunities.

The blueprint will honour John Major's election commitment to push along the drive to revitalise the inner cities.

The aim is to do for cities such as Manchester, Liverpool and Bristol what the Docklands development did for London in the Eighties – while avoiding the mistakes that were made in the capital, where communications failed to keep pace with building.

Around 50,000 acres – an area the size of the City of London and the West End – is expected to be used to attract new businesses.

Another third of the target space could be used for up to 60,000 new homes and the remainder for parkland and leisure areas to improve the quality of life for residents.

Ministers know the importance of green areas in persuading people to live and work in the regenerated areas.

The homes plan, equivalent to all the housing in a city the size of Birmingham, would dramatically reduce pressure for new building on green field sites for years to come.

The regeneration agency – the idea of Michael Heseltine when he was environment supremo – will reclaim derelict areas and use compulsory purchase powers if needed.

Incentives will be offered to industry to move in. Particular emphasis will be placed on modern communications.

The Treasury will be asked to make sure there is enough cash available to build new road links and light railway systems.

Source: *Daily Mail*, 25 May 1992

1 What are the characteristics of an 'inner city area'? *(4 marks)*

2 Outline the plans described in the article for the regeneration of inner city areas. *(6 marks)*

3 Do you think the plans will succeed? Outline your reasons carefully. *(5 marks)*

Unit 72 The Redistribution of Income

Poorest 'hit by changes in benefits'

Social security reforms aimed at giving more help to the needy have left the poorest worse off, a report today claims. Two-thirds of people on income support said they were living in more hardship.

Nearly all claimed they had been forced to cut down on food and fuel and many reported ill health.

Hardship Britain: Being Poor in the 1990s, showed many people were relying on families and friends for basic necessities.

Based on two research studies, the report published by the Child Poverty Action Group draws on interviews with 140 claimants in the wake of the 1988 social security changes.

These included the replace-ment of one-off payments for essentials with the social fund – a system of grants and loans – and the introduction of a flat-rate premium in place of spe-cial needs allowances.

Under the new system, claimants also have to pay water rates and 20 per cent of poll tax bills.

The report highlighted major problems in the new sys-tem at a time when the number of children living on the safety net has more than doubled to more than two million.

It includes quotes from mothers who regularly miss meals to make sure their chil-dren won't go hungry.

The studies were carried out by Bradford University's social fund research project and the Family Service Unit.

Source: Express and Star, 6 April 1992

1 State *three* reforms made to the social security system in 1988.   *(3 marks)*

2 Explain why the reforms have made poor people worse off.   *(6 marks)*

3 (a) How could the government improve the position of the poor in society?
(b) What might be the opportunity cost of your sugges-tions?   *(6 marks)*

Unit 79 The Exchange Rate Mechanism

Pound falls to post-poll low

The pound fell yesterday to its lowest level against the D-mark since the day before the general election.

International investors ignored a strong statement by Mr John Major, the prime min-ister, ruling out a devaluation of the pound. They sold ster-ling in large quantities and bought D-marks.

The UK government insist-ed it would hold sterling's posi-tion against the D-mark in the European exchange rate mech-anism even if other European governments forced a realign-ment. But it could not halt a sharp fall in sterling's value.

The foreign exchange mar-kets were unmoved by Mr Major's promise to bring down UK inflation to 'nil if possible'.

Instead they bid for D-marks, acting on rumours that the German central bank, the Bundesbank, would raise inter-est rates this week.

Source: Financial Times, 14 July 1992

1 Explain why the European exchange rate mechanism is important for the value of the pound.   *(5 marks)*

2 Why does the rate of UK inflation affect the value of the pound?   *(5 marks)*

3 Outline how a rise in German interest rates might affect the value of sterling.   *(5 marks)*

This Data Response Question refers to **Unit 79** on *page 196*.

Essay Questions
Units 70–72

1 'The UK is suffering from rising unemployment but falling inflation.'
(a) Describe *two* different measures which the govern-ment could take to help reduce unemployment.   *(4 marks)*
(b) Describe *two* different measures which the govern-ment could take to help reduce inflation even further.   *(4 marks)*
(c) To what extent would these measures also help increase the economic growth of the UK?   *(6 marks)*
(d) How effective will these measures be in reducing unemployment and inflation?   *(6 marks)*

2 'Britain is divided into two regions – the South rich and prosperous, the rest of the country poor and disadvan-taged.'
(a) Describe *four* ways in which differences in living stan-dards between regions could be measured.   *(8 marks)*
(b) Give *two* reasons why the South is more prosperous than the rest of the UK.   *(6 marks)*
(c) What policies could a government pursue to reduce regional inequalities?   *(6 marks)*

The Theory of Comparative Advantage

In Japan, it costs 1000 yen to produce a bottle of whisky: in Britain it costs £2. In Japan it costs 8000 yen to produce a simple camera: in Britain, it costs £20. This can be summarised like this:

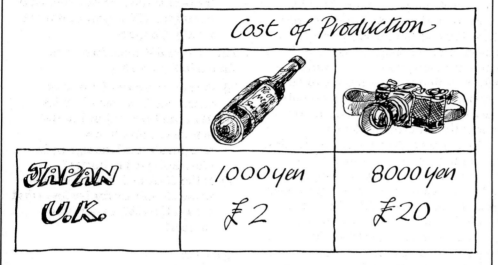

Cost of Production		
JAPAN	1000 yen	8000 yen
U.K.	£2	£20

STUDY POINTS

1. What is the opportunity cost of producing 1 camera in Japan i.e. how many bottles of whisky could have been produced for the same cost as one camera?

2. What is the opportunity cost of producing 1 camera in the UK?

3. Which country can produce whisky more cheaply (relative to cameras)?

4. Which country can produce cameras more cheaply (relative to whisky)?

5. Each year, the Japanese buy 8 million bottles of whisky and 1 million cameras. How much in total would it cost the Japanese if all cameras and all whisky were produced in Japan?

6. Each year, the British buy 20 million bottles of whisky and 1 million cameras. How much in total would it cost the British if all cameras and all whisky were produced in the UK?
Japan and the UK decide to trade whisky for cameras at an exchange rate of 1 camera for 9 bottles of whisky.

7. How many cameras can Japan make instead of the 8 million bottles of whisky she produces?

8. How many cameras will she now produce if she also carries on producing the 1 million cameras as before?

9. How many bottles of whisky can the UK now produce (including the 20 million bottles produced before) if she switches resources from the production of cameras to whisky?

10. Japan offers to trade 1 million cameras for whisky with the UK. How much whisky can she obtain in exchange?

11. How many cameras and how much whisky is now available for sale in Japan? Is Japan better or worse off than before trade took place?

12. How many cameras and how much whisky is now available for sale in the UK? Is the UK better or worse off than before trade took place?

'Italy sold 28 million pairs of leather shoes to Britain in 1983 at an average price per pair of £6. So it might come as a surprise to learn that Britain managed to sell 321 000 pairs to the Italians at an average price of £12 per pair, and it's quality which appears to be the characteristic which captures the Italians to buy British.' (*Source: The Guardian*, 4 June 1985)

Why should Italians buy British shoes when Italy is one of the world's leading producers of shoes? Why is Italy a more important producer of shoes than Britain anyway?

Specialisation

To answer these questions, we need to develop the theory of *specialisation*. Specialisation, discussed in Unit 7, means that producers specialise in producing products or performing tasks. One example of specialisation is the division of labour. If specialisation is to make economic sense, producers must specialise in what they are best at producing.

Figure 73.1 gives some sample figures for the production of shoes in the UK and in Italy. For the sake of argument, assume that Italy and the UK only produce shoes and that the only cost of production is labour. It can be seen from the table that Italy is better at producing ordinary shoes than the UK because it costs only 10 man-hours to produce a pair of ordinary shoes in Italy, but 20 man-hours in the UK. Italy is said to have an **ABSOLUTE ADVANTAGE** in the production of ordinary shoes. On the other hand, the UK has an absolute advantage in the production of quality shoes – i.e. the UK is better at producing quality shoes than Italy. So it would make sense for Italy to make ordinary shoes and exchange them for quality shoes made in the UK.

But what would happen if Italy

were better at producing both ordinary shoes and quality shoes than the UK? i.e. Italy has an absolute advantage in the production of both ordinary shoes and quality shoes. It still pays for each country to specialise. Which country will produce what depends upon which country is relatively better at producing each product. Look at Figure 73.2. Italy can produce both quality shoes and ordinary shoes at less man-hour cost than the UK. In Italy, it costs just 10 man-hours to produce a pair of ordinary shoes, whereas in the UK it costs 20 man-hours. Quality shoes cost 30 man-hours in Italy, but 40 in the UK. Italy therefore has an absolute advantage in both the production of ordinary shoes and quality shoes.

Figure 73.1

Cost of production (man hours)	Italy	UK
1 pair of ordinary shoes	10	20
1 pair of quality shoes	25	16

Figure 73.2

Cost of production (man-hours)	Italy	UK
1 pair of ordinary shoes	10	20
1 pair of quality shoes	30	40

Comparative Advantage

However, we can show that it will be to the advantage of both countries, if each specialises and then they trade. In Italy, it takes three times as long to produce a pair of quality shoes as it does a pair of ordinary shoes (30 man-hours compared to 10 man-hours). So the opportunity cost of producing a pair of quality shoes is

three times that of producing a pair of ordinary shoes. In the UK, a pair of quality shoes costs only twice as much as a pair of ordinary shoes (40 man-hours compared to 20 man-hours). So the UK is relatively better at producing quality shoes than Italy. The UK is said to have a COMPARATIVE ADVANTAGE in the production of quality shoes. Italy, on the other hand, can produce ordinary shoes relatively more cheaply than the UK. It costs Italy ⅓ a pair of quality shoes to produce one pair of ordinary shoes (10 man-hours compared to 30 man-hours), whereas it costs the UK ½ a pair of quality shoes to produce one pair of ordinary shoes (20 man-hours compared to 40 man-hours). So Italy has a comparative advantage in the production of ordinary shoes.

By concentrating on the production of ordinary shoes, in which it has a comparative advantage, a country like Italy can export these and import other products such as quality shoes, which would be relatively more expensive to produce in Italy. The UK should concentrate on producing and exporting what it is relatively best at doing – in our example, that was the manufacture of quality shoes. The theory of comparative advantage helps us to understand why one of the world leaders in the manufacture of shoes should be importing shoes from the UK.

CHECKPOINTS

1 What is meant by 'specialisation'? Name *four* examples of specialisation in the world economy.

2 (a) It costs the UK £3 to produce a record and £1 to produce a blank cassette. What is the cost

of a record in terms of cassettes?

(b) Japan can produce either 100 000 records or 200 000 cassettes for the same cost. What is the cost of a record in terms of cassettes?

(c) Which country has the comparative advantage (i.e. has the lowest relative cost) of producing (a) records; and (b) cassettes?

(d) If the UK and Japan were to trade cassettes for records, what would the UK export and what would it import?

3 The USA and France face costs shown in Figure 73.3

(a) What is the cost of 1 unit of chemicals in terms of barley (i) in the USA; (ii) in France?

(b) Which country has a comparative advantage (i) in chemicals; (ii) in barley?

(c) If the USA and France were to trade chemicals for barley, what would the USA export and import?

Figure 73.3

Costs of production (man-hours)	USA	France
1 unit of barley	2	5
1 unit of chemicals	1	2

COURSEWORK SUGGESTION

Take a traditional UK manufacturing industry which has declined since 1945, such as steel, the motorcycle industry, textiles or shipbuilding. Describe the decline and analyse the effects it has had on the UK economy. Which countries in the world are now producing these goods? Why has the comparative advantage in the production of these goods shifted to other countries? Consider the extent to which the UK could ever regain its comparative advantage in this industry.

KEY TERMS

ABSOLUTE ADVANTAGE – where one producer is better at producing a product than another producer.

COMPARATIVE ADVANTAGE – where one producer can produce a good at a relatively cheaper cost in terms of other goods than another producer.

Protectionism

Producer subsidy equivalent – the amount of subsidy that farmers receive. This is made up of two parts:

- Direct government subsidies to farmers.
- Artificially high prices received by farmers. Governments raise domestic prices, for instance, by imposing tariffs and quotas on agricultural produce coming into the country. The difference between what consumers actually pay to farmers and what they would pay if they could buy from the cheapest world source is included in the producer subsidy equivalent. It is an implicit tax on consumers.

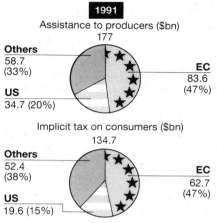

Figure 74.1 The cost of agricultural support in the rich industrialised (OECD) countries of the world, 1991

1991

Assistance to producers ($bn)
177

Others
58.7
(33%)

EC
83.6
(47%)

US
34.7 (20%)

Implicit tax on consumers ($bn)
134.7

Others
52.4
(38%)

EC
62.7
(47%)

US
19.6 (15%)

Figure 74.2 Producer subsidy equivalent per farmer, 1989

Australia	4
Austria	9
Canada	13
EC	8
Finland	26
Japan	15
New Zealand	2
Norway	32
Sweden	25
Switzerland	26
US	20

Source: OECD

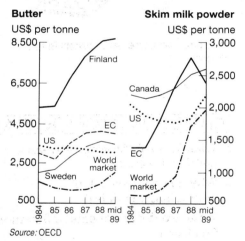

Figure 74.3 Prices paid to farmers

Butter
US$ per tonne
8,500 · 6,500 · 4,500 · 2,500 · 500
Finland, EC, US, World market, Sweden
1984 85 86 87 88 mid 89

Skim milk powder
US$ per tonne
3,000 · 2,500 · 2,000 · 1,500 · 1,000 · 500
Canada, US, EC, World market
1984 85 86 87 88 mid 89

Source: OECD

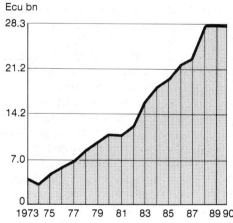

Figure 74.4 How much it cost to support farmers

Ecu bn
28.3 · 21.2 · 14.2 · 7.0 · 0
1973 75 77 79 81 83 85 87 89 90

In 1986, the World Bank published a report on the cost of agricultural support policies. It pointed out that:

- In the EC, the subsidy from consumers and taxpayers to dairy farmers was $410 per cow – this was more than the income of half the world's people; in the USA, the subsidy per cow was $835;
- US policies which kept sugar from being imported into the USA meant that its world price was only 4 cents a lb compared to 24 cents a lb being paid to US farmers; if the US had allowed free trade in sugar, the world price would have risen to an estimated 11 cents a lb.

S T U D Y   P O I N T S

Look at the definition of 'producer subsidy equivalent'.

1 When the farmer sells his produce, explain how he is being subsidised by (a) the consumer and (b) the taxpayer.

Look at Figure 74.1 which shows how much farmers were subsidised by consumers and taxpayers.

2 How much, in $bn, did EC farmers receive in 1991 in subsidies (a) directly from taxpayers and (b) because the price paid by consumers was above the world price?

3 How did this compare with the subsidies given to US farmers?

Look at Figure 74.2.

4 (a) Which two countries gave the largest subsidies to their farmers?
(b) If the value of the US$ were $2 = £1, how much in £ would the subsidies per farmer for these countries have been?

5 How does the EC compare with other countries in giving subsidies?

Look at Figure 74.3.

6 How does the EC price paid to farmers compare with the world price for (a) butter and (b) skim milk powder?

Look at Figure 74.4.

7 What happened to the cost of supporting farmers in the 1970s and 1980s?

8 Using your knowledge of economic theory, explain why rising high support prices led to increased output which in turn led to rising total support costs for agriculture in the EC.

Considering all the data:

9 Who has benefited and who has lost from the support given to agriculture in the EC, the USA and other rich countries round the world?

Reasons For Protectionism

There has been an increase in protectionism in the world economy since the mid-1970s. PROTECTIONISM is the restriction of imports into a country through government regulations. There are a variety of protectionist measures including:

- TARIFFS or *customs duties*. These are taxes imposed on imported goods. They raise the price of imports to consumers and so make them less attractive.
- QUOTAS. These are limits on the quantity of a product that can be imported into a country (e.g. no more than 100 000 cars a year can be imported).
- *Regulations*. A country may, for instance, have unique safety regulations, which means that potential imports are 'unsafe' and so cannot be sold in that country. Or the country may make it very difficult for importers to get import licences for goods.

Protectionism can give rise to major benefits for an economy. Fewer imports can mean that domestic industries will produce what would otherwise have been imported. This creates not only jobs, but extra income for the domestic economy. Domestic production may also lead to exports, as firms gain expertise in the production of goods.

Another argument in favour of protectionism is the *infant industry* argument. An economy may wish to start up a particular industry, such as steel making or car manufacturing. In the early stages, the industry is bound to be uncompetitive with foreign competition. It will have high start-up costs and not produce large enough quantities to reap sufficient economies of scale. Protecting an industry like this from imports will allow it to grow and prosper. When it is eventually strong enough, import controls can be removed.

Reasons in favour of Free Trade

The opposite of protectionism is FREE TRADE. The great advantage of free trade is that consumers can buy the products that are most competitive, whether they are produced at home or abroad.

But it is not only consumers who may benefit. Many economists argue that free trade rather than protectionism is the way to create jobs and prosperity. Their argument is that protectionism encourages protected industries to be inefficient. They have no incentive to become efficient and produce goods that consumers want to buy at the keenest prices. Such industries are unlikely ever to develop into strong industries capable of conquering export markets. Free trade, on the other hand, forces firms to become efficient or else they go bankrupt. If a firm can beat off imports at home, then it stands a good chance of being a successful exporter. Competition brought about by free trade produces efficient industries and thus leads to jobs and prosperity. What is more, if all countries follow free trade policies, each country will specialise in those products in which it has a comparative advantage and this, as Unit 73 showed, produces gains to consumers in all countries.

Increased protectionism can be self-defeating if other countries retaliate. If the UK were to ban all imports of Japanese cars, there would be little benefit for the UK if Japan were to retaliate by banning an equivalent value of UK imports.

Despite all these arguments in favour of free trade, it is true to say that some of the most successful economies in the world today – such as Japan and West Germany – have pursued or currently pursue protectionist policies. With high unemployment worldwide, it is perhaps not surprising that many countries see protectionism as an easy way of protecting jobs in their country.

Would protectionist measures benefit British industry?

K E Y T E R M S

PROTECTIONISM – the restriction of imports into a country by government measures.

TARIFFS – taxes on imported goods. Also often called *customs duties*.

QUOTAS – limits on the quantity of a commodity that can be imported.

FREE TRADE – trade without protectionist barriers between countries.

Exports and Imports

STUDY POINTS

Consider Figure 75.1

1 What has happened to exports as a share of total spending in the UK economy since 1951?

2 Why are exports now more important for British industry and British workers than in 1951?

Figure 75.1 Share of exports in total UK spending (exports of goods and services at market prices, final expenditure on goods and services at 1985 market prices)

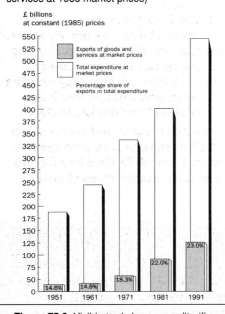

Consider Figure 75.2

3 Explain how the UK's visible trade changed over the period 1973 to 1991.

4 Calculate the difference in value of (a) imports and (b) exports of mineral fuels and lubricants in 1973 and 1991. Why has there been this large change?

5 Why is the shrinking share of manufactured goods in total UK exports of importance to the British economy?

Consider Figure 75.3

6 Which are now the most important and the least important areas of the world with which Britain trades? How has this changed since 1973?

7 Suggest reasons why this change in the direction of visible trade might have taken place.

Figure 75.3 Visible trade by area

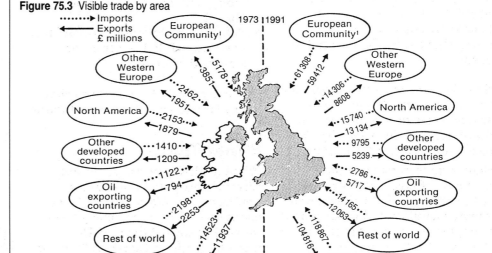

[1]Figures refer to the 12 member countries in 1991   The UK joined the European Community in 1973

Figure 75.2 Visible trade by commodity (figures in brackets are % of total)

| | Exports | | Imports | |
| | £ millions | | | |
	1973	1991	1973	1991
Food, beverages and tobacco	849 (7)	7749 (7)	2832 (20)	12362 (10)
Basic materials	420 (4)	2013 (2)	1692 (12)	5065 (4)
Mineral fuels and lubricants	374 (3)	7144 (7)	1320 (9)	7582 (6)
Semi-manufactured goods	4013 (34)	29790 (28)	3731 (26)	31414 (26)
Finished manufactured goods	5910 (50)	56312 (54)	4704 (32)	62224 (52)
Other	371 (3)	1808 (2)	244 (2)	1714 (2)
Total	11937	104816	14523	118867

Sources: CSO, *Economic Trends Annual Supplement 1992*; *United Kingdom Balance of Payments 1991*; *Monthly Digest of Statistics*, April 1992

Britain has a long history as a trading nation. When Britain was the most advanced industrial country in the world in the nineteenth century, it **IMPORTED** (i.e. brought into the country) raw materials from all over the world. It **EXPORTED** (i.e. sold abroad) goods manufactured from these raw materials. Since the Second World War, Britain has become even more dependent on foreign trade. As Figure 75.1 shows, the share of exports in total expenditure in the UK has risen from 14.6% in 1951 to 23.0% in 1991. If exports and imports were to cease suddenly, the British economy would collapse overnight – which shows just how *interdependent* Britain is with the rest of the world.

Visible Trade

Approximately two-thirds of Britain's exports and imports consist of trade in goods – or VISIBLES, as they are called in foreign trade jargon. Figure 75.2 shows UK exports and imports by commodity, and how this has changed over the period 1973–91. As mentioned, the UK has traditionally imported raw materials – basic materials such as iron and mineral fuels and lubricants such as oil – and semi-manufactured goods such as steel bars, and then turned these into manufactured goods, some of which have then been exported. This traditional pattern, which to some extent still held true in 1973, has fundamentally changed. Two very important changes can be seen in the statistics:

- Britain has become a major exporter of oil. From virtually nothing in 1973, oil came to account for over 20% of total visible exports by 1985 before falling back to 7% in 1991.

- Britain's trade in manufactured goods has suffered a major reversal. Traditionally, the UK has exported far more manufactured goods than it has imported – as was the case in 1973. By 1991, the situation had been reversed. Britain now imports far more manufactured goods than it exports. Deindustrialisation cost 3 million lost jobs in manufacturing between 1973 and 1991.

Figure 75.3 shows Britain's main trading partners and the changes that have occurred since the UK joined the European Community (the EC) in 1973. The statistics show that trade with the EC has grown rapidly, so that today 50–60% of all visible trade is conducted with Britain's EC partners.

Equally, trade with the 'rest of the world' has declined in relative importance. No longer is British trade dominated by the pattern of buying raw materials from developing countries and selling them back manufactured goods.

Invisibles

Approximately one-third of the total value of the UK's trade is made up of INVISIBLES – trade in services. These include services such as:

- banking and insurance;
- tourism;
- interests, profits and dividends on money lent and borrowed from abroad;
- defence – maintaining British forces overseas, while US forces are stationed in Britain.

Britain's export of services has shown strong growth since the Second World War.

Money Flows

When the UK exports, goods and services flow *out* of the country. Foreigners, in return, pay for those goods and services, so money flows *into* the country. When the UK imports, goods and services flow *into* the country, but money flows *out* to pay for them. So if the UK buys wine from France, an import for the UK, money goes out of the UK. Similarly, if a Briton takes a holiday in France, money leaves the UK and so this, too, is classified as an import. On the other hand, a French firm buying British shirts would be an export, because money would flow into the UK. Equally, a German firm buying insurance from a UK company would be an export for the UK, as money would flow into the UK to pay for the premium.

CHECKPOINTS

1 Distinguish between:
   (a) an import and an export;
   (b) a visible and an invisible.

2 State whether the following are (i) an export or an import for the UK; and (ii) visible trade or invisible trade:
   (a) a British car sold to the USA;
   (b) French cheese sold in Britain;
   (c) a British tourist holidaying in Spain;
   (d) British Airways buying a plane from Boeing (USA);
   (e) the American Air Force maintaining an air base in East Anglia;
   (f) the British government maintaining an embassy in Iran;
   (g) the British government buying American nuclear missiles;
   (h) an Italian oil company sending its profits from its North Sea oilfield from the UK to Italy.

3 How has the size and composition of UK trade changed over the past twenty years? Outline two factors that have caused these changes.

COURSEWORK SUGGESTION

Take one particular category of exports and imports (e.g. chemicals or textiles). Describe how exports and imports of this product have changed over time, geographically, in volume and by value. Analyse why these changes have occurred. Consider the effects on the UK economy. Sources of statistics include *Abstract of British Historical Statistics* (by B. R. Mitchell and P. Deane, published by Cambridge University Press, 1962); and *Annual Abstract of Statistics*, *United Kingdom Balance of Payments* and *Overseas Trade Statistics of the United Kingdom* (all published by HMSO).

KEY TERMS

EXPORTS – products sold to foreigners. Products leave the country in return for money coming in.

IMPORTS – products bought from foreigners. Products enter the country in return for an outflow of money.

VISIBLE TRADE – trade in goods.

INVISIBLE TRADE – trade in services.

The Balance of Payments

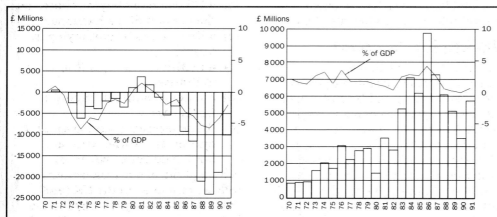

Figure 76.1 The UK balance of trade, 1970–91

Figure 76.2 UK invisible balance, 1970–91

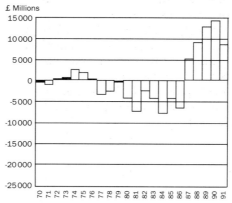

Figure 76.3 The current balance, 1970–91

Figure 76.4 Net transactions in UK external assets and liabilities

Source: (for all figures) CSO, *Economic Trends Annual Supplement 1992*

The Balance of Payments Account

Unit 75 considered the UK's pattern of trade and distinguished between exports and imports, and visibles and invisibles. This unit will consider other transactions made abroad, and how all these are brought together in the balance of payments account.

The **BALANCE OF PAYMENTS ACCOUNT** shows all the UK's financial transactions with foreigners. There are two main parts to the account. The **CURRENT ACCOUNT** shows the income and expenditure of the UK over a period of time. Its income is the money received from exports of visibles (goods) and invisibles (services). Its expenditure is the money paid to foreigners for imports to the UK. The **CAPITAL ACCOUNT** shows the investments, savings and borrowings of the UK, over a period of time.

The balance of payments must always balance – i.e. the money leaving the country must exactly equal the money coming in. This is no different from your own accounts. The money you spend and save must be exactly the same as the money you receive and borrow. Over any particular period of time, the different parts of the account need not balance. The UK can export more than it imports and use the surplus created to invest abroad, just as you can save money by not spending all the money you earn. Or the UK can import more than it exports and pay for this by borrowing from abroad or running down savings.

The Current Balance

Since 1945, exports and imports have tended to grow in value each year, even after inflation has been taken into account. This shows that the UK is becoming more and more economically interdependent with the rest of the world.

Of particular interest, though, is the balance between exports and imports.

STUDY POINTS

1 The balance of trade is the difference between the value of the exports of *goods* and the imports of *goods*. Describe how the balance of trade changed over the period 1970–91.

2 Invisible trade is trade in services. The balance on invisible trade is invisible exports minus invisible imports, i.e. exports of services minus the import of services. Why has invisible trade been very important to the British economy since 1970?

3 The current balance is the difference between total exports (both of goods and services) and total imports. Describe how the current account has changed since 1970 (a) in money terms; (b) as a percentage of total output (GDP) in the economy.

4 Suggest reasons why it might be undesirable for the current account to be negative (i.e. for imports to be greater than exports).

5 The account records the international borrowing, saving and investing by the UK abroad and by foreigners in Britain. If a British company, for instance, lends money abroad, then money will flow out of the country and this is shown by a minus figure on the account. If a foreign company were to buy shares in Britain, then money would come into the country and this would be shown by a plus sign on the account. The balance on the capital account is the difference between money coming into the country to be saved and invested and money leaving the country to be saved and invested. What does it mean if the account shows a minus sign?

6 In which years was the capital account (a) positive and (b) negative? Which is the better position to be in? Explain your answer.

7 Why do you think a country cannot go on borrowing money for ever?

Figures 76.1–76.3 show three balances:

- the **BALANCE OF TRADE** which is the difference between visible exports and visible imports;
- the **INVISIBLE BALANCE** – invisible exports minus invisible imports;
- the **CURRENT BALANCE** – total exports minus total imports (or the balance of trade plus the invisible balance).

An example of how these three balances are calculated is shown in Figure 76.5.

It can be seen that the UK tends to run a balance of trade deficit – that is, the nation tends to import more goods than it exports. On the other hand, the invisible balance is always in surplus – that is, the UK exports more services than are imported. The current balance – the sum of the balance of trade and the invisible trade – swings from surplus to deficit. Oil has been a major factor in changes in the current balance in the 1970s and 1980s. The fourfold increase in the price of oil in 1974 helped push the current balance into massive deficits in 1974 and 1975. On the other hand, production of North Sea oil, which started slowly in 1976 and made the UK self-sufficient in oil by the early 1980s, allowed the current account to go into surplus from 1980. Then, in 1986, a sharp drop in oil prices halved the value of UK exports of oil and helped push the current account into deficit in the late 1980s.

The Capital Account

The capital account shows transactions made for the purpose of investment, saving and borrowing. For instance, a Japanese company buying pounds to set up a factory in the UK would be an inflow of money to the UK. So too would a British company borrowing dollars to finance expansion in Britain. On the other hand, a British bank buying shares in New York, or a British company buying a French company would represent an outflow of money from the UK. The government, too, buys and sells foreign currency. These would all be recorded on the **NET TRANSACTIONS IN UK EXTERNAL ASSETS AND LIABILITIES** section of the balance of payments. The balance on this part of the accounts is shown in Figure 76.4.

Figure 76.5 An example of the current balance (£ million)

Visible exports	700	Invisible exports	300	Total exports	1000
Visible imports	800	Invisible imports	100	Total imports	900
Balance of trade	−100	Balance on invisible trade	200	Current balance	100

CHECKPOINTS

1 In which part of the balance of payments account would the following transactions be recorded:

(a) a US company buying shares on the London Stock Exchange;

(b) a British tourist holidaying in Spain;

(c) a British company selling cars to France;

(d) a French company buying a British firm;

(e) the government buying up £100 million of sterling with its foreign currency reserves.

Which of the above transactions are inflows of money to the UK (and therefore given a 'plus' sign on the balance of payments account) and which are outflows (and given a minus sign)?

2 The figures in Figure 76.6 refer to the UK balance of payments, 1991. Calculate (a) the balance of trade, (b) the invisible balance and (c) the current balance.

Figure 76.6

	£ millions Exports	Imports
Visible	104	114
Invisible	117	114

3 Explain why a foreign loan taken out by a British firm would be given a *plus* sign on the *capital* account, whereas the interest payable on that loan would be given a *minus* sign on the *current* account.

KEY TERMS

BALANCE OF PAYMENTS ACCOUNT – the record of all financial transactions with foreigners.

CURRENT ACCOUNT – the part of the balance of payments account where the value of exports and imports is recorded.

CAPITAL ACCOUNT – the part of the balance of payments account where the value of investment, saving and borrowing is recorded.

BALANCE OF TRADE – visible exports minus visible imports.

INVISIBLE BALANCE – invisible exports minus invisible imports.

CURRENT BALANCE – exports minus imports.

NET TRANSACTIONS IN UK EXTERNAL ASSETS AND LIABILITIES – the record of investment, saving and borrowing made by foreigners in the UK and by the UK abroad.

COURSEWORK SUGGESTION

Describe how the balance of trade has changed over the past twenty years. Analyse why these changes have taken place. What effect, for instance, have changing exchange rates or North Sea oil had on the balance of trade? Consider the effects of these changes on the British economy. Sources of statistics include the *Annual Abstract of Statistics*, *United Kingdom Balance of Payments*, and *Overseas Trade Statistics* (all published by HMSO).

Exchange Rates

Sharp fall in sterling

The pound fell sharply following heavy selling pressure. Financial markets were unsettled as they waited for what could turn out to be worse than expected balance of payments figures tomorrow.

Dollar falls in hectic trading

A 1% cut in US interest rates yesterday led to a fall in the US dollar. Sellers switched into sterling leading to a rise in the value of the pound.

Reserves hit record levels

Bank of England foreign currency reserves hit record levels last month. The Bank of England bought foreign currency for sterling in a bid to prevent the pound from rising.

Oil price rise raises sterling

A sharp rise in the oil price yesterday sent sterling up as buyers thought that this would benefit the UK current account position.

Pound supported as Deutschmark rises

A rise in the value of the Deutschmark yesterday saw the Bank of England stepping into the market. It bought pounds to counteract the heavy selling pressure as investors switched into Deutschmarks.

- 'The pound staged a dramatic recovery in the world's currency markets yesterday.'
- 'Dollar up as pound falls to record low.'
- 'The trade-weighted index stood at 76.2, unchanged from yesterday.'

Headlines such as these occur frequently. They all refer to the value of the pound sterling. What is this value and how is it determined?

The Value of the Pound

The pound can be seen as a commodity, like tomatoes or shoes or lawnmowers. Pounds are bought and sold all over the world. They are bought and sold in exchange for other types of money – French francs, Spanish pesetas, US dollars, German deutschmarks, etc. You may have sold pounds to a bank or a bureau de change to get foreign currency for a holiday. When anything is bought and sold, it is bought and sold at a price. This price represents the value of the pound, and is known as the FOREIGN EXCHANGE RATE. So the price of the pound is quoted as so many US dollars per pound, so many French francs per pound and so on.

Price

Like anything that is bought and sold, the price of the pound is fixed by the forces of demand and supply. Pounds are:

- *demanded* (i.e. bought) to pay for British exports, and to invest and save in the UK;
- *supplied* (i.e. sold) to pay for imports from abroad, and to invest and save outside the UK.

When demand for the pound goes up – more exports perhaps are sold, or foreign money comes into London attracted by high interest rates – then the price of the pound will go up too. When the supply of pounds increases – caused perhaps by increased imports or money leaving the country to be

S T U D Y   P O I N T S

Read the quotes carefully.

1 What is an exchange rate?

2 What determines the price of a commodity like tomatoes or bread? What determines the price of a currency?

3 From the quotes, make a list of:
   (a) the times when pounds were being sold, i.e. *supplied* onto the market and state why this was happening.
   (b) the times when pounds were being bought, i.e. *demanded* by the market and state why this was happening.

4 Explain how the value of the pound changed in each of the quotes and, using demand and supply analysis, explain why it was changing in this way.

invested abroad – then the value of the pound will go down.

There are a number of reasons why the value of any currency fluctuates from year to year. The main ones are:

- *Changes in the current balance* (the current balance is exports minus imports). If, say, the balance goes from being positive (or 'in the black') to being negative (or 'in the red'), then more pounds will be supplied than before to pay for those imports, relative to the number of pounds demanded by foreigners to pay for exports. So the value of the pound will go down. The value of the pound will tend to go up, however, if the current account is in surplus. Inflation is one major factor causing imports to increase faster than exports, pushing the current account into the red. If Britain's inflation rate is higher than that of other countries, British goods will become less price-competitive, encouraging imports and making it more difficult for British firms to export.

- *Changes in interest rates.* A rise in interest rates in the UK encourages other countries to invest in the UK. The demand for pounds rises, increasing the value of the pound. When domestic interest rates fall, the value of the pound tends to decline.

- *Speculation.* If the buyers and sellers of currency feel that the value of the pound is going to go down in the future, they will not buy or demand pounds now. So the value of the pound will fall. If, on the other hand, they believe that the value of the pound is going to rise, they will buy pounds now and try to make a profit out of a rising pound. FOREIGN CURRENCY SPECULATORS – people, firms, banks, whose aim is to make money by simply buying and selling currencies – are a major influence on the value of any single currency, like the pound, today.

- *Buying and selling of currency by central banks* like the Bank of England. If the Bank of England wants to see the value of the pound go up, it will buy pounds. If it wants to see it fall, it will sell pounds.

Expressing the Value of the Pound

The value of the pound can be given in terms of any single currency: £1 = $1.20, £1 = 11 francs, £1 = 2 deutschmarks, etc. But it is difficult to judge quickly whether the value of the pound has gone up or down, if, for instance, it has gone up against the dollar, but down against the French franc. To get over this problem, the UK government calculates an average value of the pound against the currencies of our major trading partners. This average is called the '*trade weighted index*' or the 'STERLING EXCHANGE RATE INDEX'.

A Diagrammatic Analysis

Changes in the value of the pound can be explained using a demand and

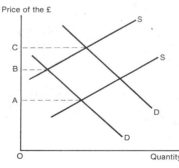

Figure 77.1

supply curve. Consider Figure 77.1. The shift in the demand curve from D to D' (i.e. at any given price, more pounds are demanded in the market) could be caused by a rise in UK exports, a rise in interest rates in London, or speculation that the pound will rise in future. This shift in the demand curve would cause the value of the pound to rise from OB to OC. A shift to the right in the supply curve (i.e. at any given price more pounds are supplied onto the market) would cause the value of the pound to fall from OB to OA. This increase in supply could have been caused by a rise in imports, a fall in interest rates in London, or speculation that the value of the pound will fall in future.

C H E C K P O I N T S

1 The value of the pound is £1 = $1.5, £1 = 12 French francs and £1 = 2 deutschmarks. How many:
    (a) French francs can you buy for £5;
    (b) US dollars can you buy for £100;
    (c) German deutschmarks can you buy for £50 000?
    What is the value of 1 deutschmark in French francs?

2 Explain how the value of the pound is determined.

3 Explain whether owners of pounds sterling will buy or sell pounds:
    (a) if there is a rise in UK imports;
    (b) if there is a rise in UK exports;
    (c) if interest rates rise in New York.

4 Using a demand and supply diagram, illustrate the effects of (a) to (c) in question 3 above.

5 What is the 'sterling exchange rate index' and why is it calculated?

C O U R S E W O R K   S U G G E S T I O N

Chart how the value of the pound has changed over the past twelve months (a) against the US dollar and (b) against the German Deutschmark. Explain why the value of the pound has changed. Analyse the likely effects of this change in value on the economy as a whole and your local area in particular. Try to decide whether the changes are likely to prove beneficial or not.

K E Y   T E R M S

FOREIGN EXCHANGE RATE – the price at which one currency is bought and sold for another currency.

FOREIGN CURRENCY SPECULATOR – a person or organisation that makes money by buying and selling foreign currencies in anticipation of changes in their value.

STERLING EXCHANGE RATE INDEX – an average value of the pound against the currencies of the UK's major trading partners.

The Significance of the Balance of Payments and Exchange Rates

Figure 78.1 Current balance, 2000–2005

	£ millions
2000	- 653
2001	+3235
2002	+6993
2003	+4923
2004	+3246
2005	+ 624

Figure 78.2 Exchange rate against major trading partners, 2000 = 100

2000	100
2001	103
2002	102
2003	105
2004	108
2005	110

Figure 78.3 Unemployment 2000–2005

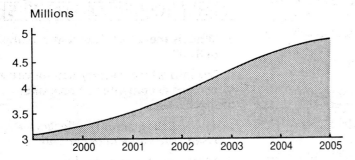

Figure 78.4 Inflation 2000–2005

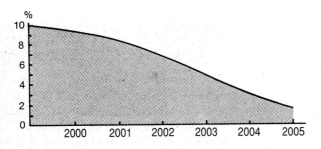

DEMOCRATIC PARTY MANIFESTO

Economic Policy

Unemployment is the main economic problem that faces our country today. It not only directly affects the lives of millions of unemployed workers and their families but also represents a huge cost to the rest of society. The Democratic Party is committed to reducing unemployment by:

- extra public spending of £10 billion on roads, schools, hospitals, sewers and grants to private firms for investment;
- cutting the exchange rate by 20% to make our country more competitive;
- stopping investment overseas and, if necessary, borrowing money from abroad to pay for new investment in private industry.

STUDY POINTS

You are the newly elected Democratic government of a country in 2000. Your manifesto commits you to certain economic policies.

1 What effect will the rise in public spending have on:
   (a) total spending in the economy and, therefore, on
   (b) imports, and, therefore on
   (c) the current balance?

2 How will the fall in the exchange rate affect:
   (a) the ability of exporters to compete abroad;
   (b) total exports;
   (c) the ability of companies to compete against foreign imports;
   (d) total imports;
   (e) the current balance?

3 What effect might reducing overseas investment by domestic companies have on:
   (a) investment at home in industry;

(b) the supply of dollars for sale on the foreign exchange markets and, therefore, on the exchange rate of the pound;
   (c) the competitiveness of domestic industry?

4 What are likely to be the effects of your policies on:
   (a) unemployment;
   (b) the incomes of workers;
   (c) investment by overseas industry;
   (d) inflation?

- 'Current account record deficit.'
- 'Pound slides again.'
- 'Record investment abroad.'

Units 76 and 77 considered the balance of payments and exchange rates. But why are they important?

The Current Account

In the second half of the 1970s, many Third World countries ran large current account deficits. They paid for this by borrowing large sums of money. But during the 1980s, they found that banks and governments wouldn't lend to them any more because they couldn't afford to repay their debts with the interest owed.

The Third World debt crisis is an example of what can happen to a country if it runs a persistent current account deficit. What is true for Argentina or Brazil is true for the UK too. We can't afford to run current account deficits year after year because eventually our foreign creditors (foreigners whom we owe money to) will want repaying. To repay debt would mean running a current account surplus.

The Price of the Pound

Is a high pound or a low pound good for Britain? Think of what happens if the pound falls. Foreigners need less of their currency to buy the same amount of pounds. So British firms can drop their prices in foreign currency terms and get the same amount back in pounds sterling. They should be able to sell more as a result.

But a fall in the value of the pound means that we have to pay more pounds to buy the same amount of foreign currency. That means that the price of imports goes up for us.

So a low pound should mean more exports and more jobs in the UK but will cause higher prices. By the same reasoning, a high pound will mean fewer exports and fewer jobs in the UK but prices will be lower. Hence, there is no simple answer as to whether a high or low pound is 'good' for Britain.

Fluctuations in the Pound's Value

Between the end of the Second World War and 1972, the value of the pound was fixed against other currencies. Over that period, it only changed twice in value, once in 1949 and next in 1967.

Between 1972 and 1990, the value of the pound was allowed to change on a day-by-day basis. The pound went up and down in value. In 1985, for instance, the pound fell to nearly $1=£1. Yet just five years before in 1980, it had risen to over $2.40 to the pound.

Between October 1990 and September 1992, the UK was a member of the Exchange Rate Mechanism. This fixes the value of the pound against other European currencies but allows the pound to go up and down freely against non-European currencies like the dollar or the yen. Then in September 1992, Britain was forced to leave the ERM.

Is it better to have free (or often called floating) exchange rates or fixed exchange rates?

Businesses usually prefer fixed exchange rates. If exchange rates are constantly going up and down, exporting and importing businesses often don't know how much they are going to get for their exports or pay for their imports. There are ways round this sometimes. A firm might be able to sign contracts where payment is in pounds rather than a foreign currency (thus passing the risk to the foreign company it is dealing with). Or it could buy money forward – agreeing a price now for money in the future. But it's not always possible to do this. So floating exchange rates discourage international trade.

On the other hand, fixing exchange rates limits the ability of governments to change the value of the pound. It might want to do this to boost exports, or reduce inflation as will be discussed in Unit 79.

CHECKPOINTS

1 What is meant by a current account deficit?

2 Explain why a country cannot run a current account deficit on a long-term basis.

3 Explain the economic effects of a rise in the value of the pound.

4 Why don't businesses like fluctuating exchange rates?

COURSEWORK SUGGESTION

Find out what has happened to the current account over the past three years. Find out also what it is predicted to be over the next year. Analyse whether the current account reflects a strong or weak economy. Would it be better for the UK if the current account were to change?

The lower the value of the pound the more American tourists will come to the UK and buy British goods.

The pound	Bank Buys	Bank Sells
Australia $	2.18	2.14
Austria Sch	24.50	23.30
Belgium Fr	71.80	68.00
Canada $	2.195	2.095
Denmark Kr	12.98	12.28
Finland Mkk	8.02	7.52
France Fr	11.07	10.52
Germany Dm	3.49	3.31
Greece Dr	214.00	199.00
Hong Kong $	12.30	11.80
Ireland Pt	1.155	1.095
Italy Lira	2385.00	2265.00
Japan Yen	261.00	247.00
Netherlands Gld	3.91	3.72
Norway Kr	11.07	10.52
Portugal Esc	232.00	220.00
South Africa Rd	4.05	3.35
Spain Pta	221.00	209.00
Sweden Kr	11.24	10.69
Switzerland Fr	2.91	2.76
USA $	1.60	1.53
Yugoslavia Dnr	530.00	490.00

Retail Price Index: 381.5
New York: The Dow Jones industrial average closed up 3.22 at 1,789.43.

12	+7	+2
13	+7	+3
14	+5	+5
15	+7	+1
16	+7	+4
17	+5	+5
18	+6	+8
19	+5	+7
20	+8	+3
21	+6	+2
22	+6	+5
23	+7	+2
24	+5	+5
25	+8	+5
26	+5	+5
27	+6	+5
28	+8	+5
29	+7	

The Exchange Rate Mechanism

Europa Bank

Commission rates on foreign exchange transactions

£1 – £5000	2%
£5000 – £20 000	1%
£20 000 – £100 000	0.5%
£100 000+	0.1%

Exchange rate value of the pound

	US dollars	German Deutschmarks
1 January	1.78	2.96
1 February	1.76	2.98
1 March	1.67	3.05
1 April	1.60	2.95
1 May	1.55	2.92
1 June	1.47	2.90
1 July	1.32	2.83
1 August	1.28	2.80
1 September	1.35	2.80
1 October	1.38	2.82
1 November	1.43	2.83
1 December	1.44	2.85

The value of the pound is determined on a minute-by-minute basis in the foreign exchange markets, as explained in Unit 77. But between October 1990 and September 1992, the UK was a member of the Exchange Rate Mechanism (ERM) of the European Monetary System (EMS) and it plans to rejoin the ERM in the near future.

The ERM is a system which stabilises the value of participating European currencies. When the UK joined, it committed itself to keeping the value of the pound within a band. Against the Deutschmark, this band was between 2.78 Deutschmarks = £1 and 3.13 Deutschmarks = £1. Firms which export and import knew that the value of the pound would not go outside of those ranges and so this gave a fair amount of stability to exchange rates.

Fixing the Value of the Pound

The Bank of England fixed the value of the pound on a day-to-day basis by buying and selling currencies.

To understand how this worked, think about why the value of the pound might fall. If it is falling, it is because there are more sellers than buyers. So to stabilise the value of a falling pound, the Bank of England has to buy pounds. It buys pounds with foreign currencies kept in the foreign currency reserves. In June 1992, these reserves were worth about $45 billion.

Equally, if the value of the pound is threatening to rise too high, the Bank of England will start to sell pounds and buy foreign currencies.

A central bank in the ERM is supported in this buying and selling by other central banks of countries in the ERM. If, for instance, the French franc is going down against the Deutschmark, the French central bank will be buying francs, but so too will the German Bundesbank, the German central bank.

Even though a central bank has billions of dollars of reserves, it can still be overwhelmed by selling pressures. The Bank of England, for

STUDY POINTS

1 You are a tourist going on holiday with your family in the USA in July. You booked your holiday in January and calculated you would need $1500 in currency for spending money. You got out your calculator and the newspaper which showed the exchange rate was £1 = $1.78. You worked out that it would cost you £842.70. (1500 ÷ 1.78). You order the currency for delivery on 1 July. On 1 July, the bank gives you a bill for £1159.09. Explain why you got it so wrong.

2 Another family books a holiday in Germany for July. If they wanted 2500 Deutschmarks in spending money: (a) how much did they think it would cost at 1 January exchange rates; (b) how much did it actually cost at 1 July exchange rates?

3 A UK exporting business signs four contracts on 1 January with payment to be made in the currency of the buying company. It has worked out its prices by taking its costs of production (in £) and adding 10% as profit. It has assumed that 1 January exchange rates will apply. (a) Two are sales to US companies, each worth $100 000. Payment for the first is on 1 August, the second on 1 December. (b) Two are sales to German companies, each worth 100 000 DM. One is for payment on 1 March, the other on 1 August. Things don't work out for the company as it expected. By calculating the amount in pounds it actually received for each contract, explain why.

4 Why are changes in the value of pound not liked by tourists or businesses?

5 Would tourists and businesses have preferred to buy and sell with dollars or Deutschmarks during the year shown above? Why?

6 Suggest ways in which exporting and importing businesses could reduce their risk from fluctuating exchange rates.

instance, lost around half its reserves in just a few weeks in September 1992, when the pound came under heavy selling pressure. In the end, the pound was forced out of the ERM and was allowed to float.

Devaluation

A country in the ERM still has the option to change the central value of its currency against other ERM currencies. If it shifted the band of values of its currency down, this would be called DEVALUATION. If it shifted it upwards, it would be a REVALUATION.

One important reason why the Bank of England was forced to devalue the pound in September 1992 was that the UK current account had been in too great a deficit for too long a time. A deficit means that, at any exchange rate value, imports are greater than exports, so sellers of pounds (UK buyers of imports) are constantly greater than buyers of pounds (foreigners buying UK exports). A devaluation should improve the current account position.

A fall in the value of the pound will mean that the price of British exports to foreigners will fall. A £20 000 car, for instance, sold at $2 = £1 would cost an American $40 000. At $1 = £1, it would only cost $20 000. Foreigners are therefore likely to buy more British exports.

Imports into the UK, on the other hand, will be more expensive to British consumers. So the volume of imports should decline.

The exact effect on the balance of payments depends upon the elasticities of demand for imports and exports. Evidence suggests that the demand for imports in the UK is inelastic, whilst exports are elastic.

So the total value of imports is likely to rise following devaluation. This is because, although fewer imports are bought by volume, each import costs more. If a 10% rise in price led to only a 5% fall in quantity demanded,

the total value of spending on imports would rise by about 5%.

But spending on exports should rise more. The price of exports remains the same to the UK exporter (whilst exports become cheaper to the buyer). Sales now increase because of the cheaper price. If sales increased by 10%, the total value of exports would rise by 10% too.

If export values go up, more pounds will be demanded by those buying our exports. This will more than offset any increase in selling pressure as pounds are sold by UK companies buying imports.

Monetary Union

The UK has committed itself in the Maastricht agreement to move towards full monetary union in the European Community. This will be done in three stages.

Firstly, the pound will have to rejoin the ERM. Secondly, the pound will become completely fixed against other ERM currencies. That will be achieved through buying and selling currencies and also by using interest rates. Britain won't be able to devalue the pound to get itself out of difficulties. It will have to use other policies to correct current account deficits discussed in Unit 81.

Thirdly, a new single currency for Europe will be established. You won't need French francs or Spanish pesetas for a foreign holiday because everyone will be using the same currency.

The great advantage of monetary union is that exporters and importers within the EC won't have to worry about exchange rate fluctuations. Over 50% of our trade is now with Europe. Selling from London to Paris will be no different from selling from London to Birmingham. Firms also won't have to pay commission to banks to change money. Of course, the US dollar and the Japanese yen will still exist. These currencies will be going up and down

against the new European ECU. But in trade terms, they aren't so important.

The disadvantage is that Britain will lose sovereignty. The Bank of England will disappear to be replaced by a new European Central Bank. It will decide monetary policy and exchange rate policy. Britain will lose the ability to control its own policy.

CHECKPOINTS

1 What is the ERM?

2 How are exchange rates stabilised in the ERM?

3 Explain how devaluation helps improve the current account.

4 What are the advantages and disadvantages of monetary union for the UK?

COURSEWORK SUGGESTION

Find out about the Maastricht agreement of December 1991. Describe what was agreed. How far has the EC reached in the move towards monetary union? What are the current obstacles to further progress? Evaluate whether or not monetary union will benefit the UK.

KEY TERMS

DEVALUATION – a fall in the value of a currency when it is fixed against other currencies.

REVALUATION – a rise in the value of a currency when it is fixed against other currencies.

Data Response Questions
Units 73–79

Unit 73 The Theory of Comparative Advantage

FORD of EUROPE
– labour productivity

HOURS PER VEHICLE*	1989	1990	1991 – Forecast
Cologne – Fiesta	33.5	29.9	28.5
Valencia – Fiesta	35.0	33.3	34.1
Dagenham – Fiesta	59.4	52.2	40.0
Saarlouis – Escort	29.5	33.9	30.5
Halewood – Escort	58.7	63.8	43.0
Genk – Transit	48.7	45.7	45.1
Southampton – Transit	70.4	73.2	64.0

*Figures based on salaried and hourly-paid employees.
Source: Internal Ford report.

Source: Financial Times, 23 December 1991

The table shows how long Ford workers at seven of its plants take on average to make Fiesta and Escort cars and Transit vans. Cologne and Saarlouis are in Germany. Valencia is in Spain. Genk is in Belgium. Southampton, Halewood and Dagenham are in the UK.

1 In which car plant were workers most productive making (a) Fiestas in 1989; (b) Transits in 1991? *(2 marks)*

2 Assume all costs were identical between countries for Ford (e.g. wage rates and raw material costs were the same). In 1991, consumers didn't buy enough cars and vans to keep all Ford car plants fully operational. Which car plants would you have recommended should go on short-time for (a) Fiestas, (b) Escorts and (c) Transits? Explain your reasoning. *(6 marks)*

3 During the 1980s, Ford expanded production of cars in Spain, Germany and Belgium but not in the UK. How can the theory of comparative advantage explain this? *(7 marks)*

Unit 74 Protectionism

Trade war fears

EUROPE and the United States hovered on the brink of a catastrophic world trade war last night.

If neither side backs down consumers and industry will be hit by spiralling prices and tariffs.

Last night Britain demanded that the U.S. drop a threat to impose crippling import tariffs on a list of £555 million of EC goods.

Agriculture Minister John Gummer branded the American move strident, antagonistic and demanding.

He warned Washington had

By KATE IRONSIDE
Political Correspondent

'better behave' and start compromising if it really wanted to end the deadlock in the current Gatt talks on world trade.

President Bush has already drawn up a hit-list of goods, and £57 million worth of British trade could suffer.

The drink, cheese and confectionery industries would be hardest hit. In the EC as a whole a wide range of goods would be affected by the U.S.

Source: Daily Express, 30 May 1992

1 What is meant by a 'trade war'? Illustrate your answer from the article. *(5 marks)*

2 Why do countries threaten to have trade wars do you think? *(5 marks)*

3 Who would lose out if there were a trade war between the USA and the EC? *(5 marks)*

Unit 75 Exports and Imports

Trade gap hits £1bn as shops wait

Britain's trade gap widened to more than £1 billion last month for the first time in over a year.

But though the figures are disappointing, the surge of imports which caused the bigger deficit points to a long-awaited revival in consumer spending.

During April, imported goods worth £10.15 billion came into the UK, while £8.79 billion of UK made products were sold abroad, leaving a visible gap of £1.36 billion.

But invisible exports brought £300 million more into Britain than went out. That left an overall deficit of £1.06 billion, almost double the March gap of £591 million.

Source: Daily Mail, 27 May 1992

1 What was the value of UK (a) visible exports and (b) visible imports in April 1992? *(2 marks)*

2 (a) Give two examples of visible exports.
  (b) Give two examples of invisible imports. *(4 marks)*

3 Why does Britain need to export goods and services? *(4 marks)*

4 Explain the link between a 'revival in consumer spending' and a widening 'trade gap'. *(5 marks)*

Unit 77 Exchange Rates

Behind the fall in sterling

THERE ARE three reasons why sterling is in crisis again. First, and most important, the sterling exchange rate is linked to the price of oil. Just as sterling was very strong during the second oil price explosion of 1979–80, so it has been tending to fall as the price of oil has fallen over the past couple of years.

Secondly, the markets may believe that domestic monetary policy is too loose – too much money in the economy will help create inflation and a loss of competitiveness as well as allowing extra spending on imports. This factor is often over-emphasised in the City of London.

The third factor is the government's failure to intervene at the right time in defence of sterling. The government's failure to increase interest rates at the right time meant that, when the pound did start to fall rapidly, the rise in interest rates had to be even greater than if prompt action had been taken.

Source: adapted from the Financial Times, 15 January 1985

1 What is meant by a sterling 'crisis'? *(4 marks)*

2 What two forces determine the price of a currency? *(2 marks)*

3 Explain, in terms of these two forces, why, according to the article, the pound was falling. *(9 marks)*

The Data Response Question for **Unit 79** can be found on page 221.

Essay Questions
Units 73–79

1 (a) Explain the difference between an export and an import. *(4 marks)*
  (b) Give *two* examples of *visible* exports for Britain. *(4 marks)*
  (c) What is meant by a 'deficit' on the current account? *(4 marks)*
  (d) What are the implications for a country if it has a current account deficit? *(8 marks)*

2 'Pounds falls in hectic trading.'
  (a) What is meant by a 'falling pound'? *(6 marks)*
  (b) How is the value of the pound determined? *(8 marks)*
  (c) What are the consequences for exports and imports of a falling pound? *(6 marks)*

The Data Response Question for **Unit 76** can be found on *page 83*. The Question for **Unit 78** can be found on *page 221* and the Question for **Unit 79** can be found on *page 183*.

The European Community

The European Community

	GDP[1] £bn	GDP[1] per head £ thousand	Population £ million
Germany[2]	636	10.1	63.1
France	555	9.8	56.4
UK	542	9.4	57.4
Italy	536	9.3	57.6
Spain	272	7.0	39.0
Netherlands	138	9.3	14.9
Belgium	92	9.2	10.0
Denmark	50	9.7	5.1
Portugal	50	4.8	10.4
Greece	48	4.7	10.1
Eire	22	6.2	3.5
Luxembourg	4	11.5	0.4

[1] Measured at purchasing power parity   [2] West Germany only

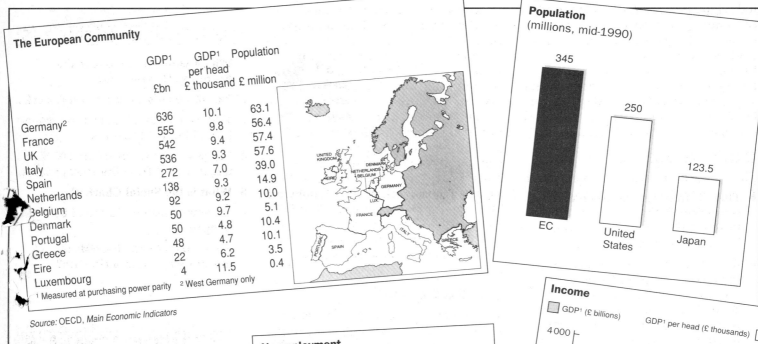

Source: OECD, Main Economic Indicators

Population
(millions, mid-1990)

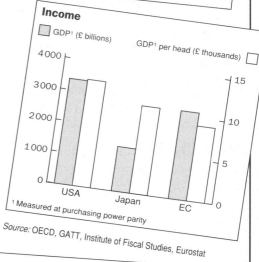

345 EC
250 United States
123.5 Japan

Income

GDP[1] (£ billions)   GDP[1] per head (£ thousands)

[1] Measured at purchasing power parity

Source: OECD, GATT, Institute of Fiscal Studies, Eurostat

GNP growth
(Annual average)

United States
1958-73 3.9%
1974-79 2.6%
1980-90 2.7%

Japan
1958-73 10.6%
1974-79 3.6%
1980-90 4.6%

European Community
1958-73 5.1%
1974-79 2.6%
1980-90 2.5%

Unemployment
(As a percentage of labour force)

United States
1980 7.2%
1987 6.2%
1990 5.5%

Japan
1980 2.0%
1987 2.8%
1990 2.1%

EC
1980 6.4%
1987 11.0%
1990 8.4%

European Community trade
(Percentage shares, 1989)

Imports to
Japan 12.2%
United States 16.6%
Developing countries 22.0%

Exports from
Japan 17.5%
United States 20.0%
Developing countries 20.3%

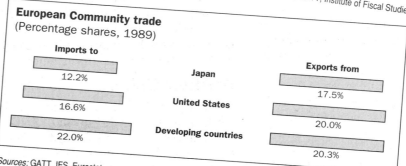

Sources: GATT, IFS, Eurostat

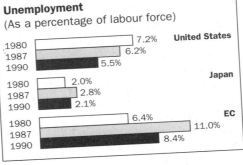

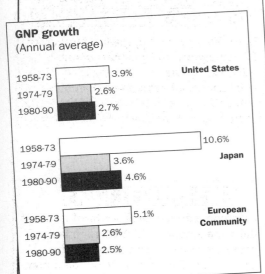

STUDY POINTS

Your task is to prepare a report about the European Community. In your report, you need to:
- describe the European Community – naming the member countries and giving a brief history of the Community;
- compare the economies of the countries within the EC – for instance, comparing population and national income;
- compare the EC with the two other major economies of the world, the USA and Japan.

The EC

The European Community (the EC, or sometimes called the Common Market) was established in 1957, when six countries – France, West Germany, Italy, Belgium, The Netherlands and Luxemburg – signed an agreement called the Treaty of Rome. Since then another six countries have joined, including the UK in 1973. Other countries, such as Sweden and Austria, want to join the EC. Almost every non-EC country in Europe has some special agreement on trade with the EC.

Customs Unions

The EC is a CUSTOMS UNION. This means:

- There is free trade between member countries. So there are no taxes (or *tariffs*) imposed when goods enter or leave a country for instance.

- All EC countries place exactly the same restrictions on goods and services imported from non-EC countries. An important part of this is the COMMON EXTERNAL TARIFF. For instance, a shirt imported from the USA will have the same tariff or tax placed upon it if it is imported into the UK as it would if imported into France or Greece.

The 1992 Process

Tariffs are just one sort of restriction on trade between countries. Countries have used other ways of keeping out foreign goods and services. For instance, governments have refused to buy goods made by foreign companies. Safety standards have been different in each country, making it difficult and costly for firms in one country to export products to another country.

'1992' is the name given to the process of sweeping away these hidden restrictions. By 1 January 1993, a British tractor manufacturer should be able to sell the same tractor in any EC country, whereas up until then each country had slightly different regulations about what must be included in the design of a tractor.

Much of the 1992 process involves *harmonisation* – agreeing the same set of rules to regulate trade across the whole of the EC.

The Social Charter

It is not just goods and services which have free movement around the community. Workers too are free to travel anywhere in the Community to take up a job. You are just as much entitled to work in Paris or Rome as in Birmingham or Glasgow. If you work in another country, you are then entitled to receive all the benefits that workers receive in that country. You pay their taxes too of course!

The Social Charter lays down minimum standards for workers to prevent firms moving round the community looking for the cheapest place to hire labour. For instance, it says that most workers should not work more than 48 hours per week. The UK has strongly resisted signing the Social Charter and is the only EC country now not guaranteeing its workers these rights.

The EC Budget

The EC collects money from member states and has its own budget. During the 1970s and 1980s, about 70% of this went on supporting farmers through the Common Agricultural Policy, described in Unit 74.

In the future, the EC wants to spend far more on giving help to the poorer regions of the Community. A single market is likely to attract investment into the already rich areas of the EC. Geographically these are at the centre of the Community. The outlying regions, like Ireland, Scotland, Portugal, Greece and southern Italy will not benefit equally from economic growth. So the EC wants to give money to attract industry into these regions.

Political Union

Monetary union and 1992 (discussed in Unit 79) will erode the power of the UK government. Some people think that the UK has already given up too many of its powers to the EC. Others argue that it is only a matter of time before there is political union, with a European government and parliament. Parliament at Westminster would then have far fewer powers than it does today. Political union – a United States of Europe – was the dream of some of

those who helped set up the EC in the 1950s. Political union would give peace, whilst a single market would help give economic prosperity to those in Europe.

CHECKPOINTS

1 Which countries belong to the European Community?

2 Explain how a customs union works.

3 Why is harmonization an important part of the 1992 process?

4 Suggest TWO reasons why UK firms might benefit from the 1992 process.

5 What is the Social Charter?

6 On what does the EC spend its budget?

7 What might be the benefits of a monetary union to a UK firm?

COURSEWORK SUGGESTION

Describe how the European Community is moving towards greater economic integration. Analyse the effects of this on consumers and firms in the UK. Who will gain and who will lose from economic and monetary union?

KEY TERMS

Common external tariff – a tariff or tax of the same amount which all member countries of a customs union put on goods coming in from outside the union.

The Limits of Government Policy

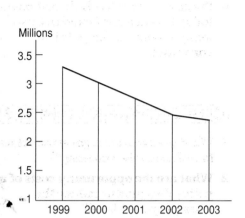

Figure 81.1 Unemployment in the UK, 1999–2003

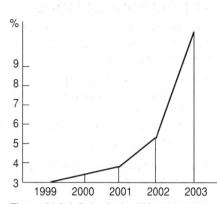

Figure 81.2 Inflation in the UK, 1999–2003

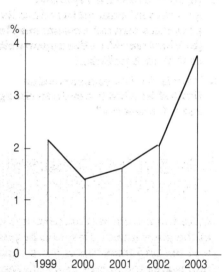

Figure 81.3 Economic growth (change in GDP), 1999–2003

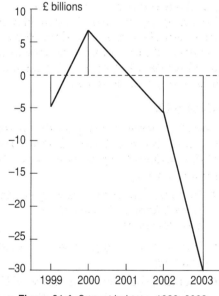

Figure 81.4 Current balance, 1999–2003

STUDY POINTS

Figures 81.1, 81.2, 81.3 and 81.4 give statistics for the British economy over the period 1999 to 2003. You are the Chancellor of the Exchequer preparing your budget in December 2004. Your task is to decide what policy measures to take. Prepare your budget statement.

(a) Comment upon the trends shown in
  (i) unemployment (ii) inflation (iii) growth and
  (iv) the current balance.
(b) State which of these trends represent problems for the UK economy.
(c) What economic policy measures could the Government take to help solve these problems?
(d) What effect would these measures have on the other two variables shown in the data?

Can the government ever get the economy to the right point of low unemployment, high economic growth, low or zero inflation and no balance of payments current deficit? At the same time, can it protect the environment and prevent too great an inequality in society? The government can manipulate the economy through:

- *fiscal policy* – manipulating taxes, government spending and government borrowing (see Unit 69);

- *monetary policy* – manipulating the rate of interest, the money supply and the volume of credit (see Unit 68);

- *exchange rate policy* – manipulating the level of the exchange rate (see Units 77 and 79);

- *trade policy* – imposing quotas and tariffs for instance (see Unit 74);

- *supply-side policies* – some of which are fiscal and monetary, but others such as trade union reform involving changes in the law (see Unit 70).

Unemployment

Imagine that unemployment is rising. If it is rising because the economy is going into recession, then the government can stimulate the economy by:

- cutting interest rates and encouraging a rise in borrowing;

- spending more itself or cutting taxes, thus increasing the PSBR (government borrowing);

- devaluing the pound, which should stimulate exports and make it easier for UK firms to compete against foreign imports;

- increasing quotas and tariffs on imported goods to keep out imports and provide more work for UK companies.

If the high unemployment is *structural*, caused by the decline of traditional industries, then the government needs to stimulate investment in the economy to recreate the jobs being lost. It can offer grants and other incentives to firms creating jobs in areas where there is high structural unemployment (see Unit 71 on regional policy). It could also cut welfare benefits and reduce income tax to encourage more workers to take low paid jobs.

But these policies have an *opportunity cost*. More government borrowing will tend to push up interest rates, and the economy needs lower interest rates to cut unemployment. The government could of course print the money to finance more spending or lower taxes. But that, with lower interest rates, will push up the money supply and cause inflation. Inflation will also go up if the pound is devalued.

Allowing the pound to fluctuate means that we cannot be a member of the Exchange Rate Mechanism. Membership of the ERM is an important policy objective of the government.

The UK can't impose quotas and tariffs because it would be in contravention of our membership of the EC and international treaties we have signed with GATT (the General Agreement on Tariffs and Trade).

Welfare benefits could be cut to the unemployed but this would increase hardship. The unemployed are already very badly off.

So the government is very much limited in what it can do. Whatever it does will make some other variables worse.

Inflation

Assume that inflation is rising in the economy. The government could:

- cut total spending in the economy by raising interest rates or cutting its own spending and raising taxes;
- raise the value of the pound to reduce import prices;
- lower tariffs and quotas to allow more foreign goods into the country, thus increasing their supply;
- try to stimulate supply of goods through supply-side policies or cut wage costs through labour market reforms.

But, as with unemployment policies, the government is boxed in. Cutting spending in the economy will push the economy into recession. Changing the value of the pound means that we cannot be a member of the ERM. Tariffs and quotas policy is now in the hands of the EC. Supply-side reforms take a long time to work.

The Current Balance

Assume that the UK has a serious current account deficit. The government could:

- cut aggregate demand in the economy thus reducing imports, by raising taxes, cutting its own spending or raising interest rates;
- devalue the pound;
- impose tariffs and quotas on imported goods;
- improve the competitiveness of British industry through supply-side measures.

But cutting aggregate demand would put the economy into recession. Changing the value of the pound means we cannot be a member of the ERM. Tariffs and quotas policy is now in the hands of the EC. Supply-side reforms take a long time to work.

Growth

The UK has had a low growth rate for the past 40 years. To reverse this, some of the policies the government needs to pursue are to:

- increase the share of GDP going to investment and research and development;
- increase spending on education and training;
- increase the competitiveness of UK industry through greater attention to quality control and product development.

But how can the government do this? If it does it through more government spending, how is it to be paid for? How can government influence firms?

The European Community

As the UK moves towards the year 2000, more and more decisions will be taken at European Community level and less and less in London. The UK government will find that it has less and less ability to change policies. But it could be argued that this doesn't really matter because:

- the UK government has failed in the past to produce a high growth, low inflation economy; the EC can't do much worse and could well do better;
- the government has little real power today because it is boxed in by so many economic and political constraints.

C H E C K P O I N T S

1 **What policies can a government use to influence the economy?**

2 **What are the opportunity costs of a policy designed to reduce the unemployment level?**

3 **(a) How could a government reduce the level of inflation? (b) What would be the opportunity costs of such a policy?**

4 **(a) How could the Japanese government attempt to reduce its persistent current account surplus? (b) What would be the opportunity cost of such policies?**

5 **Why is the UK government so limited in what it can do to change the UK economy?**

C O U R S E W O R K S U G G E S T I O N

Examine the current economic policy of the government. Describe its policies and the problems that it faces. Analyse and assess the extent to which the government is likely to succeed in its objectives.

The Developing World

Figure 82.1 GNP per capita, 1990

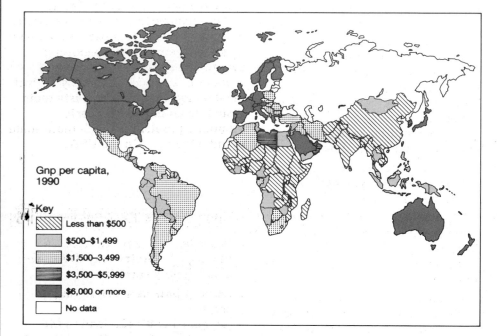

Gnp per capita, 1990

Key
- Less than $500
- $500–$1,499
- $1,500–3,499
- $3,500–$5,999
- $6,000 or more
- No data

Source: World Bank Atlas, 1991

Figure 82.2 Population projections by region

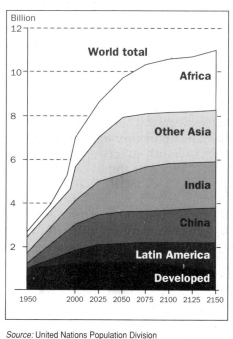

Source: United Nations Population Division

Figure 82.3 Literacy

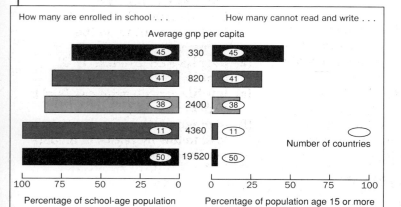

How many are enrolled in school . . . How many cannot read and write . . .

Average gnp per capita

	Average gnp
45	330
41	820
38	2400
11	4360
50	19 520

Number of countries

Percentage of school-age population   Percentage of population age 15 or more

Source: World Bank Atlas, 1991

Figure 82.4 The food supply

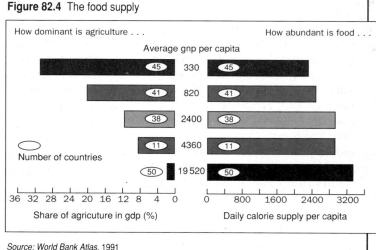

How dominant is agriculture . . . How abundant is food . . .

Average gnp per capita

Number of countries

Share of agriculture in gdp (%)   Daily calorie supply per capita

Source: World Bank Atlas, 1991

S T U D Y P O I N T S

1 Describe how the population of the world is distributed geographically (a) today and (b) in the year 2150 as projected by the United Nations.

2 Describe how the world's income is distributed. To do this, use Figure 82.1 which shows GNP per capita (i.e. income per person). The value of the dollar tends to vary between £1 = $1.50 and £1 = $2. Show that high income countries (also called 'First World' or 'developed' countries) tend to be situated in the north of the world whilst low income countries (also called 'Third World' or 'developing' countries) tend to be situated in the south.

3 What link is there between average income per person and (a) education and (b) food supplies shown in Figures 82.3 and 82.4. Why do you think there are these links?

Characteristics of the Developing World

The world's population stands at around 5 billion. Three-quarters of these people live in the DEVELOPING or THIRD WORLD, and only a quarter live in the DEVELOPED first and second worlds. The *First World* is made up of rich, industrialised, developed, Western, for the most part democratic countries, such as the USA, the UK and Japan. The *Second World* is made up of less well off, but still relatively rich, former Eastern-bloc Communist countries, such as the USSR and Poland. The developing world, where most people live, is made up of very much poorer countries in South America, Africa and Asia. Figure 82.2 shows how the world's population is distributed.

Developing countries represent the largest group of countries in the world, both by area and by population. But in terms of income and wealth, they lag behind the first two groups.

No two developing countries are the same, and therefore it is dangerous to try to generalise. However, developing countries usually show a number of the following characteristics:

- *Low incomes per person*. Figure 82.1 shows the GNP per capita (gross national product or income per person) for countries in the world today. Note that India, China, Pakistan and Bangladesh, with a quarter of the world's population, have average incomes of less than $400 a year. Note, too, that the developed countries are found mainly in the North. Hence the gap between rich and poor countries is often referred to as the 'North–South divide'.
- *Low life expectancies for their population*. Figure 82.3 shows that you are far more likely to live longer, if you live in a high-income country than if you live in a low-income country.
- *High rates of population growth*. Many children still die in developing countries, but such deaths were even more common 100 years ago. In order to maintain family size, parents had to have lots of children. Today, more children survive, but it takes time for social attitudes to change. People still have large numbers of children. There is strong evidence to suggest that as incomes rise and parents see that more children are surviving, family size will come down.
- *A less well-educated population*. By no means everybody, for instance, is able to read and write.
- *Relatively little capital*. Everything, from factories and machines to roads and schools, is far less abundant than in developed countries.
- *Low labour productivity*. A less well-educated workforce, with less capital, produces less per worker than in the industrialised countries of the developed world.
- *Poor housing*.
- *Poor sanitation*. For instance, many people in developing countries do not have access to clean piped water for drinking and washing.
- *Poor health standards*. Common diseases, no longer seen in the rich developed countries, kill millions in developing countries. Malnutrition, too, is still a big killer.

The Poverty Cycle

All aspects of poverty in developing countries are interlinked. For instance, low productivity of developing world workers means that they can only earn low wages. This, in turn, means that they cannot afford to eat sufficiently well, which leads to poor health. With low wages, they cannot afford to live in good-quality houses with adequate levels of sanitation, which again leads to health problems. High mortality (death) rates encourage parents to have large families, but this leads to too many workers chasing too few jobs and consequently to low wages. Each individual problem is part of the much larger problem facing developing countries – namely, such a lack of economic resources that many of their inhabitants cannot even satisfy their basic human needs. The basic economic problem is much more acute in India than it is in the USA.

KEY TERMS

DEVELOPED or FIRST WORLD COUNTRIES – the rich *industrialised* nations of the world, such as France and Japan.

DEVELOPING or THIRD WORLD COUNTRIES – the poorer countries of the world, such as Ethiopia and India.

Economic Development

NIGERIA

KEY STATISTICS 1991

GDP (US$)	32.0 billion
GDP per head (US$)	280
Oil production (million barrels per day)	1.9
External debt (US$)	33.4 billion
Population	114 million
Population growth	3% per year
Infant mortality	85 per thousand
Protein energy malnutrition	60% of children under five

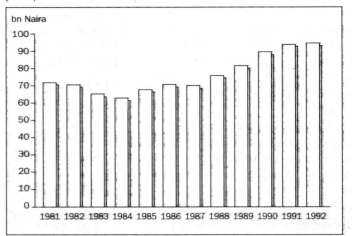

Figure 83.1 Gross domestic production (bn Naira at constant 1984 prices)

Source: Financial Times, 16 March 1992

Figure 83.2 Balance of payments, $ billion

	1990	1991	1992 (forecast)
Exports	13.7	10.6	9.5
(of which oil)	13.3	10.2	9.0
Imports	4.9	5.1	5.4
Trade surplus	8.8	5.5	5.4
Net invisibles	−3.5	−2.0	−2.0
Current account balance	5.2	3.5	2.1
Capital account balance	−4.4	−3.3	−3.4
(of which scheduled debt repayment)	−6.9	−6.0	−5.8
Overall balance	+0.8	+0.2	−1.3

Source: Financial Times, 16 March 1992

Figure 83.3 Oil price

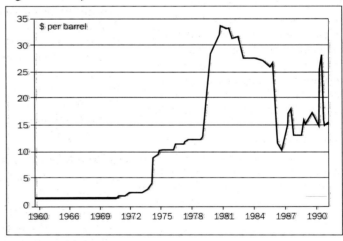

Source: Financial Times, 16 March 1992

STUDY POINTS

1 Look at all the data given. Describe four problems which faced Nigeria in 1991.

Nigeria borrowed a lot of money from foreign banks in the 1970s and early 1980s.

2 Look at the Key Statistics.
  (a) How much did Nigeria owe in 1991?
  (b) How much was that debt as a proportion of GDP?
  (c) How much was that debt per person in Nigeria?

Study Figure 83.2

3 (a) How much did Nigeria have to pay in debt repayments in 1991?
  (b) What proportion of visible exports had to be spent repaying debt?
  (c) Nigeria was predicted to have a major problem in 1992 repaying debt because the overall balance on the current and capital accounts was negative. How do you think the Nigerian government could get around this problem and what would be the opportunity costs of these solutions?

Study Figures 83.2 and 83.3

4 (a) How important is oil for Nigeria?
  (b) How has the world price of oil changed since 1973?
  (c) How do you think this has affected Nigeria's standard of living?

Look at all the statistics

5 Assuming that oil production hasn't changed since 1980, suggest three reasons why income per person in Nigeria was $1000 in 1980 but only $280 in 1991.

How Countries Grow

If you look back to Unit 65, you will see that countries can increase their national income by improving the quantity or quality of their factors of production – land, labour and capital.

Developing countries are no different from rich countries like the UK in this respect. They can grow if:

- they exploit their raw materials more. This means developing reserves of commodities such as copper, oil, gold and iron ore. It also means bringing more land into use for agriculture;

- they invest in people. Education and training are essential. But so too is making sure that valuable workers are not impaired or destroyed through ill-health and disease;

- they invest in capital. Capital is everything from fertiliser to factories to roads and health clinics.

Financing Growth

Developing countries can grow if money is set aside for investment. Money can come from two sources. The money could come from within a country. Individuals and firms could save money and it could then be used for investment. The government could also finance investment through raising taxes.

Alternatively, the money could come from abroad. The money could be borrowed by firms or by governments. Or the money could be given by foreign governments or aid agencies in the form of grants. Finally, the money could come in the form of profits on exports from a developing country.

Trade

The most important way in which First World countries can help Third World countries is through trade. Trade creates incomes and jobs as First World countries buy Third World exports. The money received can then be used to buy goods and services from the First World. Some of those goods and services will be investment products – machines, factories, education abroad or technical know-how for instance. This inflow of investment goods should stimulate economic growth.

Free trade has an additional advantage. To compete on world markets, Third World countries have to produce goods of the right quality at the right price. Competition with other world producers provides a powerful incentive for Third World producers to adopt the best production methods. This doesn't necessarily mean employing the latest Western technology. But it does mean using their relatively cheap labour in the most efficient way possible.

Protectionism

Unfortunately for Third World countries, all rich countries keep out many Third World imports through trade barriers. Third World countries find it difficult if not impossible for instance to export many food products to the First World. Clothing and textiles industries too have been protected in First World countries.

By denying Third World countries the opportunity to produce and sell goods which they are efficient at producing, First World countries are deliberately helping to keep Third World countries poor. First World countries do it to save jobs and companies in their own economies. But they suffer too because their consumers have to pay much higher prices for products than they would if they could buy them from Third World producers.

Commodity Prices

Another problem facing Third World countries is that commodity prices – copper, coffee, cocoa, coal – have been falling over the past 50 years. That means that countries which are dependent upon these for most of their exports have to produce more and more to buy the same amount of First World imports. Some of the world's poorest countries are dependent upon just one commodity for most of their exports. Third World countries need to diversify – make and export different types of goods. But that takes money for investment which is difficult to get as we will see in the next unit.

CHECKPOINTS

1 What causes a Third World country to grow?

2 How can economic growth be financed?

3 Why does foreign trade help growth in Third World countries?

4 (a) Why do most First World countries restrict imports of wheat? (b) Why does this harm the economic interests of some Third World countries?

5 Why is the long-term decline in world commodity prices (a) good news for First World countries and (b) bad news for many Third World countries?

COURSEWORK SUGGESTION

Find out what has happened to the price of a particular commodity, like copper or coffee, over the past 30 years. Explain why prices have changed. Find out which countries are the main producers of the commodity. How have these price changes affected their economies? What is likely to happen to prices in the future and what are the implications of this for producing countries?

Data Response Questions
Units 80–83

Unit 80 The European Community

£3.6m boost to ease pit jobs gloom

Communities in southern Staffordshire hit by the run down of the mining industry have been given a £3.6 million boost by the European Commission.

The cash forms part of the £124.2 million Rechar aid package released following the settling of an 18-month squabble between the British Government and Eurocrats.

News of the grant was welcomed by Staffordshire councillors today who said the cash would be used to help fund development projects in Cannock and Rugeley.

Councillor Mike Tappin, chairman of the county's economy and employment committee, said: "It's wonderful news and will help us get Cannock and Rugeley back on their feet."

He said the money would be used on the redevelopment of the former Lea Hall Colliery in Rugeley.

The pit closed in 1990 with the loss of 1100 jobs and now the county wants to buy the site off British Coal and turn it into an industrial estate.

The cash will also fund new training initiatives at Cannock's Itec centre and help finance environmental projects.

Source: Express and Star, 27 February 1992

1 Why did 'communities in southern Staffordshire' get an EC grant? *(1 mark)*

2 What will the money be used for? *(2 marks)*

3 Where does the EC get its money from to give out in grants like this? *(4 marks)*

4 What do you think might be the effects of the grant on (a) unemployment and (b) the standard of living in the local area? *(8 marks)*

Unit 81 The Limits of Government Policy

Tax cuts will bump start the economy

Norman Lamont needs to add lashings of two vital ingredients – boldness and imagination – as he prepares his budget. He must overcome his natural caution and serve up an economic offering that combines tax cuts for workers and incentives for industry.

Such a package would restore confidence and bury the recession which is so doggedly refusing to lie down.

Nothing less than 1p off income tax will do for workers. But this should only be the beginning and not the end of Mr Lamont's reforming budget.

The need for industry to be inspired is made all the more urgent as interest rates soar above inflation putting the real cost of borrowing into the stratosphere.

Over the past six months, prices have been rising at an annual rate of just 2.6 per cent compared to base interest rates at 10.5 per cent. The result has been bankruptcy for some firms and wafer-thin profit margins for others.

The Chancellor's hands are tied over interest levels because of the need to protect the value of the pound and prevent a return to the evil of inflation.

So he must find other ways of helping businesses back to prosperity and job creation. He must devise new incentives for small firms. He must give more financial encouragement to investment and training. He must ease the burden of corporation tax and produce a package to drive the car industry out of the doldrums.

Source: Adapted from the Daily Express, 20 January 1992

1 What, according to the article, was true about (a) inflation and (b) economic growth at the time the article was written? *(4 marks)*

2 Take any *three* of the policies mentioned in the article and for each one explain its likely effect on (a) unemployment (b) inflation (c) economic growth and (d) the current account on the balance of payments. *(12 marks)*

3 To what extent could the *Daily Express*'s budget proposals be described as 'supply-side' policies? *(4 marks)*

Unit 82 The Developing World

Gap between rich and poor widens

The gap between rich and poor countries has widened and a huge 73 per cent of the world's 3.9 billion people now live in conditions of human suffering, a report claimed today.

The US-based private Population Crisis Committee's second "human suffering index" found a strong link between high rates of population growth and hardship.

"The 1991 index shows that an appalling three-quarters of the world's people live in countries where human suffering is the rule, rather than the exception," committee vice-president Sharon Camp said.

In the poorer countries incomes fell in the past five years while the birth rates rose.

"Slowing population growth would help these countries buy the time they need to create real economic opportunity for the poor majority," she said.

The index looked at 10 areas – life expectancy, childhood immunisations, daily calorie supply, clean drinking water, secondary school enrolment, gross national product, inflation, political freedom, civil rights and communications technology – to assess the quality of life.

Mozambique, Somalia, Afghanistan, Haiti and Sudan were the five worst countries in all categories and all had population growth rates of close to 3 per cent. At that rate their populations will double in less than 30 years.

Source: Express and Star, 18 May 1992

1 How many people live in the Third World according to the Population Crisis Committee? *(1 mark)*

2 Explain *four* ways in which Third World countries have a lower standard of living than the rich countries of the world. *(8 marks)*

3 Why might reduced population growth in a country help improve the standard of living for its inhabitants? *(6 marks)*

Unit 83 Economic Development

World Bank turns development spotlight on poor

In its annual World Development Report, the World Bank outlined a two-pronged strategy for helping the world's poorest people. One billion people, one-fifth of the world's population, live on £200 or less a year.

The World Bank recommended that economic growth should be based on efficient labour-intensive techniques of production. Markets should be free so that workers, firms and farmers have the right incentives to produce. Governments need to build appropriate infrastructure such as roads, hospitals and schools. An efficient banking system needs to be set up to channel savings to producers. Technological innovation should be part of everyday life.

But economic growth in itself will not necessarily benefit everyone. The poorest in society might well be by-passed. So governments must provide adequate social services, such as primary education, basic health care and family planning services. Safety nets must be provided to help the most vulnerable – such as the destitute, the sick, orphans and the aged.

Source: Adapted from the Financial Times, 16 July 1990

1 What is the income of the billion poorest people in the world? *(1 mark)*

2 Explain how two of the measures recommended by the World Bank would increase economic growth in the Third World. *(6 marks)*

3 How might (a) the aged and (b) orphans in the Third World be helped? *(4 marks)*

4 What might be the opportunity cost for Third World governments of helping the poorest in their societies? *(4 marks)*

Essay Questions
Units 80–83

1 (a) What is the 'European Community'? *(8 marks)*
  (b) Describe briefly how the Common Agricultural Policy works. *(8 marks)*
  (c) Explain *one* benefit to the UK of its membership of the EC. *(4 marks)*

2 (a) Describe *four* features of poor developing countries of the world such as those found in Africa or Asia. *(8 marks)*
  (b) Analyse ways in which the developed countries of the world, such as the UK, could help the economic development of the developing countries. *(12 marks)*

Capital Transfers to the Third World

STUDY POINTS

Look carefully at the photographs. Assume that you are the government of a Third World country. You want to help solve some of the problems in your country illustrated by the photographs. Your country can't afford to do it, so you are thinking of getting money from First World countries.

1 What economic problem do you think is illustrated in each of the photographs?

2 Taking each photograph in turn, which of the following do you think would be the most likely way of tackling the problem illustrated in that photograph?
   (a) Seeking inward investment from a multinational company.
   (b) Obtaining a loan from a large international bank.
   (c) Getting grant aid from a First World government or charity.

3 What would be the advantages and disadvantages for your country of each of the solutions you have proposed?

Foreign Investment

One way for Third World countries to get money for investment is for them to allow foreign companies to set up in their country. These companies – often called MULTINATIONAL COMPANIES – bring money into the company to set up factories and plant. Often, part of the production will then be exported back to First World countries. All this creates income and jobs as well as export earnings. However, multinational companies will also want to send back profits to their home country in the First World. If few jobs are created, few goods are exported and a lot of profits are sent back, then multinational companies can damage Third World countries.

Loans

Another way for Third World countries to get investment money is to borrow it from the First World. Just as a firm often borrows money to finance expansion, so too can a country. In the 1970s, Third World countries borrowed a lot of money. In the 1980s, many found that they couldn't afford the repayments and almost went bankrupt. This occurred for a number of reasons.

- Much of the money borrowed was wasted on poor investment projects, so few exports were created to pay for the repayments.

- Some of it wasn't used for investment at all. Military dictatorships used money to pay for purchases of defence equipment. Government officials wasted money on buying luxury imported goods. So no exports were created at all.

- Most importantly, the cost of repayment went up dramatically in the early 1980s. Loans were usually in US dollars and the value of the dollar soared in the early 1980s.

Are the developing countries exploited by the developed world?

Third World countries had to export more goods to get the same number of dollars as before. What's more, US interest rates soared, vastly increasing the interest rate repayments.

The problem facing Third World countries came to be called the Third World debt crisis. In many years during the 1980s, the Third World gave more financial capital back to the First World than it received in investment, new loans and foreign aid. As a result of income going from the poor to the rich, some Third World countries were poorer in 1990 than they were in 1980.

Aid

Aid forms only a fraction of money transfers from the First World to the Third World. Some 'aid' is simply loans from First World governments to Third World governments. They have helped contribute to the Third World debt crisis.

Other aid is in the form of SOFT LOANS. These are loans that carry little or no interest. Nevertheless the loans still have to be repaid.

Too much aid in the form of loans in the past has been spent on the wrong projects. Large steel mills and enormous dam projects have often given little or no financial return. Even worse is when the money is wasted on buying arms.

A small proportion of aid is in the form of grants. Today, many countries are channelling grants through multilateral aid agencies. These include charities like Oxfam or the Red Cross. They also include the World Bank, a bank set up to help Third World countries. Aid projects are increasingly aimed at helping the poorest in Third World countries. They also increasingly are assessed for their impact on the environment. Funding projects to ranch cattle in the Brazilian rain forest might help some Brazilians earn higher incomes but will positively damage the environment.

C H E C K P O I N T S

1 **What are the costs and benefits to a Third World country of Coca-Cola setting up a manufacturing plant in that country?**

2 **How can a country develop its economy through borrowing money from abroad?**

3 **How did the Third World debt crisis develop in the 1980s?**

4 **The British government provides foreign aid for a developing country to build a steel plant. What will be the effects of this on (a) the developing country and (b) the UK?**

C O U R S E W O R K S U G G E S T I O N

Use *British Aid Statistics* (published by CSO, and available from your local large reference library) to describe the pattern of UK overseas aid in recent years. Describe who receives foreign aid and what sort of projects are supported. Analyse how foreign aid patterns have changed. Try to decide whether the UK ought to give more foreign aid, and whether current aid is effective in helping poor people in developing countries.

K E Y T E R M S

MULTINATIONAL COMPANIES – companies usually owned in one country but which produces goods and services in a number of countries.

FOREIGN AID – gifts or loans of money from the rich developed countries to poorer developing countries.

SOFT LOANS – loans at low rates of interest.

Economic Systems

FREE MARKET ECONOMY

COMMAND ECONOMY

PLANNING MINISTRY

No two economies are organised in exactly the same way, but they all have to solve three fundamental problems:

- *What* should be produced in the economy? For instance, what quantities of food or televisions or banking services should be produced?

- *How* should production be organised? For instance, should machinery be used; how many workers should be employed; should production take place in London or Glasgow?

- *For whom* should production take place? Should everybody be entitled to an identical share of production, or should some receive more than others?

Economists distinguish between four different economic systems which resolve these problems in different ways. These will now be looked at in turn.

Traditional Or Subsistence Economies

A SUBSISTENCE ECONOMY is one where there is little specialisation and little trade. People tend to live in family groups, and these families grow most of their own food, make their own houses, gather their own fuel and provide their own leisure activities – i.e. to a great extent they are self-sufficient. It is called a 'subsistence' economy because it is very difficult, without a great deal of specialisation and trade, to do more than subsist (i.e. provide the basic necessities for living). It is a 'traditional' economy because it is the type of economy that has existed all over the world since man began being economically active. It is only in relatively recent history that more 'advanced' types of economy have developed.

What, how and for whom to produce are decisions that are answered by looking to the past. If a society has managed to survive for

S T U D Y P O I N T S

There are two islands close to each other in the South Seas.

1 To start with, they are subsistence economies. What this means is that every household on the islands produces most of the things it needs to survive – from housing, to food to clothing. There is no money, so any trading that takes place is barter trade (i.e. swapping one good for another).
   (a) Think of all the disadvantages that this type of economy has.
   (b) Are there any advantages do you think?

One person from each island leaves and goes to university. One goes to the USA, the other to North Korea. When they come back, they tell everyone on their island about the wonders of the countries they have seen.

   The person who went to the USA persuades her islanders to change to a free market system of production. Money is introduced and people work for money. They then spend the money they have earned on goods and services. Instead of every household trying to produce everything, firms are set up which specialise in the production of goods and services.

2 What do you think might be the advantages of this new system?

3 What would the effect of the introduction of this system on (a) a handicapped person who can't work; (b) a 75 year old who is ill; (c) a child who is orphaned; (d) a worker whose skills are in very great demand on the island; (e) a worker whose skills are commonplace?

The person who went to North Korea persuades her islanders to change to a planned economy. Everything is owned by the state. Money is issued, but most goods and services, like housing and health, are given free to islanders. Food and clothing is bought from state shops. Workers work for the state and are paid by the state.

4 What do you think might be the advantages of this new system compared to a subsistence economy?

5 What would the effect of the introduction of this system on the people described in question 3?

An example of China's 'modernisation' – a supermarket in Beijing.

some time, then what was done in the past must have been successful. So in traditional economies there is often resistance to change and to new ideas. No two traditional economies are the same, so it is impossible to describe typical economic mechanisms by which resources are allocated.

Free-market Economies

A FREE-MARKET ECONOMY is one where decisions are made through the market mechanism. The forces of demand and supply, without any government interference, determine how resources are allocated.

What to produce is decided upon by the level of profitability for a particular product. Buyers cast their spending 'votes' in the market place. For instance, consumers may buy 200 000 British cars a year. That may not be enough to make the car company in Britain profitable. Car sellers would need either to sell more cars, or to sell the same number of cars at a higher price, in order to earn a reasonable or 'normal' rate of profit. Investors are then discouraged from investing in that industry. They will put their money into higher-profit industries. As a result, fewer British cars will be produced. What is produced is therefore fixed by what it is most profitable to produce in an economy.

How production should be organised is equally determined by what is most profitable. Firms are encouraged through the market mechanism to adopt the most efficient methods of production.

As to for whom production should take place, production is *allocated* to those who can afford to pay. Consumers with no money cannot afford to buy anything. Millionaires can purchase large quantities of goods and services.

Command Economies

A COMMAND ECONOMY is one where all economic decisions are made by the government. The government decides what to produce, how it is to be produced and how it is to be allocated to consumers. This involves a great deal of planning. Hence such economies are often called PLANNED ECONOMIES. Planned economies tend to be run by governments who, in theory at least, want to see greater economic equality between consumers. By state planning, goods and services can be produced to satisfy the needs of all the citizens of a country, not just those who have the money to pay for goods.

Mixed Economies

A MIXED ECONOMY is one where some goods and services are produced in the free-market sector of the economy, but others are produced by the state – i.e. it is a mixture of a pure free-enterprise market economy and a pure command economy.

KEY TERMS

TRADITIONAL or SUBSISTENCE ECONOMY – an economy where specialisation and trade are limited, and where there is a great degree of self-sufficiency.

FREE MARKET or FREE ENTERPRISE ECONOMY – an economy where resources are allocated through the market mechanism.

COMMAND or PLANNED ECONOMY – an economy where resources are allocated by the state through a system of planning.

MIXED ECONOMY – an economy where some resources are allocated via the market mechanism and some via the state.

Economic Systems Compared

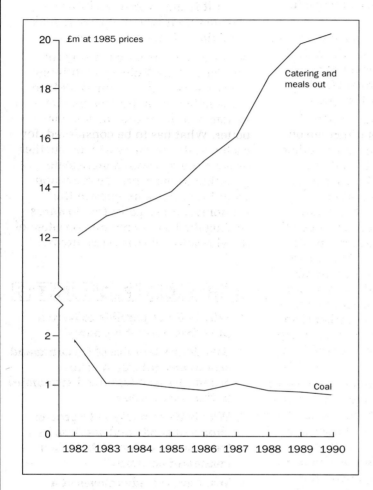

Figures 86.1 Spending on coal, and catering and meals out (£ millions at 1985 prices)

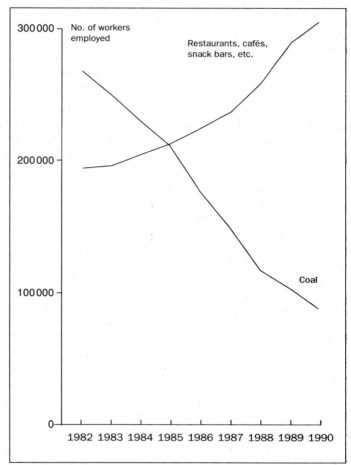

Figure 86.2 Number of workers employed in the coal industry and restaurants, cafes, snack bars, etc., Great Britain

Source: CSO, *Annual Abstract of Statistics*

STUDY POINTS

Coal

1 (a) What happened to spending by consumers on coal between 1982 and 1990?

 (b) Why do you think this change might have taken place? (Hint: how did people heat their houses in, say, 1950; do they still heat them in the same way today?)

2 What happened to the number of coalminers and the number of pits over the same period?

3 Suggest why the change in spending on coal should have led to the change in the number of pits and coalminers.

Catering and meals out

4 (a) What happened to spending by consumers on meals out between 1982 and 1990?

 (b) What reasons can you suggest which would explain this change in spending?

5 What happened to the number of workers employed in restaurants, cafés, etc., over the same period?

6 Suggest why the change in spending on meals should have led to the change in the number of workers in the restaurant and café business.

The allocation of resources

7 How have the spending 'votes' of consumers changed what is being produced in the UK?

8 Who have been the winners and losers from the shift of resources from the coal industry into the catering industry?

Free-market versus Command economies

There are no pure free-market economies nor pure command economies in the world today. The USA, however, is the most important 'free-market' economy. About 75% of total output is produced by the private sector. The other 25% is produced by the government. As was shown in Unit 55, *public* goods, such as defence, would not be provided by the free-market mechanism. Other *merit* goods, such as education, would not be provided in sufficient quantity. So any modern state has to allocate resources for these goods via a taxation and government-spending programme.

In a command economy, it is impossible to regulate all markets. Even in the most planned economies of the world, such as in China or North Korea, some goods and services are provided through a free-market mechanism. An economy where 75% of the goods are provided by the state would be called a command economy. In a mixed economy, such as the UK or France or Norway, the balance between state provision and free-market provision is more or less equal.

Efficiency

Would it be better for the UK to have more production or to be less organised by the free-market mechanism or by the state? The Conservative Party argues that more free-market production would increase efficiency. The Labour Party argues the contrary. To decide who is right is not easy because a variety of aspects of efficiency need to be considered.

Take, as an example, the provision of medical care. In the USA, it is provided mainly by the free-market mechanism. Consumers have to pay for any medical services they use. In the UK, medical care is provided by the state through the National Health Service. Almost all services are free to consumers (although they are not free to society of course – they are paid for through taxes). Aspects of efficiency that need to be considered include:

- *Distribution of resources.* In a free-market system, resources are allocated to consumers only if consumers are able to pay for them. In the USA, if you are ill, but have no money, you cannot get treatment. In the UK, treatment is given on the basis of need. If the health services do not have the resources to treat patients, then the patients either go untreated or are placed on waiting lists.

- *Choice.* In the USA, consumers have the freedom to choose which doctor to go to, or which hospital to use. Under the UK National Health Service, there is far less choice.

- *Cost.* The UK spends a lower proportion of its total income on health care than almost any other advanced country. It could be argued that British health care is not as good as that of other economies. On the other hand, it could be that Britain's state health system is much cheaper, but still provides the same level of service. A state system allows economies of scale to be achieved. Doctors are encouraged to think about what is best value for money, rather than how they can profit from charging for treatment which is of dubious value.

- *Quality.* State-provided services are often accused of being poor quality. Workers know that they do not have to sell products in a competitive market, so they do not strive to provide good-quality products. On the basis of this argument, the National Health Service would provide a better service to customers if it were privatised.

The quality and quantity of goods available for consumption and how they are distributed are very important aspects of the efficiency of an economy. Other aspects include:

- The degree to which an economy is stable. An economy racked by high inflation, or continuing bouts of high unemployment, is less efficient than a more stable economy.

- The rate at which the economy grows. A fast-growing economy that provides increases in the standards of living of its citizens is more efficient than one that grows only slowly or not at all.

- The degree to which the long-term interests of the economy are taken into consideration. An economy that destroys the environment, or its historical heritage, may be able to achieve high rates of growth today, but it is impoverishing future generations who will have to pick up the bill for such growth.

Because there are so many ways of comparing the efficiency of different types of economy, it is impossible to say whether or not the free-market system or a command economy is better. What has to be considered, for each country in the world, is whether or not a move towards more state planning or more private provision would improve efficiency in the economy, and so go further towards solving the basic economic problem of the allocation of scarce resources.

CHECKPOINTS

1 Why is it not possible to have a pure free-market economy?

2 Give *four* examples of (a) command economies, (b) free-market economies and (c) mixed economies in the world today.

3 Why is there likely to be greater choice of goods and services in a free-market economy than in a command economy?

4 What are the advantages of a free-market economy compared to a command economy? What are the disadvantages?

COURSEWORK SUGGESTION

Find out about the workings of a command economy, such as the USSR or Poland. Describe how resources are allocated in the economy. Analyse the successes and problems of the economy. Consider the impact on efficiency in the economy, if more markets were freed.

Economic Change in Eastern Europe

Handlowy is a chain of bakery shops, selling bread, cakes, etc. It is proposed to privatise each shop as a separate concern and then sell the bakery. Currently, each shop is run by a manager with an average of three assistants. The chain currently makes a small profit.

Palam Pilo is the country's major manufacturer of lighting equipment – everything from light bulbs to light fittings to commercial lighting equipment. It employs 30 000 people, and has 20 factories round the country. The company is in parts as technologically advanced as some Western companies, and even before economic change exported 20% of its output to the West. It is currently making a very small loss.

Fabryka Chemicala is a chemical company. It operates on three sites. It has made substantial losses for the past two years. Cost of manufacture is about 50% greater than similar plants in the West. It would cost US$500 million to bring the plants up to Western environmental standards. The land on which the plant is built is also heavily contaminated and it is impossible at this stage to estimate how much it would cost to clean up the sites.

EGH Elta is a small manufacturer of high-quality cut-glass products. It enjoys a national reputation for its products although in the past it has not exported goods. It is currently running at a profit. Its workforce of 500 is highly skilled.

Telecommunicata SA is the country's national telephone company. It enjoys a monopoly throughout the country. Currently running at a loss, it employs 100 000 workers. The telecommunications industry is badly in need of extra investment if it is to fulfil its role in the economic development of the country.

STUDY POINTS

You are the government of an Eastern European country. For the past 30 years, nearly all enterprises have been owned by the state. You now wish to privatise as much industry as possible. There are a number of possible ways of doing this.

• Companies could be sold to the highest bidder. This might be a foreign firm (probably a western multinational company) or it might be to individuals or private enterprises in your own country.

• Companies could be given to their workers.

• Your government could issue vouchers free of charge or for a small sum to citizens. They could use these vouchers to 'buy' shares in state enterprises. These companies would then be owned by private citizens.

1 What are the advantages and disadvantages of each of the three ways of privatising companies? Think about issues such as future investment, employment, efficiency and fairness.

2 (a) Explain which of the 5 enterprises above you think would be of interest to the following (in your answer think carefully about who would be able to afford to buy the company): (i) a foreign multinational company; (ii) a local entrepreneur; (iii) workers at the enterprise; (iv) citizen investors in the country.

(b) Are there any enterprises which the state is going to find difficult to sell? Explain your answer.

Why Change?

In 1917, the Russian Czar Nicholas II lost his throne. Government passed eventually into the control of the Communist Party. During the 1920s and 1930s, the Russian economy was transformed from a free enterprise economy into a command economy. Then Eastern European countries such as Poland and Czechoslovakia which were occupied by the Russians at the end of the Second World War also had a command structure imposed on them.

Incomes in these economies grew but, in the 1960s and 1970s, they grew even faster in the free market and mixed economies in the West (Western Europe, the USA and Japan). It was clear to many that command economies were failing to deliver the sort of living standards taken for granted in the West. What's more, the command economy structure in the East was linked to totalitarian government where citizens didn't have basic rights such as freedom of speech or freedom of movement.

So in the 1980s, communist governments in Eastern Europe began to move slowly away from command economy structures. At the end of the 1980s, communist governments were forced out of power by popular revolutions. Today, new governments in Eastern Europe are busy getting rid of their command economies and replacing them with those based on free market principles.

Privatisation

In a command economy, land and capital are owned by the state. In a free market economy, they are owned mainly by private individuals and companies. So moving from a command economy to a free market economy means transferring ownership of land and capital from the state to the private sector. This process is known as privatisation.

Privatisation is not easy. For a start, the government has to decide who will become the owners of the privatised companies. If the companies are given away to their workers, then those who work for valuable companies will get more than those who work for companies which have little or no value. Non-workers then get nothing. If shares are given away to citizens on an equal basis, then it's fair but the shares can't be sold off to foreign companies who might bring in investment money to help the firm grow. If shares are sold to foreign companies, they will only be interested in making the firm profitable and this could affect how many workers are employed as well as which factories are kept open and which closed. If companies are sold to citizens, they are unlikely to be able to put up enough money to buy large companies.

Output and Unemployment

In a command economy, instructions are sent out from the central planning office telling factories what to produce, what supplies they will get and who they have to send finished goods to. In a free market, those instructions are sent out via spending decisions.

Going from one system to the other inevitably means disruption. An enterprise which before was told who to sell to now has to find buyers for its products. Equally it can now choose who to buy from. So some enterprises now get orders, but others don't. The ones that don't get orders either have to borrow money from the government to survive, or they have to sack workers and produce less.

The result is that unemployment has gone up from virtually zero to 10–15% in Eastern Europe. At the same time, output has fallen by up to 20% in one year.

Eventually, the economic links will get re-established. But in the meantime, it means falling output and rising unemployment.

Inflation

In a command economy, if there weren't enough goods and services to meet demand, then they were rationed. There were long waiting lists for houses and flats. If you wanted food in the shops, you had to queue.

In a free market economy goods are rationed via prices. If there is a shortage, prices go up until supply equals demand.

Moving to a free market economy means that prices must be set at market levels. Because prices of essentials like food were set well below the market price before, it means that prices have to go up. Poland and Russia saw inflation of 1000% when they raised prices in 1990 and 1992.

Whether prices continue rising depends upon how much money the government continues to print. If it tries to stop its firms going bankrupt by lending them money, then inflation could be very high.

Is It Worth It?

Unemployment, falling output and high inflation are the costs that Eastern Europe and Russia have faced in transforming their command economies into free market economies. Many people are poorer today than they were ten years ago.

However, they have political freedom. Queues have disappeared. They can see the range of high quality goods, many imported from the West, now available in the shops. They know that living standards keep on increasing in the West. They hope that all the negative transitional costs will be worthwhile in the long term.

C H E C K P O I N T S

1 Why did the countries of Eastern Europe and Russia become command economies?

2 Why is privatisation necessary if an economy is to change from a command structure to a free market economy?

3 Explain why output falls and unemployment goes up when a command economy is broken up.

4 Why have economic changes in Eastern Europe led to high inflation?

5 What are the costs and benefits of economic change in Eastern Europe?

C O U R S E W O R K
S U G G E S T I O N

Choose an Eastern European country. What was it like as a command economy? How has it changed? Have the economic reforms undertaken been worthwhile?

Data Response Questions
Units 84–87

Unit 84 Capital Transfers to the Third World

Global pattern of direct investment ($bn, annual averages)

	1975-79	1980-84	1985-89	1990	1991
OUTFLOWS					
Industrial countries	34.7	41.0	128.4	209.5	165.5
US	15.9	9.6	22.8	33.4	29.5
Japan	2.1	4.3	23.8	48.0	30.7
European Community	14.2	20.9	59.4	97.5	80.5
Developing countries	0.6	1.4	6.5	12.9	11.8
Asia	0.3	0.8	5.6	11.2	10.3
Latin America	0.1	0.2	0.4	1.1	1.0
TOTAL	**35.3**	**42.4**	**134.9**	**222.4**	**177.3**
INFLOWS					
Industrial countries	19.9	36.2	98.1	148.7	115.2
US	6.1	18.6	48.2	37.2	22.2
Japan	0.1	0.3	0.1	1.8	1.4
European Community	11.4	14.2	38.4	85.9	67.7
Developing countries	7.0	16.4	19.5	30.9	42.7
Asia	1.9	4.7	10.8	19.9	25.7
Eastern Europe	0.0	0.1	0.1	0.5	2.3
Latin America	3.6	5.4	5.7	7.8	12.0
TOTAL	**26.9**	**52.6**	**117.6**	**179.6**	**157.9**

Source: Financial Times, 16 June 1992

Note: Discrepancy in total outflows and inflows is due to official reporting errors. The figures for 1991 are partly estimated.

Direct investment is investment by multinational companies. Outflows are flows of money for investment out of a country or group of countries. Inflows are flows of money coming into a country for investment.

1 How much did multinational companies based in the USA invest abroad in 1991? *(1 mark)*

2 How much was invested by multinational companies in Asia in 1990? *(1 mark)*

3 What was the net inflow or outflow of money in developing countries (a) in 1990 and (b) between 1980 and 1989? *(3 marks)*

4 Which country was the biggest net exporter of capital between 1975 and 1991? *(1 mark)*

5 Why do multinational companies invest in other countries apart from their home country? *(5 marks)*

6 To what extent do multinational companies benefit the countries where they invest? *(4 marks)*

Unit 85 Economic Systems

Government spending as a proportion of national income (% of GDP)

	1979	1991
United States	31.7	36.1
Japan	31.6	31.5
Germany	47.6	48.0
France	45.0	50.4
Italy	39.7	53.7
UK	41.0	40.0
Sweden	60.7	59.5
Netherlands	56.1	56.2

Source: OECD, Historical Statistics

1 What are the differences between a mixed economy, a free market economy and a command economy? *(6 marks)*

2 None of the countries in the data is a command economy. Explain why you can tell this from the data. *(3 marks)*

3 Name the two economies in the data which are most like (a) a free market economy and (b) a mixed economy. Explain your reasoning for choosing these countries. *(4 marks)*

4 Which countries have moved towards a more mixed economy in the 1980s? Explain your reasoning. *(2 marks)*

Unit 86 Economic Systems Compared

China moves towards the market

Workers in Chinese state factories have grown accustomed to a world where no one can be sacked unless caught gambling or fighting on the job or failing to turn up at work with no good reason.

In China, a centrally planned economy, this is the state sector system of the 'iron ricebowl'. It guarantees workers not only a job for life, but free medicine and schooling, subsidised food and subsidised housing. The system also has a secure 'iron chair' for the factory managers, good or bad, and the same 'iron wages' paid to workers whether they work or not.

But now, times are changing. Central planning is giving way to the market mechanisms. So now official state policy is to try and get rid of the system.

The aim is to make the state enterprises competitive and profitable. A third of them are losing money. They cost the state billions of yuan (Chinese currency) in subsidies every year, and the more competitive collectives, private businesses and foreign joint ventures are growing much faster.

These private sector businesses now account for almost half China's total industrial production, up from less than 25 per cent in 1980.

Source: Adapted from the *Financial Times*, 1 May 1992

1 China is a 'centrally planned economy'. What does this mean? *(4 marks)*

2 What are the advantages for state workers of living in the Chinese centrally planned economy? *(4 marks)*

3 What are the disadvantages of a centrally planned economy? Give examples from the article in your answer. *(7 marks)*

Essay Questions
Units 84–87

1 'The USA is considering imposing import restrictions on Japanese computers.'
(a) What are 'import restrictions'? Give examples of *two* different types of import restrictions. *(8 marks)*
(b) Why might a country like the USA want to impose import restrictions? *(6 marks)*
(c) What are the costs to a country of import restrictions? *(6 marks)*

2 (a) In the UK, part of our output is produced by private firms and part by government. Explain how private firms and government decide what to produce and who should receive what they have produced. *(8 marks)*
(b) What type of economy is the USSR? Who decides what to produce and who should receive that production in the USSR? *(6 marks)*
(c) What is the role of profits in a free market economy? *(6 marks)*

Unit 83 Economic Development

Food too rich for Russians

Millions of Russians and Ukrainians woke up yesterday to find they were suddenly poor.

As price controls were lifted for the first time in 70 years, many crowded into shops to see how bad the damage was.

In cruel winds and flurries of snow, men and women accepted with resignation that the value of roubles in their pockets and savings accounts had shrivelled almost to nothing.

Russian President Boris Yeltsin kept limits on the costs of a few essentials – including bread and babyfood – but even they were allowed to rise between three and five times.

Everything else was allowed to find its own level, in the hope that Russia's stricken economy will come to life under market pressure.

The shoppers were sad but resigned. Galya, 45, a worker in a staff design bureau, said: 'Bread I can afford. But now I'm not so sure I shall be buying meat again. We'll survive somehow.'

The price rises are designed to get rid of the queues which were a form of rationing goods. Before today, most goods were cheap but they were rarely available in the shops. One shopper said: 'I last saw milk about a week ago, cheese six weeks ago.'

Source: Daily Express, 3 January 1992

1 Before 1992, prices of essential goods in Russia were fixed at a very low price.
(a) What do you think was therefore true about demand for these goods?
(b) Why did this system lead to severe shortages in the shops? *(4 marks)*

2 What happened to prices on 2 January 1992 in Russia? *(1 mark)*

3 (a) What will now happen to demand for goods?
(b) Why will this get rid of shortages in the shops? *(4 marks)*

4 Who will gain and who will lose out from the price reform do you think? *(6 marks)*

Data Response Questions
Units 40, 41, 62, 63 and 79

Units 40 and 41 Sole Proprietorships and Partnerships, Joint-stock Companies

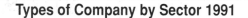

Types of Company by Sector 1991

All Businesses

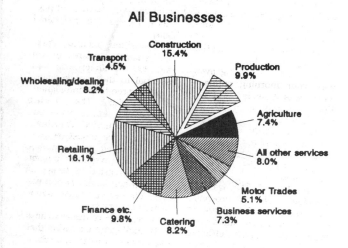

Sole Proprietors

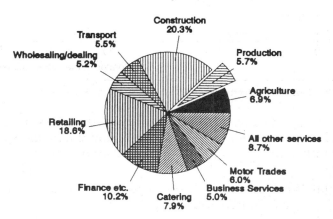

Partnerships

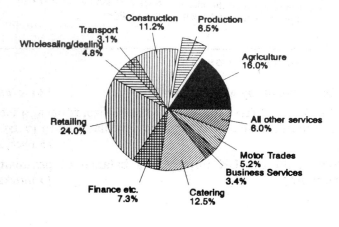

Companies and Public Corporations

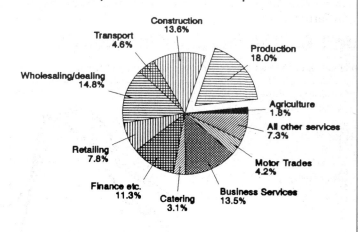

1 What are the legal differences between a sole proprietorship, a partnership and a limited company? (*10 marks*)

2 (a) In which industries are sole proprietorships and partnerships most likely to be found?
  (b) Suggest reasons why this is the case. (*10 marks*)

3 (a) In which industries are limited companies and public corporations most likely to be found?
  (b) Suggest reasons why this is the case. (*10 marks*)

Unit 62 The Causes of Inflation (1)

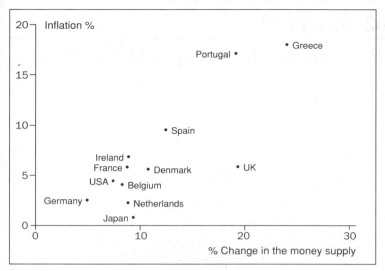

Source: European Commission: European Economy, *Annual Economic Report* 1991–92

1 Do the data in the diagram suggest that there is a link between changes in the money supply and the rate of inflation? Give evidence to support your answer.

(4 marks)

2 (a) What economic theory suggests that increases in the money supply cause inflation?

(b) Explain this theory. *(6 marks)*

3 Japan had a much higher rate of economic growth than the other countries in the diagram. How might this explain its inflation rate? *(5 marks)*

Unit 63 The Causes of Inflation (2)

Inflation (% change on previous year)   **UK pay settlements**

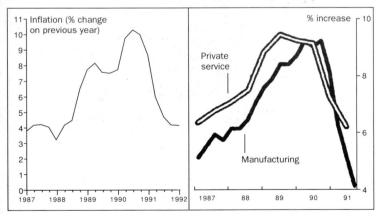

1 What happened to (a) inflation and (b) wage increases between 1987 and 1991? *(4 marks)*

2 (a) What is the cost-push theory of inflation?

(b) Does the evidence in the graphs support this theory? *(8 marks)*

3 What other costs apart from wages might lead to cost-push inflation? *(3 marks)*

Unit 78 The Significance of the Balance of Payments and Exchange Rates

How your home flies the flag for foreign countries

Wherever you are, whatever you're doing, just pause for a moment and take a look around you.

Perhaps you're reading this in the kitchen at home.

That kettle whistling away with your morning cuppa – where was it made? Probably Korea, according to government statistics.

How about the cooker? As we now import three times as many as in 1979, it's a fair bet that, too, has come from a foreign country.

The fridge? The washing machine? The microwave? Even the toaster? So many of the products that make your kitchen the hi-tech, efficient centre of your family's home are developed in Britain but made abroad.

Mr Major and Mrs Thatcher must take much of the blame for the yawning trade gap, which will be revealed as even wider when the balance of payments figures are published today.

Opposition Labour Party spokesman Gordon Brown said that manufacturing was essential to the economy and to solving the trade imbalance.

He said: 'The Tories believed you didn't need manufacturing to survive. They built up the service industries and they destroyed our manufacturing base. We can't accept the human price in terms of lost jobs and bankrupt companies. We say you must manufacture to survive.'

It is a sign of the weakness of Britain's manufacturing that even though we are in a recession which has depressed consumer demand, the Japanese and our EC competitors continue to target our country as a market place.

Source: Adapted from the *Daily Mirror*, 23 March 1992

1 What is meant by a 'trade gap'? *(2 marks)*

2 Why is it important for the UK that kettles, fridges, washing machines, etc., are made abroad rather than in Britain? *(8 marks)*

3 How could the UK improve its balance of payments position? *(5 marks)*

Index